DUMBARTON OAKS
MEDIEVAL LIBRARY

Jan M. Ziolkowski, General Editor

TWO WORKS ON TREBIZOND

MICHAEL PANARETOS

BESSARION

DOML 52

Two Works on Trebizond

MICHAEL PANARETOS

BESSARION

Edited and Translated by

SCOTT KENNEDY

DUMBARTON OAKS
MEDIEVAL LIBRARY

HARVARD UNIVERSITY PRESS
CAMBRIDGE, MASSACHUSETTS
LONDON, ENGLAND
2019

Printed in the United States of America
Second printing

Library of Congress Cataloging-in-Publication Data
Names: Kennedy, Scott, editor, translator. | Container of (expression): Panaretos, Michaēl. Peri tōn megalōn Komnēnōn. | Container of (expression): Bēssariōn, Cardinal, 1403–1472. Enkōmion eis Trapezounta. | Container of (expression): Panaretos, Michaēl. Peri tōn megalōn Komnēnōn. English. | Container of (expression): Bēssariōn, Cardinal, 1403–1472. Enkōmion eis Trapezounta. English.
Title: Two works on Trebizond / Michael Panaretos, Bessarion ; edited and translated by Scott Kennedy.
Other titles: Dumbarton Oaks medieval library ; 52.
Description: Cambridge, Massachusetts : Harvard University Press, 2019. | Series: Dumbarton Oaks medieval library ; 52 | Text in Greek with English translation on facing pages ; introduction and notes in English. | Includes bibliographical references and index.
Identifiers: LCCN 2018017732 | ISBN 9780674986626 (alk. paper)
Subjects: LCSH: Comnenus family—History—Early works to 1800. | Trebizond Empire—History—Sources—Early works to 1800. | Trebizond Empire—Civilization—Sources—Early works to 1800. | Pontus—History—Early works to 1800. | Byzantine Empire—History—1081–1453—Early works to 1800.
Classification: LCC DF609 .T96 2018 | DDC 956.5/80151—dc23 LC record available at https://lccn.loc.gov/2018017732

Contents

Introduction

In April 1204, days before the Fourth Crusade sacked Constantinople, Alexios and David Komnenos, scions of the Byzantine Komnenos dynasty and grandsons of the former emperor Andronikos I (r. 1183–1185), seized the city of Trebizond (modern Trabzon) on the Black Sea coast of Anatolia. In what appears to have been an unsuccessful bid to seize the Byzantine throne, the Komnenos brothers unwittingly became the founders of the first of three successor states that emerged from the Crusaders' dismemberment of the Byzantine empire.[1] Their ambitions to rule in Constantinople quickly dissipated after the loss of Sinope in 1214, but their empire, which stretched along the coast of the Black Sea from Oinaion (modern Ünye) to Georgia, endured for more than two and a half centuries. Although the fortunes of the restored empire of Byzantium (1261–1453) declined until by the later fourteenth century practically only Constantinople remained under the control of the ruling Palaiologan dynasty, the Komnenoi emperors of Trebizond were particularly adept at holding on to their territory despite Georgian, Turkish, and Mongol attacks. Their final emperor, David Komnenos (r. 1459/60–1461), did not surrender to the Ottoman Turks until August 1461, eight years after their conquest of Constantinople in 1453.

The empire of Trebizond was an important trading hub

for travelers along the Silk Road and acquired a great reputation for its wealth. As a unique outpost of the Eastern Roman world with its own culture and dialect of Greek, this mysterious empire has long fascinated European writers, from Miguel Cervantes in *Don Quixote* to Dorothy Dunnett in her popular Niccolò series.[2] Regrettably, the remnants of the empire's own literary production are few.[3] The city produced some figures of note in Byzantine ecclesiastical history, such as Saint Athanasios, the founder of the Great Lavra on Mount Athos, and John Xiphilinos, the patriarch of Constantinople (1063–1075), and, in the fourteenth century, it was known as a center of astronomical and mathematical studies.[4] The most famous surviving texts produced by its native sons are, however, the laconic chronicle on the emperors of Trebizond attributed to Michael Panaretos and Cardinal Bessarion's encomium of the city. They are the cornerstone of any study of the empire of Trebizond and Pontic Hellenism. This volume offers a translation of these two documents, including the first-ever English translation of Bessarion's *Encomium on Trebizond,* in the hope that they will encourage further study of this elusive empire and its culture.

On the Emperors of Trebizond, attributed to Michael Panaretos

The Alleged Author, Structure, Genre, Sources, and Language of the Text

The chronicle *On the Emperors of Trebizond,* which survives in an apograph copy in Marcianus gr. 608/coll. 306, dating from the 1440s,[5] extends in its coverage from 1204 down to

some point after 1426. It appears to have been essentially a collection of notices and entries of historical interest, resembling so-called Byzantine short chronicles. The short chronicles are brief notices scribbled in the margins and on blank folios of manuscripts. Like Panaretos's text they are characterized by a laconic style and an interest in precisely dating events, sometimes down to the hour.[6] The entries in Panaretos's chronicle are generally arranged in strict chronological order, with some exceptions, such as the death of Manuel III (r. 1390–1416/17), erroneously dated by the chronicler to 1412 (chap. 107), which is then followed by an entry for 1395.[7] Readers should not always trust its accuracy, however, as scholars sometimes have in the past,[8] for although there are few sources against which to test it, when we can verify its information, it is not always accurate.[9]

As the reader will quickly notice, no one claims authorship of the chronicle in the title or its opening sections. The attribution of the chronicle to Michael Panaretos is based on chapter 81, in which he explicitly claims authorship of the entry, as well as on the use of the first person in entries ranging from 1340 to 1386.[10] We know nothing about Michael Panaretos beyond what he tells us in his chronicle, but if we accept him as the writer of the chronicle from its beginning until Alexios III's death in 1390, his biography would run something like this. He was probably born sometime around 1320 and served Alexios III (r. 1349–1390) as *protosebastos* and *protonotarios* from 1351 to 1379.[11] As *protonotarios,* or chief secretary, he was in charge of the imperial secretariat and probably served as the emperor's personal secretary.[12] However, Alexios also dispatched him on several diplomatic missions to Constantinople, such as that of 1363

in which he helped secure a marriage alliance with the Byzantine emperor John V (r. 1341–1391).

One of the purposes of the chronicle, then, may have been to keep track of the Grand Komnenoi's relationships with their subjects and neighbors. As imperial secretary, Panaretos needed to be able to reference past history when drafting official letters and documents.[13] Occasionally, we can even hear the secretary's complaints. When the rebel Niketas Scholaris fled to Kerasunt in 1355, Panaretos remarks, "Who could possibly describe all the messages and dispatches that passed between the two cities from then on?" (chap. 54; see also 100). In this regard, Panaretos's chronicle was similar to the better-known fifteenth-century chronicle of George Sphrantzes.[14]

Most scholars generally assume that Panaretos was solely responsible for the chronicle up to the death of Alexios III in 1390 (chap. 106), or at least 1386 (105). After this point, the author of the chronicle is unknown. Scholars have traditionally spoken of "the continuator of Panaretos," but there is no clear reason for arguing that there was a single continuator rather than several. For example, the chronicle refers to the death of Manuel III (1390–1416/17) in chapter 107 before backtracking in chapter 108 to discuss the death of the Georgian-born empress Eudokia in 1395. This disruption in the chronicle's chronology suggests that the chronicle originally extended only to chapter 107. In any case, it is technically incorrect to describe *On the Emperors of Trebizond* as the work of Panaretos alone.

As for the sources of the chronicle, some interesting theories have been advanced. The empire of Trebizond's first modern historian, Jakob Fallmerayer, famously proposed

that the wall paintings of the emperors described by Bessarion in his encomium (chap. 102) may have numbered among Panaretos's sources.[15] More likely is Lampsides's suggestion that Panaretos, as chief secretary, drew upon the palace archives as well as oral traditions then in circulation.[16] On a linguistic level, readers with some knowledge of Greek will quickly notice the vast difference between Bessarion's prolix, archaizing style and the terse, sometimes contemporary style employed by the chronicle. On a number of occasions, the chronicler's Greek reveals the influence of his native Pontic dialect, such as his ambiguity over how to grammatically decline the surname of the emperor Andronikos I (r. 1222–1235): Gidos or Gidon (chap. 2).[17]

Bessarion's *Encomium on Trebizond*

The Author

Bessarion (originally named Basil), a Greek who would become both a cardinal of the Catholic church and one of the leading lights of the Italian Renaissance, was born at the beginning of the fifteenth century in Trebizond.[18] The exact date of his birth has been the subject of considerable controversy, with dates ranging from 1400 to 1408,[19] but 1403 seems the most preferable year.[20] Basil was one of fifteen children born to parents of only modest means.[21] In his youth, he showed exceptional intellectual promise, and his parents convinced the metropolitan of Trebizond, Dositheos, to take him into his care. When Dositheos had to return to Constantinople in 1416/17, Basil accompanied him and studied at the school of the celebrated metropolitan of Selymbria, John (Ignatios) Chortasmenos, in Con-

stantinople.[22] There he also joined the school of an instructor referred to simply as Chrysokokkes, where he met the Renaissance humanist Francesco Filelfo.[23] Under their tutelage, Basil completed his education and came to think of Constantinople as a second home;[24] he tells us himself that Trebizond was his birthplace, but Constantinople was where he was really raised and educated.[25] In 1423, Basil was tonsured and adopted the monastic name Bessarion after the Egyptian anchorite of that name for whom he wrote a panegyric.[26]

At the court of the Palaiologan emperors in Constantinople, Bessarion quickly ascended the ranks and won promotions due to his literary talents. In 1425 he delivered a funeral oration for the emperor Manuel II Palaiologos (r. 1391–1425).[27] In the following year, the new sole emperor John VIII Palaiologos dispatched Bessarion on his first diplomatic mission, to seek a marriage alliance with the emperor Alexios IV of Trebizond (r. 1417–1427). In August 1426 John VIII's previous wife, Sophia of Montferrat, had fled to her home in the West after years of neglect by her husband, and the emperor now hoped to marry one of the princesses of Trebizond, who were renowned for their beauty.[28]

Bessarion's exact role during this embassy is unclear, as he was probably too young to lead it, but he certainly served as its orator, delivering a panegyric of Alexios IV during negotiations.[29] Before the two parties could strike an accord, however, the Trapezuntines were rocked by the death of Theodora Kantakouzene, the wife of Alexios IV, in November 1426. Her death derailed negotiations for some time and left Bessarion free to write three consolatory monodies for the emperor and a poem on the empress.[30] In the second

and third monodies, Bessarion repeatedly urges the emperor to return to work, as he was apparently too consumed by grief to do much else.[31] Bessarion's embassy ultimately succeeded in its objective, for the bride-to-be, Maria Komnene, sailed to Constantinople in August 1427 and married the emperor John VIII.[32]

After this point, we know little about Bessarion's career. Scholars have suggested that it was around 1430/31 that he traveled to Mistra, near modern Sparta in the Peloponnese, the capital of the provincial government, which was then ruled by John VIII Palaiologos's brother, the *despotes* of the Morea Theodore II (r. 1407–1443). There, under one of the greatest philosophers and intellectuals of the age, George Gemistos Plethon, he studied a broad range of topics, such as philosophy, history, geography, and mathematics. He also participated in the court at Mistra, writing monodies and poetry on Theodore's wife Cleope after she died in 1433.[33] Bessarion's stay at Mistra ended in 1436 when John VIII summoned him back to Constantinople and gave him a position there as an instructor at the monastery of Saint Basil.[34]

A year later, in November 1437, the emperor made Bessarion bishop of Turkish-occupied Nikaia in Asia Minor.[35] This was a largely titular assignment, probably meant to bolster Bessarion's credentials, as he left Constantinople a week later in the company of the Byzantine delegation to the church council of Ferrara-Florence (1437–1439). The emperor's objective was the reunification of the Churches, something that he, and later Bessarion, believed would secure Western aid against the impending threat posed by the Ottomans. At the council, Bessarion initially opposed Union of the Churches, but later became one of its staunch

supporters.[36] After the council ended, he came back to Constantinople for a few months before returning to Italy and assuming the cardinal's hat at the invitation of Pope Eugenius IV (1431–1447), in 1440.

Now permanently residing in Italy, Bessarion spent a number of years writing apologetic works on behalf of Union and carrying out his duties as cardinal, which included reforming the Basilian monastic order in southern Italy. In 1450 he was appointed as papal legate to rule the troubled city of Bologna. In 1453 Constantinople fell to the Ottomans, and Bessarion began to collect any rare and important manuscripts he could obtain in order to preserve the literary heritage of Byzantium.[37] The extensive library that he subsequently assembled and bequeathed to Venice would form the foundation of the present day Biblioteca Marciana. After the death of Pope Nicholas V (1447–1455), Bessarion was almost elected pope at the conclave, but his fellow cardinals allegedly feared his ethnic background and well-known discipline. Under subsequent popes, Bessarion would attempt to instigate a crusade against the Turks, as matters back East worsened for the Byzantines with the fall of both the Peloponnese and his native Trebizond in 1460–61. During the 1460s, Bessarion also engaged in one of the great literary debates of the century with George of Trebizond over whether Plato's or Aristotle's philosophy better conformed to Christian belief. The fruit of this dispute was Bessarion's famous *Refutation of Blasphemies against Plato (In Calumniatorem Platonis)*. This was one of the first books ever printed on a printing press,[38] and it took full advantage of the press to sway public opinion.[39]

Bessarion died on November 18, 1472, at Ravenna, on his

way back from a failed diplomatic mission to France. He was buried in the church of the Twelve Apostles at Rome in the eponymous Bessarion chapel.

The Encomium on Trebizond: *Structure, Models, Sources, Style, and Date*

City panegyrics were already a well-established genre of ancient literature when Bessarion wrote his encomium. Some of the earliest templates were provided by Pericles's funeral oration, as recorded in Thucydides, and Isocrates's *Panathenaicus* and *Panegyricus.* The genre was, as far as we know, not particularly popular in the Hellenistic and early Roman period but was revived in the second century CE by Aelius Aristides's encomium of Athens in his *Panathenaic Oration,* which became a canonical reference point. During Late Antiquity, rhetoricians such as Menander Rhetor laid out extensive guidelines for praising a city. But Greek orators largely abandoned the genre again until the thirteenth century.[40] In an era when Constantinople's earlier monopoly over the empire was severely attenuated, regional centers and other cities took on increasing importance, encouraging eastern Romans to think about what defined their cities and to celebrate them with encomia.[41] When Bessarion wrote his encomium in the fifteenth century, he was following in the footsteps of Theodore II Laskaris, Theodore Metochites, Nikephoros Choumnos, Manuel Chrysoloras, John Eugenikos, and Isidore of Kiev, who had praised Nikaia, Constantinople, Thessalonike, and Trebizond.[42]

Although some of his contemporaries were writing encomia at the same time as Bessarion, he does not seem to have

actually used any of them as sources or direct models. Instead, he adopted the standard Byzantine practice of ignoring contemporary writings and going directly back to Late Antique precepts and examples. The two major exemplars that Bessarion consulted were Libanios's *Antiochian Oration* and Aelius Aristides's *Panathenaic Oration.*[43] For more detailed instructions, Menander Rhetor's treatise on epideictic speeches was the rhetor's essential handbook.[44] The encomium of a city had three major topics a rhetor needed to discuss: its origins, location, and deeds. This often entailed describing the city's ancestry, central location, geography, history, and finally its buildings.

Beyond these rhetorical texts, Bessarion also drew on a wide range of authors from different genres to construct the history of Trebizond and its geography.[45] His ancient sources include Homer, Hesiod, Herodotus, Xenophon, Demosthenes, Strabo, Plutarch, Ptolemy, and Appian. His sources for the city's Byzantine history are less clear. Lampsides has suggested a lost verse chronicle of world history, basing his argument on the presence in the text of a poetic line describing the Turks overrunning Asia Minor following the battle of Mantzikert in 1071.[46] Stylistically, Bessarion's Greek is challenging and demanding. He also does not always express himself clearly, and at various points I have signaled textual difficulties to the reader in the Notes to the Translation.

Odysseas Lampsides, the encomium's most recent editor, dated the work to 1436/37, based on Bessarion's statement that nearly fifteen hundred years had passed since Trebizond fell to Rome after Pompey's defeat of Mithridates VI (r. 120–63 BCE), the king of Pontos, in 64 BCE.[47] Byzan-

tine estimates of chronology are not always accurate, but the position of the encomium in Bessarion's chronologically arranged autograph collection of his juvenile works (Marcianus gr. 533) supports a date between 1434 and 1436.[48] However, there has recently been some interest in reassigning the document to Bessarion's visit to Trebizond in 1426–27.[49]

Audience and Afterlife of the Encomium

As the debate over dating suggests, the audience for which Bessarion wrote his encomium is a mystery, but it is helpful to remember that he may have envisioned different audiences for the text throughout his life. In the text itself, his imagined audience is clearly his fellow Trapezuntines, whom he addresses as "my fellow citizens" (chaps. 4, 122) and "our citizens" (116). Scholars have consequently argued that the text dates from a specific visit to Trebizond sometime between 1436 and 1437 intended to drum up support for Union with the western Church or to strengthen the bonds between the emperors of Trebizond and Byzantium.[50] The text, however, does not mention a specific occasion or addressee.[51] In chapter 36, Bessarion refers to the Mediterranean sea as "this sea," which would imply that he was in the Peloponnese or at Constantinople. Indeed, there is no evidence that Bessarion ever visited his fatherland after 1427. Thus, I would suggest that he wrote the text in Mistra or Constantinople as an intellectual exercise and circulated it among his friends back in Trebizond.

From the perspective of the text's actual readers (that is, its reception), the encomium appears to have circulated

largely among Byzantine and Italian intellectuals in Italy. For example, an apograph of the encomium (Madrid gr. 4619), copied from Bessarion's autograph manuscript Marcianus gr. 533, made its way into the library of the famed scholar Constantine Laskaris.[52] Bessarion is also known to have had the work translated into Latin during his later years in order to bolster his Latin literary profile.[53] Bessarion's panegyrist Bartholomeo Sacchi (also known as Il Platina) appears to have read this translation when he wrote his encomium of the cardinal.[54]

Principles of Translation and Transliteration

Panaretos and Bessarion present a variety of challenges to the translator and the reader. The former is written in simple Greek but is laconic to the extreme, while the latter is verbose and obscure at times. I have tried to remain as faithful to the Greek as I can while also rendering these texts in lucid English. I have profited at times from modern translations of both and acknowledge my debt here.[55] Greek names are generally transliterated as close to the original spelling as possible when they would be unfamiliar to an English audience (that is, "Alexios" for Ἀλέξιος, but "John" rather than "Ioannes" for Ἰωάννης). Foreign names present something of an issue. To the extent possible, they are rendered in the form that the individual would have used in his own language, thus Greek for Greeks, Turkish for Turks, and so forth. Many individuals who are named in Panaretos are obscure and are known only from his chronicle; when feasible, I have provided notes elaborating on them. I have translated technical terms, titles, and names of offices into their

English equivalent whenever possible (thus, "chamberlain" for παρακοιμώμενος, etc.). Terms without a common English equivalent or of uncertain meaning are transliterated in the text (for instance, "*sebastokrator*" for σεβαστοκράτωρ) and explained in the Glossary of Offices, Titles, and Technical Terms. Place-names are generally given in their Greek form, with the exception of important city names such as Constantinople and Trebizond. I indicate the modern location of a site and its proximity to modern Trabzon in the notes to the translation; for this purpose, the first volume of Anthony Bryer and David Winfield's *Byzantine Monuments and Topography of the Pontos* has been an invaluable guide. The Greek text of Panaretos dates events by the Byzantine calendar, which calculated its years from the supposed creation of the world in 5509 BCE. The Byzantine calendar year began on September 1. The modern Common Era year is calculated by subtracting 5,508 for dates falling between January and August, and 5,509 for dates falling between September and December. For the convenience of the reader, in the English translation I have converted the Byzantine dates into their equivalent Common Era years.[56]

Thanks are due to Anthony Kaldellis for first suggesting this project to me and tirelessly checking numerous drafts of the text with a sharp and critical eye. I would also like to convey my gratitude to my editors, Alice-Mary Talbot and Richard Greenfield, for their numerous suggestions and comments, which vastly improved the translation. Their insight has been invaluable for this project. Nate Aschenbrenner, John Zaleski, and Jake Ransohoff, all of them Tyler Fellows at

Dumbarton Oaks, also deserve thanks for reviewing Panaretos and Bessarion and helping to improve the notes to the texts. Ian Mladjov kindly granted permission to include the genealogical tables and the map of the empire of Trebizond and its neighboring territories. I greatly appreciate all the help and critical insight these scholars have provided over the years. The final draft of this translation was completed while I was a Junior Fellow at Dumbarton Oaks. I am grateful to Dumbarton Oaks for its hospitality, collegiality, and support in bringing this project to completion. I should also like to express my thanks to my colleagues at the Ohio State University for providing a supportive environment for this project and numerous conversations on matters related to it. Finally, fond thanks are due to Gonda Van Steen for believing like Themistokles that even the wildest colts make very good horses. However, all errors and infelicities of translation are ultimately my own.

Notes

1 On the history of the empire of Trebizond, the only general survey in English is William Miller's outdated *Trebizond: The Last Greek Empire* (London and New York, 1926). This is updated by the collected articles in Anthony Bryer, *The Empire of Trebizond and the Pontos* (London, 1980), and Bryer and Winfield, *Pontos*. The most modern surveys are Sergei Karpov, *Istoria Trapezoundskoy imperij* (Saint Petersburg, 2007), translated into Greek by Eugenia Kritsephskagia and Angelike Eustathiou, *Ιστορία της αυτοκρατορίας της Τραπεζούντας* (Athens, 2017), and Alexios Savvides, *Ιστορία της Αυτοκρατορίας των Μεγάλων Κομνηνών της Τραπεζούντας (1204–1461)* (Thessalonike, 2009).

2 Miller, *Trebizond,* 117–19; Alexander A. Vasiliev, "The Empire of Trebizond in History and Literature," *Byzantion* 15 (1940–41): 316–77, here 371–77; Dorothy Dunnett, *The Spring of the Ram* (New York, 1987; repr., 1999).

3 Rosenqvist, "Byzantine Trebizond," 29–51.

4 Libadenos, *Travels,* 59–60.

5 Peter Schreiner, "Bemerkungen zur Handschrift der trapezuntinischen Chronik des Michael Panaretos in der Bibliotheca Marciana (Marc. gr. 608/coll. 306)," in *Mare et Litora: Essays Presented to Sergei Karpov for his 60th Birthday,* ed. Rustam Shukurov (Moscow, 2009), 613–25.

6 Peter Schreiner, *Die byzantinischen Kleinchroniken,* vol. 1 (Vienna, 1975), 21–23. For more depth, see idem, *Studien zu den Βραχέα Χρονικά* (Munich, 1967), 129.

7 For further examples of entries out of chronological order, see Pampoukis, *Ποντιακά,* 2:32–33.

8 Lampsides, "Μιχαὴλ," 24–29; Asp-Talwar, "The Chronicle of Michael Panaretos," 173–74.

9 For example, Panaretos himself incorrectly states that the emperor Alexios III's illegitimate son Andronikos was born around 1355/56 (chap. 99). Andronikos was born in 1353/54 according to his tombstone. He also wrongly gives the date of Michael VIII's death as December 10 rather than 11 (chap. 6). Finally, the chronicler may incorrectly label the emir of Chalybia, Süleyman Bey, as Alexios's brother (chap. 104).

10 Lampsides, "Μιχαὴλ," 13–14.

11 Lampsides, "Μιχαὴλ," 9–17; Karpov, *Istoria,* 453–55; Savvides, *Ιστορία,* 198–201.

12 Alexander Kazhdan, "Protonotarios," *ODB,* 3:1748.

13 For example, Panaretos (chap. 6), tells the reader to note that the Byzantine emperor Michael VIII Palaiologos was still alive when the Trapezuntine emperor John II (r. 1280–1292) married his daughter.

14 See Ricardo Maisano's introduction to Sphrantzes, *Chronicle* 37–38*.

15 Fallmerayer, "Original-Fragmente," 9.

16 Lampsides, "Μιχαὴλ," 39.

17 On Panaretos's Ponticisms, see Lampsides, "Μιχαὴλ," 18–19.

18 There is no full biography in English. For a short summary of his life, see Alice-Mary Talbot, "Bessarion," *ODB,* 1:285. The standard scholarly biographies are Ludwig Mohler, *Kardinal Bessarion als Theologe, Humanist und Staatsmann,* vol. 1 (Paderborn, 1923); and Lotta Labowsky, "Bessarione," in *Dizionario Biografico degli Italiani,* ed. Alberto M. Ghisalberti (Rome, 1967), 9:686–96. For his life up to 1458, see Elpidio Mioni, "Vita del cardinale

Bessarione," *Miscellanea Marciana* 6 (1991): 11–215. For a brief outline, see Marino Zorzi, "Cenni sulla vita e la figura del cardinale Bessarione," in *Bessarione e l'Umanesimo: Catalogo della mostra* (Venice, 1994), 1–19.

19 For an overview of the controversy, see Brigitte Tambrun Krasker, "Bessarion de Trébizonde à Mistra: Un parcours intellectuel," in *"Inter graecos latinissimus, inter latinos graecissimus": Bessarion zwischen den Kulturen,* ed. Claudia Märtl, Christian Kaiser, and Thomas Ricklin (Berlin, 2013), 1–35, here 7–9.

20 See Scott Kennedy, "Bessarion's Date of Birth: A Reassessment" (forthcoming in *Byzantinische Zeitschrift*).

21 Apostoles, *Funeral Oration* 132; Bessarion, *In Calumniatorem Platonis* 4.7.3. The number of Bessarion's siblings is preserved only in the Greek version of *In Calumniatorem Platonis.*

22 Apostoles, *Funeral Oration* 133.

23 Tambrun Krasker, "Bessarion," 13–14.

24 Platina, *Panegyricus,* in PG 161, col. 105.

25 See Bessarion's prologue to Marcianus gr. 533. The Greek text is published in Henri Saffrey, "Recherches sur quelques autographes du cardinal Bessarion et leur caractère," in *Mélanges Eugène Tisserant,* vol. 3 (Vatican City, 1963), 263–97, here 283–84; see also Schreiner, *Die byzantinischen Kleinchroniken,* 1:658–60.

26 Bessarion, *Encomium of Saint Bessarion.*

27 Bessarion, *Eulogy for Manuel Palaiologos.*

28 Doukas, *History* 20.6; Sphrantzes, *Chronicle* 14.2.

29 Bessarion, *Address to the Emperor Alexios Komnenos.*

30 The poem was blotted out with ink after the manuscript was assembled. Mioni, "Vita," 31, gives a full account and suggests Bessarion erased it because the verses were too similar to those of his poem for Cleope Malatesta.

31 For example, Sideras, *25 unedierte,* 368, where Bessarion urges Alexios to act like the biblical king David, who grieved for his son while he was sick but returned to work immediately after his son's death.

32 Sphrantzes, *Chronicle* 14.3.

33 See Bessarion, *Epitaph for Cleofa Malatesta; Monody for Cleofa Malatesta.*

34 Traditionally Bessarion was said to have been the abbot of the monastery, but he is most likely to have been only an instructor: see Tambrun Krasker, "Bessarion," 3n13.

35 For the date of his appointment, see his curriculum vitae published in Saffrey, "Recherches," 270–71.

36 Joseph Gill, "Was Bessarion a Conciliarist or a Unionist Before the Council of Florence?," *Orientalia Christiana Analecta* 204 (1977): 201–19.

37 Ludwig Mohler, *Kardinal Bessarion,* vol. 3 (Paderborn, 1942), 478–79.

38 Ludwig Mohler, *Kardinal Bessarion,* vol. 2 (Paderborn, 1926). For the debate in general, see James Hankins, *Plato in the Italian Renaissance* (Leiden, 1990).

39 Zorzi, "Cenni," 15.

40 Saradi, "The Monuments," 179–80.

41 Akışık, "Praising A City," 4–5.

42 Laskaris: Luigi Tartaglia, ed., *Theodorus Laskaris: Opuscula Rhetorica* (Munich, 2000), 68–84; Metochites: Evelina Mineva, ed., "Ο Νικαιεύς του Θεοδώρου Μετοχίτου," *Diptycha* 6 (1994/95): 307–27; Choumnos: Jean Boissonade, ed., *Anecdota Graeca,* vol. 2 (Paris, 1830), 137–87; Chrysoloras: Christina Brillo, ed., "Manuele Crisolora, confronta tra l'Antica e la Nuova Roma," *Medioevo Greco* 1 (2001): 1–26; Eugenikos: Spyridon Lampros, ed., *Παλαιολόγεια καὶ Πελοποννησιακά,* vol. 2 (Athens, 1926), 47–55; Odysseas Lampsides, "Ἰωάννου Εὐγενικοῦ Ἔκφρασις Τραπεζοῦντας: Χρονολόγησις καὶ Ἔκδοσις," *Αρχεῖον Πόντου* 20 (1955): 3–39; Isidore: Spyridon Lampros, ed., *Παλαιολόγεια καὶ Πελοποννησιακά,* 2:132–99.

43 Fatouros, "Bessarion und Libanios," 191–204; Lampsides, "Περὶ τὸ ἐγκώμιον," 175–84. For Aristides, see the many endnotes to the translation in which we have signaled his influence. For a discussion of his influence, see Eleni Saradi, "Η έκφρασις της Τραπεζούντας από τον Βησσαρίωνα: Η αρχαιότης και το ιστορικό μήνυμα," *Βυζαντινός Δόμος* 17/18 (2009–10): 33–56.

44 Menander recommends using philosophers to explain the benefits of inland cities. Bessarion employs the advice for coastal cities, citing Plato for their superiority. See Donald A. Russell and Nigel G. Wilson, ed. and trans., *Menander Rhetor* (Oxford, 1981), 36; Bessarion, *Encomium on Trebizond* 44.

45 Lampsides, "Ο 'Εις Τραπεζούντα'," 16–18; Saradi, "The Monuments," 189.

46 Lampsides, "Περὶ τὸ ἐγκώμιον," 174.

47 Lampsides, "Datierung," 291–92; repeated almost verbatim in idem,

"L'éloge," 121–22; idem, "Περὶ τὸ ἐγκώμιον," 159–60; idem, "Ο 'Εις Τραπεζούντα'," 3–5.

48 Saffrey, "Recherches," 290–91; Mioni, "Vita," 43, 45–46, places it in 1434–1436 for the same reasons. Bessarion was probably still a monk when he wrote the panegyric, since he avers that he had nothing to offer his fatherland. See *Encomium on Trebizond* 4–5.

49 Ilias Giarenis, "Ο λόγιος και ο γενέθλιος τόπος: Η Τραπεζούντα με τον τρόπο του Βησσαρίωνος," *Επετηρίς Εταιρείας Βυζαντινών Σπουδών* 53 (2007–2009): 265–80, here 275; Frederick Lauritzen, "Bessarion's Political Thought: The Encomium to Trebizond," *Bulgaria Mediaevalis* 2 (2011): 153–59, here 154.

50 Mohler, *Kardinal Bessarion,* 1:54; Mioni, "Vita," 43; Lampsides, "Datierung," 291; Saradi, "Η ἔκφρασις," 36.

51 Lampsides, "L'éloge," 121–22; idem, "Περὶ τὸ ἐγκώμιον," 159–60; idem, "Ο 'Εις Τραπεζούντα'," 4–5.

52 The manuscript is described in Gregorio de Andrés, *Catálogo de los códices griegos desaparecidos de la Biblioteca Nacional* (Madrid, 1987), 132–33.

53 Capranica, *Funeral Oration* 9.

54 Platina's knowledge of the encomium is proved by his paraphrase of it: *Panegyric,* col. 104: Trapezuntus, Sinopensium colonia, huius patria est; Sinopem condidere Milesii, Miletum Athenienses. Ex his, ut a parentibus, avis, abavis, nobilitatem referens, redundan (sic) tiam Asiani ingenii frugalitate Attica compescuit; compare Bessarion, *Encomium on Trebizond* 8, 13, 29.

55 For an overview of modern translations of Bessarion and Panaretos, see the Note on the Texts and the Bibliography.

56 For more on issues of dating and date conversion, see the Notes to the Translations, under Michael Panaretos, *On the Emperors of Trebizond,* chapter 1.

ON THE EMPERORS OF TREBIZOND

Περὶ τῶν τῆς Τραπεζοῦντος βασιλέων, τῶν Μεγάλων Κομνηνῶν, ὅπως καὶ πότε καὶ πόσον ἕκαστος ἐβασίλευσεν

Ἦλθεν ὁ μέγας Κομνηνός, ὁ κῦρ Ἀλέξιος, ἐξελθὼν μὲν ἐκ τῆς εὐδαίμονος Κωνσταντινουπόλεως, ἐκστρατεύσας δὲ ἐξ Ἰβηρίας, σπουδῇ καὶ μόχθῳ τῆς πρὸς πατρὸς θείας αὐτοῦ Θάμαρ, καὶ παρέλαβε τὴν Τραπεζοῦντα μηνὶ Ἀπριλίῳ, ἰνδικτιῶνος ζ′, ἔτους ,ςψιβ′, ἐτῶν ὢν κβ′. Καὶ βασιλεύσας ὀκτωκαίδεκα ἐκοιμήθη Φεβρουαρίου κ^η, ἡμέρᾳ α′ τῆς Ὀρθοδοξίας, ἔτους ,ςψλ′, ἐτῶν γινομένων τεσσαράκοντα.

2 Ἔτους ,ςψλ′ ἐβασίλευσεν ὁ ἐπὶ τῇ θυγατρὶ γαμβρὸς αὐτοῦ, κῦρ Ἀνδρόνικος Γίδος ὁ Κομνηνός. Ἐν δὲ τῷ ,ςψλα′ ἔτει, τῷ δευτέρῳ χρόνῳ τῆς τοῦ Γίδωνος βασιλείας, ἦλθεν ὁ Μελὶκ σουλτὰν κατὰ τῆς Τραπεζοῦντος καὶ ἐχαώθησαν ὅσοι ἦσαν ἅπαντες. Ἐβασίλευσεν δὲ ὁ Γίδων ἔτη τρεισκαίδεκα καὶ ἐκοιμήθη ἐν ἔτει ,ςψμγ′ καταλείψας τὸ βασίλειον τῷ αὐτοῦ μὲν γυναικαδέλφῳ, υἱῷ δὲ πρωτοτόκῳ Ἀλεξίου τοῦ μεγάλου Κομνηνοῦ, κυρῷ Ἰωάννῃ Κομνηνῷ τῷ Ἀξούχῳ. Ὃς καὶ βασιλεύσας ἔτη ἓξ ἐκοιμήθη ἔτους ἑξακισχίλια ἑπτακόσια τεσσαράκοντα ἕξ. Λέγεται δὲ ὅτι ἐν τῷ τζυκανιστηρίῳ παίζων ἐκρημνίσθη καὶ σπαραχθεὶς ἀπέθανε.

On the emperors of Trebizond, the Grand Komnenoi, how, when, and how long each of them reigned

Lord Alexios I the Grand Komnenos left the blessed city of Constantinople and set out on campaign from Georgia with an army provided by the zeal and efforts of his paternal aunt Tamar. He came to Trebizond and captured it in April, indiction 7, 1204, at the age of twenty-two. After he had reigned eighteen years he died on the Sunday of Orthodoxy, February 20, 1222, aged forty.

From 1222, his son-in-law, lord Andronikos I Gidos Kom- 2
nenos, reigned. In 1223, during the second year of Gidon's reign, Melik Sultan came to attack Trebizond, and nearly all his army was lost. Gidon ruled for thirteen years and died in 1235, leaving the empire to his wife's brother, the firstborn son of Alexios I the Grand Komnenos, lord John I Komnenos Axouchos. After reigning for six years, he died in the year 1238. It is said that he was playing polo in the polo grounds when he fell and died after being severely injured.

3 Ἀπεκάρη γοῦν κατὰ μοναχοὺς Ἰωαννίκιος καὶ διεδέξατο τὴν βασιλείαν ὁ δεύτερος ἀδελφὸς αὐτοῦ, κῦρ Μανουὴλ ὁ μέγας Κομνηνός, ὁ στρατηγικώτατος ἅμα καὶ εὐτυχέστατος, τῷ αὐτῷ ͵ϛψμϛʹ ἔτει. Ἐν δὲ τῷ πέμπτῳ ἔτει τῆς αὐτοῦ βασιλείας, ͵ϛψναʹ ἔτει, ἰνδικτιῶνος αʹ, μηνὶ Ἰανουαρίῳ, ἐγένετο μεγάλη πυρκαϊά. Βασιλεύσας δὲ καλῶς καὶ θεαρέστως ἔτη εἴκοσι πέντε ἐκοιμήθη μηνὶ Μαρτίῳ, ἔτους ͵ϛψοαʹ.

4 Καὶ ἐβασίλευσε προτροπῇ τούτου καὶ ἐκλογῇ ἐκ τῆς δεσποίνης κυρᾶς Ἄννης τῆς Ξυλαλόης υἱὸς αὐτοῦ, κῦρ Ἀνδρόνικος ὁ Κομνηνός, ἔτη τρεῖς, καὶ ἐκοιμήθη ἔτους ͵ϛψοδʹ.

5 Καὶ ἐβασίλευσεν ὁ ἐκ τῆς κυρᾶς Εἰρήνης τῆς Συρίκαινας υἱὸς τοῦ κῦρ Μανουήλ, κῦρ Γεώργιος ὁ Κομνηνός, ἔτη δεκατέσσαρα. Ὃς καὶ παρεδόθη παρὰ τῶν ἀρχόντων ἐπιβούλως ἐν τῷ ὄρει τοῦ Ταυρεζίου καὶ ἐζωγρήθη μηνὶ Ἰουνίῳ.

6 Τῷ γοῦν αὐτῷ ἔτει διεδέξατο τὰ σκῆπτρα ὁ βος ἀδελφὸς αὐτοῦ, ὁ κῦρ Ἰωάννης ὁ μέγας Κομνηνός. Καὶ μετὰ ἐνιαυτὸν ἕνα ἐπῆλθεν αὐτῷ ἡ ἀποστασία τοῦ Παπαδοπούλου· ἀλλ᾽ ἐλευθερωθεὶς ἀπῆλθεν εἰς τὴν Πόλιν καὶ συνεζεύχθη τῇ θυγατρὶ μὲν κῦρ Μιχαὴλ βασιλέως τοῦ Παλαιολόγου, ἀδελφῇ δὲ κῦρ Ἀνδρονίκου βασιλέως τοῦ Παλαιολόγου, κυρᾷ Εὐδοκίᾳ Κομνηνῇ τῇ Παλαιολογίνῃ, τῇ πορφυρογεννήτῳ. Ἰστέον δὲ ὅτι, ἔτι ζῶν ὁ κῦρ Μιχαὴλ ὁ βασιλεύς, ἐγένετο ὁ γάμος τοῦ μεγάλου Κομνηνοῦ Ἰωάννου μετὰ τῆς Παλαιολογίνης. Καὶ τοῦ μὲν Παλαιολόγου ἀποθανόντος Δεκεμβρίου ιʹ, διεδέξατο αὐτὸν ὁ υἱὸς αὐτοῦ κῦρ

Ioannikios was then tonsured as a monk and his younger brother, lord Manuel I the Grand Komnenos, who was the greatest and most successful general, succeeded to the imperial office in that same year, 1238. In the fifth year of his reign, in the month of January, indiction 1, 1243, there was a great fire. After reigning well and in a God-pleasing manner for twenty-five years, he died in the month of March 1263. 3

And so, his son by lady Anna Xylaloë, lord Andronikos II Komnenos, whom Manuel had urged and selected to take the throne, became emperor and reigned for three years. He died in 1265/66. 4

The son of lord Manuel by lady Eirene Syrikaina, lord George Komnenos, then reigned for fourteen years. He was treacherously betrayed by his *archontes* at the mountain of Tabriz and was taken captive in June. 5

And so in that same year, his younger brother, lord John II the Grand Komnenos, succeeded to the imperial scepter. After a year, Papadopoulos's rebellion overthrew him. But he was freed and left for Constantinople, where he married the daughter of the emperor lord Michael Palaiologos, the sister of the emperor lord Andronikos II Palaiologos, lady Eudokia Komnene Palaiologina, who was born in the purple. Note that the emperor lord Michael was still alive when the marriage of John the Grand Komnenos and Palaiologina took place. When Palaiologos died, on December 10, his 6

Ἀνδρόνικος στηλιτεύσας τὸν αὐτοῦ πατέρα διὰ τὸ λατινόφρον.

7 Μετὰ δὲ τὸ ,ςψϟ′ ἔτος, Ἀπριλίου μηνός, ἦλθεν ὁ βασιλεὺς Ἰβηρίας Δαβὶδ καὶ ἐπεριώρισε τὴν Τραπεζοῦντα, ἀλλὰ ἀπεστράφη κενός.

8 Ἐν δὲ τῷ ,ςψϟα′ ἔτει, μηνὶ Ἀπριλίῳ εἰκοστῇ πέμπτῃ, ἰνδικτιῶνος ια^{ης}, κατέλαβεν ἐκ τῆς Κωνσταντινουπόλεως ἐν Τραπεζοῦντι ὁ μέγας Κομνηνὸς κῦρ Ἰωάννης σὺν τῇ Παλαιολογίνῃ, οὔσῃ ἐγκύῳ, καὶ ἐγεννήθη ὁ μέγας Κομνηνός, ὁ κῦρ Ἀλέξιος, τῷ ,ςψϟβ′ ἔτει. Εἶτα ἐγένετο ἡ τοῦ Κομνηνοῦ κῦρ Γεωργίου ἐπιδρομὴ καὶ κατάσχεσις, ὃν καὶ Πλάνον ἔλεγον, καὶ μετ᾽ αὐτοῦ ἡ ἐπίθεσις καὶ τὸ βασίλειον καὶ ἡ ἐξαίφνης φυγὴ κυρᾶς Θεοδώρας τῆς Κομνηνῆς, θυγατρὸς πρώτης τοῦ μεγάλου Κομνηνοῦ κῦρ Μανουὴλ ἐκ τῆς ἐξ Ἰβηρίας Ρουσουντάνας. Καὶ πάλιν ἀπεκατέστη εἰς τὸ σκαμνὶν ὁ Καλοϊωάννης ὁ Κομνηνὸς καὶ βασιλεύσας τὰ πάντα ἔτη ὀκτωκαίδεκα ἐκοιμήθη ἐν τοῖς Λιμνίοις μηνὶ Αὐγούστῳ εἰς τὰς ις′, ἡμέρᾳ ς′, ἰνδικτιῶνος ι^{ης}, ἔτους ,ςωε′. Ἐν γὰρ τῇ βασιλείᾳ αὐτοῦ παρέλαβον οἱ Τοῦρκοι τὴν Χαλυβίαν καὶ γέγονε παρ᾽ αὐτῶν μεγάλη ἐπιδρομή, ὥστε ἀοίκους γενέσθαι τὰς χώρας ὅλας. Ἐπεὶ καὶ ζῶν ἔτι ἐκομίσθη τὸ λείψανον αὐτοῦ ἐν Τραπεζοῦντι καὶ ἐτάφη ἐν τῷ ναῷ τῆς Χρυσοκεφάλου.

9 Καὶ ἐβασίλευσεν ὁ υἱὸς αὐτοῦ, ὁ κῦρ Ἀλέξιος ὁ μέγας Κομνηνός, καὶ ἤγαγε γυναῖκα αὐτῷ τὴν θυγατέρα τοῦ Πεκάϊ ἐξ Ἰβηρίας.

10 Ἀπῆλθεν ἡ Παλαιολογίνα χήρα εἰς τὴν Πόλιν μηνὶ

son lord Andronikos succeeded him and condemned his father for his Latin sympathies.

After 1282, in April, the king of Georgia, David, came and besieged Trebizond, but turned back empty-handed. 7

On April 25, indiction 11, 1283, lord John II the Grand Komnenos reached Trebizond from Constantinople along with Palaiologina, who was pregnant. Lord Alexios II the Grand Komnenos was born in 1283/84. Then the raid and capture of lord George Komnenos, whom they called the Vagabond, took place, and after him the coup, reign, and sudden flight of lady Theodora Komnene, the eldest daughter of lord Manuel the Grand Komnenos and Rusudani of Georgia. Kaloïoannes Komnenos was again restored to the throne and, after reigning eighteen years in all, he passed away at Limnia on Friday, August 16, indiction 10, 1297. During his reign, the Turks took Chalybia and launched a great invasion that rendered all of the lands uninhabitable. While he was still warm, his remains were brought to Trebizond and interred in the church of the Theotokos Chrysokephalos. 8

And then his son, lord Alexios II the Grand Komnenos, became emperor and took as his wife the daughter of Pekaï from Georgia. 9

Now a widow, the empress Eudokia Palaiologina de- 10

Ἰουνίῳ ιγ^{η}, ἔτους ,ϛωϛ', ἰνδικτιῶνος ια^{ης}, καὶ πάλιν ἦλθεν χήρα ἔτους ,ϛωθ', μηνὶ Μαρτίῳ, ἰνδικτιῶνος ιδ'.

11 Ἐκστρατεύσας ὁ βασιλεὺς κῦρ Ἀλέξιος κατὰ τῶν Τουρκῶν καὶ ἐν τῇ Κερασοῦντι καταλαβὼν ἐπίασε τὸν Κουστουγάνην ἔτους ,ϛωι', μηνὶ Σεπτεμβρίῳ, ὅτε καὶ ἐσκοτώθησαν Τοῦρκοι πολλοί. Ἐν δὲ τῷ αὐτῷ ἔτει, Δεκεμβρίῳ ιγ', ἡμέρᾳ δ', ἐκοιμήθη ἡ δέσποινα κυρὰ Εὐδοκία ἡ Παλαιολογίνα.

12 Μηνὶ Νοεμβρίῳ λ', ἡμέρᾳ ϛ', ἔτους ,ϛωια', ἐγένετο πυρκαϊὰ μεγάλη ἐντὸς τοῦ κάστρου. Ἐν δὲ τῷ ἐπιόντι ἔτει ἐπυρπολήθη ἡ ἐξάρτησις μηνὶ Ἰουνίῳ παρὰ τῶν Λατίνων, ὅτε καὶ ἐγένετο μέγας πόλεμος.

13 Ἥρπαξεν ὁ Παριάμης τὰς τζέργας ἔτους ,ϛωκβ', μηνὶ Ὀκτωβρίῳ εἰς τὰ β', ἡμέρᾳ γ', ἑσπέρας.

14 Ἔτους ,ϛωκζ' ἐγένετο μεγάλη πυρκαϊὰ παρὰ τῶν Σινωπιτῶν καὶ ἐλυμήνατο τὸ πῦρ πάντα τὰ ὡραῖα τῆς πόλεως, τά τε ἐντὸς καὶ ἐκτός.

15 Ἐκοιμήθη ὁ μέγας Κομνηνός, ὁ κῦρ Ἀλέξιος, μηνὶ Μαΐῳ γ', ἡμέρᾳ ε', ἰνδικτιῶνος ιγ', ἔτους ,ϛωλη', βασιλεύσας ἔτη λγ' παρὰ μῆνας γ'.

16 Καὶ ἐβασίλευσεν ὁ υἱὸς αὐτοῦ, ὁ κῦρ Ἀνδρόνικος ὁ μέγας Κομνηνός, καὶ ἐφόνευσε τοὺς δύο αὐταδέλφους αὐτοῦ, τόν τε Ἀζαχουτλοῦν κῦρ Μιχαὴλ καὶ κῦρ Γεώργιον τὸν Ἀχπουγᾶν. Ἐβασίλευσεν δὲ ὁ κῦρ Ἀνδρόνικος ἔτος α' καὶ μῆνας η', καὶ ἐκοιμήθη μηνὶ Ἰανουαρίῳ η', ἡμέρᾳ δ^{η}, ἰνδικτιῶνος ιε', ἔτους ,ϛωμ'.

17 Καὶ ἐδέξατο τὴν βασιλείαν ὁ υἱὸς αὐτοῦ κῦρ Μανουήλ, ὀκταετὴς ὤν, καὶ ἐκράτησε μῆνας η'. Ἐν γὰρ τῇ βασιλείᾳ

parted for Constantinople on June 13, 1298, indiction 11, and returned again in March 1301, indiction 14, still a widow.

The emperor lord Alexios led an army against the Turks and, reaching Kerasous, seized Koustouganes in September 1301, and many Turks were killed at that time. On Wednesday, December 13, of that same year, the empress, lady Eudokia Palaiologina, passed away. 11

On Friday, November 30, 1302, a great fire broke out within the citadel. In June of the following year, the shipyard was burned by the Latins when a great battle took place. 12

Bayram seized the covered market stalls on the evening of Tuesday, October 2, 1313. 13

In 1318/19, a great fire was started by men from Sinope and the fire destroyed all of the city's splendors both within and without. 14

Lord Alexios II the Grand Komnenos passed away on Thursday, May 3, indiction 13, 1330, after reigning for thirty-three years, less three months. 15

And then his son, lord Andronikos III the Grand Komnenos, became emperor and he killed his two brothers, lord Michael Azachoutlou and lord George Achpougas. Andronikos reigned for one year and eight months and passed away on Wednesday, January 4, indiction 15, 1332. 16

And so, his son lord Manuel II, who was eight years old, succeeded to the imperial office and held it for eight 17

αὐτοῦ ἦλθεν ὁ Παριάμης μετὰ φωσσάτου πολλοῦ ἕως τὸν Ἀσώματον καὶ ἐσκοτώθησαν Τοῦρκοι πολλοὶ καὶ ἔφυγον ὁ κόσμος· ὅτε καὶ ἡρπάγησαν ἄλογα πολλὰ Τούρκικα μηνὶ Αὐγούστῳ λʹ, ἡμέρᾳ αʹ, ἔτους ͵ςωμʹ.

18 Κατὰ δὲ τὸν Σεπτέμβριον μῆνα κβʹ, ἡμέρᾳ γʹ, ἰνδικτιῶνος αʹ, ἔτους ͵ςωμαʹ, ἦλθεν ὁ μέγας Κομνηνὸς κῦρ Βασίλειος ἐκ τῆς Κωνσταντινουπόλεως, υἱὸς μὲν τοῦ μεγάλου Κομνηνοῦ τοῦ κυροῦ Ἀλεξίου, ἀδελφὸς δὲ δεύτερος κῦρ Ἀνδρονίκου, καὶ παρέλαβε τὸ βασίλειον· ὅτε καὶ τὸν μέγαν δοῦκαν, Λέκην τὸν Τζατζιντζαῖον, καὶ τὸν υἱὸν αὐτοῦ, τὸν μέγαν δομέστικον τὸν Τζάμπαν, τοῦ ζῆν ἀπεστέρησε, τὸν δὲ ἀνεψιὸν αὐτοῦ κῦρ Μανουὴλ ἐπεριώρισε, τὴν δὲ μεγάλην δούκαιναν τὴν Συρίκαιναν ἐλίθασαν. Ἐν δὲ τῷ Φεβρουαρίῳ μηνὶ καʹ, ἡμέρᾳ αʹ τῆς Ὀρθοδοξίας, τῷ αὐτῷ ͵ςωμαʹ ἔτει, ἰνδικτιῶνος αʹ, ταραχθεὶς ὁ ἐκτομίας μέγας δοὺξ Ἰωάννης, ἐσφάγη ὁ κῦρ Μανουὴλ μαχαίρᾳ.

19 Μηνὶ Σεπτεμβρίῳ ιβʹ, ἡμέρᾳ γʹ, ἰνδικτιῶνος δʹ, ἔτους ͵ςωμδʹ, ἦλθεν ἡ δέσποινα κυρὰ Εἰρήνη ἡ Παλαιολογίνα, ἡ θυγάτηρ κῦρ Ἀνδρονίκου τοῦ Παλαιολόγου, καὶ εἰς τὰ ιζʹ τοῦ αὐτοῦ μηνός, ἡμέρᾳ αʹ, εὐλογήθη τὸν βασιλέα κῦρ Βασίλειον.

20 Κατὰ δὲ τὴν εʹ τοῦ Ἰουλίου μηνός, ἡμέρᾳ ςʹ, ἔτους ͵ςωμδʹ, ἦλθεν ὁ Σιχασάνης, ὁ υἱὸς τοῦ Ταμαρτάση, εἰς τὴν Τραπεζοῦντα, καὶ γέγονε πόλεμος εἰς τὸν ἀχάντακαν τοῦ ἁγίου Κηρύκου καὶ εἰς τὸν Μινθρίον· καὶ Θεοῦ εὐδοκοῦντος ἐτράπη ὑποβρύχιος καὶ ἔφυγεν, ὅτε ἐσκοτώθη ὁ Αὐτουραΐμης, ὁ υἱὸς τοῦ Ρουστάμη.

21 Μηνὶ Μαρτίῳ γʹ, ἡμέρᾳ βʹ τῆς ἀρχινηστίμου τῆς ἁγίας

months. In his reign, Bayram came with a large army as far as Asomatos, and many Turks were killed and everybody fled, and on this occasion many Turkish horses were also seized; this occurred on Sunday, August 30, 1332.

On Tuesday, September 22, indiction 1, 1332, lord Basil the 18
Grand Komnenos, the son of lord Alexios II the Grand Komnenos and younger brother of lord Andronikos III, came here from Constantinople and seized the imperial office; this was when he took the lives of the chief admiral Lekes Tzatzintzaios and his son, the commander in chief of the army Tzambas, and he imprisoned his nephew, lord Manuel II. They stoned to death Syrikaina, the wife of the chief admiral. On February 21, on the Sunday of Orthodoxy, in that same year 1333, indiction 1, the chief admiral, the eunuch John, rebelled and lord Manuel II was put to the sword.

On Tuesday, September 12, indiction 4, 1335, the empress 19
lady Eirene Palaiologina, the daughter of lord Andronikos III Palaiologos, came here, and on Sunday, the seventeenth of that same month, she was wed to the emperor, lord Basil.

On Friday, July 5, 1336, the sheikh Hasan, the son of 20
Timurtaş, came to Trebizond and there was a battle at the ravine of Saint Kerykos and at Minthrion. With God's consent, he was turned back by a torrent of rain and fled; this was when 'Abd-al Rahīm, the son of Rustam, was killed.

On March 3, 1337, on Monday of the first week of Lent, 21

μ′ ἐγένετο ἔκλειψις τοῦ ἡλίου ἀπὸ ὥρας δ′ ἕως ὥρας ζ′ καὶ ἐταράχθη τὸ κοινὸν κατὰ τοῦ βασιλέως, ὥστε καὶ ἔξωθεν τοῦ κουλᾶ συναχθέντες λίθους ἔσυραν εἰς αὐτόν, ἔτους ,ϛωμε′.

22 Μηνὶ Ὀκτωβρίῳ ε′, ἰνδικτιῶνος ζ′, ἔτους ,ϛωμζ′, ἐγεννήθη ὁ Κομνηνὸς κῦρ Ἰωάννης, ὁ ἐπονομασθεὶς Ἀλέξιος, ὁ υἱὸς τοῦ κῦρ Βασιλείου ὁ δεύτερος.

23 Εὐλογήθη ὁ βασιλεὺς ὁ κῦρ Βασίλειος τὴν ἐκ Τραπεζοῦντος δέσποιναν κυρὰν Εἰρήνην μηνὶ Ἰουλίῳ η′, ἔτους ,ϛωμζ′.

24 Ἐκοιμήθη ὁ βασιλεὺς κῦρ Βασίλειος ὁ μέγας Κομνηνὸς μηνὶ Ἀπριλίῳ εἰς τὰ ϛ′, ἡμέρᾳ ε′, ἰνδικτιῶνος η′, ἔτους ,ϛωμη′. Ἐβασίλευσεν ἔτη ζ′ καὶ μῆνας ϛ′. Οἱ δὲ παῖδες αὐτοῦ κῦρ Ἀλέξιος καὶ Καλοϊωάννης ἐστάλθησαν εἰς τὴν Πόλιν σὺν τῇ μητρί.

25 Καὶ ἐκράτησε τὴν βασιλείαν ἡ Παλαιολογίνα κυρὰ Εἰρήνη, χήρα οὖσα. Καὶ εὐθέως ἐταράχθησαν οἱ ἄρχοντες καὶ ἐγένοντο δύο μέρη· καὶ ὁ μὲν Τζανιχίτης, ὁ μέγας στρατοπεδάρχης κῦρ Σεβαστὸς σὺν τοῖς Σχολαρίοις καὶ Μειζομάταις καὶ κῦρ Κωνσταντῖνος ὁ Δωρανίτης καὶ οἱ Καβαζῖται καὶ ὁ Καμαχηνὸς καί τινες τοῦ κοινοῦ καὶ τῶν ἀλλαγίων τῶν βασιλικῶν ἐκράτησαν τὸν ἅγιον Εὐγένιον, οἱ δ᾽ Ἀμυτζανταράνται καί τινες τῶν ἀρχόντων καὶ τοῦ βασιλικοῦ ἀλλαγίου ἐκράτησαν σὺν τῇ δεσποίνῃ τὸν κουλᾶν.

26 Κατὰ δὲ Ἰούλιον μῆνα β′, ἡμέρᾳ α′, ἔτους ,ϛωμη′, ἐλθὼν ὁ μέγας δοὺξ Ἰωάννης ὁ ἐκτομίας ἐκ τῶν Λιμνίων μετὰ φωσσᾶτον πολύ, ἐγένετο πόλεμος, σύραντες καὶ τὸ

there was an eclipse of the sun from the fourth to the seventh hour, and the people rebelled against the emperor, so that they gathered outside the citadel and threw rocks at him.

On October 5, indiction 7, 1338, lord John Komnenos, who later was named Alexios, was born. He was the second son of lord Basil. 22

The emperor lord Basil was wed to the empress, lady Eirene from Trebizond, on July 8, 1339. 23

The emperor lord Basil the Grand Komnenos died on Thursday, April 6, indiction 8, 1340. He reigned for seven years and six months. His sons, lord Alexios and lord Kaloïoannes, were sent to Constantinople, along with their mother. 24

The widowed lady Eirene Palaiologina then seized the imperial office. The *archontes* immediately rebelled and split into two factions. Tzanichites, lord Sebastos the chief quartermaster, along with the Scholarioi, the Meizomatai, lord Constantine Doranites, the Kabazitai, Kamachenos, some of the people, and some of the palace guards seized the monastery of Saint Eugenios, while the Amytzantarantai, some of the *archontes,* and some of the imperial guards seized the citadel with the empress. 25

On Sunday, July 2, 1340, the chief admiral, the eunuch John, came from Limnia with a large army. There was a battle and they even deployed a siege engine against the 26

μάγγανον κατὰ τῆς μονῆς· καὶ ἐπυρπολήθη ἡ μονὴ καὶ πάντα τὰ ὡραῖα αὐτῆς ἀπεκαύθησαν. Καὶ ὁ Τζανιχίτης καὶ ἕτεροι ἄρχοντες ἐπεριωρίσθησαν εἰς τὰ Λιμνία καὶ ἐκεῖ τὸ ζῆν ἀπέδωκαν.

27 Τῷ αὐτῷ γοῦν ἔτει, περὶ τὸν Αὔγουστον μῆνα, ἀπῆλθε τὸ φωσσᾶτον ἡμῶν εἰς τὸν παρχάριν καὶ κουρσεύσαντες τοὺς Ἀμιτιώτας ἐπῆραν κοῦρσα πολλά, ὅτε ἐσκοτώθησαν καὶ υἱοὶ τοῦ Δολίνου.

28 Μηνὶ Ἰουνίῳ ιε′, ἡμέρᾳ ς′, ἰνδικτιῶνος θ′, ἔτους ,ϛωμθ′, ἐκοιμήθη ὁ βασιλεὺς Ῥωμαίων κῦρ Ἀνδρόνικος ὁ Παλαιολόγος.

29 Τῷ αὐτῷ μηνὶ καὶ τῷ αὐτῷ ἔτει ἐσκοτώθησαν οἱ ἄρχοντες εἰς τὰ Λιμνία.

30 Πάλιν γοῦν τῷ αὐτῷ ἔτει, Ἰουλίῳ δ′, ἡμέρᾳ δ′, ἤλθασιν οἱ Ἀμιτιῶται Τοῦρκοι καὶ ἐτράπησαν οἱ Ῥωμαῖοι ἄτερ πολέμου καὶ ἐσκοτώθησαν Χριστιανοὶ πολλοὶ καὶ ἐκαύθη ἡ Τραπεζοῦς ὅλη, ἐντὸς καὶ ἐκτός, καὶ ἐκαύθησαν λαὸς πολύς, καὶ γυναῖκες καὶ παιδία. Μετὰ δὲ τὴν πληγὴν ἐκ τῆς δυσωδίας τῶν καυθέντων ἀλόγων ζῴων καὶ ἀνθρώπων γέγονε καὶ αἰφνίδιος θάνατος. Πρὸ τούτου γὰρ ἡ θυγάτηρ τοῦ μεγάλου Κομνηνοῦ κῦρ Ἀλεξίου, ἡ κυρὰ Ἄννα ἡ λεγομένη Ἀναχουτλοῦ, τὴν μοναδικὴν ἀποβαλομένη στολὴν ἀπῆλθεν εἰς τὴν Λαζίαν καὶ ἐκράτησεν αὐτήν. Μετὰ δὲ τὸ γενέσθαι τὸν ἐμπρησμὸν καὶ τὴν ἐπιδρομὴν ἦλθεν ἡ Ἀναχουτλοῦ καὶ παρέλαβε τὴν βασιλείαν, ἔχουσα καὶ φωσσᾶτα Λάζικα, μηνὶ Ἰουλίῳ ιζ′, ἡμέρᾳ γ′, τῷ αὐτῷ ἔτει. Ἡ δὲ Παλαιολογίνα κατέβη τῆς βασιλείας, βασιλεύσασα ἔτος α′ καὶ μῆνας γ′.

monastery. The monastery was destroyed by fire and all of its beautiful adornment was burned. Tzanichites and the other *archontes* were banished to Limnia and lost their lives there.

In that same year, around August, our army went to the summer pastures, and by plundering the Ak Koyunlu Turks, they took a great deal of plunder. This was also when the sons of Dolinos were killed. 27

On Friday, June 15, indiction 9, 1341, the emperor of the Romans, lord Andronikos III Palaiologos, died. 28

In that same month and year, the *archontes* at Limnia were killed. 29

Again, in that same year, on Wednesday, July 4, the Ak Koyunlu Turks came here and the Romans were routed without even putting up a fight and many Christians were killed. All of Trebizond was set on fire, both inside and outside the walls, and a great number of people were burned too, including women and children. After this disaster, there was a sudden deadly epidemic caused by the stench of the burned animals and people. Before this, the daughter of lord Alexios II the Grand Komnenos, lady Anna, who was called Anachoutlou, renounced her nun's habit, went to Lazia, and seized it. After the fire and the assault happened, Anachoutlou came and took over the empire with an army of Laz on Tuesday, July 17, of that same year. Palaiologina was deposed from the imperial office after a reign of one year and three months. 30

31 Εἰς δὲ τὰς λʹ τοῦ αὐτοῦ Ἰουλίου μηνός, τῷ αὐτῷ ἔτει, ἡμέρᾳ βʹ, ἦλθεν ἐκ τῆς μεγαλοπόλεως ὁ ἀδελφὸς κῦρ Ἀλεξίου, ὁ κῦρ Μιχαὴλ ὁ Κομνηνός, ἔχων μετ᾽ αὐτοῦ κάτεργα γʹ καὶ τὸν Σχολάριν κῦρ Νικήταν, κῦρ Γρηγόριον τὸν Μειζομάτην. Καὶ τὸ μὲν βραδὺ καταβάντες οἱ ἄρχοντες μετὰ ὁρκωμοτικοῦ καὶ ὁ μητροπολίτης κῦρ Ἀκάκιος μετὰ τοῦ Εὐαγγελίου καὶ παρέλαβον αὐτὸν ὡς αὐθέντην, τῷ δὲ πρωῒ οὐκ οἶδα ὁ λαὸς πῶς αὐτὸν ἐπεριώρισαν. Τὰ δὲ κάτεργα ἥρπαξαν οἱ Λαζοὶ καὶ πολλοὺς διὰ βελῶν ἀπέκτειναν.

32 Τῇ οὖν γʹ τοῦ Αὐγούστου μηνός, ἡμέρᾳ ςʹ, τοῦ αὐτοῦ ἔτους ͵ςωμθʹ, πάλιν ἤλθασιν οἱ Ἀμιτιῶται Τοῦρκοι· ἀλλὰ Θεοῦ εὐδοκοῦντος οὐκ ἴσχυσαν πρὸς ἡμᾶς, ἀλλὰ ἀπῆλθον κατησχυμμένοι κενοί.

33 Μηνὶ τῷ αὐτῷ ζʹ, τῷ αὐτῷ ἔτει, ἐστάλθη ὁ Κομνηνὸς κῦρ Μιχαὴλ περιωρισμένος εἰς τὸ Οἴναιον, εἶτα εἰς τὰ Λιμνία.

34 Τῷ αὐτῷ μηνὶ ιʹ καὶ τῷ αὐτῷ ἔτει ἐστάλθη ἡ Παλαιολογίνα κυρὰ Εἰρήνη μετὰ Φράγκικον κάτεργον εἰς τὴν Πόλιν.

35 Μηνὶ Σεπτεμβρίῳ ιʹ ἔφυγεν ὁ Σχολάρις κῦρ Νικήτας καὶ ὁ Μειζομάτης κῦρ Γρηγόριος, ὁ Δωρανίτης κῦρ Κωνσταντῖνος καὶ ὁ υἱὸς Ἰωάννης καὶ ὁ ἀδελφὸς τοῦ Μειτζομάτη Μιχαὴλ καὶ ἕτεροι ἐκ τοῦ μέρους αὐτοῦ καὶ ἀπῆλθον μετὰ Βενέτικον κάτεργον εἰς τὴν Πόλιν· οἵτινες καὶ χρονίσαντες τὰ περὶ τὸν Αὔγουστον μῆνα ιζʹ ἦλθον μετὰ Κομνηνὸν κῦρ Ἰωάννην, τοῦ κῦρ Μιχαὴλ τὸν υἱόν, ἔχοντες δύο κάτεργα τῶν αὐτῶν καὶ τρία Γενουΐτικα, καὶ

On Monday, July 30, of that same year, Alexios's brother, lord Michael Komnenos, came from Constantinople with three galleys, along with lord Niketas Scholaris and lord Gregory Meizomates. In the evening, the *archontes* went down to meet him with written oaths of allegiance, as did the metropolitan Akakios with the Gospel, and they recognized him as their master; but in the morning the people somehow imprisoned him, although I do not know how. The Laz seized the galleys and killed many with arrows. 31

On Friday, August 3 of that same year of 1341, the Ak Koyunlu Turks returned but, with God's consent, they did not prevail over us and departed empty-handed and ashamed. 32

On the seventh of that same month in the same year, lord Michael Komnenos was banished to Oinaion, then to Limnia. 33

On the tenth of that same month in the same year, lady Eirene Palaiologina was sent on a Frankish galley to Constantinople. 34

On September 10, lord Niketas Scholaris, lord Gregory Meizomates, lord Constantine Doranites, his son John, Meitzomates's brother Michael, and others of their faction fled and went on a Venetian galley to Constantinople. After staying there until about August 17, they came back with lord John III Komnenos, the son of lord Michael, with two galleys of their own and three Genoese ones, and took over 35

παρέλαβον τὴν Τραπεζοῦντα μηνὶ Σεπτεμβρίῳ δʹ, ἡμέρᾳ δʹ, ἔτους ,ϛωναʹ. Καὶ ἐστέφθη τῷ αὐτῷ μηνὶ Σεπτεμβρίῳ εἰς τὰ θʹ εἰς τὴν Χρυσοκέφαλον ἐν τῷ ἄμβωνι· ὅτε καὶ ἐν τῇ ἐλεύσει αὐτοῦ ἐπὶ πᾶσιν αἱ χῶραι συνήχθησαν ἐπὶ τὸ αὐτὸ καὶ γέγονε διωγμὸς βαρὺς καὶ ἁρπαγὴ πολλή. Τότε ἐσκοτώθησαν καὶ οἱ ἄρχοντες οἱ Ἀμυτζαντάριοι, καὶ ἡ τοῦ κῦρ Γεωργίου μήτηρ, ἡ Σαργαλή, παρεδόθη τῇ πνιγμονῇ καὶ σὺν αὐτῇ ἀπεπνίγη καὶ ἡ Ἀναχουτλοῦ, βασιλεύουσα ἔτος αʹ καὶ μῆνα αʹ καὶ ἡμέρας ηʹ.

36 Μηνὶ Ἰουνίῳ, ἔτους ,ϛωναʹ, ἦλθαν οἱ Ἀμιτιῶται εἰς πόλεμον καὶ ἀπῆλθαν κενοί.

37 Ἐπειδὴ τὸν κῦρ Μιχαὴλ κρατῶν μέγας δοὺξ ὁ εὐνοῦχος ἐν τοῖς Λιμνίοις Μαρτίῳ μηνὶ ἀπεκτάνθη, ἀπῆλθεν ὁ μέγας δούξ, ὁ Σχολάρις, καὶ παρέλαβε τὸν κῦρ Μιχαήλ, καὶ ἦλθε καὶ ἐβασίλευσε μηνὶ Μαΐῳ γʹ, ἡμέρᾳ βʹ, ἔτους ,ϛωνβʹ. Ἐστέφθη δὲ μηνὶ τῷ αὐτῷ καʹ. Τὸν δὲ υἱὸν αὐτοῦ καταβιβάσας ἐπεριώρισεν εἰς τὸ σπήλαιον τοῦ ἁγίου Σάβα, βασιλεύσας ὁ κῦρ Ἰωάννης χρόνον αʹ καὶ μῆνας ηʹ.

38 Ἐπεὶ δὲ οἱ πρῶτοι ἄρχοντες τοῦ ζῆν ἀπεστερήθησαν, ἐτιμήθη ὁ Σχολάρις ὁ κῦρ Νικήτας μέγας δούξ, Γρηγόριος ὁ Μειζομάτης μέγας στρατοπεδάρχης, Λέων ὁ Καβαζίτης μέγας δομέστικος, Κωνσταντῖνος ὁ Δωρανίτης πρωτοβεστιάριος καὶ ὁ υἱος αὐτοῦ ἐπικέρνης, Ἰωάννης ὁ Καβαζίτης μέγας λογαριαστής, ὁ υἱὸς τοῦ Σχολάρι παρακοιμώμενος, Μιχαὴλ ὁ Μειζομάτης ἀμυρτζαντάριος, Τζανιχίτης ὁ Στέφανος μέγας κονοσταῦλος.

39 Μηνὶ Νοεμβρίῳ, ἔτους ,ϛωνδʹ, κατεσχέθησαν παρὰ τοῦ βασιλέως τοῦ κῦρ Μιχαὴλ μέγας δοὺξ ὁ Σχολάρις, μέγας

Trebizond on Wednesday, September 4, 1342. John III was crowned on September 9, in the pulpit of the church of the Theotokos Chrysokephalos. And it was then, when the whole region from all around had gathered in the same place for his arrival, that a terrible persecution and much confiscation took place. At this time the Amytzantarioi *archontes* were killed and lord George's mother, Sargale, was condemned to strangulation, and with her Anachoutlou was also strangled, after she had reigned for one year, one month, and eight days.

In June of the year 1343, the Ak Koyunlu came to make war and departed empty-handed. 36

Because the chief admiral, the eunuch John, who held lord Michael in Limnia, was killed in March, the chief admiral Scholaris went and took possession of lord Michael. Michael came here and reigned from Monday, May 3, 1344. He was crowned on the twenty-first of that same month. As for his son John, he deposed him and banished him to the cave of Saint Sabas. Lord John III had reigned one year and eight months. 37

Since the chief *archontes* had lost their lives, lord Niketas Scholaris was honored as chief admiral, while Gregory Meizomates was made grand chief quartermaster, Leo Kabazites was made commander in chief of the army, Constantine Doranites was made treasurer of the wardrobe, and his son was made *epikernes,* John Kabazites was made chief comptroller, Scholaris's son was made chamberlain, Michael Meizomates was made head of the imperial bodyguard, and Stephanos Tzanichites was made grand *konostaulos.* 38

In November 1345, the chief admiral Scholaris, commander-in-chief Meizomates, and others of their faction 39

δομέστικος ὁ Μειζομάτης καὶ ἕτεροι αὐτῶν. Τότε ἐστάλθη καὶ ὁ Κομνηνὸς κῦρ Ἰωάννης εἰς τὴν Πόλιν. Ἐν δὲ τῷ ,ςωνε′ ἔτει ἐπιάσθη ὁ ἅγιος Ἀνδρέας καὶ τὸ Οἴναιον.

40 Μηνὶ Σεπτεμβρίῳ, ἰνδικτιῶνος α′, ἐγένετο αἰφνίδιος θάνατος, ἡ πανούκλα, ὥστε ἀπεβάλλοντο πολλοὶ τέκνα καὶ συνεύνους, ἀδελφοὺς καὶ μητέρας καὶ συγγενεῖς, καὶ διεκράτησεν ἕως μῆνας ζ′.

41 Τῷ αὐτῷ ,ςωνς′, ἐν μηνὶ Ἰανουαρίῳ, ἐπιάσθη ἡ Κερασοῦς καὶ αἰχμαλωτίσθη καὶ ἐπυρπολήθη παρὰ Ἰανουαίων.

42 Ἐν δὲ τῷ αὐτῷ ἔτει, ἐν μηνὶ Ἰουνίου κθ′, ἰνδικτιῶνος α′, ἦλθαν ἐν Τραπεζοῦντι Τοῦρκοι πολλοί, ἤγουν ἀπὸ τὸ Ἐρζικάϊν Ἀχχὴς Ἀϊναπὰκ καὶ ἀπὸ τὸ Παΐπερτ ὁ Μαχμὰτ Εἰκεπτάρις καὶ ἀπὸ τῶν Ἀμιτιωτῶν ὁ Τουραλίπεκ καὶ ὁ Ποσδογάνης καὶ Τζιαπνίδες σὺν αὐτοῖς, καὶ ἐκράτησαν πόλεμον ἡμέρας γ′ καὶ ἀπῆλθαν κατῃσχυμμένοι καὶ πεπληγωμένοι φυγάδες, ἀποβαλλόμενοι ἐν ὁδῷ Τούρκους πολλούς.

43 Μηνὶ Μαΐῳ ε′, ἡμέρᾳ γ′, ἔτους ,ςωνζ′, ἦλθαν ἐνταῦθα ἐκ τοῦ Καφᾶ κάτεργα Φράγκικα β′ καὶ ἐξῆλθεν καὶ ἡμέτερον κάτεργον ἓν μέγαν ἐκ τῆς Δαφνούντας καὶ ἕτερον μικρὸν καὶ βαρκόπουλα ἱκανὰ καὶ ἐκρότησαν πόλεμον καὶ παραχωρήσει Θεοῦ ἐνίκησαν οἱ Φράγκοι καὶ ἐσκοτώθη ὁ μέγας δοὺξ Ἰωάννης ὁ Καβαζίτης καὶ κῦρ Μιχαὴλ ὁ Τζανιχίτης καὶ ἕτεροι πολλοί. Τὸ δὲ κάτεργον ἐκαύθη καὶ οἱ ἐν τῇ στερεᾷ Φράγκοι ἡρπάγησαν καὶ περιωρίσθησαν, τὰ δὲ κάτεργα ἀπῆλθον.

44 Κατὰ δὲ τὸν Ἰούνιον μῆνα ιε′, ἔτους ,ςωνζ′, πάλιν ἦλθαν ἐκ τοῦ Καφᾶ κάτεργα γ′ καὶ μία βάρκα ἐξ Ἀμινσῶ, καὶ

were arrested by the emperor lord Michael. It was then that lord John III Komnenos was sent to Constantinople. In 1346/47, Saint Andreas and Oinaion were taken.

In September, indiction 1, there was a sudden deadly epi- 40
demic, the plague, as a result of which many lost their children, spouses, siblings, mothers, and kinsmen. It lasted for seven months.

In January 1348, Kerasous was taken, enslaved, and 41
burned by the Genoese.

On June 29 of that same year, indiction 1, many Turks 42
came to Trebizond. They included Akhi Ayna Bey from Erzincan, Machmat Eikeptaris from Bayburt, Tur Ali Bey and Boz Doğan from the Ak Koyunlu, as well as the Çepni. They waged war for three days and took flight in shame after suffering heavy casualties, abandoning many Turks on the way.

On Tuesday, May 5, 1349, two Frankish galleys came here 43
from Caffa. A single large galley of ours, another small one, and several little barques set out from Daphnous and joined battle with them, but with God's permission the Franks won. The chief admiral John Kabazites, lord Michael Tzanichites, and many others were killed. Our galley was burned and the Franks on the mainland were seized and imprisoned. The galleys departed.

On June 15, 1349, three galleys came again from Caffa 44
along with a barque from Aminsous. After many discus-

μετὰ πολλῶν λόγων καὶ ὀχλήσεων καὶ ζητήσεων γέγονεν ἀγάπη καὶ παρεδόθη πρὸς αὐτοὺς τὸ Λεοντόκαστρον. Τότε γὰρ ἀσθένεια ἐνίκησε τὸν βασιλέα τὸν κῦρ Μιχαήλ, ὅτε καὶ ὁ Σχολάρις ὁ κῦρ Νικήτας ἐκ τοῦ Κεχρινᾶ ἐλθὼν γέγονε μέγας δοὺξ λαβὼν τὴν θυγατέρα τοῦ Σαμψών. Ἐβασίλευσε δὲ ὁ κῦρ Μιχαὴλ χρόνους ε′ καὶ μῆνας ζ′ ἥμισυν.

45 Μηνὶ Δεκεμβρίῳ ιγ′, ἡμέρᾳ α′, ἔτους ͵ϛωνη′, κατεβιβάσθη ἐκ τῆς βασιλείας ὁ κῦρ Μιχαὴλ ὁ Κομνηνὸς καὶ εἰς τὰ κβ′ τοῦ αὐτοῦ μηνός, ἡμέρᾳ γ′, εἰσῆλθεν εἰς τὴν Τραπεζοῦντα καὶ παρέλαβε τὴν βασιλείαν ὁ $\beta^{\text{ος}}$ υἱὸς κῦρ Βασιλείου τοῦ Κομνηνοῦ, ὁ κῦρ Ἰωάννης, ὁ ἐπονομασθεὶς κατὰ τὸν πάππον κῦρ Ἀλέξιος, σὺν τῇ δεσποίνῃ καὶ μητρὶ αὐτοῦ, κυρᾷ Εἰρήνῃ τῇ μεγάλῃ Κομνηνῇ. Καὶ ἐστέφθη ἐν τῷ ναῷ τοῦ ἁγίου Εὐγενίου μηνὶ Ἰανουαρίῳ εἰς τὰ κα′, κατὰ τὴν τοῦ ἁγίου ἑορτήν. Τὸν δὲ κῦρ Μιχαὴλ περιορίσας ἐν τῷ σπηλαίῳ τοῦ ἁγίου Σάβα ἀπέκειρε κατὰ μοναχόν· καὶ μετὰ χρόνον α′ ἀπεστάλθη εἰς τὴν Πόλιν μετὰ τοῦ τατᾶ κῦρ Μιχαὴλ τοῦ Σαμψών, ὅτε γέγονε καὶ ἡ συμπενθερεία πρὸς τὸν βασιλέα.

46 Τῷ αὐτῷ γοῦν ἔτει, τῷ ͵ϛωνη′, ἐγένετο σύγχυσις καὶ ταραχὴ μέσον τῶν ἀρχόντων, καὶ Ἰουνίου μηνὸς ἐπιάσθη ὁ μέγας στρατοπεδάρχης κῦρ Θεόδωρος ὁ Δωρανίτης, ὁ λεγόμενος Πιλέλης, καὶ ὁ ἀδελφὸς αὐτοῦ πρωτοβεστιάριος Κωσταντῖνος ὁ Δωρανίτης καὶ πᾶσα ἡ γενεὰ αὐτοῦ, καὶ περιωρίσθησαν ἕκαστος αὐτῶν εἰς τὰ τῶν ἀρχόντων ὀσπίτια· μετὰ δὲ $\zeta^{\text{ην}}$ τοῦ μηνὸς πάλιν ἀνεκλήθησαν.

sions, difficulties, and demands, peace was made and Leontokastron was surrendered to them. Then the emperor Michael was overcome by illness, which was when lord Niketas Scholaris came from Kenchrina, became chief admiral, and married Sampson's daughter. Lord Michael reigned for five years and seven and a half months.

On Sunday, December 13, 1349, lord Michael Komnenos 45
was deposed from the imperial office and on Tuesday, the twenty-second of the same month, Basil Komnenos's younger son, lord John, who was renamed Alexios III after his grandfather lord Alexios II, came here and took possession of the empire along with the empress, his mother lady Eirene the Grand Komnene. He was crowned in the church of Saint Eugenios on January 21, on the feast day of the saint. As for lord Michael, he was banished to the cave of Saint Sabas and tonsured as a monk. One year later, he was sent to Constantinople along with the *tatas,* lord Michael Sampson. That was when the marriage alliance with the emperor happened.

In that same year 1349/50, confusion and conflict arose 46
among the *archontes* and, in June, the chief quartermaster, lord Theodore Doranites, who was called Pileles, was arrested along with his brother, the treasurer of the wardrobe Constantine Doranites, and all his family, and each of them was confined to the homes of the *archontes.* But after the seventh of the month, they were recalled.

47 Ἐν μηνὶ Ἰανουαρίῳ, τῷ ͵ϛωνθʹ ἔτει, ἐπιάσθη ὁ γενόμενος πρωτοβεστιάριος Λέων ὁ Καβαζίτης καὶ ἀνεβιβάσθη εἰς τὸ πρωτοβεστιαρᾶτον ὁ Πιλέλης· ὅτε καὶ ὁ τατᾶς Μιχαὴλ ὁ Σαμψὼν ἀπῆλθε μετὰ κάτεργον εἰς τὴν Πόλιν ποιεῖν τὴν συμπενθερείαν καὶ λαβεῖν τὴν δέσποιναν καὶ ἐλθεῖν.

48 Τῷ αὐτῷ γοῦν ἔτει, Μαΐῳ μηνί, ἡμέρᾳ εʹ, ἐπιάσθη ὁ κουλᾶς παρὰ τοῦ Πιλέλη καὶ τῶν σὺν αὐτῷ, ἐζωγρήθη δὲ ὁ μέγας δοὺξ ὁ Σχολάρις. Ἀναταραχθεὶς δὲ ὁ λαὸς πάλιν ἐλευθερώθη, καὶ ἀπῆλθεν ὁ βασιλεὺς εἰς τὴν Τρίπολιν. Ὁ δὲ Πιλέλης καὶ ὁ υἱὸς αὐτοῦ καὶ ὁ γαμβρὸς αὐτοῦ καὶ οἱ τοῦ Ξενίτου παῖδες συλληφθέντες ἐστάλθησαν καὶ περιωρίσθησαν εἰς τὸν Κεχρινᾶν.

49 Μηνὶ Σεπτεμβρίῳ γʹ, ἰνδικτιῶνος εʹ, ἔτους ͵ϛωξʹ, ἦλθεν ἡ δέσποινα ἡ Κομνηνή, ἡ Καντακουζηνή, μετὰ κάτεργον ἐκ τῆς Πόλεως, ἡ θυγάτηρ κῦρ Νικηφόρου τοῦ Καντακουζηνοῦ τοῦ σεβαστοκράτορος, πρώτου ἐξαδέλφου ὄντος τοῦ βασιλέως Ρωμαίων κῦρ Ἰωάννου τοῦ Καντακουζηνοῦ, καὶ εἰς τὰ κηʹ ἡμέρας πρῶτον ἐγένετο εὐλόγησις αὐτῆς μετὰ τοῦ βασιλέως ἐν τῇ μονῇ τοῦ ἁγίου Εὐγενίου.

50 Τῷ αὐτῷ γοῦν ἔτει, τῷ ͵ϛωξʹ, Σεπτεμβρίου κβʹ, ἀπήλθαμεν μὲ τὴν δέσποιναν, τοῦ βασιλέως τὴν μητέρα, εἰς τὰ Λιμνία κατὰ τοῦ κεφαλατικεύοντος ἐκεῖσε Κωνσταντίνου τοῦ Δωρανίτου, ἀδελφοῦ τοῦ πρωτοβεστιαρίου τοῦ Πιλέλη, καὶ λείψαντες μῆνας γʹ πάλιν ἤλθαμεν.

51 Κατὰ δὲ τὸν Ἰανουάριον μῆνα, τῷ αὐτῷ ἔτει, εἰσῆλθεν ὁ πικέρνης Ἰωάννης ὁ Τζανιχίτης καὶ ἐκράτησε τὴν Τζάνιχαν, τὸ κάστρον, ἀνάρχῳ χειρί· καὶ κατὰ τὸν Ἀπρίλιον

In January 1351, Leo Kabazites, who had become treasurer of the wardrobe, was arrested and Pileles was raised to the rank of treasurer of the wardrobe. At the same time, the *tatas* Michael Sampson left on a galley for Constantinople to make the marriage alliance, take charge of the empress, and return. 47

On May 5 of that same year, the citadel was seized by Pileles and his supporters, and the chief admiral Scholaris was taken prisoner. But the people rose up and he was freed again, and the emperor left for Tripolis. Pileles, his son, his son-in-law, and Xenitos's children were arrested and banished to Kechrina. 48

On September 3, indiction 5, 1351, the empress Komnene Kantakouzene, the daughter of the *sebastokrator* Nikephoros Kantakouzenos, who was first cousin to the Roman emperor, lord John VI Kantakouzenos, came here from Constantinople by galley and on the twenty-eighth her wedding to the emperor took place in the monastery of Saint Eugenios. 49

On September 22 of that same year, namely 1351, we went with the empress, the emperor's mother, to Limnia to attack Constantine Doranites, the brother of the treasurer of the wardrobe Pileles, who was acting as governor there. After spending three months there, we returned here. 50

In January of that same year, the *pikernes* John Tzanichites entered and seized the stronghold of Tzanicha, violating the 51

μῆνα, τῷ αὐτῷ ἔτει, ἀπῆλθεν ὁ βασιλεὺς ἐκεῖσε καὶ ἡ δέσποινα, καὶ ἐποίησεν εἰρηνικὴν κατάστασιν. Καὶ κατὰ τὸν Ἰούλιον μῆνα, τῷ αὐτῷ ἔτει, ἐπαρεδόθησαν τῇ ἀγχόνῃ ὁ Πιλέλης καὶ ὁ υἱός του καὶ ὁ γαμβρός του ἐν τῷ Κεχρινᾷ κάστρῳ.

52 Τῷ αὐτῷ ,ϛωξ′ ἔτει ἀπῆλθεν ἡ ἀδελφὴ τοῦ βασιλέως, κυρὰ Μαρία ἡ μεγάλη Κομνηνή, καὶ συνεζεύχθη τὸν Χουτλουπέκην, τὸν υἱὸν τοῦ Τουραλῆ, ἀμηρᾶν ὄντα τῶν Ἀμιτιωτῶν, μηνὶ Αὐγούστῳ.

53 Τῷ αὐτῷ μηνὶ καὶ ἔτει ἦλθαν τὰ Βενέτικα τὰ κάτεργα κατὰ τῶν Γενουβίσων καὶ ἔκαυσαν καράβια πολλά.

54 Τῷ αὐτῷ μηνὶ Ἰουνίῳ, ἔτους ,ϛωξβ′, ἀπῆλθεν ὁ Σχολάρις φυγαδίας εἰς τὴν Κερασοῦντα· καὶ ἔκτοτε τὰ γενηθέντα διὰ μέσον μηνύματα καὶ ἀποκρισιαρίκια τίς δύναται γράφειν;

55 Μηνὶ Μαρτίῳ κε′, ἔτους ,ϛωξγ′, ἦλθεν ὁ μέγας δοὺξ ὁ Σχολάρις καὶ ὁ υἱὸς αὐτοῦ ὁ παρακοιμώμενος κατὰ τῆς Τραπεζοῦντος μετὰ ἓν κάτεργον καὶ βάρκας ια′, ὅτε ἀπῆλθε σὺν αὐτῷ καὶ ὁ πρωτοβεστιάριος Βασίλειος ὁ Χούπακας, καί, πολλῶν λόγων καὶ ὀχλήσεων γενομένων, πάλιν ἐγένετο κατάστασις καὶ ἀπῆλθον εἰς Κερασοῦντα.

56 Ἐν τῷ αὐτῷ ἔτει ,ϛωξγ′, μηνὶ Μαΐῳ, ἰνδικτιῶνος η′, ἁρματώσας ὁ βασιλεὺς κάτεργα δύο καὶ ξύλα μικρὰ ἱκανὰ <καὶ> ἀπῆλθεν ἅμα τῇ μητρὶ καὶ δεσποίνῃ καὶ τῷ μητροπολίτῃ κατὰ τοῦ Σχολάρι ἐν Κερασοῦντι, ὅτε καὶ ὁ μὲν Σχολάρις ἦν ἐν τῷ Κεχρινᾷ, ὁ δὲ παρακοιμώμενος ἐν Κερασοῦντι. Μετὰ δὲ τὴν μάχην καὶ τὸν πόλεμον ἐγένετο κατάστασις καὶ προσκυνήσασα ἡ Κερασοῦς τὸν βασιλέα.

rule of law. During April of that same year, the emperor and the empress went there and made peace. During July of that same year, Pileles, his son, and his son-in-law were condemned to hanging in the fortress of Kechrina.

That same year, 1351/52, the emperor's sister, lady Maria the Grand Komnene, left and married Kutlu Bey, Tur Ali's son, the emir of the Ak Koyunlu, in August. 52

In that same month and year, Venetian galleys came here to attack the Genoese and burned many light boats. 53

In the same month of June, 1354, Scholaris went into exile to Kerasous, and who could possibly describe all the messages and dispatches that passed between the two cities from then on? 54

On March 25, 1355, the chief admiral Scholaris and his son, the chamberlain, came to attack Trebizond with a galley and eleven barques. At the same time, the treasurer of the wardrobe Basil Choupax went with him. After many discussions and difficulties, a settlement was reached again and they went back to Kerasous. 55

In that same year, 1355, in May, indiction 8, the emperor fitted out two galleys and a large number of smaller vessels and went, along with his mother, the empress, and the metropolitan, to attack Scholaris in Kerasous. At this point Scholaris was in Kechrina but the chamberlain was in Kerasous. After a battle and some fighting, a settlement was reached and Kerasous paid homage to the emperor. But the 56

Ὁ δὲ παρακοιμώμενος ἐξελθὼν ἀπῆλθεν εἰς τὸν πατέρα αὐτοῦ ἐν τῷ Κεχρινᾷ, καὶ ἦσαν ἅπαντες οἱ περὶ τὸν Σχολάριν ἐκεῖ. Καὶ ὁ μὲν βασιλεὺς τὸν στόλον καὶ τὴν δέσποιναν ἀφεὶς ἐν τῇ Τριπόλει ἦλθεν ἐνταῦθα, καὶ λαμβάνει στρατὸν καβαλλαρικὸν καὶ ἀπῆλθε, τό τε διὰ θαλάσσης καὶ τὸ διὰ ξηρᾶς διάστημα περιώρισεν ἅπαντας ἐν τῷ Κεχρινᾷ· ὅτε καὶ πόλεμος ἐγένετο, προσκυνήσαντες τὸν βασιλέα καὶ ἀνευφήμησαν. Ὁ μὲν βασιλεὺς καὶ οἱ σὺν αὐτῷ ἅπαντες ὑπέστρεψαν, ὁ δὲ Σχολάρις καὶ οἱ σὺν αὐτῷ ἀπέμειναν ἐκεῖ· ὅτε ἦλθε καὶ ὁ πρωτοβεστιάριος ἐκ τῶν Λιμνίων καὶ οἱ περὶ αὐτόν.

57 Περὶ δὲ τὸν Αὔγουστον μῆνα, τοῦ αὐτοῦ ,ςωξγʹ ἔτους, ἐκστρατεύσας ὁ δοὺξ Χαλδίας, Ἰωάννης ὁ Καβαζίτης, ἀπῆλθε καὶ ἐπίασε τὴν Χερίαναν καὶ ᾐχμαλώτευσεν αὐτήν· ὅτε ἐλευθερώθη καὶ ἡ Σορώγαινα καὶ γέγονεν εἰς τὴν βασιλικὴν ὑποχειριότητα.

58 Τῷ αὐτῷ ἔτει ἐξῆλθε καὶ ὁ κῦρ Μιχαὴλ ὁ μέγας Κομνηνὸς ἐκ τῆς Πόλεως καὶ ἦλθε μέχρι καὶ τοῦ Σουλχατίου καὶ πάλιν ὑπέστρεψε.

59 Μηνὶ Ὀκτωβρίῳ, ἰνδικτιῶνος θʹ, ἔτους ,ςωξδʹ, ἀπῆλθεν ὁ μέγας δομέστικος ὁ Μειζομάτης καὶ ὁ μέγας στρατοπεδάρχης ὁ Σαμψὼν εἰς τὰς Τριπόλεις καὶ ἕως τοῦ Κεγχρινᾶ καὶ παρέλαβον τὸν Σχολάριν καὶ τοὺς περὶ αὐτόν, καὶ ἦλθον, καὶ γέγονεν εἰρηναία κατάστασις.

60 Μηνὶ Νοεμβρίῳ κζʹ, ἡμέρᾳ ςʹ, ἰνδικτιῶνος θʹ, τοῦ ,ςωξδʹ ἔτους, ἀπήλθομεν μετὰ τοῦ βασιλέως κατὰ τῆς Χερίανας ἀπὸ διαβολικῆς συνεργίας. Καὶ πρῶτον μὲν ἐκουρσεύσαμεν, ἐπολιορκήσαμεν καὶ ᾐχμαλωτίσαμεν, περὶ δὲ τὴν ς^{ην}

chamberlain left the city and went to join his father in Kechrina, where all of Scholaris's supporters were. And the emperor left the fleet and the empress in Tripolis and came here, took a force of cavalry and left again. He blockaded everyone at Kechrina by land and sea. At this time there was also a battle, and after paying homage to the emperor they acclaimed him. The emperor and all his supporters then returned here, but Scholaris and his supporters remained there. At that time as well the treasurer of the wardrobe came here from Limnia with his supporters.

Around August of the same year, 1355, the governor of 57
Chaldia, John Kabazites, marched out with an army, took Cheriana, and enslaved it. At this time also Sorogaina was freed and came under the emperor's authority.

In that same year, lord Michael the Grand Komnenos left 58
Constantinople, came as far as Soulchation, and then returned.

In October, indiction 9, 1355, the commander-in-chief 59
Meizomates and the chief quartermaster Sampson went to Tripolis and advanced as far as Kechrina. They took Scholaris and his supporters into their custody and returned here. And a peaceful settlement was reached.

On Friday, November 27, indiction 9, year 1355, we went 60
with the emperor to attack Cheriana at the devil's behest. At first we plundered, besieged, and took captives, but

ὥραν ἐφύγομεν φυγὴν ἄκοσμον ὀλίγων Τούρκων διωκόντων ἡμᾶς. Τότε τοίνυν ἐσκοτώθησαν Χριστιανοὶ ὡσεὶ ν′ καὶ ἐχαώθησαν καὶ ἄλογα πολλὰ καὶ ὁ δοὺξ Χαλδίας, Ἰωάννης ὁ Καβαζίτης, ἐπιάσθη καί, εἰ μὴ Κύριος ἦν ἐν ἡμῖν, ἀπωλόμην ἂν καὶ αὐτὸς ἐγώ· ἀλλὰ Θεοῦ εὐδοκοῦντος ἴσχυσέ μου ὁ ἵππος καὶ κατόπιν βαίνων τοῦ βασιλέως ἐλευθερώθημεν καὶ μετὰ τρεῖς ἡμέρας κατελάβομεν ἐν Τραπεζοῦντι.

61 Τότε τοίνυν ἐγέννησε καὶ ὁ βασιλεὺς υἱόν, τὸν κῦρ Ἀνδρόνικον, ἐξ ἄλλης γαστρὸς καὶ οὐκ ἀπὸ τῆς δεσποίνης.

62 Μηνὶ Δεκεμβρίῳ ιθ′, ἰνδικτιῶνος ι′, ἔτους ͵ςωξε′, ἐκινήσαμεν μετὰ τοῦ βασιλέως εἰς τὰ Λιμνία ποιήσαντες τὴν πρόκυψιν τῆς Χριστοῦ γεννήσεως εἰς Κερασοῦντα, τῶν δὲ Φώτων εἰς τὸ Ἰασόνιν, ὅτε ἐσκοτώθησαν καὶ Τοῦρκοι ιδ′. Ἀπελθόντες γοῦν εἰς τὰ Λιμνία καὶ πάλιν στραφέντες, λείψαντες τὰ πάντα τρεῖς μῆνας, πάλιν κατελάβομεν ἐν Τραπεζοῦντι ὑγιεῖς.

63 Περὶ τὸν Ἀπρίλιον μῆνα εἰς τὰ ς′, τῇ μεγάλῃ ε′, τοῦ αὐτοῦ͵ςωξε′ ἔτους, ἐγεννήθη τῷ βασιλεῖ θυγάτηρ, ἡ κυρὰ Ἄννα, ἐκ τῆς δεσποίνης ἡμῶν τῆς κυρᾶς Θεοδώρας, ἰνδικτιῶνος ι′.

64 Μηνὶ Μαΐῳ, ἰνδικτιῶνος ι′, ἔτους ͵ςωξε′, ἀπῆλθεν ὁ βασιλεὺς μετὰ φωσσᾶτον εἰς τὸν παρχάριν καὶ ἐγύρισε τὸν τοιοῦτον παρχάριν ὅλον.

65 Μηνὶ Νοεμβρίῳ ια′, ἡμέρᾳ ζ′, ἰνδικτιῶνος ια′, τοῦ ͵ςωξς′ ἔτους, ἦλθεν ἡ δέσποινα τῆς Σινώπης, ἡ κυρὰ Εὐδοκία, ἡ θυγάτηρ κῦρ Ἀλεξίου τοῦ μεγάλου Κομνηνοῦ.

66 Μηνὶ τῷ αὐτῷ ιγ′, ἡμέρᾳ β′, ἰνδικτιῶνος ια′, τοῦ αὐτοῦ

around the sixth hour we fled in disorder when a handful of Turks pursued us. At that time about fifty Christians were killed, many horses were lost, the governor of Chaldia, John Kabazites, was captured, and if the Lord had not been with us, I myself would have been lost. But with God's consent, my horse was strong and following behind the emperor we remained free. And three days later we reached Trebizond.

Then the emperor had a son, lord Andronikos, from the 61
womb of another woman and not by the empress.

On December 19, indiction 10, 1356, we set out with the 62
emperor for Limnia and held Christmas festivities at Kerasous and those of Epiphany at Cape Jason; at this time fourteen Turks were killed. We went to Limnia and then turned back and reached Trebizond in good health after an absence of three months, more or less.

Around April 6, Holy Thursday, indiction 10 of that same 63
year 1357, a daughter, lady Anna, was born to the emperor by our empress, lady Theodora.

In May, indiction 10, 1357, the emperor went with an army 64
to the summer pastures and patrolled all of the pastures.

On Saturday, November 11, indiction 11, 1357, the mistress 65
of Sinope, lady Eudokia, the daughter of lord Alexios II the Grand Komnenos, came here.

In that same month and year 1357, on Monday the 66

͵ϛωξϛʹ ἔτους, ἀμελησάντων ἡμῶν τὴν φύλαξιν εἰσῆλθεν εἰς τὴν Ματζούκαν ὁ Χατζυμύρις, ὁ υἱὸς τοῦ Παϊράμη, μετὰ φωσσάτου πολλοῦ καὶ ἐκούρσευσεν αἰχμαλωσίαν πολλήν, καὶ ζῷα καὶ πράγματα, ἤγουν ἀπὸ τὴν Παλαιοματζούκαν καὶ ἕως εἰς τὸ Δικαίσιμον.

67 Τῷ αὐτῷ ἔτει, μηνὶ Ἰανουαρίῳ κβʹ, ἦλθεν ἐκ τῆς Κωνσταντινουπόλεως ἀποκρισιάρις Ἰωάννης ὁ Λεοντόστηθος.

68 Μηνὶ Αὐγούστῳ κβʹ, ἡμέρᾳ δʹ, ἰνδικτιῶνος ιαʹ, τοῦ ͵ϛωξϛʹ ἔτους, ἦλθεν ἡ δεσποινάχατ ἡ κυρὰ Μαρία, ἡ τοῦ βασιλέως ἀδελφή, εἰς τὴν Τραπεζοῦντα, ἥτοι ἡ τὸν Ἀμιτιώτην συζευχθεῖσα Χουτλουπέκην.

69 Μηνὶ Αὐγούστῳ εἰς τὰ κθʹ, ἡμέρᾳ δʹ, ἀπῆλθεν ἡ θυγάτηρ τοῦ βασιλέως κυροῦ Βασιλείου, ἡ κυρὰ Θεοδώρα, πρὸς τὸ συζευχθῆναι τὸν ἀμηρᾶν Χατζυμύριν, τὸν υἱὸν τοῦ Παϊράμη, ἔχουσα νυμφοστόλον τὸν Χούπακα κῦρ Βασίλειον, τὸν Σχολάριν, ἰνδικτιῶνος ιαʹ, ἔτους ͵ϛωξϛʹ.

70 Μηνὶ Σεπτεμβρίῳ ιζʹ, ἡμέρᾳ βʹ, μετὰ τὸ ἀπόδειπνον ἐγεννήθη τῷ βασιλεῖ υἱός, ὃν καὶ ἐκάλεσε κατὰ τὸν πάππον Βασίλειον, ἰνδικτιῶνος ιβʹ, ἔτους ͵ϛωξζʹ.

71 Μηνὶ Ἀπριλίῳ, ἰνδικτιῶνος ιγʹ, ἔτους ͵ϛωξηʹ, εἰσῆλθεν ὁ βασιλεὺς εἰς τὴν Χαλδίαν κτίζειν τοῦ Κούκου, ἐλθὼν δὲ ἐκ τοῦ Παϊπερτίου ὁ Χοτζιαλατίφης μετὰ τʹ καβαλλαρίων ἐνεπόδισεν· ὅτε καὶ τὸν Καβαζίτην Ἰωάννην παρέλυσε τοῦ κεφαλατικίου.

72 Μηνὶ Μαΐῳ εʹ, ἡμέρᾳ δʹ, ἰνδικτιῶνος ιδʹ, τοῦ ͵ϛωξθʹ ἔτους, ὥρᾳ εʹ, ἐγένετο ἔκλειψις ἡλίου, οἵα οὐκ ἐγένετο ἐν τῇ καθ᾽ ἡμᾶς γενεᾷ, ὥστε ἐφάνησαν καὶ ἀστέρες ἐν τῷ

thirteenth, indiction 11, Hacı Emir, Bayram's son, entered Matzouka with a large army, due to our neglect in guarding it, and plundered it, taking many captives and seizing both livestock and property from Palaiomatzouka as far as Dikaisimon.

On January 22 of that same year 1358, the emissary John Leontostethos came here from Constantinople. 67

On Wednesday, August 22, indiction 11, 1358, the *despoinachat,* lady Maria, the emperor's sister, who was married to the Ak Koyunlu Kutlu Bey, came to Trebizond. 68

On Wednesday, August 29, indiction 11, 1358, the daughter of the emperor lord Basil, that is lady Theodora, left to be married to the emir Hacı Emir, Bayram's son, with lord Basil Choupax Scholaris as the bridal escort. 69

On Monday, September 17, indiction 12, 1358, after compline, a son was born to the emperor Alexios III. He was named Basil after his grandfather. 70

In April, indiction 13, 1360, the emperor entered Chaldia to build Koukos. But *hoca* Latif came from Bayburt and thwarted him with three hundred cavalrymen. This was also when Alexios III removed John Kabazites from the governorship of Chaldia. 71

On Wednesday, May 5, indiction 14, 1361, at the fifth hour there was a solar eclipse during which the stars appeared in the sky, something that had not happened in our generation. 72

οὐρανῷ, καὶ ἐκράτησεν ὥραν α′ ἡμίσειαν. Ὁ δὲ βασιλεὺς κῦρ Ἀλέξιος καὶ ἡ μήτηρ αὐτοῦ, ἡ κυρὰ Εἰρήνη, καί τινες τῶν ἀρχόντων, κἀγὼ σὺν αὐτοῖς, εὑρέθημεν κατὰ συγκαιρίαν ἐν τῇ κατὰ τὴν Ματζούκαν μονῇ τῆς Σουμελᾶς, ποιήσαντες δεήσεις πολλὰς καὶ παρακλήσεις.

73 Τῷ αὐτῷ ‚ςωξθ′ ἔτει, ἤτοι πρὸ ἓξ μηνῶν, Δεκεμβρίῳ μηνὶ εἰς τὰ ς′, ἀπῆλθεν ὁ βασιλεὺς εἰς τὰ Λιμνία, ἔνθα ποιήσας ὡσεὶ γ′ ἥμισυν μῆνας πάλιν ἦλθε.

74 Τῷ αὐτῷ ‚ςωξθ′ ἔτει ἦλθεν ἐκ τῆς Πόλεως ἀποκρισιάρις ὁ Λεοντόστηθος ὡς ἀπὸ τοῦ βασιλέως κῦρ Ἰωάννου τοῦ Παλαιολόγου, ζητῶν συμπενθερείαν μετὰ τοῦ βασιλέως ἡμῶν.

75 Τῷ ‚ςωξθ′ ἔτει, ἰνδικτιῶνος ιδ′, μηνὶ Ἰουνίῳ λ′, ἡμέρᾳ δ′, ὥρᾳ τοῦ ἀποδείπνου, ἐκοιμήθη ὁ μέγας δούξ, Νικήτας ὁ Σχολάρις· ὅτε καὶ ὁ βασιλεὺς μεγάλως ἐλυπήθη ἐπιστὰς ἐν τῇ προπομπῇ τῆς ἐξόδου αὐτοῦ, φορέσας καὶ λευκὰ διὰ τὴν θλῖψιν, καθὼς εἴθισται τοῖς ἄναξι.

76 Μηνὶ Ἰουλίῳ κγ′, ἡμέρᾳ ς′, ἰνδικτιῶνος ιδ′, τοῦ ‚ςωξθ′ ἔτους, ὁ ἀπὸ τοῦ Παϊπερτίου κεφαλὴ Χοτζιαλατίφης, λαβὼν ἐπιλέκτους στρατιώτας ὡσεὶ υ′ καὶ πρός, εἰσῆλθεν κατὰ τὴν Ματζούκαν πρός τε τὴν Λαχαρανὴν καὶ Χασδένιχαν. Οἱ δέ γε Ματζουκαῖται προκαταλαβόντες τὰς διεξόδους ἔκτειναν ὡσεὶ σ′ Τούρκους καὶ πλείους ἁρπάσαντες καὶ ἄλογα καὶ ἅρματα πολλά, καὶ αὐτὸν τὸν Χοτζιαλατίφην καρατομοῦσι καὶ τῇ ἐπαύριον θριαμβεύουσι τὰς κεφαλὰς αὐτῶν ἀνὰ τὴν Τραπεζοῦνταν ὅλην.

77 Μηνὶ Δεκεμβρίῳ ιγ′ ἀπήλθομεν εἰς τὴν Χαλυβίαν μετὰ τοῦ βασιλέως εἰς τὸ ὀσπιτόκαστρον τοῦ Χατζυμύρι, υἱοῦ

It lasted an hour and a half. The emperor lord Alexios III, his mother lady Eirene, and some of the *archontes,* and I myself with them opportunely found ourselves at the Soumela monastery in Matzouka and we made many supplications and prayers at that time.

In the same year, some six months before, on December 6, 1360, the emperor left for Limnia, where he spent about three and a half months before returning here. 73

That same year, 1360/61, Leontostethos came from Constantinople as an emissary from the emperor lord John V Palaiologos to seek a marriage alliance with our emperor. 74

At the hour of compline on Wednesday, June 30, indiction 14, year 1361, the chief admiral Niketas Scholaris passed away. The emperor greatly mourned his passing at that time and led his funeral procession, wearing white for mourning as is the custom for rulers. 75

On Friday, July 23, indiction 14, 1361, the chieftain of Bayburt, *hoca* Latif, entered Matzouka near Lacharane and Chasdenicha with a select group of soldiers numbering around four hundred or more. But the people of Matzouka took control of the passes before his return, killed about two hundred Turks, and captured more of them, as well as many horses and arms. As for *hoca* Latif himself, they beheaded him and on the following day they carried their enemies' heads in triumph through all of Trebizond. 76

On December 13, indiction 15, 1361, we left for Chalybia with the emperor and went to the fortified manor of Hacı 77

τοῦ Παϊράμη, ἤγουν μετὰ τὴν ἐν Κερασοῦντι εἰσέλευσιν αὐτοῦ καὶ ἔσμιξιν μεθ᾽ ἡμῶν. Ἀπὸ δὲ Χαλυβίας ἤλθομεν διὰ ξηρᾶς εἰς τὴν Κερασοῦντα, ἀκολουθούντων ἡμῖν τοῦ ἀμηρᾶ Χατζυμύρι καὶ Τούρκων, μικροῦ δεῖν δουλικῶς, ἰνδικτιῶνος ιε′, ͵ςωο′ ἔτους.

78 Μηνὶ Ὀκτωβρίῳ, ἰνδικτιῶνος ιε′, τοῦ ͵ςωο′ ἔτους, ὁ ἀπὸ τοῦ Ἐρζιγκὰ Ἀχχὶ Αἰναπὰκ κατελθὼν περιεκάθισε κάστρον τὴν Γόλαχαν ὡσεὶ ἡμέρας ις′, στήσας καὶ μάγγανον καὶ πολέμους κροτήσας σφοδρούς. Ἀλλὰ σὺν Θεῷ μηδέν τι δυνηθεὶς πρᾶξαι ἀπῆλθε μετ᾽ αἰσχύνης κενός· ὅτε καὶ ὁ βασιλεὺς ἀνέκτισεν τὸν ἐν τῇ Κορδύλῃ ναὸν τοῦ ἁγίου Φωκᾶ καὶ μονὴν τοῦτον ἐποίησεν.

79 Τῷ αὐτῷ ͵ςωο′ ἔτει ἐκίνησεν ὁ αἰφνίδιος θάνατος τοῦ βουβῶνος καὶ ἐκράτησεν τὸν αὐτὸν ἐνιαυτὸν ὅλον· πρὸς δὲ τὸ καλοκαίριν καὶ θέρος γέγονε σφοδρότατος καὶ ἐλυμήνατο καὶ ἀποίκισε πολλούς.

80 Περὶ δὲ τὸν Μάρτιον μῆνα, τοῦ αὐτοῦ ͵ςωο′ ἔτους, ἀπῆλθεν ὁ βασιλεὺς καὶ ἡ δέσποινα καὶ ἡ μήτηρ αὐτοῦ εἰς τὰ Μεσοχάλδια ἅμα μὲν διὰ τὸν αἰφνίδιον θάνατον, ἅμα δὲ καὶ διὰ τὴν ἀπόδρασιν τοῦ Κομνηνοῦ Ἰωάννου ἐκ τῆς Ἀδριανουπόλεως καὶ ἔλευσιν τούτου ἐν τῇ Σινώπῃ, ἔνθα καὶ ἐκοιμήθη. Ὅτε καὶ οἱ βασιλεῖς ἐλθόντες ἐκ Χαλδίας οὐκ εἰσῆλθον ἐν Τραπεζοῦντι εἰς τὸ κάστρον διὰ τὸν σφοδρότατον διωγμὸν τοῦ θανάτου, ὑπῆρχε γὰρ μὴν Ἰούνιος, ἀλλ᾽ ἐσκήνωσαν εἰς τὸν ἅγιον Ἰωάννην τὸν Ἁγιαστήν, εἰς τὸν Μίνθρον βουνόν· ὅτε καὶ πρέσβυς ἦλθεν ἐκ τοῦ τζαλαπῆ Τατζατίνη διὰ τὴν συμπενθερείαν. Τότε μικροῦ δεῖν ἐπανέστησάν τινες τῷ βασιλεῖ. Ἀποδρὰς ἐκ

Emir, Bayram's son, that is after he came to Kerasous and met us. From Chalybia we went by land to Kerasous, followed by the emir Hacı Emir and some Turks, almost as if they were our servants.

In October, indiction 15, 1361, Akhi Ayna Bey from Erzincan came and invested the citadel of Golacha for about sixteen days. He set up a siege engine and fought violent battles. But with God's aid, he was not able to accomplish anything and went away empty-handed in shame. This was when the emperor rebuilt the church of Saint Phokas in Kordyle and made it a monastery. 78

In that same year, 1361/62, the bubonic plague suddenly broke out and lasted for the whole year. In the summer it grew the most violent, killing and displacing many from their homes. 79

Around March of that same year, 1362, the emperor, the empress, and his mother departed together for Mesochaldia both because of the plague and because of John Komnenos's escape from Adrianople and arrival at Sinope, where he died. When the imperial family came back from Chaldia, they did not enter into Trebizond proper because of the virulence of the plague, for it was June at this time, but camped out at Saint John the Sanctifier on Mount Minthros. At this time as well, an ambassador came from *çelebi* Taccedin, seeking a marriage alliance. Then certain individuals nearly raised an insurrection against the emperor. Lord John 80

τῆς εἱρκτῆς καὶ ὁ υἱὸς τοῦ Κομνηνοῦ κυροῦ Ἰωάννου καὶ ἀπῆλθεν εἰς τὸν Καφᾶν, εἶτα εἰς τὸν Γαλατᾶν.

81 Μηνὶ Ἀπριλίῳ, ἰνδικτιῶνος α΄, τοῦ ͵ςωοα΄ ἔτους, ἀπήλθαμεν μετὰ τοῦ βασιλικοῦ κατέργου εἰς τὴν μεγάλην Πόλιν, ὅ τε μέγας λογοθέτης κῦρ Γεώργιος ὁ Σχολάρις καὶ ὁ πρωτοσεβαστὸς καὶ πρωτονοτάρις Μιχαὴλ ὁ Πανάρετος, ὁ ταῦτα γράφων, καὶ προσεκυνήσαμεν προσκυνήσεις φοβεράς· εἴδαμεν καὶ τὸν βασιλέα κῦρ Ἰωάννην τὸν Παλαιολόγον καὶ τὸν βασιλέα κῦρ Ἰωάσαφ μοναχὸν τὸν Καντακουζηνόν, τὸν πατριάρχην κῦρ Κάλλιστον καὶ τὰς δεσποίνας καὶ τοὺς υἱοὺς τοῦ βασιλέως, καὶ αὐτὸν δὴ τὸν καπετᾶνον καὶ ποτεστάτην τῶν ἐν τῷ Γαλατᾷ Γενουΐτῶν Λεονάρδο Τεμουντάτο, ὅτε ἐποιήσαμεν τὴν συμφωνίαν τῆς συμπενθερείας, ἵνα λάβῃ ὁ τοῦ βασιλέως τοῦ Παλαιολόγου ὁ υἱὸς τὴν θυγατέρα τοῦ βασιλέως τῆς Τραπεζοῦντος κῦρ Ἀλεξίου τοῦ μεγάλου Κομνηνοῦ, καὶ ἤλθαμεν μηνὶ Ἰουνίῳ ε΄ τῷ αὐτῷ ͵ςωοα΄ ἔτει, μηνὶ Αὐγούστῳ ιε΄, νὰ ἐσμιχθῶμεν τὸν αὐτοῦ γαμπρὸν τὸν Χουτλουπέκην, τὸν υἱὸν τοῦ Τουραλῆ, ἀλλὰ μὴ ἐσμιχθέντες διὰ τὸν ἐπεισπεσόντα τοῖς Τούρκοις αἰφνίδιον θάνατον, μεθ᾽ ἡμέρας κζ΄ πάλιν ἐστράφημεν ἐν Τραπεζοῦντι.

82 Μηνὶ Ὀκτωβρίῳ κζ΄, ἡμέρᾳ ζ΄, ἰνδικτιῶνος β΄, ἔτους ͵ςωοβ΄, καθεζομένου τοῦ βασιλέως ἐν τῷ ποταμῷ τοῦ ἁγίου Γρηγορίου, κατὰ τὸν Καταβατόν, αἴφνης περιέπεσον αὐτῷ οἱ ἐκ τῶν ἀρχόντων Καβαζῖται, ὁ μέγας λογοθέτης κῦρ Γεώργιος ὁ Σχολάρις καὶ ἕτεροι, καὶ ἐδίωξαν αὐτὸν ἀπ᾽ ἐκεῖ μέχρις αὐτοῦ τοῦ κουλᾶ. Καὶ οἱ μὲν Καβαζῖται διὰ ξηρᾶς φυγόντες συνελήφθησαν καὶ ἐκρατήθησαν, ὁ δὲ

Komnenos's son also escaped from prison and went off to Caffa and then Galata.

In April, indiction 1, 1363, we, that is the grand *logothetes* lord George Scholaris and the *protosebastos* and chief secretary Michael Panaretos, who is writing this, went by imperial galley to Constantinople, and we paid our respects in fulsome homage. We saw the emperor lord John V Palaiologos, the emperor-monk lord Ioasaph Kantakouzenos, the patriarch lord Kallistos, the empresses, the emperor's sons, and the *capetan* and chief magistrate of the Genoese at Galata, Leonardo di Montaldo. This was when we concluded a marriage agreement whereby the son of the emperor John V Palaiologos would marry the daughter of the emperor of Trebizond, lord Alexios III the Grand Komnenos. On June 5 of the same year, 1363, we came back here in order to meet his brother-in-law, Kutlu Bey, Tur Ali's son, on August 15. But we did not meet him because a sudden deadly epidemic fell upon the Turks, so after twenty-seven days we returned to Trebizond. 81

On Saturday, October 27, indiction 2, 1363, while the emperor was sitting by the Saint Gregory River near Katabatos, some of the Kabazitai *archontes,* the grand *logothetes* lord George Scholaris and others, suddenly attacked him and pursued him from there as far as the citadel itself. The Kabazitai fled overland, but were captured and arrested, while 82

μέγας λογοθέτης σὺν τοῖς περὶ αὐτὸν ἀπῆλθεν εἰς τὴν Κερασοῦντα, εἶτα εἰς τὴν Ἀμινσοῦν· ὅτε καὶ ὁ μητροπολίτης Τραπεζοῦντος Νήφων ὁ Πτερυγιωνίτης, κοινωνὸς ὢν τῆς βουλῆς, περιωρίσθη ἐν τῇ μονῇ τῆς Σουμελᾶς ἐν Τραπεζοῦντι. Τῇ δὲ κθʹ τοῦ Δεκεμβρίου μηνός, ἡμέρᾳ ϛʹ, πάλιν ἦλθεν ὁ μέγας λογοθέτης μεσάζοντος εἰς τοῦτο τοῦ Ντζιανώτη Σπίνουλα καὶ Στεφάνου τοῦ Δακνοπίνη.

83 Τῷ αὐτῷ ἔτει, ἤτοι τῷ ͵ϛωοβʹ, ἰνδικτιῶνος βʹ, μηνὶ Μαρτίῳ ιθʹ, ἐν ἡμέρᾳ τῇ μεγάλῃ Τρίτῃ, ἐκοιμήθη ὁ μητροπολίτης Τραπεζοῦντος κῦρ Νήφων νόσῳ προσπαλαίσας πλευρίτιδι, ἔτι ὢν ἐν τῇ Σουμελᾷ, καὶ ἐνεταφιάσθη ἀρχιερατικῶς εἰς τὴν Χρυσοκέφαλον, εἰς τὸν τάφον τοῦ μητροπολίτου κῦρ Βαρνάβα. Καὶ ἐψηφίσθη ὁ σκευοφύλαξ Ἰωσὴφ ὁ Λαζαρόπουλος καὶ ἀπῆλθεν εἰς τὴν Πόλιν.

84 Μηνὶ Δεκεμβρίῳ ιϛʹ, ἡμέρᾳ βʹ, περὶ τὸν ὄρθρον, ἰνδικτιῶνος γʹ, τοῦ ͵ϛωογʹ ἔτους, ἐγεννήθη τῷ βασιλεῖ υἱός, ὃς ἐκλήθη Μανουήλ.

85 Μηνὶ Ἀπριλίῳ ιγʹ, τῷ αὐτῷ ͵ϛωογʹ ἔτει, τῇ μεγάλῃ Κυριακῇ τοῦ Πάσχα, ἱσταμένου τοῦ βασιλέως εἰς τὸ μαϊτάνιν, ἐγένετο ὄχλησις μέσον τοῦ κονσούλου καὶ τοῦ παΐλου· ὅτε ἦλθε καὶ ὁ μητροπολίτης κῦρ Ἰωσήφ, χειροτονημένος εἰς τὸν θρόνον Τραπεζουντίων, καὶ τῇ Τρίτῃ τῆς διακαινησίμου γέγονεν ἡ εἰσέλευσις αὐτοῦ.

86 Μηνὶ Ἰουλίῳ ιδʹ, ἰνδικτιῶνος γʹ, τοῦ ͵ϛωογʹ ἔτους, κατέβη ὁ τοῦ βασιλέως γαμβρὸς Χουτλουπέκης, ὁ ἀμηρᾶς, μετὰ τῆς αὐτοῦ ὁμοζύγου κυρᾶς Μαρίας δεσποινάχατ, τῆς μεγάλης Κομνηνῆς, ἐν ταύτῃ τῇ εὐδαίμονι πόλει Τραπεζοῦντος καὶ ἡνώθη τῷ βασιλεῖ καὶ εἰσῆλθεν εἰς τὸ παλάτιν,

the grand *logothetes* with his supporters went to Kerasous, and then Aminsous. At the same time, the metropolitan of Trebizond, Nephon Pterygionites, who was privy to the plot, was confined to the monastery of Soumela in Trebizond. But on Friday, December 29, the grand *logothetes* came back here through the mediation of Dzianotes Spinoula and Stephanos Daknopines.

In that same year, 1364, indiction 2, on March 19, Holy 83
Tuesday, the metropolitan of Trebizond, lord Nephon, died after a battle with pleurisy, while still at Soumela. He was interred with all the honors of an archbishop in the church of the Theotokos Chrysokephalos, in the tomb of the metropolitan, lord Barnabas. The *skeuophylax* Joseph Lazaropoulos was elected metropolitan and departed for Constantinople.

On Monday, December 16, indiction 3, 1364, around mat- 84
ins, a son was born to the emperor and he was named Manuel.

On Easter Sunday, April 13, of the same year, 1365, as the 85
emperor was standing in the marketplace, a dispute broke out between the consul and the Venetian ambassador. This was also when the metropolitan lord Joseph came here after his consecration to the see of Trebizond. And his ceremonial entrance happened on the Tuesday of Easter week.

On July 14, indiction 3, 1365, the emperor's son-in-law, the 86
emir Kutlu Bey arrived with his wife, the *despoinachat* lady Maria the Grand Komnene, at this blessed city of Trebizond, and was met by the emperor and entered the palace.

καί, σκηνώσας κατὰ τὸν ἅγιον Ἰωάννην τὸν Ἁγιαστὴν ὡσεὶ ἡμέρας η′, πάλιν μετ᾽ εἰρήνης ἀπῆλθε τιμηθεὶς μεγάλως.

87 Εἰς δὲ τὸ ἐπιὸν ἔτος ἀνῆλθεν ὁ βασιλεὺς εἰς τὸν παρχάριν. Καὶ ἡμεῖς ἅπαντες σὺν αὐτῷ ἀναβάντες ἐκ Σπέλιας εἰς τὴν Φιανόην καὶ παροδεύσαντες τὸ Γαντοπέδιν καὶ Μάρμαρα καὶ διαβάντες τὸν ἅγιον Μερκούριον ἀνήλθομεν εἰς τὸν Ἀχάντακαν, πεζοὶ καὶ καβαλλάριοι ὑπὲρ τοὺς δισχιλίους· καὶ ποιήσαντες μετὰ τοῦ ἀμηρᾶ ἡμέρας δ′, πάλιν ὑπεστρέψαμεν μηνὶ Ἰουνίῳ, ἰνδικτιῶνος ε′, τοῦ ͵ϛωοε′ ἔτους, καταβάντες ἐν τῇ Λαζικῇ μετὰ δυνάμεως διά τε ξηρᾶς καὶ διὰ θαλάσσης ἅμα βασιλεῖ καὶ τῇ τούτου μητρὶ τῇ δεσποίνῃ, κατέχοντες ἅμα καὶ τὴν τοῦ βασιλέως θυγατέραν, κυρὰν Ἄννην τὴν μεγάλην Κομνηνήν, ἥτις συνεζεύχθη τῷ βασιλεῖ τῶν Ἰβήρων καὶ Ἀβαζγῶν, κῦρ Παγκρατίῳ τῷ Παγκρατιανῷ, ἐν τῇ χώρᾳ Μακροῦ Αἰγιαλοῦ. Ἐλθόντες δέ, παρευθὺς ἀνῆλθεν ὁ βασιλεὺς εἰς τὸν παρχάριν τῆς Λαραχανῆς, εἰς τὸ Λιμνίον, καὶ ἀπῆλθεν ἕως Χαλδίας.

88 Μηνὶ Νοεμβρίῳ ιβ′, ἰνδικτιῶνος ϛ′, ἔτους ͵ϛωοϛ′, ἐξῆλθεν ὁ μητροπολίτης κῦρ Ἰωσὴφ ἐκ τοῦ θρόνου τῆς Τραπεζοῦντος καὶ ἀπῆλθεν ἐν τῇ μονῇ τῆς Ἐλεούσης.

89 Καὶ περὶ τὰς ιθ′ τοῦ Ἰουλίου μηνός, τοῦ αὐτοῦ ͵ϛωοϛ′ ἔτους, ἀπῆλθον εἰς τὴν Κωνσταντινούπολιν διὰ τὸ κοῦρσον, ὃ ἐποίησαν τὰ ἀζάπικα παρασκάλμια τοὺς Ἀρανιώτας· ὅτε καὶ ὁ πεφιλημένος μου υἱὸς Κωνσταντῖνος, φεῦ, φεῦ μοι τῷ ἀθλίῳ καὶ ἁμαρτωλῷ, ἐν τῇ θαλάσσῃ πεσὼν τῇ ἑορτῇ τῆς Μεταμορφώσεως κατὰ τὴν μονὴν τῆς ἁγίας

He camped near the church of John the Sanctifier for about eight days and then left peacefully, having received great honors.

In the following year, the emperor went up to the sum- 87
mer pastures. And we all went up with him from Spelia to Phianoe, traveling by way of Gantopedin and Marmara. We then went up to Achantakas, crossing over Saint Merkourios with more than two thousand infantry and cavalrymen. After spending four days with the emir we returned in June, indiction 5, 1367, descending into Lazike with land and sea forces, along with the emperor and the dowager empress; we also took with us the emperor's daughter, the lady Anna the Grand Komnene, who was married to the king of the Georgians and Abasgians, lord Bagrat Bagration in the region of Makrou Aigialou. After coming back here, the emperor went straight up to the summer pastures along the Larachane River, namely to Limnion, and advanced as far as Chaldia.

On November 12, indiction 6, 1367, the metropolitan, 88
lord Joseph abdicated from the see of Trebizond and left for the Eleousa monastery.

Around July 19 of the same year, 1368, I departed for Con- 89
stantinople because of the raid that the pirate ships made against the Araniotai. This was also when my beloved son, Constantine—alas, alack, wretched sinner that I am—fell into the sea on the feast of the Transfiguration at the monas-

Σοφίας τέθνηκεν, ἐτῶν ὢν ιε΄· μεθ᾽ ὃν καὶ ὁ ἕτερός μου ποθεινότατος υἱὸς Ρωμανός, ἐτῶν ὢν ιζ΄, δυσουρικῷ προσπαλαίσας νοσήματι κεκοίμηται· λείποντός μου μῆνας γ΄ ἥμισυν ὑπέστρεψα.

90 Τῷ αὐτῷ ,ςωος΄ ἔτει, μηνὶ Μαρτίῳ, εἰσελθὼν ὁ Γλιτζιασθλάνης ἐπολιόρκει τὴν καθ΄ ἡμᾶς Χαλδίαν, ὅτε καὶ ἐκστρατεύσας ὁ βασιλεὺς ἀνέβη ἐκεῖ.

91 Μηνὶ Ἰανουαρίῳ, ἰνδικτιῶνος ζ΄, ἔτους ,ςωοζ΄, κατὰ τὴν ἡμέραν τῶν Φώτων, ἐπιάσθη ἡ Γόλαχα παρὰ τῶν Τούρκων κλωπικῶς, δι᾽ ἣν αἰτίαν ἠφανίσθη ἡ Χαλδία, οἱ μὲν ἐν τοῖς πολέμοις, οἱ δὲ ἐν τῷ ἐκεῖσε δολίῳ σπηλαίῳ.

92 Τῷ αὐτῷ ,ςωοζ΄ ἔτει, περὶ τὴν ἔκβασιν τοῦ Ἰανουαρίου, ἀπῆλθεν ὁ βασιλεὺς εἰς τὰ Λιμνία μετὰ στόλου καλοῦ καὶ λείψας τετραμηνιαῖον ὑπέστρεψεν.

93 Μηνὶ Μαΐῳ, ἰνδικτιῶνος η΄, ἔτους ,ςωοη΄, ἐξῆλθεν ὁ βασιλεὺς μετά τινων ὀλιγοστῶν στρατιωτῶν εἰς τὸν παρχάριν περὶ τὰ μέρη τοῦ Μαρμάρων. Καὶ κατὰ τὴν κα΄ τοῦ αὐτοῦ μηνός, ἡμέρᾳ γ΄, ἐξαίφνης συνήντησαν Τούρκους ὡσεὶ καβαλλαρίους πεντακοσίους καὶ πεζοὺς τριακοσίους. Ἦσαν δὲ περὶ τὸν βασιλέαν ὡσεὶ ἑκατὸν καβαλλάριοι· ὅτε καὶ κροτήσας πόλεμον νικᾷ κατὰ κράτος ὁ βασιλεὺς καὶ διώκει αὐτούς, στείλας καὶ κεφαλὰς Ἀγαρηνικὰς ἐνταῦθα καὶ τὴν τούτων σημαίαν.

94 Μηνὶ Αὐγούστῳ ιγ΄, ἡμέρᾳ γ΄, ἰνδικτιῶνος η΄, τῷ ,ςωοη΄ ἔτει, εἰσῆλθεν ὁ μητροπολίτης κῦρ Θεοδόσιος εἰς τὴν Τραπεζοῦντα καὶ ἐνεθρονιάσθη· ὃς ὥρμητο μὲν ἐκ Θεσσαλονίκης, μονάζει δὲ ἐν τῷ ἁγίῳ Ὄρει χρόνους κ΄, καταλαμβάνει δὲ τὴν εὐδαίμονα Κωνσταντινούπολιν, γενόμενος

tery of Saint Sophia and is dead, aged fifteen. After him, my other dearest son Romanos, who was seventeen years old, has now passed away after battling a urinary disease. After an absence of three and a half months, I returned here.

In March of that same year, 1368, Kılıç Arslan invaded and besieged our part of Chaldia. The emperor then marched out with an army and went up there. 90

In January, indiction 7, 1369, on Epiphany, Golacha was treacherously seized by the Turks. For this reason, Chaldia was obliterated, some of its people dying in battle, others in the treacherous cave there. 91

In that same year, 1369, around the end of January, the emperor left for Limnia with a good-sized fleet and, after an absence of four months, returned here. 92

In May, indiction 8, 1370, the emperor left with a very small number of soldiers for the summer pastures in the Marmara region. On Tuesday, the twenty-first of that same month, they suddenly encountered some five hundred Turkish cavalrymen and three hundred infantrymen. There were about a hundred cavalrymen surrounding the emperor. This was the situation when the emperor joined battle with them, decisively overpowered them, and chased them away. He sent back here the heads of the Hagarenes and their battle standard. 93

On Tuesday, August 13, indiction 8, 1370, the metropolitan lord Theodosios entered Trebizond and was enthroned. He came from Thessalonike and was a monk on the Holy Mountain for twenty years before going to the blessed city of Constantinople and becoming superior of the monastery 94

ἡγούμενος ἐν τῇ μονῇ τῶν Μαγγάνων· εἶτα ψήφῳ συνοδικῇ χειροτονεῖται καὶ στέλλεται.

95 Μηνὶ Αὐγούστῳ ϛʹ ἀπήλθαμεν ἐν τῇ Λαζικῇ καὶ πρὸς τὸ ἔκβαν τοῦ μηνός, περὶ τὰ εἰσιτήρια τοῦ ͵ϛωπαʹ ἔτους, ἐσμίγαμεν τὸν βασιλέα τὸν Παγκράτιν· εἶτα ἀπήλθαμεν εἰς τὸ Βαθύν, στήσαντες τὰς τέντας ἔξω, ἔχοντες καὶ κάτεργα βʹ καὶ ξυλάρια ὡσεὶ μʹ. Ἐκεῖ γοῦν ὁμιλήσαντες καὶ τῷ Γουρέλῃ, ἐλθόντι εἰς προσκύνησιν τοῦ βασιλέως, καὶ ἓξ ἡμέρας ποιήσαντες, πάλιν ἐστράφημεν, ἰνδικτιῶνος ιαʹ.

96 Μηνὶ Ἰανουαρίῳ ιγʹ, ἀπελθόντος τοῦ βασιλέως κατὰ τῆς Χεριάνης καὶ χιόνος πολλῆς γενομένης καὶ χειμῶνος πολλοῦ ἐπεισπεσόντος, γέγονε τροπὴ καὶ ἐφθάρησαν Χριστιανοὶ ρμʹ, οἱ μὲν ἔργον σπάθης γενόμενοι, οἱ δέ, καὶ μᾶλλον οἱ πλείονες, ὑπὸ τοῦ κρύους ἀπέθανον, ἰνδικτιῶνος ιαʹ, ἔτους ͵ϛωπαʹ.

97 Μηνὶ Νοεμβρίῳ ιαʹ, ἡμέρᾳ ϛʹ, τοῦ ͵ϛωπβʹ ἔτους, ἰνδικτιῶνος ιβ^{ης}, ἦλθεν ὁ τοῦ βασιλέως τῶν Ῥωμαίων κῦρ Ἰωάννου Παλαιολόγου υἱός, ὁ κῦρ Μιχαήλ, μετὰ δύο μεγάλων κατέργων καὶ ἑνὸς μικροτέρου κατὰ τοῦ βασιλέως ἡμῶν· καὶ σταθεὶς ἡμέρας εʹ παλίνορσος γέγονε, μὴ ἀνύσας τι τῶν ἀδοκήτων, ὧν σὺν αὐτῷ ὁ πρωτοβεστιάριος κῦρ Ἰωάννης ὁ Ἀνδρονικόπουλος· ὅς καί, ἀπελθὼν ὁ Παλαιολόγος, αὐτὸς ἐξῆλθε καὶ γέγονεν ὑπόσπονδος τῷ βασιλεῖ ἡμῶν.

98 Μηνὶ Ἀπριλίῳ ιϛʹ, ἡμέρᾳ αʹ, ἰνδικτιῶνος ιβʹ, τῷ ͵ϛωπβʹ ἔτει, ἐπιάσθη ἡ Γόλαχα παρὰ τῶν Χαλδαίων, καὶ πάλιν γέγονεν ὑπὸ τῷ βασιλεῖ καὶ εὐθὺς αὖθις ἑάλω παρὰ τῶν ἐχθρῶν.

of Mangana. Then by vote of the synod he was elected metropolitan and sent here.

On August 6, we went to Lazike and toward the end of the month, around the beginning of the year 1372, we met king Bagrat. Then we went to Bathys and pitched our tents outside the city, having with us two galleys and around forty smaller boats. There we met with the Gurieli, who came to make obeisance to the emperor, and after staying six days there, we returned, in indiction 11. 95

On January 13, when the emperor had gone to attack Cheriana, there was a lot of snow and a great winter storm struck. This caused a rout and 140 Christians perished. Some of them died by the sword, but the others, the great majority, died from the cold, in indiction 11, 1373. 96

On Saturday, November 11 of indiction 12, 1373, the son of the Roman emperor lord John V Palaiologos, lord Michael, came to attack our emperor with two large galleys and a smaller one. And after remaining here for five days, he beat a hasty retreat without accomplishing anything remarkable. The treasurer of the wardrobe, lord John Andronikopoulos, was with him and, when Palaiologos left, he came over and became our emperor's vassal. 97

On Sunday, April 16, indiction 12, 1374, Golacha was taken by the Chaldians, and it again came under the emperor's control only to immediately be retaken by the enemy. 98

99 Μηνὶ Μαρτίῳ ιδʹ, ἡμέρᾳ ςʹ, ἰνδικτιῶνος ιδʹ, τοῦ ͵ςωπδʹ ἔτους, ἐκρημνίσθη ὁ τοῦ βασιλέως υἱός, κῦρ Ἀνδρόνικος δεσπότης ὁ μέγας Κομνηνός, ἀπὸ τοῦ παλατίου τοῦ κῦρ Ἀνδρονίκου τοῦ μεγάλου Κομνηνοῦ καὶ βασιλέως. Καὶ εὐθὺς κομισθεὶς ἐν τοῖς ἀνακτόροις τέθνηκε καὶ ἐνεταφιάσθη ἐν τῇ μονῇ τῆς Θεοσκεπάστου, ἀκολουθήσαντος ἐν τῷ ἐξοδίῳ αὐτοῦ τοῦ βασιλέως καὶ πατρὸς αὐτοῦ καὶ τῶν δεσποινῶν, τῆς τε μάμμης τούτου καὶ τῆς μητρυιᾶς. Τὰ δὲ συναλλάγματα, ἃ εἶχε μετὰ τῆς ἐξ Ἰβηρίας, θυγατρὸς μὲν Δαβὶδ τοῦ βασιλέως Τυφλισίου, ἀνεψιᾶς δὲ ἐπ᾽ ἀδελφῇ τοῦ Ἀχπουγᾶ, μεταφέρονται εἰς τὸν νεώτερον καὶ γνήσιον καὶ νόμιμον υἱὸν τοῦ βασιλέως ἡμῶν καὶ νέον βασιλέα κῦρ Μανουὴλ τὸν μέγαν Κομνηνόν. Καὶ δὴ τῆς μνηστείας προβάσης κινεῖ ὁ βασιλεὺς καὶ ἡμεῖς σὺν αὐτῷ Μαΐῳ μηνὶ ιʹ, ἰνδικτιῶνος ιεʹ, ἔτους ͵ςωπεʹ, καὶ ἀπελθόντες ἐν τῇ Λαζικῇ διεβιβάσαμεν τὸ καλοκαίριν ὅλον ἐκεῖ κατὰ τὸ χωρίον Μακραιγιαλοῦς ἕως εἰς τὰς ιεʹ Αὐγούστου μηνός. Τότε δὲ κατέβη κἀκείνη ἀπὸ Γωνίας εἰς τὴν Μακραιγιαλοῦν καὶ τῇ ἐπαύριον κεκινήκαμεν καὶ εἰς τὰ λʹ τοῦ Αὐγούστου ἐφθάσαμεν ἐν Τραπεζοῦντι, ἡμέρᾳ Κυριακῇ. Περὶ δὲ τὰς εʹ τοῦ νέου ἔτους, Σεπτεμβρίῳ μηνί, ἡμέρᾳ Σαββάτῳ, ἰνδικτιῶνος αʹ, τοῦ ͵ςωπςʹ ἔτους, ἐστέφθη ἐν τῇ βασιλικῇ προκύψει καὶ ἐκλήθη Εὐδοκία (Κουλκάνχατ γὰρ πρότερον ὠνομάζετο), καὶ τῇ ἐπαύριον ἡμέρᾳ Κυριακῇ, Σεπτεμβρίου ςʹ, ἐγένετο καὶ ὁ γάμος καὶ ἐπεκράτησεν ἑβδομάδαν καὶ πλέον. Ἦν δὲ ὁ εὐλογήσας αὐτοὺς ὁ Τραπεζοῦντος Θεοδόσιος, στεφανοκράτωρ δὲ ὁ πατὴρ ἦν καὶ βασιλεύς.

100 Μετὰ πολλῶν λόγων καὶ πρέσβεων, Ρωμαϊκῶν λέγω

On Friday, March 14, indiction 14, 1376, the emperor's son, the despot lord Andronikos the Grand Komnenos, fell from the palace of lord Andronikos the Grand Komnenos and emperor. He was immediately carried into the royal quarters where he died. He was entombed in the Theoskepastos monastery, with his father the emperor and the empresses, his stepmother and grandmother, following in the funeral procession. The marriage alliance which he had with the woman from Georgia, who was the daughter of king David of Tbilisi, as well as the niece on the sister's side of Achpougas, passed to the younger, legitimate, and lawful son of our emperor, the young emperor lord Manuel III the Grand Komnenos. And so, as the time for the betrothal approached, the emperor, and we with him, set out on May 10, indiction 15, 1377. We went to Lazike and passed the whole summer there in the region of Makraigialous until August 15. It was on that day that the lady came down from Gonia to Makraigialous and we set out on the next day and reached Trebizond on Sunday, August 30. Around September 5 of the new year, on a Saturday, indiction 1, 1377, she was crowned empress on the imperial dais and given the name Eudokia (her previous name had been Koulkanchat). On the following day, Sunday, September 6, the wedding took place and it lasted for a week or more. It was the metropolitan of Trebizond, Theodosios, who wed them, while the one who gave them their marriage crowns was Manuel's father, the emperor. 99

After many talks and delegations, both Roman and 100

καὶ Μουσουλμανικῶν, μέσον δὴ τοῦ βασιλέως καὶ τοῦ Ταταζιατίνη τζιαλαπῆ, ἐκίνησεν ὁ βασιλεὺς κατὰ τὴν ιδʹ τοῦ Αὐγούστου μηνός, ἰνδικτιῶνος βʹ, ἔχων κάτεργα μεγάλα δύο καὶ παρασκάλμια βʹ, καὶ ἡ θυγάτηρ κυρὰ Εὐδοκία. Καὶ ἀπήλθαμεν μέχρι Κερασοῦντος. Μανδᾶτον δὲ ἦλθεν ἐκ Τραπεζοῦντος ὅτι ὁ Χλιατζιασθλάνης μέλλει καταβεῖν εἰς τὴν Τραπεζοῦνταν. Ὁ δὲ βασιλεὺς ἀφεὶς τὴν θυγατέραν ἐν Κερασοῦντι ἦλθε σὺν τοῖς ἄρχουσιν ἐν Τραπεζοῦντι καὶ ἐδυνάμωσε τὸ κάστρον καὶ διετάξατο τὴν χώραν. Περὶ δὲ τὰ τελευταῖα τοῦ Σεπτεμβρίου ἐκίνησε καὶ λαβὼν τὴν θυγατέραν ἐν Κερασοῦντι ἀπῆλθε μέχρις Οἰναίου, κἀκεῖ ἐσμιχθεὶς τῷ τζιαλαπῇ συνέζευξεν αὐτῷ τὴν θυγατέραν αὐτοῦ, τὴν κυρὰν Εὐδοκίαν, κατὰ τὴν ηʹ τοῦ Ὀκτωβρίου, ἰνδικτιῶνος γʹ, ἔτους ͵ϛωπηʹ, ὅτε παρέλαβεν ὁ βασιλεὺς καὶ τὰ Λιμνία.

101 Μηνὶ Φεβρουαρίῳ ἐκίνησεν ὁ βασιλεὺς διά τε ξηρᾶς καὶ διὰ θαλάσσης κατὰ τῶν Τζιαπνίδων. Καὶ περὶ τὰς δʹ τοῦ Μαρτίου μηνός, ἡμέρᾳ αʹ, ἰνδικτιῶνος γʹ, ἔτους ͵ϛωπηʹ, ἐποίησεν τὸ φωσσᾶτον μερίδας βʹ. Τοὺς μὲν πεζοὺς ὡσεὶ χʹ ἔστειλεν ἀπὸ τὸ Πέτρωμαν, ὁ δὲ βασιλεὺς παραλαβὼν τὸ καβαλλαρικὸν καὶ ἑτέρους πεζοὺς παμπόλλους ἐπέρνιξέν τους ὅλον τὸν Φιλαβωνίτην ποταμὸν ἄνω ἕως εἰς τὰ χειμαδίας, καὶ τὰς σκηνὰς αὐτῶν ἐκούρσευσεν, ἐσκότωσεν, ἔκαυσεν καὶ ἐλῄϊσεν αὐτοὺς καὶ πολλὰ ἡμέτερα αἰχμάλωτα ἠλευθέρωσεν Σιμυλικά καὶ ἐστράφη καὶ ἐστάθη μικρὸν εἰς τὸν Σθλαβοπιάστην. Οἱ δὲ χʹ, οἱ ἀπελθόντες ἀπὸ τὸ Πέτρωμαν, ἐκούρσευσαν εἰς τὸ Κοτζαυτᾶ καὶ ἐποίησαν σφαγὴν καὶ κοῦρσον καὶ πυρκαϊὰν πολλήν·

Muslim, between the emperor and *çelebi* Taccedin, the emperor set out on August 14, indiction 2, with two galleys and two other ships and his daughter, the lady Eudokia. We made it as far as Kerasous. Then a message came from Trebizond announcing that Kılıç Arslan was about to descend on Trebizond. The emperor left his daughter in Kerasous and went with his *archontes* to Trebizond, where he strengthened the citadel and organized the countryside. Around the last days of September, he set out, picked up his daughter in Kerasous, and then went as far as Oinaion, where he met the *çelebi* and married his daughter, the lady Eudokia, to him on October 8, indiction 3, 1379. This was when the emperor took possession of Limnia.

In February, the emperor set out by land and sea to attack 101
the Çepni. Around Sunday, March 4, indiction 3, 1380, he divided his army into two parts. The emperor dispatched around six hundred foot soldiers from Petroman, while he himself took charge of the cavalry and a large number of foot soldiers and conveyed them along the course of the Philabonites River as far as the winter quarters of the Çepni, where he plundered their tents, killed, burned, and despoiled them, and set free many of our people from Simylika, whom they had captured. He turned back there and stayed for a while at Sthlabopiastes. Meanwhile, the six hundred who had set out from Petroman plundered as far as Kotzauta. They engaged in much slaughter, plundering, and

καταβαίνοντες δὲ μετὰ πολέμου, ὁσάκις ἐποίουν καὶ συμπλοκὴν μετὰ τῶν διωκόντων Τούρκων, πολλοὶ ἔπιπτον ἐκ τῶν Τούρκων. Οἱ δὲ Ρωμαῖοι ἐλπίζοντες τὸν βασιλέα εἰς τὸν αἰγιαλόν, ἰσχυρὰ πολεμοῦντες καὶ κτείνοντες, ἤρχοντο. Περὶ δὲ τὸν αἰγιαλὸν τοῦ Σθλαβοπιάστου γενόμενοι, ὡς οὐχ εὗρον τὸν βασιλέα, ὡς ἐσυνεφώνησαν, μικρὸν πρὸς τροπὴν βλέψαντες ἔπεσον ὡσεὶ μβʹ Ρωμαῖοι. Οἱ δὲ πεσόντες Τοῦρκοι καὶ Τούρκισσαι καὶ Τουρκόπουλα ὑπὲρ τοὺς ρʹ ἠριθμήθησαν.

102 Μηνὶ Ἰουνίῳ ιθʹ, ἰνδικτιῶνος εʹ, ἔτους ,ςωϞʹ, ὁ τοῦ βασιλέως κῦρ Ἀλεξίου υἱός, ὁ κῦρ Μανουήλ, ἐγέννησεν υἱὸν ἐκ τῆς ἐξ Ἰβήρων κυρᾶς Εὐδοκίας, ὃν καὶ βαπτίσας ὁ πάππος καὶ βασιλεὺς κῦρ Ἀλέξιος καὶ ἡ προμάμμη καὶ δέσποινα κυρὰ Εἰρήνη καὶ ὁ μητροπολίτης Τραπεζοῦντος κῦρ Θεοδόσιος ἐκάλεσαν τοῦτον Βασίλειον κατὰ τὸν πρόπαππον.

103 Μηνὶ Ἰουλίῳ θʹ ἤρχθη ἡ νόσος τῶν βουβώνων, ἔτους ,ςωϞʹ, ἰνδικτιῶνος εʹ, καὶ ἐλυμήνατο ἐν Τραπεζοῦντι πολλοὺς μέχρι καὶ τοῦ Δεκεμβρίου καὶ τοῦ Γεναρίου μηνός. Ἐλυμήνατο δὲ καὶ τὴν Ματζούκαν περὶ πολλοῦ καὶ τὴν Τρικωμίαν καὶ τὸ μέρος τῶν Συρμένων ἕως εἰς τὴν Δρύωναν.

104 Μηνὶ Ὀκτωβρίῳ κδʹ, ἡμέρᾳ δʹ, ἰνδικτιῶνος ιʹ, τοῦ ,ςωϞεʹ ἔτους, κινήσας ὁ τοῦ βασιλέως γαμβρός, ὁ ἐκ τῶν Λιμνίων ἀμηρᾶς ὁ Τατζιατίνης, κατὰ τοῦ ἑτέρου γαμβροῦ τοῦ βασιλέως υἱοῦ, τοῦ ἐκ Χαλυβίας Χατζυμύρη, τοῦ λεγομένου Σουλαμάμπεκ, ἔχων φωσσᾶτον χιλιάδας ιβʹ, καὶ τῇ Χαλυβίῃ εἰσελθὼν ἔπεσε πρῶτος αὐτὸς ὁ Τατζιατίνης καὶ

burning. Whenever they engaged in combat with the Turks who were pursuing them as they fought their way down, many Turks fell. The Romans, who were hoping to find the emperor at the shore, were fighting fiercely and killing as they went, but when they came close to the beach of Sthlabopiastes and did not find the emperor there as they had arranged, they were more inclined to flee, and as many as forty-two Romans fell. But the number of Turkish men, women, and children who fell numbered more than a hundred.

On June 19, indiction 5, 1382, the son of the emperor lord 102
Alexios III, lord Manuel III, had a son by the lady Eudokia from Georgia; he was baptized by his grandfather the emperor lord Alexios III, his great-grandmother the empress lady Eirene, and the metropolitan of Trebizond, lord Theodosios. They called him Basil after his great-grandfather.

On July 9, indiction 5, 1382, the bubonic plague broke out 103
and killed many in Trebizond until the months of December and January. It also devastated Matzouka, Trikomia, and the district of Sourmaina as far as Dryona.

On Wednesday, October 24, indiction 10, 1386, the em- 104
peror's son-in-law from Limnia, the emir Taccedin, set out to attack the son of the emperor's other brother-in-law, Hacı Emir from Chalybia, who was called Süleyman Bey, with an army numbering twelve thousand. When he entered Chalybia, Taccedin himself fell first and was cut to pieces

κρεουργηθεὶς ἐκεῖ τέθνηκεν· οἱ δὲ περὶ αὐτὸν ἐκτάνθησαν ὡς ,γ, οἱ δὲ λοιποὶ γυμνοὶ ἔφυγον, ἀποβαλλόμενοι ἵππους ,ζ καὶ ὅπλα ἄπειρα.

105 Ἀμηρᾶς τις Τάταρις, ἔχων καὶ χάνην, ὡς λέγουσιν, ὁ δὲ Τάταρις Ταμουρλάγκης ὢν τὸ ὄνομα, ἐκ τῶν ὁρίων ἐξελθὼν Χαταΐας, ἔχων, ὥς φασιν οἱ εἰδότες, φωσσᾶτον ὑπὲρ τὰς ὀκτακοσίας χιλιάδας, ἦλθε καὶ παρέλαβε τὴν πᾶσαν Περσίαν. Εἶτα εἰσελθὼν καὶ ἐν τοῖς ἀκρωρείοις Ἰβήρων παρέλυσε πολέμου νόμῳ τὸ θαυμάσιον Τυφλίσιον, ζωγρήσας καὶ τὸν βασιλέα Παγκράτιν τὸν στρατηγικώτατον καὶ τὴν ὁμόζυγον αὐτοῦ, τὴν θυγατέραν τοῦ ἡμετέρου βασιλέως, τὴν ὡραιοτάτην κυρὰν Ἄννην καὶ τὸν υἱὸν αὐτῆς Δαβίδ, τὸν δὲ λαὸν ἔθυσε μαχαίρᾳ καὶ ἀπώλεσε. Ὁπόσα δὲ πράγματα εἷλε καὶ ὅσας εἰκόνας ἔγδειρε καὶ κατέκαυσε καὶ λίθους τιμίους καὶ μαργαριτάρια καὶ χρυσὸν καὶ ἄργυρον ἀπεφέρετο, οὐ δύναταί τις γραφῇ παραδοῦναι, μηνὶ Νοεμβρίῳ κα′, ἔτους ,ςωϟε′.

106 Ἐκοιμήθη ὁ βασιλεὺς κῦρ Ἀλέξιος ὁ μέγας Κομνηνός, ὁ υἱὸς τοῦ κῦρ Βασιλείου τοῦ μεγάλου Κομνηνοῦ ὁ δεύτερος, μηνὶ Μαρτίῳ κ′, ἡμέρᾳ Κυριακῇ τῆς ε′ ἑβδομάδος, ὥρᾳ δευτέρᾳ τῆς ἡμέρας. Ἐβασίλευσε δὲ ἔτη μ′ καὶ μῆνας γ′, ἐτῶν ὢν να′, ἔτους ,ςωϟη′.

107 Μηνὶ Μαρτίῳ ε′, τοῦ ,ςϡκ′ ἔτους, ἐκοιμήθη ὁ βασιλεὺς κῦρ Μανουὴλ ὁ μέγας Κομνηνὸς καὶ ἐτάφη εἰς τὴν Θεοσκέπαστον. Ἐβασίλευσε δὲ ἔτη κζ′.

108 Μηνὶ Μαΐῳ β′, ἔτους ,ςϡγ′, ἐκοιμήθη ἡ δέσποινα κυρὰ Εὐδοκία, ἡ οὖσα ἐξ Ἰβήρων, μήτηρ δὲ τοῦ βασιλέως κυροῦ Ἀλεξίου.

and died there. Some three thousand of those who were with him were slain, while the rest fled with nothing, abandoning some seven thousand horses and countless weapons.

There was a Tartar emir who had a khan in his power, so 105
they say. The Tartar was named Timur, and he came from the boundaries of Cathay. With an army numbering more than eight hundred thousand men, so those who know say, he came and seized all of Persia. Then he entered the Georgian highlands and destroyed the marvelous city of Tbilisi according to the rules of war, taking captive its king Bagrat, that most excellent general, and his wife, our emperor's daughter, the most beautiful lady Anna, as well as her son David, while he put the city's people to the sword and destroyed them. As to the number of objects he seized, the icons he desecrated and burned, and the precious stones, pearls, gold, and silver he carried off, who could possibly record it all? This happened on November 21, 1386.

The emperor lord Alexios III the Grand Komnenos, the 106
second son of lord Basil the Grand Komnenos, died on Sunday, March 20, in the fifth week of Lent, at the second hour of the day, 1390. He reigned for forty years and three months and was fifty-one.

On March 5, 1412, the emperor lord Manuel III the 107
Grand Komnenos died and was buried in the Theoskepastos monastery. He reigned for twenty-seven years.

On May 2, 1395, the empress Lady Eudokia, who was from 108
Georgia, the mother of the emperor lord Alexios IV, died.

109 Μηνὶ Σεπτεμβρίῳ, ἰνδικτιῶνος δʹ, ἔτους ,ϛϡδʹ, εἰς τὰ δʹ, ἡμέρᾳ Σαββάτῳ, ἦλθεν ἀπὸ Κωνσταντινουπόλεως εἰς τὸν ἅγιον Φωκᾶν ἡ δέσποινα κυρὰ Εὐδοκία ἡ μεγάλη Κομνηνὴ μετὰ κατέργου καὶ ἑνὸς γριπαρίας. Εἶχε δὲ καὶ νύμφας, εἰς μὲν τὸν αὐτάδελφον αὐτῆς, τὸν βασιλέα κῦρ Μανουήλ, χῆρον ὄντα, τὴν θυγατέραν τοῦ Φιλανθρωπηνοῦ κυρὰν Ἄννην, εἰς δὲ τὸν ἀνεψιὸν αὐτῆς, τὸν βασιλέα κῦρ Ἀλέξιον, τὴν θυγατέραν τοῦ Καντακουζηνοῦ κυρὰν Θεοδώραν. Καὶ τῇ ἐπαύριον Κυριακῇ, βροχῆς οὔσης, εἰσῆλθον εἰς Τραπεζοῦντα. Γέγονε δὲ καὶ πρέσβυς εἰς ταῦτα ὁ μέγας δούξ, Ἀμυριάλης ὁ Σχολάρις.

110 Τῷ δὲ ,ϛϡλε^{ω} ἔτει, τῆς εʹ ἰνδικτιῶνος, τῇ ιβʹ τοῦ Νοεμβρίου, ἡμέρᾳ γʹ, ὥρᾳ γʹ τῆς νυκτός, ἐκοιμήθη καὶ ἡ δέσποινα, ἡ κυρὰ Θεοδώρα Καντακουζηνὴ ἡ μεγάλη Κομνηνή, ἡ ὁμόζυγος τοῦ αὐτοῦ βασιλέως κῦρ Ἀλεξίου, καὶ ἐτάφη ἐν τῷ πανσέπτῳ ναῷ τῆς ὑπεραγίας Θεοτόκου τῆς Χρυσοκεφάλου, ἐν τῷ κοιμητηρίῳ τοῦ Γίδωνος, εἰς τὸ παράβημα. . . .

111 Τῷ δὲ αὐτῷ ἔτει, μηνὶ Νοεμβρίῳ, ἦλθε καὶ ἀπὸ Γοτθίας ἡ βασίλισσα κυρὰ Μαρία, ἡ τοῦ κῦρ Ἀλεξίου ἐκ τῶν Θεοδώρων θυγάτηρ, καὶ εὐλογήθη μετὰ εὐσεβοῦς δεσπότου, τοῦ ἀνδρὸς αὐτῆς, κυροῦ Δαβὶδ τοῦ μεγάλου Κομνηνοῦ.

On Saturday, September 4, indiction 4, 1395, the empress lady Eudokia, the Grand Komnene, came from Constantinople to Saint Phokas with a galley and another boat. She had two brides with her: for her brother, the emperor lord Manuel, who was a widower, she brought Philanthropenos's daughter, the lady Anna; and for her nephew, the emperor lord Alexios IV, she brought Kantakouzenos's daughter, the lady Theodora. On the following day, Sunday, they entered Trebizond in the rain. Amyriales Scholaris, the chief admiral, served as ambassador for this purpose. 109

On Tuesday, November 12, indiction 5, 1426, at the third hour of the night, the empress, lady Theodora Kantakouzene the Grand Komnene, the wife of the emperor lord Alexios IV, died and was buried in the most sacred church of the most holy Mother of God, the Chrysokephalos, in the cemetery of Gidon, in the vault. . . . 110

In November of that same year, the empress, lady Maria, the daughter of Alexios of Theodoro, came from Gothia, and was married to the pious despot, her husband lord David the Grand Komnenos. 111

ENCOMIUM ON TREBIZOND

Εἰς Τραπεζοῦντα

Ἀπάρχεσθαι μὲν τῶν αὐτοῖς τιμιωτάτων ἑκάστους καὶ πατράσι καὶ ἄρχουσι καὶ τοῖς ὁτουοῦν ἄλλως ἀγαθοῦ σφίσιν ὑπάρξασι νενόμισταί γε καὶ πάνυ δικαίως· δεῖ γάρ, ἄνθρωπον ὄντα, τὸ μόνον τῶν ζῴων ἐλεύθερον καὶ φιλότιμον καὶ φιλόδωρον, *μὴ μόνον εὖ πάσχειν, ἀλλὰ καὶ ἀντευποιεῖν* ἐν τῷ μέρει, καὶ πρός γε τοῦ πλέον τι δυναμένου νικώμενον τῷ φθάσαι παρασχεῖν ἂν ἐκεῖνον, τοῖς ἀμοιβαίοις γοῦν καὶ δευτέροις αὐτὸν μὴ ὑστερῆσαι, μηδὲ χείρω καὶ κατὰ τοῦτο φανῆναι, οὐδὲ τὰς δυνατάς οἱ χάριτας ἐκτιννύντα καὶ οἷς ἂν ἐνδείξαιτο πρὸς ἀξίαν εὐηργετημένος καὶ πεπονθὼς τἀγαθά. Τοσούτῳ δὲ δικαιότερον πατρίδα τιμᾶν καὶ τὴν ἐνεγκαμένην ἀσπάζεσθαι καὶ ταύτην οἷς ἄν τις ἔχοι δωρεῖσθαι, ὅσῳ γῆ μὲν καὶ *πατέρων πατήρ*, ταύτης δὲ μὴ φερούσης τὰ παρ᾽ αὐτῆς, οὔτ᾽ ἂν ἄρχοντες ἢ ὧν ἂν ἄρξαιεν εἶχον, οὐκ ὄντων οἷς ἂν τρέφοιτο τὸ ἀρχόμενον καὶ ὅλως συνίσταιτο, ἢ οἷς εὖ ἐποίουν τοὺς ὑπὸ χεῖρα, μὴ οὔσης ἑτέρωθεν εὐπορίας, οὔτ᾽ ἂν ὅπως ἢ ὅτων ἐγίγνοντ᾽ ἂν οἱ τεκόντες πατέρες, μᾶλλον δ᾽ οὐδ᾽ ἂν αὐτοὶ πρῶτον οἱ μὲν οὔθ᾽ ὅλως ἦσαν, μὴ ὅτι γ᾽ ἑτέρων πατέρες, οἱ δ᾽ οὐδὲ ἄρχοντες.

2 Ἐοίκασι γοῦν οἱ μὲν διδόναι λαμβάνοντες, ἡ δὲ μόνον διδόναι καὶ μόνη προῖκα τὰ παρὰ τῶν οἰκείων χαρίτων

Encomium on Trebizond

It is customary and altogether proper for everyone to offer what he deems most precious to his fathers, rulers, and anyone else who has benefited him. For as a human being, the only free animal that loves both receiving honor and giving gifts, *he should not only benefit at the hands of others, but should also do something good* in return *for them.* Even if he falls short of what someone with greater means could offer, he should not in any case delay in providing even second-rate recompense, nor appear inferior in this regard by not fully repaying the favors shown to him in the best way that he can and by showing how worthily the other person benefitted him and what blessings he received. This being so, it is all the more proper for him to honor his fatherland, salute the land of his birth, and present to it whatever he can, insofar as the land is the *father of his fathers.* If it did not bear its fruits, its rulers would not be able to rule what they do, since without the land's products their subjects could not be nourished or even exist, nor would they have the means to benefit them. And since there would have been no other sustenance, there would be no way or means for their parents to have been their fathers. Instead, their forebears would not have existed or, if they had, they would be other people's forefathers, and they themselves would not be rulers.

Humans seem to offer gifts only after they have received 2
something, but the earth alone keeps on giving and alone

εἰσφέρειν τῷ γένει, οὔτ᾽ οὐδενὸς αὐτῇ προϋπάρξαντι, οὔτ᾽ ἂν μετὰ ταῦτα δεομένῃ διδομένου, ὥστ᾽ οὐχ ὧν εὖ ὑπ᾽ αὐτῆς πάσχομεν μόνον, ἀλλὰ καὶ ὧν πατέρες φιλοτιμοῦνται καὶ χαρίζονται βασιλεῖς καὶ φίλοι φίλοις δωροῦνται τὴν αἰτίαν φέροιτ᾽ ἂν μόνη δικαίως καὶ τὰς παρὰ πάντων εὐφημίας καὶ χάριτας δέχοιτο. Οὕτω μετὰ παντὸς τοῦ δικαίου καὶ γιγνομένου καὶ πολλῆς τῆς ἀνάγκης ἀπάρχοιτ᾽ ἄν τις τῶν ἑαυτοῦ τῇ πατρίδι καὶ οἷς ἂν ἐνείη ταύτην ἀμείβοιτο, ὅθεν τὸ εἶναι τὸ ζῆν ἔσχομεν αὐτὸ τὸ ἔχειν οἷς ἂν τὸν εὐγνώμονα δείξαιμεν.

3 Ἄλλοι μὲν οὖν ἄλλο τι τῶν ἢ μικρὸν ἢ μεῖζον δυναμένων τῇ πατρίδι συνεισφερέτωσαν, οἱ μὲν χορηγοῦντες, ἄλλοι τριηραρχοῦντες, τοὺς πολίτας ἕτεροι λαμπρῶς ἑστιῶντες, οἱ δ᾽ ἐπισκευάζοντες πεπονηκότα τὰ τείχη καὶ νεὼς ἀνιστάντες καὶ ἱερὰ καὶ κατασκευάζοντες θέατρα, τὰ μὲν πρὸς κόσμον, τὰ δὲ πρὸς ἀσφάλειαν, τὰ δ᾽ εἰς αὔξησιν αὐτῇ καὶ ἐπίδοσιν, αὐτὴν αὐτῆς ἐκ παντὸς τρόπου βελτίω μηχανωμένων εἰσαεὶ γίνεσθαι, ὡς μὴ τὸ τὰ πέρυσι βελτίω εἶναι κρατεῖν ἐπ᾽ αὐτῆς, τὸ δ᾽ ἐς νέωτα πλουσιωτέραν ἑαυτῆς ἀεὶ καὶ φαιδροτέραν οὐκ ἐλπίζεσθαι μόνον, ἀλλ᾽ ἤδη καὶ φαίνεσθαι γινομένην, ὥστ᾽ ἐπ᾽ αὐτοὺς τἀγαθὸν πάλιν ἀντιστραφῆναι, οὐδενὸς δεομένης ἐκείνης, εὐδαίμονας αὐτοὺς ὄντας καὶ καλουμένους. Οἱ μὲν δὴ ταῦτα, καὶ πάντως αὐτῶν ἕκαστος, οὔθ᾽ ἧττον ἢ δύνανται οὔτ᾽ ἀποδιδοῖεν ἂν ὅσον ὀφείλουσι· τὸ μὲν γὰρ ἀδύνατον, εἴπερ οὐκ ἐκεῖθεν

freely contributes from its bounties to a race, since no one existed before it and it has never subsequently needed to be given anything by anyone. Consequently it is through its favors that we not only prosper, but fathers take pride, kings give freely, and friends give to friends. For this, the earth alone rightly bears responsibility and might accept acclamations and favors from everyone. Thus, it is entirely right and appropriate, compulsory even, for someone to offer something of his own to his homeland and repay it in whatever way he can, as it is the source of our existence, our life, and even the very means by which we may express our gratitude to it.

Therefore, let everyone contribute something either large or small, whatever he can, to his fatherland. Let some act as patrons, let some serve as trierarchs, let others throw lavish feasts for the citizens, while yet others restore dilapidated walls, erect churches, and construct shrines and theaters. Some of this activity will be for the adornment of their fatherland, some for its security, and the rest for its improvement and growth. People are always coming up with ways to make their land better than it was before, in any way possible, so that the sentiment that it was better in years past does not prevail over it, but rather a hope that it will always be richer and more famous in years to come, and not only the hope but also the perception that it is already becoming so. Consequently, a reciprocal relationship for the good is established for its people and, even though the land demands nothing itself, they are said to be, and actually are, prosperous. These people, then, and surely each of them individually, may neither give less than they are able, nor give as much as they should. While it would be entirely 3

εἰλήφασι τὸ δύνασθαι μόνον, ἀλλὰ καὶ σφίσιν αὐτοῖς ταῦτα πορίζονται, τὸ δὲ παντελῶς ἄγνωμον.

4 Ἡμεῖς δὲ τῶν ἄλλων ἀποροῦντες ἁπάντων καὶ πρὸς οὐδὲν ἂν ἕτερον οὔτε ὄντες οὔτ' ἐσόμενοι χρήσιμοι τῇ πατρίδι καὶ τοῦ μὲν πρὸς αὐτὴν γιγνομένου κατὰ ταὐτὰ τοῖς ἄλλοις πολίταις ἡμῖν ὄντες ὑπόχρεω, τοῦ δέ γε ταὐτὰ δύνασθαι καὶ πάνυ λειπόμενοι, οἷς ἔχομεν μόνοις ἀποδώσομεν αὐτῇ τὰ τροφεῖα καὶ τὴν δυνατὴν ἐκτίνοντες τῇ τροφῷ χάριν, τῷ καλλίστῳ μὲν ἂν τῶν σφετέρων, οὐδενὸς δὲ λειπομένῳ τῶν ἄλλων ταύτην ἀγήλαιμεν, λόγοις κοσμοῦντες οἷς ἡμᾶς ἀντὶ πάντων ὁ λόγιος ἐδοκίμασε Θεὸς ἀγαπᾶν, τὴν οὐ θρεψαμένην μόνον παραγαγοῦσαν, ἀλλὰ καὶ τούτων ἡμῖν γενομένην αἰτίαν τὰ μὲν οἷς οἴκοθεν αὐτῇ προσπαρέσχετο δαψιλῶς, τὰ δ' οἷς τὰ παρ' ἑτέρων οἵους τ' ἀπέφηνε δέξασθαι. Εἰ δ' οὐ τὸ πρὸς αὐτὴν ταύτῃ χρέος ἀφοσιωσόμεθα μόνον, ἀλλὰ καὶ τῶν ἄλλως ἂν γενομένων ἐπιτυχῶν τῶν δικαίων τῶν πρὸς αὐτὴν οὐδενὸς ἧττον, χάρις μὲν τῷ Θεῷ μὴ παντάπασιν ἀσυντελεῖς ἡμᾶς ἀνασχομένῳ φανῆναι, χάρις δὲ καὶ τοῖς λόγοις αὐτοῖς, δυναμένοις τοσοῦτον καὶ οὕτω λαχοῦσι τάξεως ἐν τοῖς οὖσιν, ὡς οὐδενὸς μὲν ἡττᾶσθαι, ἀλλὰ πλεονεκτεῖν μὲν τῶν πλείστων, τοῖς δ' ἐς ἴσον ἀκριβῶς ἔρχεσθαι.

5 Καίτοι λόγον ἀσκοῦσι καὶ τοῦτον τοῦ καθ' αὐτοὺς βίου προστησαμένοις παντός, οὐδ' ἄλλως ἐνῆν ἂν οὐδὲ πολλὰ βουλομένοις ποιεῖν, εἴπερ ἡμᾶς μὲν ἀνάγκη μᾶλλον τῶν ἄλλων τοῖς φαινομένοις εὐλόγοις ἐκ παντὸς ἕπεσθαι

ungrateful for them to do the former, the latter would be impossible, since they not only receive from their land the ability to give anything, but also the very things with which they may do so.

As for myself, I lack any of those other resources listed above and will not be good for anything other than this speech for our fatherland, either now or in the future. My debt to it is coming due, as it is for the rest of my fellow citizens, but I am far from being able to give to it the same gifts. Instead, I will offer it compensation for having reared me in the only way I can, repaying it for having nurtured me with the gift that I can offer; I thus intend to celebrate it with my very best resource, which is, however, in no way inferior to any other: I shall adorn my fatherland with words, which God the Word challenged us to love above all else, not only because it reared us, but also because it was responsible for us acquiring this skill, as it provided us with more than an abundance of talent for speaking and also made us capable of learning this from others. If, then, I do not just discharge my debt to it in this way, but do so no less than anyone else who has succeeded in some other way in paying his due to it, then thanks be to God for not permitting us to be completely imperfect, and thanks also be to the words themselves that are so powerful and enjoy such a high rank among all things in existence that they are second to none. Indeed, they surpass most things and are perfectly equal to the rest. 4

Furthermore, because I practice rhetoric and have made it the object of my entire life, I could not repay my debt otherwise, even if I actually wanted to do so, since necessity compels us to follow more than anything else what appears reasonable in every aspect of our behavior, and reason offers 5

τρόπου, τὴν δ᾽ ἐνεγκαμένην ἀγάλλειν τοῖς δυνατοῖς, ὡς οὐχ ἕτερον εὔλογον ὃν ὁ λόγος ἀπέδειξεν. Εἰ γὰρ αὐτοὶ λόγον ἄγοντες περὶ πλείστου τοῖς ἐκ τούτων προφαινομένοις τὴν ἐναντίαν βαδίσαιμεν, σχολῇ γ᾽ ἂν ἑτέροις πιθανὰ συμβουλεύσαιμεν, κατὰ λόγον καὶ τὸ εἰκὸς τὰ σφῶν αὐτῶν πείθοντες ἄγειν. Οὕτω καὶ μετὰ μείζονος ἀνάγκης ἐπὶ τὸν λόγον ἡμεῖς ἴοιμεν, καὶ πρὸς τοῦτον ἀποδυσαίμεθ᾽ ἂν τὸν ἀγῶνα ἢ οἱ τῶν ὄντων ἄλλως ἀπαρχόμενοι τῇ σφετέρᾳ.

6 Παραιτεῖσθαι δὴ νόμιμον ὂν τοῖς ἐκ τοῦ προφανοῦς μάλιστα σχῆμα τοῦ λόγου προστησαμένοις σεμνόν, καὶ σφᾶς μὲν αὐτοὺς ταπεινοῦντας, ἐξαίροντας δὲ τὰ πράγματα, τοὺς ἀκροατὰς οὕτω καταπραΰνειν, ὡς ἂν ἀμφοτέρως εὐδοκιμήσειαν, ἐφικόμενοί τε τῆς ἀξίας καὶ κατόπιν ἐλθόντες, τὸ μὲν τῆς σφῶν ἐν τῷ λέγειν δεινότητος, τὸ δ᾽ ἀποφερομένης τῶν ἐπαινουμένων τῆς φύσεως, αὐτὸς οὔτε κατὰ ταὐτὰ τοῖς ἄλλοις τόνδε διαθήσω τὸν λόγον, καὶ τοσούτου δέω χρήσεσθαι τοῖς τοιούτοις, ὥσθ᾽ ὅτι μὲν ὁ λόγος ἐργώδης τε καὶ λαμπρὸς καὶ δυσχερὴς ἀνῦσαι, μηδὲν διδαχθῆναι δεόμενος, μήτ᾽ ἴσως διδάξαι· κρατεῖ γὰρ ἐν ταῖς ἁπάντων ψυχαῖς· ὅτι δὲ καὶ αὐτὸς φαύλως πρὸς τοὺς τοιούσδε τῶν λόγων καὶ οὐχ ἱκανῶς παρεσκεύασται παντὸς μᾶλλον εἰδώς, ὅμως οὔτε ἀποκνῶ, καὶ θαρρούντως ἐπ᾽ αὐτὸ τρέψομαι τὸ ἐγκώμιον, τὸ μὲν εὖ τε καὶ καλῶς περὶ τῶν τῇ πατρίδι προσόντων εἰπεῖν καὶ τῇ κείνης ἀξίᾳ τὸν λόγον ἀποδοῦναι συμβαίνοντα, εὐκτὸν μὲν οἰόμενος εἶναι καὶ οἷον ἀντὶ πολλῶν ἂν ἀλλάξασθαι, οὐ ῥᾴδιον δέ, ἀγαπῶν δ᾽ ἂν εἰ καὶ ὁπωσοῦν τὰ τοῦ χρέους ἀφοσιώσαιμι

no other reasonable course than to celebrate the city which bore me as best I can. For if, in spite of my great preoccupation with words, the conclusions I have drawn from all of this are mistaken, my advice to others, namely that they conduct themselves in a reasonable and appropriate manner, would be even less persuasive. Thus it is actually under greater compulsion than people who make other kinds of offerings to their fatherland that I set forth upon my discourse and strip down for the competition.

It is customary for people beginning an especially solemn 6
sort of oration to explicitly make an apology for themselves, deprecating themselves and exalting their subject matter in order to win over their audience, so that they gain repute no matter the outcome of the speech, whether they deal with their subject adequately or fall short of it, as the former proves how good they are at speaking, while the latter reflects the praise due to the nature of their subject. I, however, will not compose my speech like everyone else in this regard, even though I really do need to use these kinds of tactics. For I do not need to be told that my speech's style is difficult, heavily ornamented, and irksome to read, nor do I need to tell anyone about this, as everyone must be thinking this anyway. And thus, although I am more aware than anyone that I am poorly and inadequately prepared for orations like this, still I will not hold back and will confidently turn to my encomium itself. I think it is desirable to speak well and favorably about the characteristics of one's homeland and deliver a speech worthy of its reputation, and it is also the sort of thing one does to repay one's homeland for its many gifts. It may not be easy to do this, but I am going to do it out of love, hoping to discharge some part of my debt

καὶ μὴ πάνυ τοι πόρρω τοῦ σκοποῦ βάλλοιμι. Οἶμαι δὲ καὶ τῶν νῦν τε παρόντων καὶ μετέπειτα συνεσομένων τοῖσδε τοῖς λόγοις ταύτῃ τοὺς πλείστους κρινεῖν καὶ τῶν τοιούτων κριτὰς ἀξιόχρεως.

7 Τῶν γὰρ μείζοσιν ἢ καθ᾽ αὑτοὺς ἐγχειρούντων, μή τινος μὲν συνωθούσης ἀνάγκης, οὐκ ἄν τις ἐλλελοιπότων τῆς ἀξίας ἀνάσχοιτο· ἐνὸν γὰρ ἔξω τῶν κινδύνων ἑστῶτας ἀπηλλάχθαι πραγμάτων, οἵδ᾽ ὑπὸ τῆς ἄγαν φιλοτιμίας, ὡς ἔοικεν, ἀποδύονται τὸν ἀγῶνα καὶ τὸ στάδιον ὑπεισέρχονται καὶ σφᾶς αὐτοὺς ἐν τοῖς ἀθληταῖς ἀπογράφονται. Ὥστ᾽ ἂν εἰκότως ἀντὶ θαύματος ἀποφέροιντο γέλωτα, μὴ διὰ πάντων διήκοντες καὶ πᾶσιν ἀρκούντως ἐπεξελθόντες. Εἰ δέ τις ἑκὼν ἄκων κατατολμᾷ τῶν μεγίστων, καὶ σφόδρα μὲν ἂν βουλόμενος ἐνεῖναί οἱ μὴ παρακινδυνεύειν, οὐκ ἔχων δ᾽ ὅπως, τοῦτον οὐχ ὁρῶ πῶς ἄν τις εὐλόγως τὴν διὰ πάντων ἀπαιτοίη ἀκρίβειαν ἢ πῶς δικαίως ἂν μέμψαιτο, τῆς ὑποθέσεως ἡττηθέντα.

8 Τοῦτο δὴ τοὐμὸν καὶ ὃ πᾶσα παθεῖν ἀνάγκη τοὺς Τραπεζοῦντα καὶ τὴν αὐτῆς εὐφημίαν τῷ λόγῳ ποιουμένους ὑπόθεσιν, οὐ μόνον ὅτι πολλῶν ὄντων αὐτῇ τῶν ἐς εὔκλειαν καὶ πολλῶν ἂν ἀπομερισομένων ἕκαστα δέοι γλωσσῶν, ἀλλ᾽ ὅτι καὶ πρεσβυτάτης εἴπερ ἄλλη τις ὑπαρχούσης, ἐν ἀφανεῖ γε τὰ πλείω τῶν αὐτῆς κεῖσθαι συμβέβηκεν, οὐ τὴν ἀρχὴν μόνον εἰς τὸ πλέον ἀνήκειν τοῦ φανεροῦ καὶ προχείρου λαβεῖν, ὃ περὶ τῆς μητρὸς αὐτῆς πόλεως εἴρηται καὶ πρὸς ἣν εἰ καὶ διὰ μέσων ἑτέρων ἑαυτὴν ἀναφέρει.

9 Ὥστ᾽ οὐκ ὀλίγων ὄντων τῶν ἡμᾶς διαφευξομένων καὶ οἷς ὁ λόγος ἐλλιπὴς ἔσται, τὸ μηδὲ τοῖς φαινομένοις αὖ

and not completely miss the mark. And I think that the majority of people here today and my future readers, who are judges worthy of the task, will rule in my favor.

If people undertake tasks greater than their abilities 7 while not under duress, no one will put up with them falling short of their goal; for they need not have got into that business or incurred that risk, but instead, apparently driven by their excessive desire for honor, they strip down for the contest, sneak into the stadium, and sign up for the competition. Consequently, these people will probably elicit mockery rather than admiration for not having properly equipped themselves and having marched out unprepared in every way. But if someone were, willingly or not, to venture upon the greatest tasks, fervently wishing he could avoid taking the risk, since he did not know how to brave it, I do not see how anyone could reasonably demand utter perfection or rightly censure him if he falls short of his subject.

This, indeed, is the situation I must face along with ev- 8 eryone who makes Trebizond and its praise the subject of his speech. The city not only has many features which bring it glory, each of which would take many tongues to recount in detail, but it is also just as ancient as any other city. Moreover, most information about it happens to be obscure, so where to start is not so obvious and easy to decide. This has already been said about its mother city, after which it models itself, although through some other intermediaries.

Consequently, there will be no small number of matters 9 that will escape me and make my speech defective. Yet while

ἐξαρκεῖν ἔχειν ἀφαιρεῖται τοῦ παντὸς ἐγκωμίου τῆς πόλεως, οὐ μὴν ὥστε καὶ τὴν οὖσαν αὐτῇ δόξαν συναφαιρεθεῖσαν οἴχεσθαι, ὅτι μὴ καὶ προσαυξηθῆναι μᾶλλον, ἔργῳ φανέντος τοῦ κατ᾽ αὐτὴν ὑπερέχοντος.

10 Ἡ γὰρ δὴ πόλις ἡμῖν γεγένηται μὲν οὐκ οὖσα, γενομένη δ᾽ οὐκ ἀπεγένετο, τὸ μὲν πάσαις σχοῦσα κοινόν, τὸ δ᾽ οὐ πάνυ πολλαῖς. Τῶν γὰρ ἐκ τοῦ παντὸς αἰῶνος συνοικισθεισῶν αἱ μέν, οὐδ᾽ αὐτὸ τοῦτο συνοικισθεῖσαι καλῶς, εἰς ὃ ἦσαν ἀνέδραμον αὖθις, ὡς μηδὲ τὴν ἀρχὴν γεγονυῖαι, αἱ δέ, καὶ τύχης ἀγαθῆς ἀπολαύσασαι καὶ πρὸς μέγα δυνάμεώς τε καὶ δόξης ἠρμέναι, αἱ μὲν ὁμαλῶς τε καὶ συνεχῶς, αἱ δ᾽ αὖ κατ᾽ ἀμοιβὴν καὶ ἀντιπερίστασιν, τοτὲ μὲν ἄρχουσαι, τοτὲ δὲ δουλεύουσαι, ὅμως ἅπασαι τελευτῶσαι αἱ μὲν οὐδὲ λείψανον ἑαυτῶν γνώρισμα τῆς πάλαι ποτὲ κατέλιπον τύχης, αἱ δ᾽ ὅσον τὸ τῆς φύσεως ἀνώμαλον καὶ ἀνόμοιον ἀπελέγξαι τὸν χρόνον νικήσασαι τοῖς ἄλλοις ἡττῶνται, πολλὰς ἐν τῷ μέσῳ μεταβολὰς ἀμειψάμεναι καὶ μετὰ τῆς χείρονος ἱστάμεναι μοίρας, παρὰ τοσοῦτον τῆς παντελοῦς γενόμεναι κρείττους φθορᾶς, παρ᾽ ὅσον τοῦτ᾽ ἦν αὐταῖς βέλτιον ἧς νῦν ὑπὸ τῆς τοῦ χρόνου περιπετείας εἰλήχασι τάξεώς τε καὶ καταστάσεως.

11 Ταυτηνὶ δὲ τὴν ἡμετέραν, ὥσπερ τινὶ θείᾳ μοίρᾳ συστᾶσαν ὡς ἀληθῶς καὶ θείων ἀνδρῶν ἔργον γεγενημένην, ἐνδιδόντος Θεοῦ, οὐ χρόνου πλῆθος ἠμαύρωσεν, οὐκ ἤμβλυνεν ὁ τοσοῦτος αἰών, οὐχ αἱ κυβεῖαι τῆς τύχης, οὐ

it may be insufficient to capture what there is to say about the city, and thus may detract from my praise of the city as a whole, it will *not* take away from the city's existing reputation, but rather even increase it, since my speech will make known its superior qualities.

Our city came into being from nonexistence and, once in existence, has not ceased to exist. The first attribute it shares with all other cities, the second with very few. Throughout the ages, some cities which have been established have quickly reverted to what they were before because they were not properly founded, just as if they had never even been there to start with. Others have enjoyed good fortune, obtaining great power and reputation; but while some of them did so steadily and continuously, others only did so after enduring many transformations and changing circumstances, ruling one moment and being enslaved the next. Nevertheless all of these have come to an end. Some of them have not even left a trace of their former fortune, whereas others have succeeded in rebuffing nature's inconstancy and inconsistency, defeating time only to be defeated in other ways, as they have undergone many changes in the meantime and suffered a difficult fate. For as long as they were strong enough to avoid complete destruction, they were better off than the current state of affairs and circumstances they have now come to on account of the vagaries of time. 10

As for our city, however, a city that would appear to be truly supported by some divine lot and that has been the work of divinely inspired men, the multitude of years has not obscured it, nor has so great a length of time dulled it. Neither the dice-rolls of fortune, nor the inconstancy of 11

τὸ τῶν πραγμάτων ἀνώμαλον καὶ ὁπωσοῦν ἔσχον λυμήνασθαι, ἀλλ᾽ ἅπαξ τὸ εἶναι λαχοῦσα καὶ ὑπὲρ τὰ μέτρα τῆς τῶν ὄντων φιλονεικεῖ φύσεως, ἀρξαμένη μὲν ἐξ ὅτου σχεδὸν ἐπέδωκαν Ἕλληνες, εἴξασα δὲ οὐδέπω τῷ χρόνῳ καὶ ταῖς ἐκεῖθεν μυρίαις μεταβολαῖς, ἀλλ᾽ ἦν τε καὶ ἔστιν ἡμῖν ἡ αὐτὴ ὡς ἂν χθές τε καὶ πρότριτα συνῳκισμένη, κακῶν ἀπαθὴς καὶ τῶν τοῦ βίου κυμάτων ἀνώτερος, καὶ εἴη γε, σῶτερ Θεὲ πολιοῦχε καὶ ἡγεμόνιε, μηδὲ πρότερον παύσαιτο πρὶν *ἂν ὕδωρ τε νάον καὶ δένδρεα μακρὰ τεθηλότα,* σοῦ συνέχοντος ἄνωθεν καὶ τῇ κραταιᾷ χειρὶ περιέποντος καὶ τοῦ οἰκείου μεταδιδόντος ὡς ἑνὸν ἀγαθοῦ, τῆς διαμονῆς τε καὶ διαρκείας.

12 Τὸ δὲ μεῖζον καὶ ὃ μόνης αὐτῆς ἴδιον καὶ μάλιστα πρὸς ἐπαίνου καὶ θαύματος, ὅτι καὶ βελτίων ἑαυτῆς ἀεὶ καὶ τιμιωτέρα καθίσταται, ἐπιδιδοῦσα, τοῦ χρόνου προβαίνοντος, εἰσαεὶ καὶ κατὰ τοσοῦτον τοῦ εὖ εἶναι πλεονεκτοῦσα, καθόσον αὐτῇ πλεονάζεται καὶ τὸ ἁπλῶς εἶναι καὶ ὄν τι καὶ εἶναι καὶ λέγεσθαι, ὡς ὁ λόγος προϊὼν δηλώσει σαφέστερον καὶ τοῖς ἀγνοοῦσιν ἀνθρώπων, εἴπέρ τινές εἰσι, παραστήσει.

13 Αὕτη πρώτην τοῦ γένους ἀρχὴν καὶ μητρόπολιν, εἰ δεῖ τὰ πρεσβύτερα πρότερα λέγειν, Ἀττικὴν καὶ τὴν Ἀθηναίων αὐχεῖ πόλιν, τὴν τροφὸν τῶν Ἑλλήνων, τὴν μητέρα τῶν λόγων, τῆς καλλίστης ταύτης φωνῆς τὴν διδάσκαλον. Ἀπῴκισαν μὲν γὰρ αὐτὴν Σινωπεῖς, τοὺς δ᾽ αὖ, οἰκισθέντες ὑπ᾽ Ἀθηναίων, Μιλήσιοι, τὰ κράτιστα τῆς Ἀσίας, *τὸ πρόσχημα τῶν Ἰώνων,* οἱ τῆς παραλίου ταύτης Ἑλλάδος

history, nor anything else has succeeded in destroying it, but from the moment when it first came into being, it has struggled to survive even beyond the natural limits of living beings. While it may have begun around the time when the Greeks flourished, it has never yet submitted to time and the countless changes that brings; but it was, and still is for us, the same city, as if it had only been founded yesterday or the day before yesterday, untouched by misfortunes and riding high above the waves of life. May this always be the case, God our savior, our ruler, and the protector of our city, and let it not cease as long as *water flows and tall trees are in bloom.* May you protect the city from above, take care of it with your mighty arm, and extend your own virtue to it, to whatever degree possible: I mean permanence and sufficiency.

The great thing about the city, and what is unique to it 12
and especially worthy of praise and wonder, is that it is always making itself better and more esteemed, forever improving. And to the extent that it continues to excel in its prosperity, so it excels simply by being itself, and by being and being spoken of for what it is, as my speech will clearly show and present more lucidly below for the benefit of people who may be unaware of this fact (if indeed there are any).

Our city prides itself on the origins of its race—if I must 13
start by recounting its earliest history—that is to say its Attic mother-state, the city of Athens: the nursemaid of the Greeks, the mother of literary culture, and the teacher of this most beautiful language. This is because our city was colonized by the people of Sinope, who in turn had been colonized by the people of Miletos, which had in turn been settled by the Athenians. The Milesians were a powerhouse in Asia and *the gem of the Ionians,* ruling over coastal Greece.

ἡγούμενοι, οὐκ *ἄλκιμοι* μόνον γεγενημένοι *πάλαι ποτέ,* τοῦτο δὴ τὸ λεγόμενον, ἀλλὰ καὶ μεθ᾽ ὑπερβολῆς ὅσης ἂν εἴποις.

14 Ἀθηναίων μὲν οὖν πέρι διεξιέναι καὶ τῆς αὐτῶν ἀλκῆς καὶ δυνάμεως καὶ ὡς πάσης ἐπελάβοντο γῆς, τὰ μὲν ἀποικίαις, τὰ δ᾽ ἰδίαις τε καὶ κοιναῖς φιλανθρωπίαις, ἀντὶ φυλακτηρίου κοινῇ καθιστάμενοι πᾶσιν, ἐνίοις μὲν δεομένοις αὐτῶν, τῶν δὲ καὶ μόνης τῆς χρείας ἱκανῆς παρακλήσεως γινομένης, ὅσους τε πολέμους διενεγκόντες πρὸς Ἕλληνας καὶ βαρβάρους, τοὺς μὲν πρὸς ὃν ἂν ἑκάστοτε τύχοι, ἔστι δ᾽ οὓς καὶ πρὸς τοὺς ἀπὸ πάσης τῆς οἰκουμένης σχεδόν, ὅσον ἐν πᾶσι τῶν ἐναντίων ἐκράτησαν καὶ κρείττους ἐγένοντο, καὶ ὅσα ἄν τις περὶ τούτων εἰπεῖν ἔχοι, ταῦτα μὲν οὖν ἐάσω· Ἑλλήνων τε γὰρ εἶναι οὐδένα ὅστις τὰ κατ᾽ αὐτὴν ἀγνοεῖ οὐ μᾶλλόν γε ἢ τὰ τῆς γεννησαμένης αὐτὸν ἕκαστος, καὶ ἄλλως οὐ τὸ τυχὸν ἔργον, οὐδὲ δέκα μόνον ἢ δὶς τοσούτων γλωσσῶν, οὐχ ὅτι γε πάντα τὰ κείνης, ἀλλ᾽ οὐδ᾽ ἕν τι τῶν προσόντων καὶ μίαν αὐτῆς πρᾶξιν ἀπολαβόντα κατ᾽ ἀξίαν εἰπεῖν.

15 Μιλήτου δὲ καὶ τῆς Μιλησίων δυνάμεως ὀλίγα μνησθεὶς ὅσον τῇ τε μητρὶ τὰ εἰκότα χαρίσασθαι καὶ δεῖξαι μὴ τὸ πορρωτέρω μόνον καὶ πρεσβύτερον ἡμῖν γένος οὕτως ἐπαίνου παντὸς κρεῖττον ὑπάρχον, ἀλλὰ καὶ τὸ προσεχὲς καὶ ἐγγύτερον οὐδὲν ἀποδέον ἐκείνου καὶ οἷον ἂν ἐφάμιλλον γένοιτο καὶ τῆς προαγαγούσης ἐπάξιον καὶ μάλα συμβαῖνον, ἐπ᾽ αὐτὴν εἶμι τὴν ὑμνουμένην καὶ ἣν ἐνεστησάμην ὑπόθεσιν.

16 Μίλητον τοίνυν, οἰκισάντων τῶν Ἀθηναίων, ἐς μέγα

Not only were they *mighty once upon a time,* so the saying goes, but, one might even say, exceedingly so.

I will thus permit myself to skip over the Athenians, their 14
strength and their power, as well as how they obtained the entire earth partly through colonization, partly through private and public acts of philanthropy that established them as a source of protection for all; some begged them to come, whereas for others their need alone was sufficient invitation. I pass over also how many wars they waged against Greeks and barbarians, some against whosoever happened to come along, others against opponents that had gathered together from almost the entire world; how they prevailed over their enemies in all ways and were stronger than them; and all the rest that one might say about them. There is not a Greek in the world who does not know about Athens any less than he does about the land of his birth. In any case, neither the present work, nor ten, nor twice that number of tongues could say everything there is to say about Athens or, for that matter, could even describe a single one of its attributes or deeds in an appropriate manner.

I will, however, mention a few things about Miletos and 15
the power of the Milesians, enough to confer upon a mother her due and to show not only that our race was far above all praise in the distant past, but also that lately and more recently it has not been inferior to its past self and would almost be a match for its forebear. I will then proceed to the praise of the city that I have made my main subject.

All writers and historians attest that Miletos was an 16

προβῆναι δυνάμεως, Ἰωνίας τε πάσης ἡγεμονεῦσαι καὶ τῶν ταύτῃ κατῳκημένων Ἑλλήνων προστῆναι μαρτυροῦσι μὲν λογογράφοι καὶ συγγραφεῖς ἅπαντες, μαρτυρεῖ δὲ καὶ ἃ ἐν τῷ παντὶ διεπράξατο χρόνῳ ὑπέρ τε σφῶν αὐτῶν καὶ Ἑλλήνων τῶν Ἀσιανῶν, πρὸς ὁμόρους τε καὶ ἅμα πλήθει καὶ πλούτῳ ἰσχύοντας διαμαχομένη βαρβάρους καὶ ὅμως ἀντέχουσα.

17 Οἱ γὰρ Ἀσίας καὶ *τῶν ἐντὸς Ἅλυος ποταμοῦ* πολλῶν ὄντων ἐθνῶν ἄρχοντες βάρβαροι, ἀπὸ Γύγου τοῦ τὸν δεσπότην ἀπεκτονότος Κανδαύλην ἀρξάμενοι καὶ τὴν Λυδῶν οὕτως ἡγεμονίαν περιζωσαμένου, ἀεὶ μέν τι προσεπικτώμενοι, ἀεὶ δ' ἔλαττον νομίζοντες ἔχειν καὶ τὸ μηδέν, εἴ τινες τὴν αὐτῶν μὲν οἰκοῖεν, ἐλεύθεροι δ' εἶεν ἀπὸ τοῦ ἴσου τε καὶ ὁμοίου σφίσι διαλεγόμενοι, ἐπεὶ πᾶν μὲν αὐτοῖς ἔθνος κατέστραπται, Φρύγες δὲ καὶ Μυσοὶ δουλείαν ὁμολογήσαντες ὑπετάγησαν, Βιθυνοί τε καὶ Παφλαγόνες καὶ Χάλυβες μετὰ τῶν ἡττημένων γεγένηνται, Πάμφυλοί τε καὶ Κᾶρες καὶ πᾶν γένος ὑπεῖξαν, ὥσπερ ἀστραπῆς προσιούσης ὑπεξιστάμενοι, ἀδούλωτον δ' αὐτοῖς ὑπῆρχεν οὐδὲν οὐδ' ἐλεύθερον. Ἕλληνες δὲ μόνοι καὶ μάλιστα Ἴωνες καὶ τούτων αὖθις τὰ κράτιστα, Μίλητος, ἀπρὶξ τε τῆς ἐλευθερίας ἀντείχοντο καὶ οὐδὲν ὅπερ οὐκ ἄσμενοι ὑπὲρ ταύτης ᾑροῦντο, δεινὸν μὲν ἐποιοῦντο εἰ μόνοι πάντων ἀνθρώπων ὑπεξαιροῖντο τῆς αὐτῶν δυναστείας, σφοδρὸς δ' αὐτοῖς ἔρως ἐνσκήπτει καὶ τούτους καταδουλώσασθαι.

18 Ὥσπερ δὴ χορευτῶν τοῦ κορυφαίου σφαλέντος οὐδὲν ὄφελος, καὶ στρατιᾶς ἐκ μέσου γενομένου τοῦ στρατηγοῦ ῥᾳδία ἡ χείρωσις, ἀθλητῶν τε τὸν μάλιστα εὐδόκιμον ἂν

Athenian settlement, attained great power, ruled over all Ionia, and was preeminent among the Greeks living there. A testament to this fact is all that the city accomplished over a great expanse of time for itself and the Greeks of Asia. It battled the neighboring barbarians, who were both numerous and wealthy, and yet it managed to hold its ground.

For the barbarian rulers of Asia and the many peoples *on* 17
this side of the Halys River, starting from Gyges onward—who killed his master Kandaules and thus took the Lydian throne—were always after more and always thought they had less, or even nothing, so long as there existed any people who inhabited their own land and were free, interacting with each other on an equal footing as peers. This was because every other people had been struck down by them. The Phrygians and the Mysians had delivered themselves up to slavery and had submitted. The Bithynians, Paphlagonians, and Chalybians were among those they had defeated. The Pamphylians, Carians, and every other race also obeyed them. As though fleeing before an approaching thunderstorm, not one people had remained free from slavery and at liberty. The Greeks alone and especially the Ionians, the best of whom were, in turn, the Milesians, clung fast to their freedom, and there was nothing that they would not gladly do on its behalf. However, the Lydians could not bear the thought that the Milesians alone of all people should be free of their domination, and they felt a violent lust to enslave them as well.

Just as all goes wrong when the leader of a dance troupe 18
misses the beat, an army is easily defeated when the general goes missing, and everything is ruined if you take the most

τοῦ σταδίου ἐξέλοις τὸ πᾶν συγκαθεῖλες, οὕτω καὶ βάρβαροι πεποιήκεσαν. Δόξαν γὰρ αὐτοῖς Ἰωνίαν χειρώσασθαι, ἐπὶ τὴν ἡγεμονικὴν καὶ στρατηγίδα πόλιν εὐθὺς ἔβλεψαν, καὶ πᾶν ἦν αὐτοῖς Μίλητος, καὶ ὅ φησιν ὁ συγγραφεύς, *τἄλλα πολίσματα περὶ ἐλάττονος ποιησάμενοι,* ἐπ᾽ αὐτὴν *ἤλαυνον* πανστρατί, καὶ ταύτην ἑλεῖν ἐποιοῦντο μέγα ἀγώνισμα, οὐχ ὅτι μόνον καὶ καθ᾽ αὐτὴν ἐσομένην οὐ τὴν τυχοῦσαν προσθήκην, οἷα δ᾽ ἂν γένοιτο καὶ τοῦ παντὸς ἀνταξία, ἀλλ᾽ ὅτι καὶ τὸ τῶν ἄλλων Ἑλλήνων κοινῇ φρόνημά τε καὶ ἀξίωμα Μιλήτῳ καὶ τῇ Μιλησίων ἂν συγκαθῃρεῖτο δυνάμει, καὶ λοιπὸν ἦν ἂν οὐδὲν ἔργον οὐδὲ λόγος τῆς ἄλλης Ἑλλάδος, ἀλλ᾽ ἤρκει μόνον αὐτὴν ὁμολογῆσαι τὴν δεσποτείαν καὶ τὰς ἄλλας εὐθὺς ἀναιμωτὶ προσχωρῆσαι.

19 Γύγης τε οὖν καὶ Ἄρδυς ὁ Γύγου οὐ μικρὸν μέν, ὅμως δ᾽ ἀνήνυτον ἔργον πεποιημένοι τὸ ταύτης κρατῆσαι, τέλος ἀπειρηκότες καὶ γνόντες *ἀέρα δέροντες* καὶ *τὸ ἐκ τῆς ψάμμου σχοινίον πλέκοντες,* ἐσπείσαντο, καὶ Κολοφῶνα μὲν εἷλον καὶ Σμύρνην ἐκάκωσαν καὶ Πριήνην ὑπέταξαν καὶ Κλαζομενὰς παρεστήσαντο, ὑπὸ δὲ Μιλησίων παθόντες τι μᾶλλον ἢ δεδρακότες ἀπήλλαξαν, νῷ διοικουμένοις ἐντυχόντες ἀνθρώποις καὶ ἡγεμονικοῖς τὰ πολέμια. Οἵ τε τούτους διαδεξάμενοι Σαδυάττης ὁ Ἄρδυος καὶ Ἀλυάττης ὁ Σαδυάττου, καταγνόντες αὐτῶν ὡς οὐχ ἱκανῶς παρεσκευασμένων, ἐφ᾽ ἕνδεκα μὲν αὐτοὶ τῇ πολιορκίᾳ προσεῖχον ἐνιαυτούς (τὰ μὲν ἓξ Σαδυάττης, Ἀλυάττης δὲ τὰ ἑπόμενα πέντε). Πολλάκις δὲ ἐσβαλόντες καὶ πλειστάκις συρράξαντες πόλεμον καὶ συστάδην ἀγωνισάμενοι, οὐδὲν ὅμως

popular competitor out of the stadium, this is what the barbarians attempted to do. When they decided to seize Ionia, they fixed their eyes immediately upon its administrative and military center: Miletos was all they wanted. And, as the historian says, *they cared little for the other towns* of Ionia, but *marched* upon it in full force; they made seizing it their chief objective, not just because its addition to their rule would itself be worth as much as anything else, but because the common purpose and standing of the rest of the Greeks would be completely destroyed by the loss of Miletos and the strength of the Milesians. Thereafter they would not have to reckon with or think about the rest of Greece; if they could only get this city to recognize their sovereignty, the others would submit immediately and without a fight.

Gyges and Ardys, his son, thus made an enormous but 19
fruitless effort to seize Miletos and finally gave up, recognizing that they were trying to *skin the air* and *make rope out of sand;* and so they made peace. They seized Kolophon, ravaged Smyrna, subdued Priene, and took control of Klazomenai, but, rather than accomplishing anything, they departed after suffering at the hands of the Milesians. For there they had encountered men who were governed by intellect and were authoritative in war. Their successors, Sadyattes, the son of Ardys, and Alyattes, the son of Sadyattes, disregarded what happened to them because they did not think they had been adequately prepared, and so they too spent eleven years pressing a siege (Sadyattes spent six and Alyattes the remaining five). They assaulted the city many times and even more often they fought pitched battles at close quarters. However, they gained no advantage despite

ἔσχον οὐδ' αὐτοὶ πλέον μετὰ τοσαύτης παρασκευῆς καὶ δυνάμεως ἐπιόντες καὶ Μιλησίοις ἀντικαθιστάμενοι, μόνοις τὸν τοσοῦτον διενεγκοῦσιν ἀγῶνα συμμαχίας ἐπήλυδος ἄνευ ἁπάσης. Οὐδεὶς γὰρ Ἰώνων αὐτοῖς τόνδε συνεπελάφρυνε τὸν ἀγῶνα, τὸ μὲν οὐ προσδεομένοις, τὸ δὲ καὶ τοῦ καιροῦ κατεπείγοντος πρὸς ἑαυτοὺς ἕκαστον βλέπειν καὶ τὴν οἰκείαν ἀσφάλειαν, ἀγαπητὸν ἂν οἰομένους ἑαυτὸν ἕκαστον σῴζειν καὶ τὰ οἰκεῖα φυλάττειν.

20 Οὕτως οἱ μέν, αὐτὴν ἄγοντες ἀντὶ πάντων ἐδήλουν οἷς ὡς πρὸς σκοπόν τε καὶ τέλος ἐφέροντο ταύτην πᾶν μηχανώμενοι. Ἡ δ' ἕως ἐνῆν ἀγωνισαμένη πλεῖστα καὶ μέγιστα, μέγα μαρτύριον ἐξενήνοχεν ἀνδρείας, μεγαλοπρεπείας, φρονήσεως· ἀνδρείας μέν, εἰ, τοσούτοις ἀντιπαλαμωμένη κἀπὶ τοσοῦτον χρόνον, περιεγένετο· μεγαλοπρεπείας δὲ οἷς οὐδὲν τοῦ φρονήματος καθυφῆκεν, οὐδ' ἀνάξιόν τι καὶ ταπεινὸν ἢ ἐνενόησεν ἢ ἐφθέγξατο, δουλείαν ἀκίνδυνον τῆς μετὰ κινδύνων ἐλευθερίας ἀλλαξαμένη. Ἀλλὰ μὴν πῶς ἄν τις μᾶλλον μετὸν αὐτῇ δείξειε καὶ φρονήσεως καὶ σοφίας ἢ εἰ πᾶσι μὲν αὐτὴ συμμαχοῦσα, μηδ' ἑνὸς δ' ἑτέρου προσδεηθεῖσα, αὐτὴ ἑαυτῇ ἤρκεσεν εὐβουλίᾳ τὴν πολυχειρίαν νικήσασα ἔργῳ τε δείξασα μάταιον οὖσαν τὴν δύναμιν, ἀπούσης φρονήσεως.

21 Ἆρ' οὖν ἐν μὲν τοῖς ἄνω καὶ τότε καιροῖς οὕτω διηγωνίσατο καὶ παρὰ πάντων εἶχε τὸ συγκεχωρηκός, ἐχθρῶν τε καὶ φίλων ἐνσπόνδων καὶ πολεμίων, τῶν μὲν οἷς τῶν ἄλλων ὑπεριδόντες ταύτην ἀρχήν τε καὶ τέλος τῶν ἑλληνικῶν ἡγοῦντο πραγμάτων, τῶν δ' οἷς αὐτὴν σφῶν αὐτῶν προεστήσατο, τὴν οἰκείαν αὐτῇ πιστεύσαντες σωτηρίαν.

such extensive preparations and forces when they attacked and confronted the Milesians, who endured this struggle alone without any external support. None of the Ionians tried to ease their struggle, partly because the Milesians did not ask, partly because the situation forced each to look out for himself and his own security; they thought it preferable for every man to save himself and protect his own.

The Lydians thus demonstrated how much they valued Miletos above all other cities by making it their target and goal, doing everything they could to take it. But Miletos, for as long as it could, fought exceptionally well and provided a great testament to its bravery, magnificence, and intelligence. Proof of its bravery is that it resisted so many enemies and survived for so long. Proof of its magnificence is that it did not concede any of its spirit and did not consider doing or saying anything unworthy or beneath itself by exchanging slavery without peril for perilous freedom. As for its intelligence and wisdom, how else would one prove its claim than by recalling that, although it aided everyone else, it sought help from no one else? It was enough for Miletos to have defeated the multitude of its attackers by its sound judgment and to have shown through its deeds that force is useless without intelligence. 20

Thus in those ancient times, then, Miletos exerted itself in these ways and everyone, whether friend or foe, ally or enemy, recognized it. The former looked to the city as their leader and entrusted it with their own safety and security, while the latter, although they disdained every other city, recognized it as the beginning and end of Greece. And yet as 21

Ἐπεὶ δὲ τῶν πραγμάτων αὐξομένων βαρβάροις ἔδει ποτὲ καὶ Μιλησίους ἀνθρώπους ὄντας φανῆναι καὶ τῷ κύκλῳ περιενεχθέντας τοῦ βίου μὴ τὴν κρείττονα μοῖραν ἔχειν ἀεί, ἔστιν οὕς τινας μᾶλλον ἐτίμων οἱ καταδουλωσάμενοι βάρβαροι καὶ βασιλεὺς ὁ μέγας αὐτός, οὗ τὰ τέρματα τῆς ἀρχῆς ἀνατέλλων ὁρίζει καὶ δύνων ὁ ἥλιος; Ἦ ἐτίμα μὲν διαφερόντως, τὰ δὲ πολεμικὰ κρείττους ἑτέρων ἐνόμιζεν; Ἦ τοῦτο μὲν οὐδὲ μαθεῖν ἔχρῃζεν, ἑαυτὸν δ᾽ ἑτέροις μᾶλλον καὶ τὴν οἰκείαν σωτηρίαν ἐν τῷ παρισταμένῳ τῆς χρείας ἐπίστευεν; Οὐδαμῶς· ἀλλ᾽ ὡς ἐλευθέρων ἐλευθέροις (εἰ οἷόν τ᾽ εἰπεῖν) προσφερόμενος, ᾐδεῖτο μὲν τὸ ἀρχαῖον αὐτῶν πρόσχημα καὶ ἣν περιεζώννυντό ποτε τῶν Ἰώνων ἡγεμονίαν, τῆς δὲ καρτερίας αὐτῶν καὶ τῆς ἐν πολέμῳ δεινότητος ἔργῳ πεπειραμένος, οὔτ᾽ ἐξεστράτευε, Μιλησίων ἀπόντων, παρόντες τε τοῦ βασιλέως σωτῆρες καὶ τῶν βασιλέως πραγμάτων, ἕως οὐκ ἦν ἄλλως ποιεῖν, διετέλουν γιγνόμενοι καὶ καλούμενοι.

22 Ἐπεί τε τὴν ἐλευθερίαν ὠδίνοντες καταδουλουμένους τοὺς Ἕλληνας ὁρᾶν οὐκ ἠνείχοντο, πρῶτοί τε τῆς ἀποστάσεως ἦρξαν, τοῦ καιροῦ παρασχόντος, καί, τοὺς ἄλλους ἐπισπασάμενοι, αὐτοὶ παντὸς ἄρχοντες ἀγαθοῦ καὶ τῷόντι τὸν ἡγεμόνα δεικνύντες, μέχρι τε Σάρδεων ἀνῆλθον αὐτῶν καὶ τὰ Περσῶν ἐκάκωσαν πράγματα καὶ τὴν δυνατὴν ὑπὲρ Ἑλλήνων παρὰ βαρβάρων Ἕλληνες ἔλαβον δίκην, ἡγουμένων τε καὶ ἐνδιδόντων τῶν Μιλησίων, σφόδρα καὶ τοῦτο ποιούντων ἑλληνικὸν καὶ σοφόν, τῶν μὲν πραγμάτων ἀντικρουόντων ὑπείκειν, ἁρπάζειν δὲ τὸν

the barbarians prospered, even the Milesians showed perforce that they were only human and could not forever hold the upper hand when buffeted by the wheel of life. But were there any others whom the conquering barbarians and the Great King himself, whose realm was bounded by the rising and the setting of the sun, honored more? Did he honor them especially because he thought that they were better at war than other cities? Or did he not need to learn this fact but instead entrust himself and his own safety and security to others when he had to? Neither was the case. Instead, as a free man would behave around free men (if that is possible to say), he would not march out without taking a contingent of Milesians with him, because he respected their ancient preeminence and the power which their city once held over the Ionians, and because he himself had actually experienced their vigor and cunning in war. The Milesians continued to be and to be called the king's companions and the saviors of the king's affairs so long as there was no other choice.

Because they worked so hard for their liberty, the Mile- 22
sians could not bear to see the Greeks being enslaved. They were thus the first to revolt when the opportunity presented itself, and won the rest of the Greeks over to their cause. They were responsible for every good thing that happened during this time, showing what a leader really is when they marched inland as far as Sardis itself and ravaged the lands of the Persians. The Greeks exacted a mighty vengeance on the barbarians on behalf of all the Greeks with the help and leadership of the Milesians. Their actions were very Greek and wise: yield when things are going against you and seize the opportunity when it presents itself. They neither

καιρὸν παραστάντα, ὡς μήτε τοῖς ἀδυνάτοις ἐπιχειρεῖν, ἀναισθησίας ἐπιφερομένους ἔγκλημα, μήτε τοῦ καιροῦ παρασχόντος καθεύδειν.

23 Τοιαύτη μὲν δή τις ἡ Μίλητος καὶ τοσαύτη, καὶ οὕτως ἡ πρὸς μητρὸς ἡμῖν, εἶπεν ἄν τις, μήτηρ διὰ παντὸς ἥκει θαύματος, ὃ περὶ Εὐρώπην Ἀθῆναι καὶ τὸ τῆς Ἀττικῆς ἔδαφος, τοῦτο περὶ τὴν Ἀσίαν αὐτὴ καὶ ἀρχῆς ἕνεκα καὶ εὐδαιμονίας ἀναφανεῖσα. Τοιαύτη δὲ οὖσα καὶ σφόδρα τῶν Ἀθηνῶν ἐπαξία ἑτέραν ἑαυτὴν ἐν τῷ τοῦ Εὐξείνου Πόντου καλλίστῳ τὴν Σινώπην οἰκίζει, ἀνθρώπων τε πλήθει στενοχωρουμένη καὶ δυνάμεως ἱκανῶς ἔχουσα. Οὐ γὰρ ἦν ἀπὸ τῆς ἑτέρας ἐπὶ τὴν ἄλλην θάλασσαν μεταβαίνειν, μὴ περιουσίᾳ χρωμένην δυνάμεως καὶ τῶν ἐν μέσῳ πάντων ἢ τελέως ἐπικρατήσασαν ἢ λόγον ποιουμένην οὐδένα. Ἅτε δὲ καὶ δυνάμει καὶ πλούτῳ ἀνθρώπων τε πλήθει τὸ συγκεχωρηκὸς ἔχουσα παρὰ πάντων, πρός τε τὴν ἀποικίαν ἀπεῖδε, καί, κατ᾽ ἐξουσίαν ἑαυτῇ τὸν κάλλιστον χῶρον ἐκλεξαμένη, τοὺς παρ᾽ ἑαυτῆς, ᾤκισε φέρουσα ἔνθα συνοίσειν τε αὐτοῖς ἔμελλε μάλιστα καὶ κατῳκημένους ἀσφαλές τε εἶναι καὶ πρὸς τὰς χρείας εὐπόριστον αἷς ὁ τῶν ἀνθρώπων συνέχεται βίος.

24 Ἐν καλῷ μὲν γὰρ τῆς θαλάσσης κειμένη, ἐν ἀσφαλεῖ δὲ καὶ τῆς ἠπείρου, ἠπειρῶτίς τε καὶ θαλάσσιος οὖσα, οὐδέτερον αὖ ἀκριβῶς εἶναι δοκεῖ, καὶ τοιαύτη δοκοῦσα τὰ παρ᾽ ἑκατέρων ὅμως, ἠπείρου τε καὶ θαλάσσης, δέχεται δαψιλῶς, ἅτε καὶ πρὸς ἀμφοτέρας εὖ ἔχουσα θέσεως ἕνεκα. Προβέβληται μὲν γὰρ ἐς τὸ πέλαγος ὁ τῇδε χῶρος, μέχρι πολλοῦ προτεινόμενος, τὴν θάλασσαν ἡμερῶν καὶ τοὺς

undertook the impossible, which would have earned them the charge of stupidity, nor did they sleep when the opportunity presented itself.

This then was the sort of city that Miletos was and the extent of its greatness. Thus our mother on our mother's side, you might say, reached the pinnacle of all admiration. What Athens, the bedrock of Attica, was for Europe in terms of its power and prosperity, Miletos was for Asia. Such a city, so worthy of Athens, founded another version of itself, Sinope, in one of the most beautiful areas of the Black Sea, and what Sinope lacked in population it made up for in strength. At that time, it was not possible to cross from the Aegean Sea to the Black Sea without a formidable force to either seize all the lands in between or to be able to ignore any threat they posed. Since Miletos was well known for the strength, wealth, and number of its people, it set its sights on establishing a colony, and it selected the finest possible location for itself. It settled its people where it would be in their best interests for the safety of the settlement and for keeping it well supplied to fulfill the needs by which human life is constrained. 23

The city of Sinope occupies a good site by the sea and a secure location on land, so that it is both a coastal and an inland city, although it does not exactly fit into either category. This being the case, it nevertheless abundantly possesses the attributes of each, that is of the sea and the land, given that it is well situated in both regards. The site projects out into the sea over a great distance, calming the sea, 24

ἐνταῦθα καταίροντας ὑποδεχόμενος καὶ χεῖρα προτείνων καὶ μεταδιδοὺς ἀναπαύλης καὶ ἀσφαλείας οἷς ἐν κύκλῳ λιμέσι καὶ ὅρμοις διείληπται, μᾶλλον δ' οἷς λιμὴν ὅλος ἐστὶ καὶ σύμπας ὁ πρὸς ἥλιον ἀνίσχοντα κόλπος εἰσέχων, εἰς νήσου δ' ἀποτορνευόμενος σχῆμα, καὶ περιηγμένος ἐν κύκλῳ ἰσθμῷ τινι μίγνυται τῇ ἠπείρῳ ἀπὸ θαλάσσης εἰς θάλασσαν οὐ μάλα πολλῷ διέχοντι διαστήματι, καὶ χερρόνησος γίνεται. Ἡ δὲ πόλις ἐπ' αὐτῷ τῷ ἰσθμῷ, ἐπὶ μὲν μῆκος παρατεταμένη μέχρις οὗ πλείστου ἠδύνατο, κατιοῦσα δ' ἐπ' εὖρος ἑκατέρωθεν μέχρι θαλάσσης, καὶ καθαρῶς ἤδη νῆσον τὴν χερρόνησον ἀποδείξασα οἷς, αὐτῆς τε κειμένη μέσον καὶ τῆς ἠπείρου, διέστησεν αὐτὰς ἀπ' ἀλλήλων. Καὶ γοῦν ἀκριβῶς οὖσαν θαλάσσιον οὐδὲν ἧττον αὐτὴν καὶ θαλάττης οὐκ ὀλίγον ἀπέχουσαν ἠπειρῶτιν καλέσαις, ἐκ τοῦ εἴσω καὶ πρὸς θάλατταν αὐτῆς μέρους ἤπειρον περιβεβλημένην τοσαύτην, ὡς καὶ προαστείων λόγον ἐπέχειν καὶ ἀμπελῶνας ἀποπληροῦν καὶ βουσὶ καὶ ἀρότροις ἀνεῖσθαι καὶ πρὸς καρπῶν φορὰν ἐξαρκεῖν.

Οὕτω δὲ ἔχουσα καὶ ποταμῶν δύο μεγίστων τε καὶ καλλίστων τῶν ἀνὰ πᾶσαν τὴν γῆν τὴν μέσην εἴληχε θέσιν καὶ ἐναντίαν, ἔνθεν μὲν Νείλου τοῦ τὴν Αἴγυπτον ἄρδοντος, ὑδάτων ἀρίστου καὶ γονιμωτάτου, ἀπ' ἄρκτων δέ γε τοῦ Ἴστρου, πρὸς τὰς ἀμφοτέρων ἐκβολὰς βλέπουσα καὶ ἀμφοῖν ἐναντίον κειμένη, *Ἴστρου* τοῦ πηγάζοντος μὲν *ἐκ Κελτῶν καὶ Πειρήνης πόλεως, μέσην* δὲ *σχίζοντος* ἅπασαν *τὴν Εὐρώπην* καὶ πρὸς τὸν Εὔξεινον ἐκβάλλοντος Πόντον, τῆσδε τῆς πόλεως ἔναντι, ἀφ' ἧς ἄν τέ τις ἐπὶ *τὴν ὀρεινὴν*

welcoming ships putting into port, extending the hand of friendship, and granting rest and safety to them. It does so through harbors and anchorages that encircle it at intervals, and especially the complete and entire eastern bay, which is effectively a harbor. The site is rounded off in the shape of an island and leads around via a curved isthmus to the point where it meets the land, separating sea from sea by a short distance and thus forming a peninsula. Situated on this isthmus, the city extends as far as possible in length, while in width it descends as far as the sea on both sides; it has, thereby, effectively made the peninsula an island, in that, by lying between the sea and the land, it separates one from the other. Indeed, while the city is clearly by the sea, you might also call it an inland city because part of it is quite far from the sea and it encompasses so much land on both its landward and seaward parts that it has room for suburban estates, is filled with vineyards, is given over to oxen and the plow, and has plenty of room for cultivating crops.

Situated in this way, Sinope also occupies a spot facing, 25
and in between, two of the greatest and most beautiful rivers in the entire world: the Nile River, which irrigates Egypt and has the best and most fertile waters, and the Danube River coming from the north. It faces the mouth of both rivers and lies opposite the pair of them. *The Danube* has its source *in the lands of the Celts and the city of Peirene, and it divides* all of *Europe in half,* emptying into the Black Sea opposite this city. From there, if you were to go to *mountainous*

ἴοι *Κιλικίαν,* ἄν τ᾽ ἐκεῖθεν ἐς Αἴγυπτον, ὅπου ῥέων Νεῖλος ἐκβάλλει, εὐθεῖά τε αὐτῷ ἡ ὁδὸς ἔσται καὶ ἀπαρέγκλιτος καὶ τὸ ὅλον εἰπεῖν ἀτραπός.

26 Οὕτως ἐν καλῷ τε κεῖται τῆς γῆς τόδε τὸ μέρος αὐτῆς, καὶ τοῖς ἁπανταχόθεν δορυφορεῖται καλοῖς, οἷς αὐτούς τε Μιλησίους πρὸς τὸν οἰκεῖον ἐπηγάγετο ἔρωτα καὶ πρότερόν ποτε Κιμμερίοις τὴν πολλὴν ἔστησε πλάνην. Οὗτοι γάρ, ὑπὸ Σκυθῶν τῶν νομάδων ἐκ τῶν ὑπὲρ τὸν Καύκασον καὶ Ἀράξην ποταμὸν *τόπων ἐξαναστάντες* καὶ εἰς τὸ πρόσθεν ἀεὶ καταδιωκόμενοι, οὐ πρότερον τῆς φυγῆς ἔληξαν, οὐδὲ τῆς τῶν διωκόντων ἔσχον ὠμότητός τε καὶ τυραννίδος ἀπαλλαγῆναι, πρὶν ἐπ᾽ αὐτὴν τήνδε τὴν χερρόνησον ἐξικέσθαι καὶ ταύτην οἰκίσαι, οὕτω μὲν θέσεως εὖ, οὕτω δ᾽ ἀσφαλείας καλῶς ἔχουσαν γνόντες, ὥστ᾽ εἰ μὴ τοῖς Ἕλλησι τῶν τῆς οἰκουμένης τιμιωτάτων πεπρωμένων καὶ τοῦτον αὐτοὺς ἔδει τὸν χῶρον κοσμῆσαι Ἑλληνίδα τε πόλιν ἐνταῦθα συστῆναι, κἂν ἐς τόδε Κιμμερίων ἦν ἔθνη τῇδε οἰκοῦντα καὶ τῆς ἐνταῦθα γῆς ἄρχοντα. Νῦν δ᾽ οὐδ᾽ ἐς δύο που γενεὰς διατετριφότας ἐκεῖσε Λυδοὶ μὲν ἀνέστησαν, Ἕλληνες δὲ καὶ οἱ ἀπὸ Μιλήτου πεμφθέντες, Λυδῶν οὐκ ἐπιστρεφόμενοι, τῆς τε γῆς ἐπελάβοντο καὶ τείχεσι τὸν ἰσθμὸν περιέλαβον, ὡς τὴν τοιάνδε τῆς γῆς ἀπόμοιραν τοὺς τοιούσδε τῶν ἀνδρῶν οἰκεῖν δέον ᾖ.

27 Τούτων τε καὶ πολλῶν ἄλλων ὄντων τῶν ἐν ἐπαίνου καὶ θαύματος, οὐδὲν ἧττον καὶ Διογένης ὁ Σινωπεὺς εἰς κόσμον τε καὶ δόξαν αὐτῇ συντελεῖ, ἐνταῦθα μὲν καὶ γεννηθεὶς καὶ τραφείς, ἐν δὲ πάσῃ σχεδὸν οἰκουμένῃ πολιτευσάμενος καὶ γῆς ἁπάσης πολίτης γενόμενος, σοφίας μὲν ἐπ᾽

Cilicia and, from there, to Egypt where the Nile flows and empties its waters, the road would be straight, direct, and a direct path between them.

The region of Sinope thus lies in a good natural location and is protected on all sides by these good features. It was with these that it wooed the Milesians themselves and, earlier, halted the long wanderings of the Cimmerians. These people, who *had been compelled* by the Scythian nomads *to leave the regions* beyond the Caucasus mountains and the Araxes River, and had been constantly driven forward, did not cease their flight and were unable to free themselves from the cruelty and tyranny of their pursuers until they came to this peninsula and settled it, recognizing what a fine, secure location it was. As a result, if fate had not given the most desirable parts of the world to the Greeks and if necessity had not compelled them to adorn this spot by establishing a Greek city there, the Cimmerian nations would even now still live there and rule over that part of the earth. But as it stands, although they had not been living there for more than two generations, the Lydians forced them to emigrate, whereupon the Greeks, those who were sent from Miletos, took control of the land with no regard for the Lydians and walled off the isthmus, because it is only right for men such as this to occupy a land such as this. 26

Among all the many other Sinopites worthy of praise and admiration, Diogenes of Sinope contributed no less to the city's honor and glory. Although he was born and raised there, he lived almost all over the known world and was a citizen of the entire earth. He became extremely wise, and 27

ἄκρον ἐληλακὼς ὅση τε θεωρίας ἔχεται καὶ λόγων ἅπτεται θειοτέρων, ὅση τε πρακτικὴ καὶ ἠθική, κοσμοῦσα τὸν ἄνθρωπον καὶ ῥυθμίζουσα τὴν ψυχὴν καὶ τὰς αὐτῆς ἀτάκτους ὁρμὰς ἀναστέλλουσα, κοινὸς δ᾽ εὐεργέτης ἀναφανεὶς ἅπασι καὶ τυράννους ἐλέγχων καὶ νουθετῶν τοὺς πολλοὺς αὐτῶν τε καθαπτόμενος βασιλέων καὶ ἰδιώτας διδάσκων καὶ πᾶσι κοινὸν ἑαυτὸν εἰς μέσον ἀγαθὸν προτιθέμενος.

28 Αὕτη μὲν οὖν, Μιλησίων ἄποικος οὖσα κἀκείνους αὐχοῦσα πατέρας, ἐπείπερ τῶν προαγαγόντων ἀξίως καὶ ὡσὰν εἰκὸς ἦν ἐκ ῥίζης ἀνασχοῦσαν τοιαύτης ἐς αὔξησιν ἐπιδοῦσαν καὶ τῶν καθ᾽ αὑτὴν οὐδεμιᾶς ἔλαττον ἔχουσαν κατ᾽ οὐδέν, ἔδει μηδ᾽ ἀποικίαις ἐνδεῖν μηδὲ ταύτῃ τῶν ἄλλων ἡττᾶσθαι, μοίρας αὐτῇ θείας συλλαβομένης, καὶ τοῦτο δεδύνηται. Δεδύνηται δὲ βέλτιον μὲν ἢ κατὰ τὰς ἄλλας, μεῖζον δὲ ἢ καθ᾽ αὑτήν, αὑτήν τε καὶ τὰς ἁπανταχοῦ πόλεις ἐν τούτῳ νικήσασα, συνοικίσασα μὲν τὴν Τραπεζοῦντα καὶ ἡμετέραν ταυτηνὶ πόλιν, ἡττηθεῖσα δ᾽ αὐτῆς οὐδ᾽ ὅσον ἂν ηὔξατο· καὶ ὃ τοῖς ἄλλοις *πατράσιν εὐκτὸν* μέν, οὐ ῥᾴδιον δ᾽ ἴσως, τῶν *παίδων ἡττᾶσθαι*, τούτου καὶ τετύχηκεν αὕτη, καὶ σφόδρα νενίκηται, καὶ τὰ δευτερεῖα φέρουσα χαίρει ὡσὰν οὕτω λαμπρότερον κοσμουμένη.

29 Οὐ γὰρ ὅσον αὐτήν τε ταύτην τὴν ἀποικισαμένην ἡ καθ᾽ ἡμᾶς ὑπερεβάλλετο πόλις, ἀλλὰ καὶ τῶν ἄλλων οὐκ ἄν τις εὕροι τὴν νικῶσαν ῥᾳδίως. Ταῖς τε γὰρ τῶν ἀρίστων ἀρίσταις ἐφάμιλλον παρέχεται ἑαυτήν, καὶ πρὸς τὴν Ἀττικὴν καὶ τὴν πόλιν τῶν Ἀθηνῶν ἐξεικασμένη τοῖς πλείοσιν ἐκείνης εἰκὼν καὶ ἀκριβὲς ὡς ἐνῆν ἀπείργασται

was as well-versed in every kind of theory and conversant with divine concepts, as with practical and ethical considerations that adorn man, regulate the spirit, and restrain its disorderly urges. Diogenes was a public benefactor to everyone. He rebuked tyrants and admonished many of them. He scolded kings themselves, taught private citizens, and showed himself off publicly to everyone like the public blessing that he was.

As a colony of the Milesians that could proudly claim them as its forefathers, and since it was indeed worthy of its forebears, which was only natural given the roots from which they had sprung, Sinope could not in turn fail to establish colonies itself or fall short of other cities in this respect, since it was growing in greatness and proving in no way inferior to any of those nearby. And, in accordance with divine will, it proved equal to the task. It was actually able to do better than all the others and outperform even itself, for it outdid itself and cities everywhere in this respect when it founded Trebizond, our city, and was then surpassed by it in all the ways for which it could have hoped. While *being surpassed by their children is something for which* other *fathers can only hope,* as it is perhaps not something easy to do, Sinope has accomplished precisely this. It has thus been sorely defeated by Trebizond, yet it gladly takes second place, as if it were thereby even more splendidly adorned. 28

Our city not only surpassed the city that founded it, but it would also be hard to find another city that could better it. Indeed, it even rivals the best of the best cities, and it has thus come to resemble an image of Attica and the city of Athens in many of its attributes, in fact as close an imitation 29

μίμημα. Ὃ γὰρ ἐφ᾽ ἡμῶν καὶ τῆς φύσεως αὐτῇ δεδιδάγμεθα πείρᾳ καὶ τῷ παθεῖν,—ὡς ἄρα στίγματά τινα καὶ οὐλὰς ἐν βραχίοσι καὶ προσώπῳ φερόντων τινῶν, ἐν μὲν παισὶ καὶ παίδων ἴσως παισὶν οὐκ ἂν ἴδοις τὴν ὁμοιότητα, ἐς δὲ τρίτην γενεὰν καὶ τετάρτην ἐπισημαίνει τά γε τοιαῦτα, καὶ τὴν ἴσην οὐλὴν ἐπὶ ταὐτοῦ τόπου τῷ πάππῳ ἢ ἐπιπάππῳ τὸν υἱωνὸν ἢ υἱὸν υἱωνοῦ εὕροις ἂν φέροντα—τοῦτο κἀνταῦθα κρείττονα τρόπον συμβέβηκεν. Οὐ γὰρ οὐλῶν δή τινων καὶ στιγμάτων οὐδ᾽ ἀγεννῶν τινῶν καὶ φαύλων ἡμῖν ἡ πόλις παραδειγμάτων εἰκόνα σῴζει καὶ τύπον, ἀλλὰ τὴν Ἀθηνῶν κοινότητα καὶ φιλανθρωπίαν καί τινα τρόπον ἕτερον τὸ αὐτόχθον ἐκείνων καὶ τῆς δυνάμεως τὴν περιουσίαν καὶ κράτος ἐν πολέμοις καὶ μάχαις καὶ ὅσα κόσμος Ἀττικῆς καὶ ταύτης μόνης καθέστηκεν οὐ παντελῶς ἐν τοῖς ὑπ᾽ αὐτῆς οἰκισθεῖσι σωθέντα ἀκριβῶς ἡμεῖς μεμιμήμεθα, καίτοι διὰ τρίτης πρὸς αὐτὴν ἀναφέροντες καὶ παίδων αὐτῇ παῖδες ὄντες καὶ πρὸς αὐτὴν ἀπεικάσμεθα τέλεον καὶ τοῦ παραδείγματος οὐκ ἐκπίπτομεν, ὥστ᾽ ἄν τις ἐκείνοις τὰ ἡμέτερα παραβάλλοι, καὶ σφόδρ᾽ ἂν τοῦ σκοποῦ τύχοι καὶ πολλῶν τῶν συλληψομένων καὶ συνοισόντων αὐτῷ τῶν ἐπαίνων τὸν ἔρανον.

30 Τοῦ μὲν γὰρ παντὸς μέση καὶ γῆς τῆς καθόλου οὔτ᾽ αὐτὴ κεῖται ἡ ἡμετέρα, οὔτ᾽ ἂν αὐτὸς φαίην. Μάλιστα μὲν γὰρ μιᾶς τοῦτο γίνεται καὶ τόπου ἑνός, καὶ τὰς ἄλλας οὐκ ἔστι ταὐτοῦ τούτου τυχεῖν, οὐδ᾽ ἂν πολλὰ ἀγωνίσωνται, ὥσθ᾽ ὅταν τις ἁπασῶν ταύτῃ καταψηφίσηται, καὶ τούτου χωρὶς οὐκ ἂν ἔχοιμεν οἷς αὐτοὺς τῆς μέμψεως ἐξελοίμεθα

as possible. What we have learned through trial and error about ourselves and our nature has happened here in a better way than elsewhere. It is true that there are people who have birthmarks and moles on their arms and faces, and, although you would not find a similar mark in their children and perhaps in their children's children, come the third or fourth generation these characteristics show up again, and you might thus find that the grandson or great-grandson has the same mole in the same place as his grandfather or great-grandfather. But our city does not preserve the image or imprint of moles, birthmarks, or ignoble and paltry things like that. Rather, we have truly imitated the accessibility of the Athenians, their benevolence, and, put another way, their native traits, as well as the abundance of their power, their might in wars and battles, and all the qualities that adorned Attica and it alone. These qualities have not fully survived among the other cities founded directly by Athens, yet we accurately represent her, despite tracing our descent back to her through three generations and being the children of her children; we perfectly resemble her and do not fall short of her example. In consequence, if anyone were to compare us to the Athenians, he would be right on the mark, for there are many points that he could collect and assemble for a celebration of Trebizond's virtues.

30 Our city of Trebizond does not lie at the center of everything or even of the entire earth, nor would I myself claim this. For this is certainly true of only one city and one place, and the same thing cannot possibly be the case for the rest, nor would people dispute it very much. So, if one were to evaluate all the cities in the world based on their centrality, we would lack this attribute and would not possess the attributes necessary to escape censure and number our-

καὶ μετὰ τῶν ἐπαινουμένων ἂν θείημεν, τότε καὶ ταύτην ἢ μέσην δεκτέον ἢ μὴ ἔχοντας ἐγκαλύπτεσθαι καὶ μετ' αἰσχύνης περιιέναι, τὸ μεῖζον εἰς δόξαν ὑφαιρεθέντας. Ἔπειτα, εἰ μὲν τῷ μέσην εἶναι καὶ τὸ πάντων εὐθὺς ἀρίστην πεφυκέναι συνηκολούθει, εἶχεν ἂν λόγον περιεργάζεσθαι· εἰ δὲ τοῦτο μὲν οὐδ' ἄν τις καὶ τοῖς οὖσιν ἀπομαχόμενος εἴποι, πολλαὶ δὲ διαφοραὶ γῆς βελτίους τε καὶ κρείττους, μείους τε καὶ μείζους, αὐτῆς ἑαυτῆς ὡς ἐπὶ τὸ πολὺ βελτίονος οὔσης τοῖς πλείοσιν αὐτῆς μέρεσιν, ἔνθα τὸ μέσον χώραν οὐκ ἔχει, τί ἄν τις ἣν ἐπαινεῖ ἀπό τε τῶν οὐκ ὄντων καὶ ὧν οὐ μέγα τὸ θαῦμα κοσμοίη, τὰ ὄντα οἱ παρ' οὐδὲν θέμενος καὶ τὸν ἀληθῆ κόσμον αὐτῆς παριδὼν καὶ κατ' ἄμφω τοῦ πρέποντος ἁμαρτών; Τὸ μὲν οὖν τῆς γῆς μέσον οὐκ ἂν ἡμῖν ἡ πόλις ἐπέχοι, τὸ δ' αὐτῆς κάλλιστον ὄψις τε μαρτυρεῖ καὶ πεῖρα παρέστησε καὶ ὁ λόγος προϊὼν ἀποδείξει.

31 Εἰ δή με καὶ μεσότητος χρὴ μνησθῆναί τινος, μέσην ἂν αὐτὴν φαίην οὐκ Ἀττικῆς τινος καὶ Ἑλλάδος, μικροῦ χωρίου καὶ γῆς ὀλίγης, μικροῖς διαστήμασι μετρουμένης καὶ στενοῖς ὅροις ὁριζομένης, ἀλλὰ τοῦ τῆς Ἀσίας ὡς εἰπεῖν πλείστου καὶ τῶν Ἀσιανῶν ἐθνῶν τε καὶ πόλεων. Ἐκ μὲν γὰρ τοῦ πρὸς ἀνίσχοντα ἥλιον Πέρσαι καὶ Μῆδοι καὶ Σάπειρες καὶ τὰ Κόλχων ἔθνη περιοικοῦσι τὴν ἡμετέραν, ἐκ δέ γε θατέρου Καππαδόκαι καὶ Κίλικες καὶ Γαλάται περιστοιχοῦσιν ἡμᾶς καὶ Λυδοί, ὥσπερ τινὰ δορυφορίαν ἡμῖν συμπληροῦντες καὶ χορείαν τινὰ περιελίττοντες ἐναρμόνιον, ὥσπερ ἐν κύκλῳ, καὶ στεφανοῦντες μὲν ἡμᾶς τοῖς παρ' ἑαυτῶν καὶ ὧν ἑκάστη φέρει καλῶν, δεχόμενοι δὲ τὰ

selves among the praised; we would thus either have to demonstrate our city's centrality or, without this attribute, feel embarrassed and go around ashamed, deprived of the most important component of our glory. If being the city at the center of everything directly implied that it was also the best city of all, then it would make sense to show concern for this matter and elaborate upon it. But if one were not to say this, countering with facts, that there are many different cities on earth, better and stronger, smaller and greater, but that for the most part the one which is in itself better is, in the majority of places, *not* in the center of the country there, why would the encomiast glorify a city with falsehoods that elicit no great admiration, disregarding the facts, ignoring its true glory, and failing to write properly on both counts? Thus, while our city may not be at the center of the earth, its appearance attests, experience of it has confirmed, and the following words will reveal what is best about it.

If I must say something concerning centrality, then I 31
would not say that Trebizond is at the center of an Attica or Greece, a minor region and a small land, measured in small distances and bounded by narrow boundaries. Instead, I would say it lies at the center of a vast expanse of Asia, so to speak, as well as of the peoples and cities of Asia. For the Persians, Medes, Sabiri, and people of Kolchis live near our eastern border, while the Cappadocians, Cilicians, Galatians, and Lydians surround us to the west. It is as if they form a bodyguard around us or swirl around us in a harmonious dance, as if in a circle. They crown us with their virtues and the goods that each of their lands produces, while they

παρ' ἡμῶν καὶ (ὅ φασιν) *ἐξαντλοῦντες* μὲν *ἀμφοτέραις*, πλείω δὲ λείποντες ἢ λαμβάνουσιν. Αὐτή τε γὰρ παρ' αὐτῆς ἡ πόλις ἡμῖν οὐκ ἔστιν ἧς τινος ἔλαττον ἴσχει οἷς φέρει καὶ γεωργεῖ, καὶ τὰ παρ' ἐκείνων ὑποδεχομένη ταμεῖον κοινὸν καὶ ἐργαστήριον οἰκουμένης καὶ *θάλασσα*, φασίν, *ἀγαθῶν ἀναπέφηνεν*.

32 Οὐ γὰρ δὴ πρὸς οὓς εἴρηται μόνον οὕτω θέσεως δεξιῶς ἔχει, ὥσπερ τι κέντρον πρὸς τὰ κύκλῳ πανταχοῦ σχεδὸν ἴσην ἔχουσα τὴν ἀπόστασιν, ὡς, ὅθεν ἄν τις ἐπ' αὐτὴν ὁρμηθῇ, κοῦφον εἶναι τὴν πόλιν καὶ μονονοὺ πάντοθεν ἴσην καὶ ὅμοιον, ἀλλὰ καί, πρὸς τοὺς τῆς ἑτέρας ἠπείρου καὶ πόλεις τὰς Εὐρωπαίας οὐδὲν ἧττον ἔχουσα συμμιγνῦναι, τὴν ἀρίστην εἴληχε τάξιν καὶ θέσιν καὶ ἧς οὐδ' ἂν αὐτὴ κρείττονα ηὔξατο. Τοῦ γὰρ πρὸς ἕω σύμπαντος Πόντου καὶ τῆς τῇδε θαλάσσης τὴν μέσην σχεδὸν χώραν ἐπέχουσα, πρός τε τὰ παρ' ἑκάτερα παραπλεῖν ἀσφαλῶς ἔχει καὶ ῥᾷστα, τὰ μὲν ἐκφέρουσα, τὰ δ' ἀντεισάρουσα, τῇ τε ἀντιπέρας ἠπείρῳ οὐκ ἐκ πολλοῦ διαστήματος οὐδὲ πολλοῦ πόνου καὶ πλοῦ μιγνυμένην οὐκ ἔστιν ὃ τῶν καλῶν αὐτὴν διαφεύγει καὶ ὧν ἡ σύμπασα φέρει. Οὕτως ἡμῖν περίεστι καὶ μεσότητος, καὶ τοιούτων ἄρα καὶ τοσούτων ἐθνῶν καὶ χωρῶν τὴν μέσην εἰλήχαμεν, εἴπερ τῳ φέρειν καὶ τοῦτο δοκεῖ εἰς ἔπαινον καὶ θαύματος λόγον.

33 Πελάγους τε καὶ θαλάσσης τοιαύτης τὸ μέσον ἐπέχομεν, ἣν οὐδεὶς ἂν διὰ τέλους οὐ λογογράφος οὐ ποιητὴς ᾄσαι, κἂν πολλὰ φθέγξαιτο καὶ τοῦτο μόνον ἔργον προστήσαιτο. Τῷ γὰρ Εὐξείνῳ δὴ Πόντῳ πρῶτα μὲν αὐτὸ τοὔνομα τοῦτο, πολλὴν φιλανθρωπίαν τε καὶ κοινότητα

receive what we produce and *collect it in both hands* (so the expression goes), though they lack more than they receive. By itself our city is no less robust than any other in terms of what it produces and grows, but by accepting their products it has become the world's common storehouse and workshop, *a sea of bounties,* as they say.

The city is not only favorably situated in the ways I have 32
already described, but, as the center of a circle, everything around it is nearly equidistant, so that from whatever side you approach the city, it is easily accessible, virtually the same from any direction. Moreover, being no less in contact with the people on the other continent, Europe, and the cities there, it enjoys the best position and location and could not hope for a superior one. For the city occupies what is roughly the central region of the whole eastern Pontos and the Black Sea, making it safe and quite easy to sail to the regions on either side of it in order to import and export goods. Since it also has connections with the land which lies opposite, no great distance away and without requiring too much effort or sailing, there are no goods beyond its reach and nothing the whole world does not bring to it. We thus excel even in terms of centrality and occupy a central place among these many peoples and regions, assuming, that is, one thinks this has any bearing on our reputation and is a reason for wonder.

We also occupy the central point of a very great sea, 33
which no orator or poet could succeed in celebrating, even if he were to expend many words upon it and devote an entire work to it alone. First of all, even the name of the Black Sea attests to its great benevolence and accessibility, and, in a

μαρτυροῦν, πάντα συλλήβδην αὐτοῦ κατηγορεῖ τἀγαθά, ὡς μὴ τὸν πολλὰ μὲν εἰρεσίαις ἐνιδρώσαντα, πολλὰ δὲ πρωρεύσαντα καὶ διασκεψάμενον πνεύματα, κύματα, κλύδωνας, πλείω δὲ πηδαλιουχήσαντα μόνον, ἀλλὰ καὶ τὸν θαλάσσης καὶ τοῦ κατ' αὐτὴν ἄπειρον πλοῦ τοῦτο μόνον ῥηθὲν θαρσύνειν τε καὶ πτεροῦν πρὸς τὸν πλοῦν, καὶ κυμάτων καὶ πνευμάτων ὑπερορῶντα καὶ πᾶσαν τῆς ψυχῆς ἀπεληλακότα δειλίαν.

34 Ἔπειτ' αὐτῇ τε πείρᾳ γνόντας καὶ πράγματι ὡς ἀλύπως καὶ ἀσφαλῶς, ὡς ἐνὸν τοὺς πλέοντας ἑκασταχοῦ παραπέμπει, οὐκ ἔστιν αὐτῷ παραβαλεῖν οὐδ' ὁντινοῦν ἕτερον, οὐ κόλπον, οὐ πέλαγος. Οὐ Χάρυβδιν γάρ, οὐ Σκύλλαν προτείνεται, οὐκ ἄμπωτιν, οὐ πλημμυρίδα ποιεῖ καὶ παλίρροιαν, τοτὲ μὲν ἐπὶ ξηρᾶς ὥσπερ προσηλῶν καὶ πατταλεύων τὰ σκάφη, τοτὲ δὲ βυθίζων καὶ δεικνὺς ὑποβρύχια, οὐδὲ Σικελικὸς ἐνταῦθα πορθμὸς καὶ πελάγους Ἀτλαντικοῦ ῥαχίαι καὶ *πέτραι* τινὲς *ὕφαλοι* καὶ *σπιλάδες,* αἷς ἀνάγκη τοῦ πνεύματος τοὺς πλέοντας συρρηγνύντος, τῶν μὲν αἰσθάνεσθαι μόνον, οὐκ ἔχειν δ' ὅπερ ἂν διαπράξωνται, πρὸ ὀφθαλμῶν σφίσι τοῦ ὀλέθρου κειμένου, τῶν δ' οὐδὲ συνεῖναι πληττουσῶν, ἀλλὰ φθάνειν τὴν πεῖραν τὴν αἴσθησιν τῶν κακῶν, πρὶν οἷ τύχης κεχώρηκε σφίσι τὰ πράγματα γνῶναι τοῦ ἁλμυροῦ πίνοντας ὕδατος, ἀλλ' ὅλος δι' ὅλου ἑαυτοῦ ὁμαλός τε καὶ συνεχὴς τέταται, ἐφ' ὅσον πλεῖστον ἐχρῆν ἥκων μήκους τε καὶ πλάτους, ὡς μήτε ἀδιεξίτητος εἶναι διὰ τὸ μέγεθος, μήτ' αὖ ὑπεροπτέος τῷ συνεστάλθαι πρὸς τὸ μηδὲν καὶ μικροῖς ὅροις ἀπείργεσθαι, ἀλλ' ἡμερῶν μὲν οὐκ ὀλίγων σοι τριφθήσεται πλῆθος πανταχῇ περι-

word, highlights everything that is good about it. The mere mention of its name is enough to impart courage, not only in anyone who has labored long and hard at the oars, who has stood for a long time at the bow of the ship and tested the winds, waves, and surf, or who has steered many ships, but even in someone who is inexperienced with sailing over the sea; it is enough to make him sprout wings for the voyage, taking no notice of the waves and winds and banishing all thought of cowardice from his mind.

In addition, because people know from trial and error 34
that travelers can sail anywhere along the coast safely and without trouble, there is no other bay or sea anywhere else that is comparable to the Black Sea. It does not harbor a Scylla or a Charybdis. It has no ebb and flow from the rise and fall of tides, which alternately leave ships' hulls high and dry on the shore and then submerge them, showing them underwater. There is no Sicilian strait here, nor the rocky shores and *hidden reefs* and *shoals* of the Atlantic Ocean, against which the force of the wind dashes sailors, some of whom notice the rocks only when peril is right before their eyes and consequently there is nothing they can do, while others do not even realize that they are striking them, but only recognize their evil plight and the evil hand dealt them by fortune when they are swallowing seawater. Here, in contrast, the Black Sea spreads out smoothly and consistently everywhere, while its length and breadth are so perfect, that it is neither infinite in size, nor, on the other hand, despicable for being so small that it amounts to almost nothing at all and for being enclosed within tiny boundaries. While you

πλέοντι, διὰ παντὸς δὲ ὅμως ἔξεστι διελθεῖν καὶ πάντα τὸν Πόντον διερευνήσασθαι, μηδὲν αὐτοῦ καταλιπόντα ἀκίχητον.

35 Τὴν γὰρ ἐν ἑκατέρῳ φυγὼν ἀμετρίαν, ἐπίσης τε καὶ μικρότητα καὶ μέγεθος ἀτιμάσας, ἐπὶ τοῦ μέσου τε καὶ ὀρθοῦ τετήρηκεν ἑαυτόν, τιμήσας τὸ μέτριον, νικῶν μὲν ὧν βέλτιον κατὰ μέγεθος, ἡττώμενος δ' ἅ γε νικᾶν οὐκ ἐχρῆν, ὡς νίκην εἶναι καὶ τὴν ἧτταν αὐτῷ κἀνταῦθα μόνον νικᾶσθαι οὗ νικᾶν οὐ συνήνεγκεν ἄν. Ὥστε, δέκα τῶν μεγέθει διαφερόντων κόλπων θαλάττης γνωριζομένων, οὔτε πρῶτός ἐστιν οὗτος οὔθ' ὕστατος, ἀλλ' ὁ μέσος ἤδη καὶ ἕκτος. Οὕτω καὶ οὗτος τὸ μέσον τετίμηκε.

36 Θάλαττα δὲ καὶ πέλαγος ὢν καὶ καλούμενος, αὐτὸ τοῦτο μόνον ἐστὶν ὃ κέκληται, πέλαγος, οὐ νήσους, οὐκ ἠπείρους προβάλλων ἐν τῷ μέσῳ οὐδ' ἀγροὺς καὶ κώμας καὶ πόλεις ἐν μέσῃ θαλάττῃ δεικνύς, ὡς ἔργον εἶναι τὴν ἀληθῆ κλῆσιν αὐτῷ φωράσαι καὶ ὅθεν ἂν αὐτὸν ὀνομάσαιμεν, πότερον ἤπειρον ἢ θάλατταν ὑγρὰν ἢ ξηράν, χέρσον ἢ πέλαγος, τοῦτο δὴ τὸ τῆς ἄλλης θαλάττης, ᾗ νόθην ἂν φαίην ταύτην προσεῖναι τὴν κλῆσιν, ἀλλοτρίῳ ἐπιθεμένην ὀνόματι, τὴν δ' ἡμετέραν ταυτηνὶ θάλασσαν μόνην γνησίως τε καὶ κυρίως τοῦτο καλεῖσθαι καὶ μόνην συμβαίνειν οἷς ὀνομάζεται, ὥστε καὶ τοὺς τῇδε τὸν πλοῦν ποιουμένους οὐδὲν οὐδαμῶς ὑποπτεύειν, ἀλλ' ὅλοις ἱστίοις θαρρεῖν φερομένους καὶ νύκτωρ καὶ μεθ' ἡμέραν μέσον τὸ πέλαγος τέμνοντας, οὐ νήσους, οὐ σκοπέλους ὑφορωμένους, οὐ δεδιότας ναυάγια, οἷς πολλοῖς περιπίπτειν ἀνάγκη τοὺς Ἑλλησπόντῳ τε καὶ Αἰγαίῳ καὶ τῇ τῇδε παραβαλλομένους

might spend many days sailing all around it, it is, however, always possible to traverse and explore the whole Pontic sea, for nowhere is out of reach within it.

35 By avoiding immoderation in either respect and being neither too small nor too large, the Black Sea has kept itself perfectly centered and has thus valued moderation. It wins in size where it is good to win, and is defeated only when it would not be expedient to win, considering those defeats to actually be a victory, and thence accepts being conquered only where to conquer would not be to its advantage. While it may not be the first or last among the ten known seas of notable size, it is the sixth and so the middle one. In this way, even the sea treasures its central position.

36 The Black Sea is and is called both a "sea" and an "open sea." It is the only body of water properly called an "open sea," as it has no islands or larger bodies of land emerging in its midst and thus has no fields, villages, and cities in the middle, as a "sea" does. Consequently, it is hard to figure out the correct term we should use for this "sea" of ours: a body of land or a "sea," wet or dry, mainland or "open sea." In fact the Black Sea is not an "open sea" but that other "sea," and it is to that one should say it is wrong to apply the term "sea," and that which needs a different name. For it is only this "sea" of ours which should truly and correctly be called a "sea" and which alone matches what is implicit in that name. Thus people sailing across the Black Sea never worry that anything may happen to them, but confidently set full sail and cut right across the middle of the "open sea" by day and night without keeping watch for islands or promontories. Nor do they fear shipwreck, something which by contrast often befalls those who sail the Hellespont, the Aegean, or this sea. Consequently, it is safer to sail on the Black Sea

θαλάττῃ ἀσφαλέστερόν τε πλεῖν ἄνευ ἁπάσης περιεργίας τὸν Εὔξεινον τῶν ὑπὸ πυρσοῖς καὶ λαμπτῆρσι καὶ πύργοις ἀλλαχοῦ καταιρόντων.

37 Περὶ πᾶσαν μὲν γὰρ ἑαυτοῦ τὴν ἀκτὴν ὅρμους τε καὶ λιμένας αὐτοφυεῖς ἐκ συμμέτρου διαστήματος παρεχόμενος, ὡς ἔστιν ἐν οἷς οὐδὲ πείσματος ὁρμούσας δεῖσθαι τὰς ναῦς, εἴσω δὲ τῶν ἑκατέρωθεν αἰγιαλῶν αὐτὸ τοῦτο μόνον ὕδωρ καὶ πέλαγος ὑπάρχων ἀμύθητον ἐφέντας μὲν εἰς αὐτὸ ταῖς χρηστοτέραις βουκολεῖ τῶν ἐλπίδων· κοῦφον γὰρ αὐτοῖς τότε καὶ νὺξ ἐπιγενομένη καὶ καταιγίδες καὶ λαίλαπες καὶ τυφῶς προσραγείς· ἔξεστι δέ γε πυθέσθαι τῶν ναυτικῶν, πᾶν οἰομένων φορητὸν μετά γε πελάγους· κατάραντας δὲ λαμπρῶς ὑποδέχεται καὶ φιλοφρόνως διαναπαύει, μεταδιδοῦσα καὶ λιμένων καὶ ἀγορῶν καὶ τῆς ἄλλης τρυφῆς· ὃ πολλοῦ δεῖ τῆς ἄλλης ἀπολαύειν θαλάσσης, ἡνίκ' ἄν, νυκτὸς ἀσελήνου ἐπιλαβούσης καὶ πνευμάτων ἐναντίων ἀπολαβόντων καὶ κύκλῳ πανταχῇ περικεχυμένων τῶν νήσων, ἔστι δ' ὅτε καὶ λαμπρὸν τῆς ἡμέρας διαλαμπούσης, σφοδρότερον συνωθοῦντος τοῦ πνεύματος, πρὶν ἢ μεταχειρίσασθαι τὰ ἱστία καὶ χαλάσαι τὰ λαίφη, λάθοιμεν ἐξοκείλαντες πρὸς τὰς τῶν νήσων ἀκτὰς καὶ ταῖς πέτραις προσρήξαντες καὶ δύντες κατὰ βυθοῦ.

38 Τοιούτου δὲ τοῦ παντὸς ὄντος Εὐξείνου, τὸ περικλύζον ἡμᾶς ἔτι μέρος αὐτοῦ πολλῷ φιλανθρωπότερόν τε καὶ ἡμερώτερον, ὥσπερ ἑαυτὸν ἐνταῦθα νικῆσαι ἐρίσαντος καὶ αὐτὸν ἑαυτοῦ βελτίω τοῦτο τὸ μέρος φανῆναι θελήσαντος, ὥστε τοὺς ἐνταῦθα ναυτικοὺς καὶ θαλάττης ἐργάτας, καίτοι λιμένων ὄντων ἡμῖν οὐκ οἶδ' εἴ τινος φερόντων τὰ

without all the concern that people show elsewhere when they put into port with the guidance of beacons, lanterns, and towers.

Along its entire coastline, there are thus anchorages and natural harbors at a moderate distance from one another, such that ships at anchor in them do not need to be tied up. Along the shore on either side, there is only water and the enormous open sea, which beguiles those setting out upon it with auspicious expectations. It is easy for them to do this even when night has fallen and when storms, tempests, and typhoons have burst forth; just ask sailors with experience of everything that can happen on the open sea. The coast thus warmly welcomes those who seek anchorage and kindly gives them respite, granting them access to harbors, markets, and other luxuries. This is certainly a great advantage over those other "seas" when the night sky is moonless, contrary winds are picking up, and islands are scattered all around, or even in broad daylight when the wind blows a sharp gust before we can get hold of the sails and slacken off the canvas; for there we barely avoid running aground on the headlands of the islands, crashing on the rocks, and sinking into the abyss. 37

If the whole Black Sea is like this, the portion of it surrounding us is even more kind and gentle. It is as if it sought to outdo itself here, wanting to prove itself better than itself in this particular section. The condition of the sea here is such that although we have harbors second to none I know 38

δεύτερα, ἔνθεν μὲν τοῦ τοῦ Ὕσσου λιμένος, ἐκεῖθεν δὲ τοῦ Ῥιζοῦντος, οὐδὲν αὐτοῖς χρῆσθαι, τὰ πλεῖστα κατ᾽ ἐξουσίαν ἐνθερίζοντάς τε καὶ ἐνεαρίζοντας, ἔστι δ᾽ ὅτε καὶ ἐγχειμάζοντας ὅπου καὶ τύχοι τῶν αἰγιαλῶν, ἐπὶ μιᾶς ἀγκύρας ἢ καὶ πολλάκις ἑνὸς πείσματος πεποιθότας καὶ χρωμένους ἀντὶ λιμένων ἀκτῇ πάσῃ καὶ πᾶσιν αἰγιαλοῖς καὶ σφᾶς αὐτοὺς καὶ τὰ σκάφη πιστεύοντας ᾧ ἂν καὶ βούλοιντο.

39 Ὥσπερ γάρ, οἶμαι, τῆς φύσεως εὐφυῶς τε καὶ δεξιῶς τὰ τῇδε πάντα διαθεμένης, ἅτε προειδομένης τὴν ἐσομένην ἐνταῦθα πόλιν καὶ ὡς τοῖς τε ἄλλοις καὶ τῷ ναυτικῷ πλεῖστον διοίσει καὶ τριήρεσι περιέσται καὶ ναυσὶ κρατήσει τῶν κατ᾽ αὐτήν. Οὕτω τῆς ἐνταῦθα θαλάσσης ἥ τε φύσις καὶ θέσις εὐφυῶς ἔσχεν, ἀντὶ λιμένων μὲν τὰς ἀκτάς, ἀντὶ δὲ ὅρμων πεπλουτηκυῖα τοὺς αἰγιαλούς, ὃ μόνον ἄπιστον πανταχῇ πιστὸν ἐνταῦθ᾽ ἀναφήνασα καὶ τὰ ἴσα δυνάμενον, οἷς μόνοις ἔνι πιστεύειν καὶ θαρρεῖν πανταχῇ, ὡς μηδὲν ἐμποδὼν εἴη τῷ πεπρωμένῳ καὶ οἷς περὶ αὐτῆς εἵμαρτο, μηδὲ κωλύσῃ μηδὲν αὐτὴν θαλάττης πειρᾶσθαι καὶ κυμάτων κατατολμᾶν καὶ ναυτικὸν βίον βιοῦν.

40 Πρὸς δὲ τοῦτο δοκῶ μοι καὶ τοὺς πρώτους ταύτην οἰκισαμένους ἰδόντας καὶ ταῦτα μαντευσαμένους περὶ αὐτῆς, ἐνταῦθα φέροντας ἐνιδρῦσαι τοὺς ἐξ ἑαυτῶν, πολλῶν τῶν ἐν μέσῳ ὑπεριδόντας. Παρ᾽ ἑκάτερα γὰρ λιμένων ἐλλογίμων ὄντων, ὡς ἂν ἐκ τοῦ σύνεγγυς ἀμφοῖν ἔχοιεν χρῆσθαι, ἐπίσης αὐτοὺς ἑκατέρων ἀπέστησαν, πρὸς μὲν τὴν παροῦσαν ἑκάστοτε χρείαν ἀρκεῖν ἂν οἰόμενοι τοὺς παρόντας αἰγιαλούς, ἐν δὲ τῷ καλοῦντι τῆς ἀνάγκης κατ᾽

about, namely the Hyssian harbor on one side and Rizous on the other, sailors and seamen do not use them. For most of the spring and summer, and sometimes even during the winter, they can dock at will wherever there is a beach, entrusting their boat to only one anchor or often even a single rope. Instead of harbors they use every headland and beach, entrusting themselves and their vessels to whatever location they want.

I think it is almost as if nature cleverly suited and dexter- 39
ously arranged everything in this spot, foreseeing the city that would emerge here and how it would surpass the others nearby with its navy, overcome them with its triremes, and conquer them with its ships. Nature and location also shaped the sea here well, endowing it with headlands instead of harbors, and beaches instead of anchorages. What is only unbelievable everywhere else, nature has made believable here, and those things which one can only believe in and trust everywhere else it has actually made possible here, so that there would be no obstacle to what was destined and fated for our city. There would be nothing to stop it from exploring the sea, braving the waves, and living the sailor's life.

I imagine our city's first founders took note of this and 40
foresaw it about our city, so they brought their families and settled here, passing over the many other sites in between. As there are noteworthy harbors on both sides of our city, they kept themselves an equal distance from each, so that they could use them both on account of their proximity. They thought that the beaches there would suffice for their day-to-day needs but, when forced by necessity, seeing as

ἐξουσίαν ἢ τόν γε κρείττω καὶ ταῖς παρισταμέναις ὥραις συμβαίνοντα πληροῦν αὐτοῖς τὴν ἀνάγκην ἢ καὶ ἄμφω τὰς ναῦς αὐτῶν ὑποδέχεσθαι, τοῦ ἑνὸς οὐ χωροῦντος, οὐδ᾽ ἀρκοῦντος τοσῷδε ναυτικοῦ πλήθει, ὃ πολλοῦ γ᾽ ἔδει αὐτοὺς δύνασθαι, θατέρῳ τῶν λιμένων ἐπικειμένης τῆς πόλεως. Τούτου τε γὰρ ἂν ἐστέρητο, οὗ τὸ πλεῖστον τοῦ χρόνου νῦν ὁρμοῦσιν αἱ πλόϊμοι καὶ τοῦ τῶν λιμένων ἑτέρου δὶς τοσοῦτον ὅσον τό γε νῦν εἶναι διέχουσα οὐδέποτ᾽ ἂν εἶχεν ὅσον νῦν ἀπολαύειν. Νῦν δ᾽ ἀμφοῖν ἐν τῷ μέσῳ κειμένη, τριπλοῦν ἀνθ᾽ ἁπλοῦ περιβέβληται τὸν λιμένα, τῶν παρ᾽ ἑκάτερα κειμένων ὥσπερ μεταδιδόντων καὶ τῇ μεταξὺ ἑαυτῶν θαλάσσῃ τῆς οἰκείας φύσεως καὶ τὸ σύμπαν αὐτῆς ἕνα τινὰ καὶ συνεχῆ διὰ παντὸς ἑαυτοῦ λιμένα δεικνύντων.

41 Ἐξ οὗ τί γίνεται; Πᾶσι μὲν συμμίγνυμεν ἔθνεσι, πᾶσι δὲ συμβάλλομεν γένεσιν, *ἄστεά τε καὶ νόον ἀνθρώπων* οὐκ ἔστιν ὧν τινων οὐ γινώσκοντες, τὰ μὲν οἷς αὐτοὶ ναυσὶν ἡμεδαπαῖς πανταχῇ διαβαίνομεν, τὰ δ᾽ οἷς ἐπήλυδες ἁπανταχόθεν καταίρουσιν, σοφώτεροί τε καὶ αὐτῶν καὶ βελτίους γινόμεθα, τὰ κάλλιστα πανταχόθεν συλλέγοντες καὶ τὸ χρήσιμον ἐκλεγόμενοι καὶ πᾶν εἶδος ἐμπορευόμενοι γνώσεως. Καίτοι τινὸς ἤκουσα λέγοντος ὡς πλεῖστον ἀπέχειν αἰγιαλῶν καὶ θαλάττης μέρος εὐδαιμονίας εἶναι ταῖς πόλεσι καὶ πρὸς ἀρετὴν ἔχειν αὐταῖς συμβαλέσθαι, ὡς ἂν ναυτικῆς ἀναρχίας καὶ ἀπειροκαλίας ἀπηλλαγμέναις καὶ τῶν παρεπομένων θορύβων καὶ ταραχῆς καὶ συγχύσεως καὶ τῆς δεινῆς ἀμαθίας. Ἐγὼ δ᾽ εἰ μὲν ἢ τοὺς ναυτικοὺς μόνους ἢ πάντας ἑώρων ταῦτα νοσοῦντας, ἢ τὴν

the city lay near each of the harbors, they either had at their disposal the one which best met their pressing needs in the circumstances, or both harbors could accommodate their ships when one was not big enough and did not suffice for such a large fleet of ships, which was something they often had to do. If Trebizond were to be deprived of the places where its ships lie at anchor most of the time, or if it were twice as far from either of the harbors as it is now, it would never have had everything that it currently enjoys. Now, however, since it lies in the middle between the two harbors, it has a triple harbor instead of just one, because those on each side share their natural role, as it were, with the sea between them and the whole appears to be one continuous harbor all around.

What is the result of all of this? We intermingle with all 41
foreign peoples, we interact with all races. There are no *cities or minds of men* about which we do not know. Some we know because we travel all over the place in our own vessels, while we know others, from among the foreign peoples, because they put into harbor here, from all over the place. We become wiser and better than them because we collect what is best from everywhere, selecting what is useful and trading in every kind of knowledge. And yet I have heard someone say that being far from the coast and the sea is part of what makes cities prosperous and contributes to their virtue, since they are freed from the anarchy and boorishness of sailors as well as from the resultant uproar, unrest, turmoil, and profound ignorance. Now if I saw that sailors either individually or as a group suffered from this illness, or that a

πολυπειρίαν ἄλλως συλλεγομένην ἀνθρώποις, καὶ τὸ εἰδέναι τήν τ᾽ ἀρετὴν οὐκ ἂν προσγενομένην οὐδ᾽ ὁτῳοῦν, ἂν μὴ πολλὴν πρότερον ἀλογίαν ἐπιτηδεύσῃ καὶ ἀμιξίαν, μηδενὶ μήτε συμβάλλων μήτε διομιλούμενος, σφόδρ᾽ ἂν ἐδεδίειν τὸν λόγον καὶ τὴν θάλατταν ἂν ἐδυσχέρανον καὶ τὰ κύματα, εἰ δὲ πόλιν μὲν εὖ ἔχειν καὶ διὰ παντὸς ἥκειν ἐπαινουμένου μὴ ὡς πλείστοις συμβάλλουσαν, οὐδεὶς ἂν συμφῆσαι.

42 Τῶν δ᾽ ἐμπορευομένων οἱ πλεῖστοι κακοί, κἂν ναυτικοὺς εἴποις κἂν ἠπειρώτας. Ἔστι δέ γ᾽ ἐς ἀγαθὸν καὶ θαλαττίων ἀπώνασθαι· οὐδὲν γὰρ ἀπώμοτον, τό τε πολλὰ μαθεῖν ἐκ τοῦ πολλὰ παθεῖν περιγίνεται καὶ τὸ ἰδεῖν τῷ εἰδέναι συμβάλλεται. Ἀρετῆς τε κυρίως οὐκ ἄν τις ἐφίκοιτο, οὐδ᾽ ἂν ἐπαινοῖτο κατ᾽ αὐτὴν καὶ θαυμάζοιτο πρὸς ἀξίαν, μὴ πολλῶν ὄντων τῶν ἀντικρουόντων περιγινόμενος καὶ κατορθῶν ἐν πολλοῖς σφάλλουσι, καίτοι καὶ τὸ εἰδέναι μόνον αὐτὸ καὶ γινώσκειν οὐκ οἶδ᾽ εἴ τις τοῦ κρατίστου μέρους ἐξέλοι τῆς ἀρετῆς. Τί δεῖ τῶν ἀναχωρήσεων καὶ προφάσεων τούτων ἢ πῶς ἀξίως δυσχερανοῦσιν ἃ μὴ χρεὼν καὶ ψέξουσι θάλατταν, καὶ κοῦφον ἂν νομιοῦσιν εἴ τις αὐτῆς στέρηται, δέον, ἐγκαλυπτομένους οἷς τούτῳ τῷ μέρει τῶν ἄλλων λείπονται, τοῦτο μὲν σιγῇ παρελθεῖν, ἑτέρωθεν δὲ τὸν ἔπαινον ἐρανίζεσθαι καὶ συμπληροῦν τὸ ἐγκώμιον;

43 Τίς γὰρ καὶ τούτων ἄνευ οὐκ οἶδεν ὅσοις ἀνάγκη τῶν ἐν μεσογείᾳ πλεονεκτεῖν τὰς ἐν θαλάττῃ κατῳκημένας εὐδαιμονίας τε εἵνεκα καὶ πλούτου καὶ ὠνίων ἀφθονίας καὶ τῆς ἄλλης ἐς τὸν βίον παρασκευῆς τε καὶ εὐθηνίας,

human being could gather a variety of experiences in some other way, and that knowledge and virtue could only come from practicing speechlessness and unsociability, by not meeting anyone or interacting with them, I would have seriously feared speech and I would scorn the sea and the waves. Yet no one would agree that a city can be well off and fully merit praise if it does not interact with as many people as possible.

You might say that most merchants are bad, whether they 42
arrive by sea or by land. However, there is something to be said for making the most of those who come by sea. There is certainly nothing to be disavowed about them, since learning a great deal results from experiencing a great deal, and seeing contributes to knowing. One could not attain virtue in the proper sense, nor would one be praised for it or appropriately admired for it, if one did not overcome the many obstacles in its way, and if one did not succeed in spite of making many mistakes; furthermore, I do not know if one could remove knowledge as such and learning from the best part of virtue. So where is the need for all these absences and excuses? That is, how can they rightly despise what they really should not and disparage the sea, claiming that being deprived of it is immaterial, when they should really conceal their feelings about coming up short in this regard compared to everyone else and pass over it in silence, devising something else with which to praise themselves and complete their encomium?

And anyway, despite all this, who does not know that 43
coastal cities necessarily do better than inland ones in terms of prosperity, wealth, abundance of goods, and everything else requisite for the plentiful provision of life's necessities,

προσέτι δὲ καὶ δυνάμεως καὶ τῆς κατὰ πόλεμόν τε καὶ μάχας ἀνδρείας καὶ ἐμπειρίας; Ταῖς μέν γε καὶ ἀμφοῖν ἔξεστιν ἀπολαύειν καὶ θαλαττίοις εἶναι κατ᾽ ἐξουσίαν καὶ γῆν ἀσπάζεσθαι καὶ τὰ τῆς χέρσου καλὰ καὶ στρατιὰν ἀγείρειν καὶ ἐπιταφρεύεσθαι καὶ χαράκωμα βάλλεσθαι καὶ πηγνῦναι στρατόπεδον καὶ στόλον δεῆσαν συγκροτῆσαι πάντων μάλιστα ῥᾷστα καὶ ἀπὸ τοῦ καταστρώματος διαμάχεσθαι καὶ λαίφεσι καὶ κώπαις καὶ πνεύμασι πιστεύειν εἰσπλέοντας, ἐκπλέοντας, διεκπλέοντας καὶ πάντοθεν ἰσχυροῖς εἶναι καὶ τῶν ἐχθρῶν περιγίνεσθαι.

44 Αἱ δ᾽ οὐδὲν μᾶλλον τῆς ἠπείρου μόνης καὶ τῶν ἐκεῖθεν καλῶν κορεννύμεναι θατέρῳ, τάχα δὲ δὴ τῷ πλείστῳ καὶ τῷ παντὶ τὸ ἔλαττον ἔχουσι, τῶν ἐκ θαλάττης καλῶν στερισκόμεναι, καίτοι, εἰ Πλάτων ἀμφοτεροδέξιον ἄνθρωπον ἐπαινεῖ καὶ θαυμάζει καὶ τυχόντα μὲν οὕτω τῆς φύσεως μακαρίζει, τοὺς δὲ μὴ τυχόντας προτρέπει πρὸς ἄσκησιν, ὡς τῷ παντί γε διαφέρον μιᾷ τε χειρὶ καὶ ἀμφοῖν ἔχειν κεχρῆσθαι, ἤπου τούς γε θαλάττης ὅλης εὐφυῶς ἔχοντας καὶ ἠπείρου ὅσον μιᾶς χειρὸς καὶ ἑνὸς μέλους σώματος τοσούτῳ μέρει τῆς οἰκουμένης μᾶλλον ἂν καὶ πρὸς πλείω τις χρήσαιτο, τοσοῦτον ἄρα καὶ μᾶλλον θαυμάσομεν καὶ ζηλώσομεν καὶ τῷ ὄντι νομιοῦμεν εὐδαίμονας, τοῦτο δὴ τὸ ἡμέτερον; Τίς γὰρ ἡμῶν ἢ πρὸς γῆν ἢ πρὸς θάλατταν εὐφυέστερον ἔχει, τίς δὲ καὶ τῶν παρ᾽ ἀμφοῖν ἐξ ἴσης ἡμῖν ἀπολαύειν;

45 Οἵ γε τοῦ Πόντου τὸ μεσαίτατον εἰληχότες καὶ τοσούτων ἐθνῶν καὶ χωρῶν Γαλατίᾳ μὲν καὶ Παμφυλίᾳ καὶ Κιλικίᾳ καὶ τοῖς Εὐφρατίοις ἀπόνως συμμίσγομεν ἔθνεσι,

as well as in strength, manliness in war and battles, and experience? Coastal cities can enjoy having it both ways. Being by the sea, they can also embrace the earth and the advantages of dry land, lead armies, dig ditches, put up a palisade, set up camp, and fight everyone very easily, even when their fleet is not there. But they can also fight from the deck and trust in their sails, oars, and winds when they are sailing in, sailing out, and sailing across. They can be strong on every side and conquer their enemies.

But inland cities must be satisfied with nothing more 44
than the land alone and its fruits, and they are inferior to coastal cities in every way most of the time, because they are deprived of the benefits of the sea. Furthermore, if Plato praises, admires, and blesses a man so much for being naturally ambidextrous that he instructs those who do not naturally possess this ability to practice it, surely, then, since one would regard those inland, being in such a part of the world, as like those who use only one hand and have only one useful bodily limb, how much more would we wonder at and envy and deem truly fortunate those who, being by the sea, are naturally so very well situated, as is our own city? For who is more advantageously situated by land and sea than us? Who enjoys both of them as well as we do?

By occupying the very middle of the Pontos region as 45
well as the midpoint among so many peoples and lands, we interact effortlessly with the peoples of Galatia, Pamphylia, Cilicia, and the Euphrates. Sailing and mostly traveling by

πλέοντές τε καὶ τὰ πλεῖστα πεζεύοντες κἀκεῖθεν κατ' ἐξουσίαν πόρρω τῶν ἑῴων τε καὶ μεσημβρινῶν ἐλαύνοντες πόλεων, διαβαίνομεν δὲ ῥᾷστά τε καὶ κουφότατα πρὸς τὴν ἀντιπέρας ἤπειρον καὶ ἀμφοτέραν τὴν Σαρματῶν γῆν καὶ Κολχίδα καὶ Ἀλβανίαν καὶ Ἰβηρίαν, κἀκεῖθεν αὖθις τῶν ἀρκτῴων ἐς ὅσον ἔνι ἀπολαύομεν, οὐδὲ τῶν δυσμικῶν τῷ τοσούτῳ διαστήματι διειργόμενοι. Ταῖς ναυσὶ γὰρ τὸ τοσοῦτον μῆκος συστέλλεται, καὶ ῥᾷον καὶ τούτοις συμβάλλομεν, αὐτοί τε παρὰ τούτους ἰόντες καὶ τοὺς ἐκεῖθεν ὑποδεχόμενοι, ὥσθ', ὥσπερ τινὸς ἐργαστηρίου κοινοῦ ἢ ἐμπορίου τῆς οἰκουμένης ἁπάσης ἡμῖν οὔσης τῆς πόλεως, τούς τε ἁπανταχοῦ τῆς γῆς ἐνταῦθα ἂν ἴδοις πολιτευομένους τὸ πλεῖστον τοῦ χρόνου καὶ οὐ πολλὰ ἂν κάμοις τὰ γνωριμώτερα τῶν γενῶν καὶ γλωσσῶν ἐξετάζων.

46 Ἀρκεῖ γὰρ ἐς τὴν τῇδε ἀγορὰν κατιόντα τῶν ἀγοραζόντων πυθέσθαι καὶ αὐτῶν τούτων περὶ ὧν ἂν δέοι μαθεῖν καὶ τῶν ἑκασταχοῦ γινομένων καὶ ὧν ἑκάστη φέρει καλῶν, οὐκ οἶδ' εἴ που καλλίω ἢ πλείω ἔστιν εὑρεῖν. Μηδική τε γὰρ ἐσθὴς καὶ Αἰγύπτιος καὶ τὰ Σηρῶν νήματα καὶ κανᾶ τῶν Σινῶν καὶ τὰ Κιλίκων ὑφάσματα οὐκ ἐλάττω παρ' ἡμῖν ἢ παρ' οὓς φύονται, καὶ ὅσα ἡ περὶ τὸν Φάσιν καὶ Τάναϊν φέρει καὶ τὴν ἐνταῦθα γῆν ἅπασαν πάντα ἂν εὕροις ἐνταῦθα καὶ ὅσα τῆς ἄλλης γῆς οὐδαμοῦ, ὥστε κἀν τούτοις ἑκάστην τε ἀνὰ μέρος νικᾶν καὶ πάσας ὁμοῦ, τὸ μὲν οἷς τὰ πασῶν ἔχει κεκτημένα πλουσίως, ἑκάστης τοῖς οἰκείοις πλεονεκτούσας, τὸ δ' οἷς καὶ τὰ παρ' ἑαυτῆς

foot from those places, we pass at will through the more distant cities of the east and south. We travel very easily and in a leisurely fashion to the lands across from ours and in both directions, such as those of the Sarmatians, Kolchians, Albanians, and Iberians. From there, too, we have at our disposal the cities of the north, as far as we can go, nor are we separated from the cities of the west by too great a distance. Because the great distance to them is shortened by the use of our ships, we easily come into contact with them; we go to them and, in turn, we welcome here people from there. Thus, as if our city were a common emporium or marketplace for the whole world, you might see people from all over the world living here for most of the year, and it would not be hard for you to examine the more important races and languages.

Just going to the market here and asking the buyers there 46
themselves is enough to find out what you need to know, both about what is happening all over the world, and what goods each country produces. I do not know if there is anywhere else that you could find higher quality or more numerous goods. More Median fabric, more Egyptian cloth, more Serian silk threads, more Sinese baskets, and more Cilician fabrics are produced in our city than where they originate, and you would find here the products of the lands around the Phasis and Tanaïs rivers and every land, as well as things that you would not find anywhere else on earth. Our city consequently triumphs over each of them separately and all of them combined, partly because it is so richly endowed with what it has acquired from all these cities, whereas they each have the advantage only when it comes to their own distinctive products, and partly because it adds in

προστίθησι δαψιλῶς, καὶ τὰ ἑτέρωθεν ἐπεισάγουσα καὶ παρ' ἑαυτῆς πλεῖστα φύουσα.

47 Ἑκάστης γοῦν τῆς ἡμέρας ὥσπερ ἐν ἑορτῇ τε καὶ πανηγύρει τοὺς μὲν ἴδοις ἂν ἐσιόντας, τοὺς δ' ἐξιόντας, καὶ οἱ μὲν προσίασιν, οἱ δὲ ἀπίασιν, οἱ μὲν ἐκ θαλάττης, οἱ δ' ἐξ ἠπείρου, πλέοντες καὶ πεζεύοντες, ὥστε τὴν μὲν τῇδε θάλατταν ὁλκάσιν ἀναγομέναις τε καὶ καταγομέναις ἀεὶ κατακρύπτεσθαι καὶ σχεδὸν ναῦν μόνον ὁρᾶσθαι καὶ λαίφη κυρτούμενά τε καὶ κοιλαινόμενα, τὴν δ' ἤπειρον πλήθειν ἀνθρώπων καὶ φορτηγῶν ζῴων, ἐμπόρων ἄλλοθεν ἄλλων προσιόντων καὶ ἀπιόντων καὶ παντοδαπὰ φερόντων τε καὶ λαμβανόντων ὤνια πάντων, τῶν μὲν πρὸς χρείαν καὶ τὴν ἀναγκαίαν ἀνθρώποις ζωήν, τῶν δὲ καὶ πρὸς τρυφὴν καὶ διαγωγὴν καὶ ῥᾳστώνην καὶ ὅσα πόλεων εὐτυχίαν καὶ περιουσίαν εὐδαιμονίας κατηγορεῖ.

48 Ἀλλ' οὕτω μὲν τῆς κατὰ γῆν τε καὶ θάλατταν εἴληχε θέσεως, καὶ οὕτως ἐν καλῷ καὶ τούτων ἀμφοῖν κεῖται καὶ δεξιῶς ἔχει πρὸς ἀμφοτέρας. Τῆς γε μὴν τῶν ὡρῶν ἁρμονίας καὶ κράσεως εἵνεκα καὶ ὡς ἐνταῦθα τῷ ὄντι κυρίως καὶ ἀληθῶς ἔξεστιν αὐτὰς διαιρεῖν ἑκάστῃ τε τούτων ἕκαστον μέρος ἀπονέμειν οἰκείως τοῦ χρόνου, τούτων μὲν οὖν οὐδεὶς ἐρίσας ἡμῖν ἀμφισβητήσιμον γοῦν ἑαυτῷ καταστήσει τὴν ἧτταν, οὐδ' ἔστιν ἥτις τῶν πόλεων τὰ ἐντεῦθεν βραβεῖα ἀποίσεται, μᾶλλον δ' οὐκ ἔστιν ἥτις οὐ παραχωρήσει τῇ ἡμετέρᾳ καὶ τοῖς δευτερείοις ἀγαπήσει καὶ στέρξει νικωμένη τῆς Τραπεζοῦντος, ὥσπερ ἄλλη νικήσασα.

49 Μόνη γὰρ ἡ παρ' ἡμῖν κατὰ φύσιν τε καὶ λόγον καὶ τὸ εἰκὸς ἢ κομιδῇ σὺν ὀλίγαις ἡμέρων ἔτυχε τῶν ὡρῶν καὶ

abundance its own products to the mix, importing things from elsewhere and producing a great deal on its own.

Every day you can see people coming and going from the market as if there were a festival or a celebration going on. Some people enter, others leave, some by sea and some by land, traveling by boat and on foot. The sea here is consequently always covered with merchant vessels docking and launching, so that it almost seems as if you are seeing just a single ship with its sails bulging out and billowing. Likewise, the land teems with people and beasts of burden, as other merchants from different places come and go, all of them bringing all sorts of goods with them and taking others away, some of which are purely functional and necessary for human life, while others are for luxury, comfort, ease, and whatever else indicates the good fortune and plentiful prosperity of cities. 47

Such is the position on land and sea that our city has obtained, situated as it is in a good location in both respects and able to benefit from both. When it comes to the harmony and mixture of seasons, however, and how here it is possible to divide them from one another properly and truly and assign to each of them a portion of the year, surely no one will contend with us on this point and thereby assure his own defeat. For there is no other city that would take the prize in this respect; or rather, there is no city that would not concede defeat to ours, willingly taking second place and being happy to have lost to Trebizond, just as it would if any other city had won. 48

For our city alone, in accordance with nature, logic, and reason, has seasons that, with the exception of a few days, 49

συμμέτρου τῆς ἐνεργείας ἑκάστων καὶ ὄντως ὡραίων καὶ αὐτὸ τοῦτο ὃ κέκληνται. Καὶ μαρτυρήσουσιν ἄνδρες ἀστρονόμοι καὶ οἱ παιδεύοντες τὰ μετέωρα καὶ οὐράνια, ὀγδοήκοντα μὲν μοιρῶν τὸ σύμπαν τῆς καθ' ἡμᾶς οἰκουμένης πλάτος καὶ ἀπὸ τῆς διακεκαυμένης μέχρι τῆς κατεψυγμένης ζώνης τιθέμενοι, ὑπὸ δὲ τεσσαρακοστὸν τρίτον παράλληλον τὴν Τραπεζοῦντα κεῖσθαι διδάσκοντες καὶ τὸ μέσον τοῦ καθόλου πλάτους μαρτυροῦντες ἐπέχειν.

Ὥστ' ἴσον τοῦ σφοδροῦ καύματος καὶ ψύχους ἀπέχουσα, οὔτε τοῦ χειμῶνος οὔτε τοῦ θέρους παρὰ τὴν ἐπωνυμίαν τετύχηκεν, ἢ τῷ ψύχει πλέον τοῦ δέοντος ἢ τῷ καύματι χρωμένη μᾶλλον ἢ χρῆν, ὡς ἢ χειμῶνα τὸ θέρος ἢ θέρους ὥραν εἶναι τὴν τοῦ χειμῶνος αὐτῇ, ὃ τῶν πόλεων αἱ πολλαὶ πάσχουσι καὶ ὅσαι πρὸς βορρᾶν μᾶλλον ἢ πρὸς νότον τὴν οἴκησιν ἔλαχον, ὅπου τῷ μᾶλλον καὶ ἧττον τὰς ὥρας ἔξεστι διαιρεῖν καὶ τούτοις ἀμυδρῶς τε καὶ σκιωδῶς καταχρωμένους ταῖς κλήσεσιν, οὐ κυρίας τὰς ὀνομασίας προσφέροντας. Ταῖς μὲν γὰρ ὄμβροις ἀεὶ καὶ χιόσι καὶ παγετῷ πηγνυμέναις οὐ τοῦ χειμῶνος μόνον ἀνάγκη ῥιγοῦν καὶ τρόπον δεσμίων ταῖς οἰκίαις ἐνεῖρχθαι τοὺς ἐν αὐτῇ, πεδητῶν βίον βιοῦντας, καὶ ταῖς ἀγοραῖς ἢ οὐδ' ὀλίγα συμβάλλοντας ἢ μόνον φανέντας εὐθὺς ὡς εἰς χηραμοὺς φεύγοντας τὰς οἰκίας ἐνδεδυκέναι, ἀλλὰ καὶ μέσου τοῦ θέρους ζητεῖν ὃ περιβάλωνται καὶ ὅθεν ἂν ἀλέαν πορίσωνται καὶ τὸ ψῦχος ἀμύνωνται· ταῖς δ' αὖ ἐκ τοῦ ἐναντίου θέρμῃ καὶ καύματι καὶ ταῖς ἡλιακαῖς φλεγομέναις ἀκτῖσι

match the proper character of each and, being truly seasonable, actually fit what they are called. Astronomers and teachers of astronomical and heavenly phenomena will attest that the entire breadth of our known world is divided into eighty parts, from the Tropical Circle to the Polar Circle, and they teach that Trebizond lies beneath the forty-third parallel and attest that it occupies the midrange of the world's breadth in a general sense.

Consequently, the city occupies a position equally distant 50
from the extremes of heat and cold, and so has both a winter and a summer that do not exceed what these seasons' names imply. It is neither colder than it ought to be, nor warmer, unlike those many cities to the south or north where the summer is like the winter or the winter like the summer. In those places, it is only vaguely possible to distinguish the seasons, and people can only apply these terms in an imperfect and obscure way without making the proper distinctions in nomenclature. In northern cities people are compelled to shiver in the winter because they are always being frozen by rain storms, snow, and ice; the people who live there are confined to their homes like people in fetters, living their lives like prisoners; they either congregate in the markets a great deal of the time or show up only to immediately return to their homes and dive into them like holes. Even during the summer they have to decide what to wear and how to get warm and avoid the cold. In southern cities, on the contrary, people are constantly afflicted by the scorching heat and the sun's burning rays; even the winters

θέρος εἶναι καὶ τὸν χειμῶνα καὶ μέσου Ποσειδεῶνος τηκομένους τοὺς ἐνοικοῦντας καὶ ζητοῦντας ὅθεν ἂν ἀναψύξωσιν.

51 Ὥστε τοὺς ὁποτέραν αὐτῶν ἑκάστοτε ἐγκωμιάζοντας τὰ πλείω χαριζομένους ἢ ἀληθεύοντας ἐν τοῖς περὶ τούτων λόγοις ἔστιν εὑρεῖν οὐ σκοποῦντας ὅ τι ἂν ἀληθεύσαιεν, ἀλλ' ὅ τι χαρίσαιντο κἂν μὴ τύχοι τἀκριβὲς οὕτως ἔχον, μόνοις δ' ἡμῖν καὶ ὅσοι τὸν ὑπὲρ τῆς ἡμετέρας λόγον ποιοῦνται ταύτην οὐκ ἔστιν ἐπενεγκεῖν τὴν αἰτίαν, οὐδὲ γράψαιτ' ἄν τις ἡμᾶς ψεύδους οὐδὲ τούτῳ τῷ μέρει. Χορείαν γὰρ ὑπὲρ ἡμᾶς αἱ ὧραι περιελίττουσιν ἐναρμόνιον, ἑκάστης τῇ γείτονι μεταδιδούσης καὶ μεταλαμβανούσης τῶν παρ' ἀλλήλων, ὡς τόν τε χειμῶνα μετέχειν ἀλέας καὶ τὴν θέρειον ὥραν συμμέτρως ψυχραίνεσθαι, κιρναμένων ἀλλήλοις τοῦ ψύχους τε καὶ τοῦ καύματος παρ' ἑκατέρας τὰς ὥρας καὶ τὴν καλλίστην οὕτως ἁρμονίαν ἀποτελούντων, ὡς αὐτάς τε ταύτας καὶ τὰς μεταξὺ τούτων ὥρας τά τε οἰκεῖα τηρεῖν ἀσυγχύτως καὶ τὰ παρ' ἀλλήλων φιλοφρόνως εἰσδέχεσθαι, οὔτε πλεονεκτούσας ἀλλήλαις, οὔτε τοῦτο πασχούσας, ἐπίσης τε τὴν παντελῆ ἀμιξίαν ἀλλήλων καὶ τὴν παντάπασιν ἕνωσίν τε καὶ μίξιν ἀποστρεφομένας καὶ σύγχυσιν, ἐξ ὧν ὑγιεινοῖς μὲν εἶναι καὶ καλῶς κεκραμένοις τὰ σώματα περιγίνεται, αὐτῇ δὲ τῇ γῇ πρός τε καρπῶν ἀφθόνους εὖ μάλα παρεσκευάσθαι γονὰς καὶ πρὸς τὰς τῶν ὡραίων προβολὰς εὖ ἔχειν, *νικώντων κἀνταῦθα μάλιστα καὶ παρὰ τὴν ἐπωνυμίαν* εἴπερ που τῆς γῆς. Ἀκρόδρυα γὰρ πάντα καὶ βάλανος ἅπας καὶ ὀπωρῶν ποικιλία, καὶ κάλλει καὶ πλήθει διαφερουσῶν, οὔτε πλείω

are summers. Even at the beginning of January, those who live there are melting and seeking ways to cool off.

Consequently, people who praise either of these sorts of 51
cities often embellish most of their attributes in their speeches rather than telling the truth, so that it is quite obvious that they are not trying to tell the truth but rather whatever may find favor, regardless of how accurate it may be. Against us alone, however, and whoever writes about our city, it is impossible to bring this charge, nor could anyone accuse us of lying in this regard. For the seasons wind around us in a harmonious dance. Each season has something in common with the next and shares in the characteristics of the other one, so that it is somewhat warm in winter and somewhat cool in summer, with attributes of the cold and heat mixed with each other in each season, creating such an utterly beautiful harmony that these particular seasons and those between them, that is, spring and autumn, both keep their own distinct characteristics and hospitably welcome in the characteristics of the others without overwhelming one another or being themselves overwhelmed. Furthermore, they avoid both complete separation from one another and, at the same time, complete union, mingling, and confusion. As a result, our bodies are healthy and well balanced, while the land is well prepared for the bountiful seeding of crops and ready for seasonal growth which here especially, if anywhere on earth, *transcends what is normal according to the name of the season.* This is because all the hard fruits, every nut, and a wide variety of soft fruits, those which stand out in their loveliness and abundance, grow neither in

οὔτε καλλίω παρ' ἄλλοις· λέγω δὲ οὐχ ὡς εἰπεῖν πλεῖστα, οὐδ' εἵνεκα λόγου, ἀλλ' ὄντως πλεῖστα καὶ ἀριθμὸν ὑπερβάλλοντα.

52 Οὕτω κατάκαρπος ἡμῖν ἡ χώρα καὶ πλήρης ἀρίστου παντός, καὶ οὐδ' ἔστιν εὑρεῖν αὐτῆς ὃ μὴ ἕν τι τῶν πάντων προάγει, μηδὲ χορηγεῖ τὴν ἀναγκαίαν συντέλειαν. Οὔτε γὰρ διὰ πάσης ἑαυτῆς ἀνέστηκεν, ἀποκορυφουμένη καὶ ὑψουμένη πρὸς ὄρη, οὔτ' αὖ ὅλη δι' ὅλης ἐξήπλωται εἰς πεδιάδας, ὡς τοῖσδε μὲν ἐξαρκεῖν, ἔστι δ' ὧν καὶ ἀπᾴδειν, μιᾶς φύσεως γῆς οὐκ ἐχούσης ἐπιτηδείως διακεῖσθαι πρὸς πάντα, ἀλλ' ὁμοίως εἰς ὄρη μεριζομένης καὶ πεδιάδας, τὰ πλεῖστα μὲν τὰ αὐτὰ γεννῶσί τε καὶ προφέρουσι καὶ τοῖς αὐτοῖς ἡμᾶς δεξιοῦνται, ὅσα δὲ ἡ ἑτέρα φέρειν οὐκ ἔχει, ταῦτα θάτερον ἐπιδαψιλεύεται μέρος, παρέχον πλουσίως ὧν ἄλλοθεν ἀπολαύειν οὐκ ἔνι. Τὰ μὲν γὰρ τὸν πάντων καρπῶν ἡμερώτατον φύει, καὶ τοῦτον τῶν ἁπανταχοῦ κάλλιστον. Οὕτως ἐριβῶλαξ ἡμῖν ἡ γῆ καὶ πίειρα, ὥστε, πολλοῦ πάντοθεν ἐπεισαγομένου σίτου διαποντίου τε καὶ χερσαίου, ἅτε πληθούσης τε ἀνθρώπων τῆς ἡμετέρας καὶ πολλῆς ἐπεισάκτου δεομένης τροφῆς, οὐδεὶς τῶν ἁπανταχοῦ τῷ παρ' ἡμῖν οὐδ' ἐγγὺς ἂν ἥκοι ποτέ.

53 Τὰ δ' ἄλσεσιν ἀνεῖται καὶ δένδρεσι, τοῖς μὲν καρποφόροις, τοῖς δ' ἄλλην οὐκ ἐλάττω συντέλειαν χορηγοῦσιν ἡμῖν οἷς ὑλοτομεῖν τε καὶ δρυτομεῖν τοῖς ἐνταῦθα παρέχουσιν, ἐξ ὧν νεώς τε ἱδρύομεν καὶ συσκευάζομεν οἴκους, ἐς δύο καὶ τρεῖς ὀρόφους ἀνάγοντες καὶ κάλλους οὐδὲν ἀπολείποντες, καὶ πήγνυμεν ναῦς μακράς τε καὶ φορτηγούς, ἔς τε πόλεμον καὶ εἰρήνην ὁμοίως τὰ μέγιστά τε καὶ

better quality nor quantity anywhere else. I say this not to amplify my material or for the sake of my oration, but because there really are a great many of them, indeed more than can be counted.

Thus our land is fruitful and full of all the best things; it is 52
impossible to find an area in which it does not surpass everywhere else or abundantly furnish us with a necessary provision of resources. Our land is neither elevated throughout, rising up and reaching its zenith in mountains, nor is it entirely spread out into plains, so that while it would be good for some things, there would be others for which it would be unsuited. Instead, our land does not have a single nature that is uniformly suitable for all things, but is proportionately divided between mountains and plains. The majority of it grows and produces the same things, paying homage to us with them. But what one part cannot grow, another region produces lavishly, providing abundantly what the other cannot. Some areas grow the most cultivated crops of all and these are the best you can find anywhere. Thus, our land is so fertile and rich that even though we import grain from far and wide by land and sea to our city, seeing as it is full of people and needs to bring in a large supply of food, no one anywhere else could ever rival our native crop.

Other areas are devoted to groves and trees. Some of 53
them are fruit-bearing, while others provide us with a no less important contribution, namely wood for local people to cut down and fell. With it, we erect churches and construct houses which are two or three stories high, and are not lacking in beauty. We also build long ships and cargo boats that perform the most important and necessary service during times of war and peace alike. While it is thus

ἀναγκαιότατα συντελούσας, ὥστε καὶ δι᾽ ὁμαλῆς ἔξεστι τῆς ὁδοῦ καὶ ψιλῆς διϊέναι, *τὸν προκείμενον δρόμον ἀνύοντας*, καὶ ὑπὸ σκιαῖς καὶ δένδροις ἀνάπαυλαν ἴσχειν καὶ καταψύχεσθαι, τὴν ἐκ τοῦ καύματος θεραπεύοντας φλόγα τοῖς τ᾽ ἀνέχουσι τῶν ὀρῶν καὶ τοῖς παρ᾽ αὐτῶν πνεύμασι τὴν ἐκ τῶν πεδίων ἀποκρουομένους ἀλέαν καὶ ἀποψύχοντας τὸν ἐντεῦθεν ἱδρῶτα.

54 Οὐ γὰρ δὴ τὸ μὲν τῆς χώρας πεδιὰς μόνον καὶ ὅλον ὕπτιον, τὸ δ᾽ ἀνέστηκεν εἰς ὄρη τε καὶ βουνούς, ὡς ἑκάτερον ἑκατέρου κεχωρίσθαι παντάπασιν, ἀλλ᾽ ἔστι μὲν εὑρεῖν ἐνταῦθα καὶ τοῦτο, ἔστι δὲ καὶ πεδία μετὰ γηλόφων ἰδεῖν καὶ βουνῶν οὐ μάλα τοι μετεώρων ἐντυχεῖν τε καὶ ὄρεσι λιβάδας ἐφ᾽ ἑαυτῶν καὶ πεδία προτεινομένοις οὐ μάλα στενά, οὐδὲ σμικροῖς ὅροις περιγραφόμενα, ὡς πανταχοῦ τὸ ἴσον τηρεῖσθαι καὶ μέτριον ἀμφοῖν ὁμοίως, ἀνὰ μέρος τὴν ἡμετέραν κοσμούντων, ὡς μήτ᾽ ἔνθα χρῆν ἐκτετάσθαι τὸν χῶρον εἰς πεδιάδας ἀποκεκορυφῶσθαι πρὸς ὄρη, μηθ᾽ ὅπου τῶν ὀρῶν ἔδει τὰ πεδία παρεμπεσεῖν, ἀλλὰ τὸν προσήκοντα τηρεῖν ἑκάτερα τόπον καὶ ὃς ἑαυτοῖς τε καὶ τοῖς ἐνταῦθα κατῳκημένοις ἔμελλε συνοίσειν.

55 Πεδία γὰρ ἐκδέχονται ὄρη καὶ βουνοὺς τὰ πεδία, καὶ συμφυὲς ἓν οἷον διὰ παντὸς ἑαυτοῦ καὶ πεδίοις τισὶ σύμμικτον ὄρος ἀποκαθίσταται μέχρις ἂν εἰς τὸν Ἀντίταυρον ἥκοι, τὸν ὀρῶν ἄριστον ἡμῖν τε σωτήριον, ὅς, ἀπὸ τοῦ Ταύρου ὄρους μέχρις Εὐφράτου καὶ τῶν Καυκασίων διήκων ὀρέων, μεγέθει τε μέγιστος καὶ μήκει μήκιστος πεφυκώς, τὴν ἡμετέραν τῆς Ἀρμενίας ὁρίζει γῆς καὶ Κιλίκων καὶ ἧς νῦν ἄρχουσι βάρβαροι πάσης. Ἔδει γὰρ δὴ τοὺς

possible to travel along smooth and cleared roads *on our appointed course,* we may also rest and refresh ourselves in the shade of the trees, finding relief from the burning heat of the day, or we can ward off the heat of the plains and cool off in the mountain highlands with the breezes that descend from them.

For one part of our land is not just plains and entirely flat, 54
while the other part is only elevated with mountains and hills, so that one part is completely distinct from the other. One can find that contrast here, but it is also possible to see plains with low hills in them as well as hills which rise quite high in the air, just as one can encounter mountains with valleys of their own, offering quite wide plains, so that everywhere they preserve balance and moderation on both counts. Each in turn adorns our land, so that the land does not rise up into mountains when it ought to give way to plains, nor does it fall away into plains where there ought to be mountains. Instead, since the region preserves what is suitable about each type of countryside, it will be of benefit both to those places themselves and to those who live there.

Our mountains include plains and our plains hills, merg- 55
ing together as one mountain range intermingled with plains which rises up until it reaches the Antitauros Mountains. They are the best mountains and our salvation. They run from the Tauros mountains as far as the Euphrates River and the Caucasus mountains. Since they are the biggest in size and longest in length, they separate our land from that of Armenia and the Cilicians, and all the land which the barbarians now rule. For people so foreign in speech and

τοσούτῳ φωνῆς τε καὶ γλώττης καὶ τῶν Ἑλληνικῶν ἠλλοτριωμένους ἠθῶν μὴ ποταμοῖς τισιν εὖ μάλα διαβατοῖς, κἂν Ἰνδὸς κἂν Γάγγης ὢν τύχοι, καὶ φάραγξιν ἀποτόμοις, οὐδ' αὐτοῖς ἀπεράτοις, καὶ οὐκ οἶδ' οἷς τισι λήροις ἑτέροις, ἀλλ' οὕτως ἐλλογίμοις ἡμῶν καὶ μεγίστοις ὅροις διείργεσθαι, πόρρωθεν καὶ τοῖς ἀγνοοῦσι παρεχομένοις τεκμήρασθαι ὅσον ἡμῶν τε κἀκείνων τὸ μέσον καὶ ὡς πλεῖστον ἀλλήλων διέστημεν παιδείᾳ τε καὶ τοῖς κατὰ φρόνησιν ἀγαθοῖς καὶ ἃ κοσμεῖ μόνα τὸν ἄνθρωπον.

56 Πρὸς γὰρ δὴ τῷ τοσοῦτος ἡμῶν τε κἀκείνων μεταξὺ κεῖσθαι ἔτι καὶ δεινῶς ἄβατον ἢ μάλιστα δύσβατον ἑαυτὸν παρεχόμενος ἀποτόμους τε καὶ κρημνώδεις ἔχει καὶ μάλα στενοὺς τὰς εἰσόδους τε καὶ διόδους καὶ οὐ πάνυ τοι περασίμους, καὶ ταύτας οὐ δύο καὶ τρεῖς οὐδὲ τέτταρας, οὐδ' ἑκάστην ὀλιγομήκη καὶ βραχὺ τὸ φαραγγῶδες καὶ ἀπότομον ἔχουσαν, ἀλλ' ἐς μὲν ὅσον ἐνῆν πλεῖστον ῥωγάσι τε καὶ κρημνοῖς καὶ στενοπόροις μηκυνομένην ὁδοῖς, ἐς ἀριθμὸν δὲ τὰς πάσας ἀποπερατουμένας ἱκανὸν καὶ ὑπὲρ ὃν οὐκ ἐχρῆν ἐκτετάσθαι. Οὐ γὰρ κατὰ τὰς ἐν Ἑλλάδι Πύλας ἡμῖν ὁ Ἀντίταυρος τὰς εἰσόδους παρέχεται, ἑνί τινι τόπῳ μόνον ὠχυρωμένας καὶ τούτῳ δὲ ἐλλιπῶς· δι' ἑτέρας γάρ ἐστιν ἀκινδύνως ἄνωθεν εἰσιέναι, καὶ μὲν δὴ καὶ εἰσίασι Πέρσαι καὶ ὁ μετὰ Ξέρξου στρατός, καὶ Λεωνίδην καὶ τοὺς τριακοσίους μετὰ τῶν σὺν αὐτοῖς συνεπάτησαν, *οὐδὲν πλέον τοῦ καλῶς ἀποθανεῖν ἐπιδείξασθαι δυνηθέντας.*

57 Οὐδὲ Θυρέαν μιμεῖται τὴν διαιρέτιν γῆς τῆς Λακωνικῆς καὶ τῆς Ἀργολικῆς μοίρας, ἣν διαβῆναι κοῦφον καὶ σμικροῦ πόνου καὶ μερίμνης ὀλίγης. Οὐδὲν δὲ πρὸς ταύτας

language from Greek customs had to be cut off from us not by some easily-crossed rivers, even if those happen to be the Indus and Ganges, or steep ravines, which are not insurmountable, or who knows what other trifling barriers, but precisely by these famous and huge mountains of ours. For a long time, these mountains have provided testimony even to people ignorant of just how much distance lies between us and them, and how different we are from each other in terms of education, intellect, and whatever else adorns human beings alone.

Besides the great size of the mountains that lie between 56
us and them, the mountains are terribly inaccessible or, better, difficult to cross. They have steep, precipitous, and extremely narrow entrances and passes that are not easily traversable at all. They do not have two, three, or four of these, nor is each of them short in length with only a small section that resembles a ravine and is precipitous. Instead, as much as possible for its whole length there are clefts, cliffs, and narrow tracks, which are sufficient in total and no more than there should be. The Antitauros Mountains do not provide us with points of access like the Gates into Greece, which are only fortified in one place and inadequately at that, since there one can enter higher up by other routes without any danger. The Persians and Xerxes's army thus entered that way and trounced Leonidas, the Three Hundred, and the men with them, *who could then do nothing but show how to die nobly.*

Nor are the Antitauros Mountains like Thyrea, the re- 57
gion dividing Lakonia from the Argolid, which is easy to cross, with little effort and few concerns. Nor does crossing

ἥ τε δι᾽ Ἄλπεων ἐξ Ἰταλίας ἐς τὴν Κελτῶν γῆν διάβασις καὶ Κιλίκιοι Πύλαι, ἔς τε Συρίαν ἀπάγουσαι καὶ τὴν Αἴγυπτον, νικᾶσθαι δὲ τὰς ἁπανταχοῦ πάσας τῶν παρ᾽ ἡμῖν πλήθει τε καὶ δεινότητι, ὡς μέγαν ὅρον τόδε τὸ ὄρος ἑστάναι τοῖς ἑκατέρωθεν ἑαυτοῦ οἷς τε πρὸς τοσοῦτον ἐκτέταται μέγεθος καὶ οἷς οὕτω δύσβατον παρέχεται ἑαυτόν, ὥστ᾽ ἐπὶ μὲν ἀνακωχῆς καὶ εἰρήνης κατ᾽ ἐμπορίαν ἀλλήλοις συμμίσγοντας ἔξεστιν ἀσφαλῶς διϊέναι, οὐδὲν δεδιότας, ἐπὶ δὲ πολέμου καὶ μάχης, δεῆσαν ἐπελθεῖν στρατιάν, ἢ οὐδ᾽ ἂν οὐδ᾽ ὅλως εἰσέλθοι, εὐαριθμήτοις τισὶ τῶν εἰσόδων φυλαττομένων ἀνδράσιν, ἢ εἰσελθοῦσα κακῶς ἀπαλλάξει καὶ γνώσεται καθ᾽ ἑαυτῆς ὁρμηθεῖσα καὶ τὸ ξίφος ὠθήσασα. Οὕτως ἡμῖν καὶ ὅρος καὶ τεῖχος καθέστηκεν ὁ Ἀντίταυρος, καὶ τῆς ἐκεῖθεν ἡμᾶς γῆς διαιρῶν, μέσος ἕστηκεν ἡμῶν ἀκλινὴς οἷόν τις διαλλακτὴς καὶ ταμίας καὶ διανομεὺς ἑκατέρας ἀρχῆς καὶ ἡγεμονίας, οὐκ ἐῶν οὐδέτερον μέρος ἐπιβουλεύειν θατέρῳ καὶ τῆς ἀλλήλων γῆς ἐπιβαίνειν ἀκόντων.

58 Ἐπὶ δὴ τῆς τοιαύτης μὲν γῆς, τοιαύτης δὲ χώρας, οὕτω δὲ κύκλῳ διειλημμένης ὄρεσι καὶ βουνοῖς καὶ πεδίοις καὶ τῇ πασῶν ἡμερωτάτῃ καὶ φιλανθρωποτάτῃ θαλάσσῃ τὴν οἴκησιν οἱ πατέρες λαχόντες ἡμῶν, τὸ ταύτης αὖ κάλλιστόν τε καὶ ἀσφαλέστατον ἐκλεξάμενοι τείχεσι περιέλαβον. Γήλοφος γάρ τις οὐ μάλα μετέωρος ἐξανέχει τῆς γῆς, φάραγξί τισιν ἑκατέρωθεν ὠχυρωμένος βαθείαις καὶ τῆς ἄλλης διειργόμενος γῆς ὥσπερ τισὶ τάφροις καὶ πολλῷ τῷ μέσῳ τάφρων ἀμείνοσι. Διὰ δὲ τούτων καὶ ποταμοί τινες ἀέναοι πρὸς θάλατταν ἐκδιδοῦσι, χειμῶνος μὲν καὶ

the Alps from Italy to the land of the Celts compare with them, or the Cilician Gates, which lead to Syria and Egypt; all these crossings everywhere are inferior in comparison to the sheer magnitude and formidable nature of ours. This mountain range rises up like a great boundary marker for those who live on either side of it. It reaches such magnitude and is so hard to traverse that, although in times of truce and peace people trading with one another can safely cross it with nothing to fear, in times of war and conflict an attacking army either does not enter it at all, because a handful of men can hold the passes, or, if it does enter it, it comes off badly, recognizing that it has actually assaulted and brandished its sword against itself. In this way, the Antitauros is both a boundary and a wall for us, separating us from the land on the other side. It stands immovable in between us like a mediator, a manager, and a regulator of each state and dominion, not permitting either side to plot against the other and tread upon its land, if the other does not want it to.

This, then, was the land that our forefathers settled, and 58
such was its nature, divided off all around by mountains, hills, plains, and a sea that is smoother and more benevolent than any other. The location which they selected to wall off was the most beautiful and secure of all. A low hill rises moderately from the ground, protected on both sides by deep ravines and cut off from the rest of the land as if by trenches, but these ravines are far better than actual trenches. Through them, perennial streams flow into the

σφοδρότερον ῥέοντες ἑαυτῶν καὶ τὸ ῥεῦμα πληθύοντες, οὐδ᾽ ἔαρος δ᾽ ἀπολείποντες, οὐδὲ μέσου τοῦ θέρους αὐτοῦ, ὡς καὶ πολλὴν οὐ μόνον ἀσφάλειαν τοῖς ἐντὸς ἑαυτῶν χορηγεῖν, ἀλλὰ καὶ ψυχαγωγίαν ἱκανὴν καὶ χρείαν αὐτοῖς ἀποπληροῦν οὐκ εὐκαταφρόνητον. Ῥύμματά τε γὰρ καὶ καθάρματα πάντα δι᾽ αὐτῶν ἔνεστιν ἀπόνως καὶ κούφως ποιεῖσθαι, δι᾽ αὐτῆς ὡς εἰπεῖν τῆς ἑκάστου σχεδὸν οἰκήματος θύρας διϊόντος τοῦ ῥεύματος.

59 Ὁ δὴ γήλοφος οὗτος, ἀπὸ θαλάττης ἀρξάμενος, ἠρέμα μὲν καὶ κατὰ μικρὸν ἐπὶ τὸ ἄναντες ἄνεισι καὶ τιμᾷ τὸ μετέωρον, προϊὼν δ᾽ εἰς ὕψος ἀποκαθίσταται σύμμετρον, ἑκατέρωθεν ὥσπερ τῆς παρ᾽ ἑκάτερα φαραγγώδους μᾶλλον ἀποχωρῶν γῆς καὶ πρὸς ἑαυτὸν συσφιγγόμενος καὶ κρημνώδη μὲν τὰ παρ᾽ ἑκάτερα ἑαυτοῦ λείπων καὶ ἀποκαθιστάς, ἑαυτὸν δ᾽ ὥσπερ στρογγύλλων εἰς μετέωρόν τινα καὶ ἐπίπεδον χῶρον καὶ ὡς ἐνῆν ἄριστόν τε πρὸς οἴκησιν καὶ πρὸς τὰς τῶν ὡρῶν κράσεις εὐαρμοστότατον. Ἐπὶ δὴ τούτου τὴν πάλαι μὲν πόλιν, νυνὶ δὲ ἀκρόπολιν ᾤκησαν δομησάμενοι, τῇ σφῶν τε ἀρετῇ μᾶλλον ἢ τῇ θέσει τοῦ τόπου πεπιστευκότες καὶ τειχῶν ἐχυρότητι, καίτοι καὶ τείχη περιεβάλλοντο καρτερά, πύργων τε εἵνεκα καὶ τῆς στεφάνης αὐτῶν καὶ ἐπάλξεων καὶ πάσης τῆς τῇδε παρασκευῆς οὐδενὸς εἶχον τὰ δεύτερα. Ἐδύναντο μὲν γὰρ ἀντ᾽ ἄλλου τινὸς ἐρύματος σφῶν αὐτῶν τὰ δόρατα προβαλέσθαι καὶ τείχεσι χρῆσθαι τοῖς ὅπλοις ὡς πάλαι ποτὲ Λάκωνες, ὡς δὲ μηδὲν αὐτοῖς πρὸς ἀσφάλειαν φέρον ἀπείη, μηδὲ τοῦτο γοῦν τὸ μέρος τῆς κατ᾽ αὐτάρκειαν

sea. During the winter, they flow much more vigorously than they do at other times, and they swell in size, but they do not dry up during the spring nor even in the middle of the summer, and thus not only provide those who live between them with much security, but also furnish them with ample pleasure and fulfill a need that is not negligible. For washing and all sorts of cleaning are painless and easy to do in these streams, since they flow past the door of practically every house.

This low hill, beginning at the sea, rises up gently and 59
gradually and reaches quite far into the air, but stops after attaining a moderate height. On the other side, however, it is separated from the land by the ravines on each side, girding itself with sharp drop-offs on each side and leaving itself separate. The hill is rounded at the top, and has a level area, which provides the best possible arrangement for habitation and is extremely well suited to the changing seasons. Upon this hill, our ancestors built and inhabited what was then the city and is now the acropolis of Trebizond, trusting in their own valor rather than in the location or strength of the city's walls, although they built strong walls around it, which were second to none on account of their towers and parapets, battlements, and all other constructions of this sort. For they could still brandish their spears instead of using a fortification for defense, using their weapons instead of walls, as the Spartans once did a long time ago, but so that nothing that contributes to security would be missing among them and they would not lack this element of

εὐδαιμονίας ἐλλίποιεν, καὶ τοῦτο καλῶς ποιοῦντες προσεπορίσαντο.

Ἐντεῦθεν Ἕλληνες ἄνθρωποι καὶ τὴν Ἑλλήνων φωνήν τε καὶ γλῶτταν προϊέμενοι καὶ τιμῶντες ἐλευθερίας τε καὶ ἰσονομίας ἀντιποιούμενοι μόνοι μέσον ᾤκουν βαρβάρων, κύκλῳ περικεχυμένων ἐς πλῆθος, καὶ τῆς Περσῶν ἀρχῆς τε καὶ δυναστείας, πολλὰ μὲν δυναμένων, πάντα δὲ καταδουλωσαμένων, πλείω δὲ περιεζωσμένων ἀρχήν τε καὶ ἐξουσίαν καὶ γῆς ὡς εἰπεῖν ἡγουμένων ἁπάσης. Ἄρτι γοῦν συνῳκισμένοι καὶ οἷα εἰκὸς τόν τε ἀριθμὸν ὄντες οὐ πάνυ πολλοὶ καὶ τὴν ἰσχὺν ἀσθενεῖς, ὅμως εὐθὺς ἐξ ἀρχῆς ἔδειξαν Ἕλληνες ὄντες, γένος ἀδέσποτον καὶ ἀδούλωτον καὶ μόνον ἐλεύθερον τήν τε ψυχὴν τά τε σώματα, Σινωπεῖς τε καὶ Μιλησίους καὶ ἔτι πρότερον Ἀθηναίους τοὺς σφῶν πατέρας μιμούμενοι, τοὺς μὲν οἵας ἴσμεν ἀποκρίσεις ἐπιόντων αὐτοῖς τῶν βαρβάρων ἀποκεκριμένους ἔργα τε διὰ πάντων ἐπιδειξαμένους τίνος οὐκ ἄξια, τοὺς δ᾽ ἐν μέσοις μὲν τοῖς βαρβάροις οἰκοῦντας, οὐδὲν δ᾽ ἐπιστρεφομένους αὐτῶν, ἀλλ᾽ ἐς ὅσον ἐξῆν ὑπὲρ ἐλευθερίας τοῖς τῆς οἰκουμένης δεσπόταις ἀνταίροντας καὶ μετέχοντας ἰσοπολιτείας αὐτοῖς, οὐδὲν οὐ τοῦ φρονήματος, οὐ τοῦ τῆς ψυχῆς ἐφεῖσαν ἐμβριθοῦς καὶ γενναίου, οὐδ᾽ ἀνάξιον οὐδὲν τῶν προγόνων καὶ τῆς Ἑλληνικῆς ἐπεδείξαντο δόξης, ἀλλ᾽ ὥσπερ οὐ γῆς μᾶλλον ἢ τῆς ἐκείνων ἐκπεμφθέντες ἀρετῆς κληρονόμοι πρὸς αὐτούς τε διεπράττοντο πᾶν ἀναφέροντες, κἀκείνους καὶ τύπον ποιούμενοι καὶ παράδειγμα, διεγίγνοντο φύσει τοῖς βαρβάροις ὄντες πολέμιοι καὶ ἀσύμβατοι καὶ μεγίστοις αὐτῶν ὅροις φωνῇ τε καὶ

self-sufficient prosperity, they rightly also provided the city with walls.

Consequently, it was Greek people, who spoke the Greek 60
language and tongue, honored freedom, and strove for equality, who lived there all on their own in the midst of the barbarians who encircled them in huge numbers. They were encircled too by the Persian empire, which had become very powerful, enslaved everything, obtained ever greater power and authority, and held sway over nearly the whole earth. When our ancestors had settled the city and, as you might expect, lacked great numbers and were not very strong, they nevertheless demonstrated immediately that they were Greeks, a race which obeys no master, is no one's slave, and is alone free in mind and body; thus they imitated their Sinopite, Milesian, and, even before that, their Athenian forefathers. We know what kind of response the latter gave when the barbarians were attacking them and the undeniably glorious deeds that they performed; and how the Milesians, though they lived in the midst of the barbarians, did not care a jot about them and stood up for their freedom against the masters of the world and remained on equal terms with them for as long as possible. Like them, our ancestors yielded nothing in terms of pride, dignity, and nobility of spirit, and did not do anything unworthy of their ancestry and reputation as Greeks; instead, as the inheritors not of their land but rather of their virtues, they did everything with reference to them, making them their model and example. They remained inherently inimical to and irreconcilable with the barbarians because of the great barriers of

ψυχῇ διϊστάμενοι καὶ κοινὸν οὐδὲν αὐτοῖς ἔχοντες. Πολέμου τε γοῦν νόμῳ κατ᾽ αὐτῶν ἐπιόντες ἰσχυρῶς ἀπεκρούοντο, λόγοις τε φιλανθρώποις παράγειν καὶ ὑποσχέσεσι τὴν αὐτῶν ὑφελέσθαι πειρωμένους ἐλευθερίαν οὐ παρεδέχοντο, ἀλλ᾽ ἐς ὅσον πλεῖστον ἐνῆν διετέλεσαν καὶ ψυχὰς καὶ τὰ σώματα τηροῦντες ἐλεύθερα.

61 Καίτοι ποσάκις εἰκὸς ἦν αὐτοὺς προσβαλεῖν καὶ μετὰ πάσης ἐπιέναι στρατείας τὰ κύκλῳ πάντα καταδουλωσαμένους ἀνθρώπους καὶ καταστησαμένους ὑποχείρια σφίσι, μόνην δὲ μίαν ταυτηνὶ πόλιν ὁρῶντας ἀφηνιάζουσαν καὶ νόμοις καὶ τρόποις καὶ ἤθεσι διαφέρουσι κεχρημένην καὶ ἀλλοτρίαν οὐ φωνὴν μόνον προϊεμένην, ἀλλὰ καὶ δεσποτείαν ἐπικεκλημένην ἑτέραν καὶ τελοῦσαν εἰς Ἕλληνας. Ὧν οὐκ εἰ μὴ πασῶν περιγεγενημένη διατετέλεκε δεινὸν ἡγεῖσθαι δεῖ καὶ ἐπίψογον, δειλίας ἢ ἀνανδρίας ποιουμένους τεκμήριον, ἀλλ᾽ ὅτι τῶν πλείστων ἐκράτησε κἀπὶ τοσοῦτον ἀντέσχε, μόνη πρὸς τοσούτους καὶ τηλικούτους ἀνταίρουσα, καὶ θαυμασόμεθα καὶ ζηλώσομεν καὶ τὴν αἰτίαν ἀνοίσομεν εἰς τὴν κατὰ ψυχὴν τῶν ἐνοικούντων ἀνδρείαν καὶ γενναιότητα καὶ τὸ τοῦ φρονήματος ἀκλινὲς καὶ ἀήττητον, ὧν οὕτως ὡς πλεῖστον αὐτοῖς περιῆν ὡς πλείσταις ἀνδρῶν γενεαῖς καὶ χρόνῳ κρείττονι μνήμης ἐν ἐλευθερίᾳ διαρκέσαι τῇ ὄντως, καὶ πάντων τῶν κύκλῳ περικεχυμένων ἐχθρῶν, πλειόνων τε καὶ ἐλαττόνων, μειόνων τε καὶ μειζόνων, καὶ τῶν ἐκεῖθεν ἐγειρομένων πολέμων οὕτως ὑπερορᾶν καὶ ἐν οὐδενὶ τίθεσθαι καὶ πολλῷ περιγενέσθαι τῷ κρείττονι, ὡς μὴ τὰ καθ᾽ αὐτοὺς μόνον, ἀλλὰ καὶ τὰ

language and spirit between them, and because they had nothing in common with them. When the barbarians marched against them in war, they were mightily repulsed. Nor did the Trapezuntines brook their attempts to win them over with kind words and underhandedly deprive them of their liberty with promises, but rather they remained free in mind and body for as long as they possibly could.

It was indeed likely on so many occasions that the bar- 61
barians, after enslaving all the surrounding people and making them their subjects, would assault and attack the people of Trebizond with their entire army, for they could not bear to see this one city alone refuse their hegemony and utilize different laws, manners, and customs, as well as not only speaking a different language, but also recognizing a different form of mastery, and numbering itself among the Greeks. For these reasons we ought not think it a bad thing and blameworthy that our city did not conquer everyone else, nor should we take this as evidence of its cowardice or a lack of manliness. Rather, we should both admire and envy the fact that it gained the upper hand for the most part and, standing alone against such powerful and numerous barbarians, resisted them for so long, and we should attribute the cause of this to the manly spirit, nobility, and unbending and invincible temperament of its inhabitants. This is why they were able to persevere in a true state of freedom for so many generations of men, an extent of time so great that it defies memory. This is also why they could overlook all their enemies encircling them, more or less numerous, smaller or greater, as well as the wars that they started, disregarding them and easily prevailing even over the mightiest. They

πρὸς ἑτέρους κατ᾽ ἐξουσίαν ὡς ἐβούλοντο διοικεῖν, τῶν ἐθνῶν καὶ γενῶν, οἷς ἂν ἑκάστοτε τὸ παραστὰν τῆς χρείας καλέσειε, συμμαχοῦντες, κἂν προσκρούειν τισὶν ἔμελλον, καὶ τούτοις αὐτοῖς τοῖς δυνατωτάτοις ἀνθρώπων οὐδὲν ἐπιστρεφόμενοι οὐδὲ πολύν τινα ποιούμενοι λόγον.

62 Τοὺς γοῦν μετὰ Κλεάρχου μυρίους Κύρῳ τῷ νέῳ κατ᾽ Ἀρτοξέρξου τοῦ τῆς Παρυσάτιδος συμμαχοῦντας καὶ τὴν Περσῶν ἀρχήν τε καὶ βασιλείαν αὐτῷ συγκατακτωμένους, ἐπείπερ αὐτῷ μὲν δυστυχὲς τὸ τοῦ πολέμου τέλος ἀπήντησεν, οὔτε τῆς ἀρχῆς ἐπιλαβομένῳ καὶ προσαπολωλεκότι τὸ ζῆν, οἵδ᾽ ἐν τῷ καθ᾽ αὑτοὺς κέρᾳ καὶ ᾗπερ ἐτάχθησαν κατορθοῦντες, ὅμως ἐπαύσαντο τὸν θάνατον Κύρου πυθόμενοι, ἀπαιτούμενοί τε σφᾶς αὐτοὺς καὶ τὰ ὅπλα φέροντας παραδοῦναι οὐδ᾽ ἄκροις ὠσὶν ὑπεδέξαντο, καίτοι μυριάσιν ἐνενήκοντα στρατοῦ κατειργόμενοι, πολλὰ δὲ τὰ μὲν ἔδρασαν, τὰ δ᾽ ἔπαθον, πόρρω μὲν τῆς Ἀσίας ἀναβεβηκότες καὶ αὖ κατιόντες ἐκεῖθεν, διὰ δὲ τῆς ἀλλοτρίας καὶ πολεμίας ἰόντες καὶ πᾶν τὸ ἀντιπῖπτον τὸ μὲν συγκόπτοντες, ἔστι δ᾽ ὑφ᾽ οὗ τοῦτο πάσχοντες. Παραμυθία δ᾽ ἦν αὐτοῖς οὐδεμία καὶ τῶν κακῶν ἀποφυγὴ καὶ μετρία πόλεών τέ τινι προσιέναι κἀνταῦθα τὸν πολὺν διαναπαύσασθαι πόνον, οὔτ᾽ αὐτοῖς εἶχεν ἀσφάλειαν, τούς τε δεξομένους οὐκ ἦν εὑρεῖν· ἐδεδίεσαν γὰρ ἅπαντες Πέρσας καὶ τὴν Περσῶν ἀρχήν, οὕτω κορυφωθεῖσαν. Ἔδει δ᾽ ὅμως διόδου καί τινος ἀναπαύλης αὐτοῖς· ἤδη γὰρ ἀπειρήκασι πολλὰ κεκμηκότες, καὶ οὐκ ἦν ἐπὶ πλέον ἀντέχειν, εἰ μή τις ἐξ ὑπογυίου τῶν περιστάντων αὐτοὺς ἀνακωχὴ κακῶν ἀπαντήσει. Τότε δὴ μόνη καὶ πρώτη τούτους ἡ ἡμετέρα

could thus manage not only their own affairs, but also those of others in whatever way they wanted. They aided peoples and nations, whenever there was pressing need and even if that meant offending others, but they neither paid any attention to these most powerful people, nor showed much concern about them.

Take, for example, the Ten Thousand and Klearchos, who 62
were allied with Cyrus the Younger against Artaxerxes, the son of Parysatis, and sought to take possession of the Persian empire and throne for him. Although the war ended badly for Cyrus after he failed to take control of the empire, and he lost his life as well in the bargain, yet I know the Ten Thousand continued to prevail on the wing to which they had been assigned, though they stopped when they heard of Cyrus's death. When they were asked to surrender and lay down their arms, they would not listen even though an army of nine hundred thousand was blocking them. They accomplished much and suffered much on their long march inland into Asia and then again on their march back to the coast, passing through strange and hostile lands and removing any obstacle in their path, though they did sometimes experience setbacks. There was no comfort for them, no refuge from their troubles, and no neutral city for them to reach, in which they might rest after their great labors. They were not safe and could find no one who would receive them, since everyone feared the Persians and the Persian empire, which was then at its peak. They needed a way out and somewhere to rest, as they were already giving up in exhaustion and could no longer resist unless they soon found some relief from their troubles. Then our city, alone and [illegible] of all,

λαμπρῶς ὑποδέχεται καὶ φιλοφρόνως διαναπαύει καὶ παραμυθεῖται καὶ ἀναψύχει, μεταδοῦσα καὶ ἀγορᾶς καὶ ὠνίων καὶ δεξαμένη συνοίκους καὶ τραπέζης αὐτοῖς κοινωνήσασα καὶ ἁλῶν καὶ πάντων ὧν εἶχε καλῶν, οὐ τὰς ἀπειλάς, οὐ τὸν ἐπηρτημένον κίνδυνον ὑπολογισαμένη, οὐδ᾽ ὡς ἀνάγκη τούτοις προσκρούειν, οὓς οὐκ ἀνήρ, οὐ πόλις, οὐ γένος οὐδὲν ὑφίσταται, ὑποχωρεῖ δὲ πάντα καὶ συναπάγεται ῥᾷον ἢ ψηφῖδες κατὰ κυμάτων φερόμεναι καὶ χειμάρρου ῥευμάτων.

63 Ἥ τε γὰρ γενναιότης καὶ τὸ ἐν πολέμοις ἀήττητον, ἥ τε φιλανθρωπία καὶ ἡμερότης, καὶ τὸ μὴ πρὸς αὐτῶν εἶναι παριδεῖν τε καὶ ἀπώσασθαι ἱκέτας ἀνθρώπους ταὐτοῦ γένους καὶ τῆς αὐτῆς φωνῆς τε καὶ γλώττης, ἐλευθερίας ἀθλητὰς καὶ γενναίους προβόλους, ταῦτ᾽ οὖν παρ᾽ οὐδὲν ἔπειθον τὴν βαρβαρικὴν ὠμότητα τίθεσθαι καὶ διαπτύειν τὰς ἀπειλὰς καὶ δεδιττομένων καταγελᾶν, εἴτε γοῦν ἥττους αὐτοὺς τῶν βαρβάρων ᾔδεσαν ὄντας καὶ διὰ τοῦτο πεισομένους ἂν ὑπ᾽ αὐτῶν ὅσα τοὺς ὡς κέντρα λακτίζοντας ἔδει, ὅμως ἀνθείλοντο τῆς τῶν ἱκετῶν σωτηρίας τὴν ἰδίαν οἱ πολῖται ζημίαν καὶ τῆς ἱκεσίου θεοῦ θεραπείας οὐδὲν ἔθεντο πρότερον, μέγιστον ἂν εἶεν ἐξενηνοχότες καὶ σαφέστατον δεῖγμα φιλανθρωπίας τε καὶ μεγαλοψυχίας καὶ τελεώτατον ὅρον ἀγάπης, σφᾶς αὐτοὺς ὑπὲρ τοῦ σῶσαι τοὺς φίλους προέμενοι καὶ θάνατον εὐκλεᾶ ζωῆς ἀκλεοῦς ἀνθελόμενοι.

64 Εἴτ᾽ ἀξιόμαχον ἰσχὺν περιβεβλημένοι καὶ κράτος ἐν μάχαις ἐπίστευον ἑαυτοῖς καὶ τῇ οἰκείᾳ ἀνδρείᾳ ὡς κούφως πᾶν οἴσοντες, καὶ μετὰ πολλῆς τῆς ῥᾳστώνης τὸν ἐπιόντα

lavishly welcomed them, and offered them hospitality, comforting and refreshing them. It opened up its market goods for sale to them, took them into its homes, and shared its table and its salt with them along with any other good things it had. It did not care about the threats or impending danger, even if that meant offending people whom no man, no city, and no people had resisted; for everyone else had simply yielded before the Persians and had been carried away more easily than pebbles tossed about by waves or a winter flood.

Their nobility and invincibility in war, their kindness and gentleness, and their refusal to overlook those who were related to them or to expel suppliants of the same race, language, and tongue, people who were champions and noble defenders of liberty—all this persuaded the citizens of Trebizond to disregard the savagery of the barbarians, spit upon their threats, and laugh at their attempts to frighten them. One possibility was that they knew they were weaker than the barbarians and consequently would suffer at their hands what people who kick against the pricks must suffer, but the citizens nevertheless chose their suppliants' safety over the harm that might come to them themselves and valued nothing more highly than serving the god of supplication; they thereby demonstrated a great and very clear example of humanity and magnanimity, indeed the ultimate mark of love, by betraying themselves to save their friends and choosing a glorious death over an inglorious life. 63

The other possibility is that they knew that their forces were strong enough to fight the barbarians in battle and they trusted that their own strength and manliness in battle would easily prevail over any opponent and that they would 64

ἀγωνισόμενοι πόλεμον, πῶς οὐ διὰ παντὸς ἂν ἥκοιεν θαύματος καὶ εἰς ἔσχατον εἶεν ἀναδραμόντες ἀνδρείας καὶ γενναιότητος, οὕτως ὀλίγοι πρὸς τοσούτους καὶ τηλικούτους ἀνταίροντες καὶ δεινὸν ἐντεῦθεν οὐδὲν οὐχ ὅσον οὐ προσδοκῶντες, ἀλλ' οὐδὲ πάσχοντες, τοῦ καιροῦ παραστάντος; Ἄσμενοι οὖν διὰ ταῦτα τοὺς πρόσφυγας ὑποδεδεγμένοι καὶ μεταδόντες ὅσων εἰκός, τῆς τε πρὸς τὸ παρὸν ἀσφαλείας αὐτῶν προὐνοήσαντο, εἴσω τειχῶν αὐτοὺς ποιησάμενοι, καὶ τῆς μετέπειτα σωτηρίας ἐφρόντισαν, καὶ ὅπως ἂν ἀσφαλέστατα διὰ φιλίων καὶ Ἑλληνίδων βαδίζοιεν πόλεων, μηκέτι δεδιότες βαρβάρους καὶ τὸν ἐκεῖθεν ὑποπτεύοντες κίνδυνον, διεπράξαντο.

Ὁ γοῦν αὐτοῖς καὶ Κλεάρχῳ ἄνω τε συναναβὰς τῆς Ἀσίας καὶ πάλιν συνεπανιὼν κατιοῦσι Ξενοφῶν Ἀθηναῖος, ἀνὴρ οὐ σοφίαν μόνον καὶ λόγον εὐδόκιμος, ἀλλ' οὐδὲν ἧττον τὴν πολιτικὴν ἄριστος ἐπιστήμην καὶ τὰ πολεμικὰ κράτιστος, στρατηγῶν μὲν αὐτῶν ἐν τῷ μέρει, τοῦ Κλεάρχου θανόντος, τὰ πλείω δ' ὅμως ὧν κατειργάσαντο ἔχων εἰς ἑαυτὸν ἀναφέρειν καὶ τὰς οἰκείας βουλάς, οἷόν τις *ἄρχων ἀρχόντων ὑπάρχων* καὶ στρατηγὸς τῶν ἀγόντων, οὗτος τοίνυν, τὰ καθ' αὑτούς τε καὶ Κῦρον συγγράφων καὶ τὴν στρατείαν ἐκείνην, τῇ ἡμετέρᾳ τὰ κάλλιστα μαρτυρεῖ, θαλάσσιόν τε καὶ Ἑλληνίδα καὶ μόνην σφίσιν ἀναφανεῖσαν φίλιον ὀνομάζων, ὡσανεὶ βοῶν καὶ διαμαρτυρόμενος ὡς ἐν οἰκουμένῃ τοσαύτῃ καὶ τοσούτῳ γῆς μέρει ἣν διῆλθον καὶ δι' ἧς διϊόντες πολλὰ τὰ μὲν ἔπαθον, τὰ δ' ἔδρασαν, μόνην ἐλευθέραν καὶ κυρίαν ἑαυτῆς

fight the impending war with great ease. And in that case how would they not earn all possible admiration and swiftly rise to the pinnacle of bravery and nobility? For they, although few, would resist such powerful and numerous enemies and, because they would encounter no unexpected misfortune, they would not suffer, when the time came? For these reasons, they gladly welcomed in the refugees and gave them what they needed, both guaranteeing their temporary security by bringing them inside the walls and also providing for their future safety by arranging for them to pass in the most secure way through friendly and Greek cities on their way home, without having to fear the barbarians any longer or be wary of danger from them.

Travelling alongside with them and Klearchos on their 65
march into inland Asia and again on the return journey was Xenophon the Athenian. He was a man reputed not only for his wisdom and skill with words, but no less for his knowledge of politics and his might in war; it was he who took partial command of the troops when Klearchos died. The greater part of what they accomplished, he could attribute to himself and his own advice, acting as a *commander of commanders* and a general among the leaders. Furthermore it was he who, in recording what happened to them, to Cyrus, and to that expedition, bears witness to the best qualities of our city, explicitly saying that it was by the sea, was Greek, and alone showed itself as friendly to them. It is as if he is loudly proclaiming and publicly testifying that after the Ten Thousand had passed, and were still passing, through so great an empire and such a great area of the world, where they suffered much and accomplished much, they saw this city of Trebizond alone as being free and its own mistress, when all

ἐθεάσαντο ταυτηνί, τῶν ἄλλων ἁπάντων δεδουλωμένων. Τοὺς γὰρ βασιλέως ἐχθροὺς οὐκ ἦν οὐδέσι χρήσασθαι φίλοις τῶν πολύν τινα λόγον ποιουμένων τοῦ βασιλέως. Ἅμα τε γὰρ ἂν αὐτοῖς ἦσαν φίλοι καὶ τοῦ βασιλέως ἐχθροί, ὥστε πρὶν πρὸς αὐτοὺς ἐπιδείξασθαι τὰ τῶν φίλων πρὸς ἐκεῖνον ἀκήρυκτον ἐχρῆν πόλεμον ἀναρριπίσαι καὶ μάχην, τοῦτο δ᾽ ἂν ὅσης εἴη δυνάμεως καὶ ὡς ἀνδρῶν ἐλευθέρων καὶ τὰς ψυχὰς ἀηττήτων οὐδεὶς ὃς ἀγνοεῖ.

66 Δεξάμενοι γοῦν αὐτοὺς ἐπὶ τῆς αὐτῆς οἱ πατέρες ἡμῶν πόλεως καὶ τὴν Περσῶν ἔχθραν ἐν δευτέρῳ θέμενοι τοῦ πρὸς αὐτοὺς γιγνομένου, μέχρι Σινώπης διαβῆναι ἐποίησαν, ἐκεῖσε καταγαγόντες αὐτούς, οὗ λοιπὸν ἦν οὐδὲν δέος οὐδ᾽ ὑποψία Περσικοῦ φόβου καὶ τῶν ἐκεῖθεν ἐπηρτημένων κινδύνων. Καίτοι, εἰ θαυμάζομεν Ἀθηναίους, Ἡρακλείδας οὐ μόνον ὑποδεξαμένους, Εὐρυσθέως ἐλάσαντος, ἀλλ᾽ ἔς τε τὸ παρὸν μεταδόντας πολιτείας καὶ τῆς ἄλλης παραμυθίας καί, τοῦ καιροῦ παρασχόντος, εἰς τὴν γῆν τὴν πατρῴαν καταγαγόντας καὶ τὴν ἐκ γένους καὶ πατρὸς αὐτοῖς προσήκουσαν ἀποδόντας ἡγεμονίαν, πῶς ἄν τις οὐχὶ θαυμάσεται τὰ ἡμέτερα καὶ τὴν φιλανθρωπίαν ὑμνήσει καὶ ζηλώσει τὴν γενναιότητα; Οὔτε γὰρ τῶν ἐκ Περσῶν ὑπεριδεῖν ἀπειλῶν τοσοῦτο δυναμένων, οὔτε τοῦ σφίσι συμφέροντος ἦν ἀμελῆσαι, μὴ γενναιότητι καὶ φιλανθρωπίᾳ διενεγκόντας. Ὅσο γοῦν ἑνὸς ἀνδρὸς Εὐρυσθέως καὶ γῆς ὀλίγης τυράννου μικρὰ δυναμένου τὰ Περσῶν ἔθνη δεινότερά τε καὶ φοβερώτερα, τοσοῦτο μεῖζον ἐροῦμεν ἐξενηνοχέναι καὶ ἐναργέστερον πάντων ἀγαθῶν δεῖγμα τοὺς ἀνηρημένους τὸν πρὸς τοὺς δεινοτέρους

the others were enslaved. It was impossible for enemies of the king to find friends among those who were so obedient to the king's will. Being friendly to the Ten Thousand was one and the same thing as being the enemy of the king, so that before they performed any acts of friendship to the former, they were necessarily in a state of undeclared war and conflict with the latter. No one can miss the point that this shows how strong they were, what free men they were, and how unconquerable were their spirits.

So then, it was our forefathers who welcomed the Ten 66
Thousand into the city and put the enmity of the Persians second to the fact that they were related to these men. They gave them safe passage as far as Sinope since, once they reached it, there would be no more fear or suspicion of the Persian terror and the dangers associated with it. Indeed, if we admire the Athenians for not only welcoming the sons of Herakles into their city after Eurystheus drove them out, but for even bestowing temporary citizenship upon them and sharing with them all other comforts until the opportunity presented itself to lead them back to their fatherland and restore them to the sovereignty that belonged to them from their family and father, how could one not admire us for what we did, praise our kindness, and admire our nobility? Our people were not so powerful that they could just overlook the Persians' threats, nor was it in their best interests to ignore them, unless they stood up for nobility and benevolence. Indeed, to the extent that the Persian peoples are more terrible and frightening than a single man, such as Eurystheus, who was an insignificant ruler of a small land, to the same extent we might say this makes those who undertake to fight more terrible opponents, seem even more pre-

τῶν ἀντιπάλων ἀγῶνα. Τὸ γὰρ τῶν πολεμίων εὐδόκιμον θατέροις, πάντως δὲ τοῖς νικῶσιν οὐκ ὀλίγα πρὸς εὔκλειαν συλλαμβάνεται καὶ ἡ τῶν ἀνταγωνιστῶν γενναιότης ἐς δόξαν τοῖς κρατήσασι φέρει. Ὥστε, εἴτ' οἴκοθεν ἡ πόλις ἡμῖν, μηδενὸς προδιδάξαντος, ἐπὶ τὰ τῶν πράξεων κάλλιστα τὴν ῥοπὴν ἔσχε, τοσοῦτο διήνεγκεν, εἴτ' Ἀθηναίους καὶ τὰς αὐτῶν πράξεις ζηλοῦσα πρὸς τοῦθ' ὥρμησε, τοσοῦτον ὑπερεβάλετο.

67 Οὕτως ἄνωθεν Ἑλληνικοῦ τε φρονήματος ἔμπλεως ἦν καὶ τὴν ἐλευθερίαν ἐτίμα, τὴν δουλείαν καὶ μέχρι τῆς κλήσεως ὡς ἐνὸν ἀποστρεφομένη καὶ δυσχεραίνουσα, ἐπεί τοι τὸ χείροσιν ἑαυτῶν ἀναγκάζεσθαι δουλεύειν τινὰς καὶ συνειδέναι σφίσι τὰς ψυχὰς πολλῷ κρείττοσιν οὖσιν ἢ ὑφ' ὧν ἄρχονται, τίνος οὐκ ἂν καταβάλοι ψυχὴν ἢ πῶς ἄν τις οὐ δεύτερα πάντα κακὰ θεῖτο καὶ πρὸς ἓν μόνον ἀγωνίσαιτο τοῦτο, τῆς μεγίστης συμφορᾶς ταυτησὶν ἀπηλλάχθαι; Τὸν γὰρ ἐλεύθερον ἄνδρα καὶ πόλιν ἢ τοῖς ἀμείνοσιν ὑπείκειν ἀνάγκη καὶ δουλεύειν τοῖς κρείττοσιν, ἀγομένοις ὑπ' ἐκείνων ἐπὶ τὰ σφίσι συμφέροντα καὶ ἐφ' ἅπερ οὐκ ἂν αὐτοὶ οἴκοθεν ἤχθησαν· οὗτος γὰρ δὴ νόμος ἀρχῆς ἄριστος καὶ δουλεία ἐλευθερίᾳ ἀντίρροπος, ἔστι δ' ὅτε καὶ κρείττων, ὅταν μὴ σφίσι τινὲς ἐξαρκοῖεν μηδὲ δύναιντο μηδενὸς παραδείξαντος ἐφικνεῖσθαι τῶν ἀρετῶν· ἢ τοῦτο οὐκ ἔχοντας οὐδὲ τοιούτων δεσποτῶν εὐποροῦντας ζῆν καθ' αὑτοὺς ὥς γ' ἐκ τῶν ἐνόντων αἱρουμένους τὰ βέλτιστα καὶ ἃ ἂν τὴν διὰ πάντων ἐλευθερίαν αὐτοῖς μαρτυρήσειεν.

68 Ἐπὶ δὴ τοιούτοις καὶ οἱ ἡμέτεροι σαλεύοντες, λογισμοῖς

eminent and an even better exemplar of all the virtues. For the glory of one side in a conflict is greatly enhanced by the good reputation of its opponents, especially if it is victorious, and the nobility of its antagonists brings repute to their conquerors. Thus our city was either so different because it was inclined to do the best deeds all on its own, without anyone having shown it how, or else it was so exceptional because it was emulating the Athenians and their deeds when it set out upon this course.

Thus long ago our city had a Greek mentality and hon- 67
ored liberty, while avoiding and loathing slavery even in name for as long as it could. If one were forced to serve an inferior people and knew that he was spiritually and intellectually far superior to the ruling people, how would one not be spiritually and intellectually disturbed by the fact or how would he not set all other ills aside and struggle for this one thing: to be free of so great a misfortune? A free man and city must in some circumstances obey their betters and serve their superiors, who direct them in their best interests and in ways that they would not have arrived at on their own; for this is the best method of government and this form of slavery is the proper counterbalance to freedom. In some circumstances, it is even preferable when people are neither self-sufficient nor capable of attaining virtue without someone showing them the way. Otherwise, if people lack this kind of government or have masters without those qualities, they must live independently and make the best of their situation, doing whatever demonstrates their commitment to freedom.

Motivated by such ideas and having acquired the habit of 68

καὶ ταῦτα προμελετῶντες, οὕτω τῶν τοιούτων ἐγένοντο λογισμῶν καὶ ταύτης τῆς δόξης, ὥστ᾽ ἐφ᾽ ὅσον μὲν ἐνῆν καὶ ψυχὰς καὶ σώματα διετέλεσαν ἐλεύθεροι ὄντες, μετ᾽ ἐλευθερίας τῆς ὄντως πολιτευόμενοι καὶ τὰ καθ᾽ αὑτοὺς διοικοῦντες, μόγις δέ ποτε καὶ τοῦτ᾽ ἐπ᾽ ὀλίγον τοῖς σώμασιν εἴξαντες, ταῖς ψυχαῖς οὐχ ὡμολόγησαν οὐδ᾽ ἐγγύς, οὐδ᾽ ἐδουλώθησαν τὰ φρονήματα τῷ μεγίστῳ ἑαυτῶν καὶ κυριωτάτῳ, τὸ ἀρχικὸν τηροῦντες καὶ τὴν ἡγεμονίαν καὶ τὸ διὰ πάντων ἐλεύθερον.

69 Δυοῖν γὰρ δὴ τούτοιν, σώμασι καὶ ψυχαῖς, δουλουμένων τῶν ἀνθρώπων ἀνθρώποις, τοὺς μὲν τὰς ψυχὰς καταβεβλημένους καὶ γνώμαις ταπεινωθέντας ἐλευθέρους οὐκ ἂν ὀνομάσαιμι, κἂν σώμασιν ἄρχοιεν, τῷ τιμιωτάτῳ ἑαυτῶν ὑπακούοντας ἄλλων. Ἂν δέ τις ἐς μὲν ὅσον ἐστὶν ἐφικτὸν ὑπερέχῃ τῶν ἐναντίων καὶ ἀμφοτέροις, ἀνάγκης δὲ συνωθούσης προδιδοίη τὰ τῆς ἐλάττονος μοίρας ὑπὲρ τοῦ σῶσαι τὸ κρεῖττον, τοῦτον τῷ ὄντι ἐλεύθερον οὐκ ἂν αἰσχυνοίμην ἀποφαινόμενος καὶ ἄρχειν, δουλείαν ὑποκρινόμενον, καὶ δεσπόζειν ἐν ᾧ δοκεῖ πρὸς ἄλλων τινῶν ἄρχεσθαι. Τίς γὰρ οὐκ οἶδεν, ὡς τὸν μὲν γνώμῃ ταπεινωθέντα καὶ σώματι δουλεύειν ἀνάγκη, ἅτε τοῦ μὲν ἑπομένου, τῆς δὲ ψυχῆς ἀγούσης ἐκ τρόπου παντός, τῇ δὲ τοῦ φρονήματος ἐμβριθείᾳ καὶ τῷ ἀταπεινώτῳ τῆς γνώμης καὶ τὰ σώματα συνεξαίρεται, καὶ συμμετέχει τῆς ἐλευθερίας πρός τε τὴν παρεστῶσαν ὥραν τοῦ χρόνου καὶ τῶν πραγμάτων διδόντων ἐς ὕστερον τελεώτερον, ὡς ἔργοις αὐτοῖς καὶ πράγμασιν οἱ ἡμέτεροι ἔδειξαν, οὐ μετὰ πολὺ τοῖς κοινοῖς δεσπόταις Ῥωμαίοις καὶ τῇ ἀρίστῃ καὶ δικαιοτάτῃ

them, our ancestors came to be so controlled by such arguments and such an opinion that they remained free in spirit and body for as long as possible, living in a state of true freedom and administering their own affairs. Hardly ever did they yield their bodies to another and even then only for a short while, but they did not even come close to surrendering in spirit. Their minds were not enslaved by the greatest or the most powerful among them. Instead, they maintained their sovereignty, hegemony, and freedom in all regards.

For when men are enslaved by other men in regard to both of these things, namely the mind and body, I would not call free those whose minds are subjugated and whose intelligence is humbled, even if they retain mastery of their bodies, because they obey others with regard to the most powerful and most important aspect of themselves. But if one were to prevail over one's enemies in both respects, body and soul, to whatever degree possible, but were to betray the lesser part in order to save the greater when necessity dictated, then I would feel no shame in declaring this person truly free and in control, and only pretending to be the slave, and to be the master while he seems to be controlled by others. After all, everyone knows that a person who is humbled in thought must necessarily also be enslaved in body, as the body follows and the mind leads in every way. Indeed, it is by the weight of the mind and the unyielding character of the intelligence that the body is elevated, participating in freedom both at the present moment and more completely in the future, when circumstances permit. Our ancestors demonstrated this principle with their very deeds and actions when, not too long afterward, they attached themselves to the Roman masters of the world and the best and most just 69

Ῥωμαίων προστεθέντες ἡγεμονίᾳ καὶ ἄσμενοι ἐκείνων ἀπαλλαγέντες οἷς πρότερον ὑπετάγησαν.

70 Μιθριδάτου φημὶ καὶ τῶν ἐξ ἐκείνου Ποντικῶν βασιλέων. Πρὸς γὰρ δὴ τούτους καὶ τοὺς ἐκ τούτου τοῦ γένους βασιλεῖς, ἐπὶ μέγα ἠρμένους, ὡς οὐκ ἦν ἔτι ἀντέχειν, τὸ μὲν οἷς πολλὰ κεκμήκασι πρότερον ἠγωνισμένοι πρός τε Πέρσας καὶ τοὺς ἄλλους βαρβάρους καὶ αὐτοὺς τοὺς ἀπὸ Μιθριδάτου, τὸ δ' οἷς αὐτοὺς ἔπειτα εἰς μέγιστον ἐπιδεδωκότας συνεῖδον καὶ πολλῆς ἄλλης ἑλληνικῆς γῆς ἐπιλαβομένους, ἐσπείσαντό τε αὐτοῖς καὶ ὑπήκουον, ἀναξιοπαθοῦντες ὅμως καὶ ταῖς ψυχαῖς δυσχεραίνοντες καὶ ἀνάξιον κρίνοντες ὅτι σώμασι γοῦν τῷ χείρονι ἑαυτῶν οἷς μὴ χρεὼν ἔδει ὑπείκειν.

71 Τὴν γὰρ ἐν Πόντῳ καὶ Γαλατίᾳ Μιθριδάτου τοῦ Ἀριοβαρζάνου ἡγεμονίαν, ταπεινὴν ἐν τοῖς ἄνω καιροῖς οὖσαν ἀπὸ μικροῦ τέ τινος ἀρξαμένην, ὅμως ὑπώπτευεν ὁ τῶν Ἀλεξάνδρου διαδόχων μέγιστος καὶ πρεσβύτατος Ἀντίγονος, ὁ βασιλεὺς Συρίας καὶ τῆς Ἀσίας τοῦ πλείστου, ἔκ τε τῶν πραγμάτων αὐτῶν τεκμαιρόμενος ἐς ὅσον ὄγκου τε καὶ μεγέθους προβήσεται καὶ πόσης γῆς ἐπιλήψεται ἔκ τέ τινος ἐνυπνίου διαταραχθεὶς οὐ μετρίως. Νομίσας οὖν, Μιθριδάτου θανόντος, παραλύσεσθαί τε τὴν βασιλείαν αὐτῷ καὶ μέρος τῆς ἰδίας ἀρχῆς γενήσεσθαι τελεώτερον, βουλὴν βουλεύεται πονηρὰν μᾶλλον ἢ σοφήν, ἀδόκητον αὐτῷ καὶ αἰφνίδιον ἐπιστῆσαι τὸν θάνατον.

72 Ἐπεὶ δὴ ξύμμαχον ὄντα κἀν τοῖς φίλοις τελοῦντα καλῶς οὐκ εἶχεν ἐκ τοῦ προφανοῦς ἀνελεῖν, εὐπροσώπου μὴ

rule of the Romans, and were gladly rid of the people by whom they had previously been subdued.

I am referring of course to Mithridates and the kings of Pontos descended from him. Against enemies such as these and kings of this line who had grown powerful, resistance was no longer possible, partly because the Trapezuntines had grown very weary from previous battles against the Persians and other barbarians, including Mithridates's own people, and partly because they were aware that Mithridates's people had grown powerful and taken control of many other Greek lands. So the people of Trebizond made peace with them and submitted to them, although they were unhappy at this unworthy treatment, were dismayed by it in spirit, and judged it unworthy to submit their bodies to someone weaker than themselves when they did not have to. 70

In prior years, the dominion of Mithridates, son of Ariobarzanes, in the Pontos and Galatia had been modest and had humble origins, but it still nevertheless aroused the suspicions of the greatest and most senior of Alexander's successors, Antigonos, the king of Syria and most of Asia. For he had conjectured from the actual circumstances how massive and great Mithridates's dominion would become and, from a dream, that he would seize many lands, and he was greatly alarmed. So, thinking that, with Mithridates dead, the latter's kingdom would collapse and become a part of his own empire in its entirety, Antigonos devised a wicked, rather than wise, plan to bring about his unexpected and sudden demise. 71

Since Mithridates was an ally and ranked among his friends, Antigonos had no obvious reason to kill him and 72

δραξαμένῳ προφάσεως, δόλῳ μετελθεῖν αὐτὸν ἐδοκίμασε παρόντα τε καὶ κατὰ συμμαχίαν αὐτῷ συνεπόμενον, καί, τῷ υἱῷ Δημητρίῳ τὸ ἀπόρρητον κοινωσάμενος, ὅρκοις αὐτὸν προκατείληφε παρ᾽ ἑαυτῷ τηρεῖν ἀνέκφορον τὸ μυστήριον μηδενί τε τὸ παράπαν εἰπεῖν μηδὲ ἕν. Τὸν δὲ φιλίᾳ τε προκατειλημμένον τἀνδρὸς καὶ ἅμα παθόντα τὴν ψυχὴν ὡς ἀδίκως πεισομένου τἀνθρώπου εὑρεῖν ὅπως Μιθριδάτην τε ῥύσεται τοῦ κινδύνου καὶ κρείττων αὐτὸς ἐπιορκίας φανήσεται, τὰ ὀμωμοσμένα τηρήσας ὡς ἐνὸν ἔμπεδα· ἀπολαβὼν γὰρ αὐτὸν κατὰ μόνας, ὡς ἐγεγόνεισαν καθ᾽ αὑτούς, γράφει μὲν αὐτὸς κατὰ γῆς τῆς λόγχης τῷ στύρακι, ὁρῶντος ἐκείνου, "Φεῦγε, Μιθριδάτα," ὁ δ᾽ εὐθὺς συναισθόμενος ἀπέδρα τε νυκτὸς εἰς Καππαδοκίαν καὶ τὸν ἐπηρτημένον αὐτῷ διέφυγε κίνδυνον.

73 Ἐκ τούτου τῆς τε φιλίας Ἀντιγόνου ἀφίσταται καὶ διετέλει διάφορός τε ὢν αὐτῷ καὶ πολέμιος καὶ τὴν ἀρχὴν ἑαυτοῦ οὐ συνέχων μόνον καὶ συντηρῶν, ἀλλὰ καὶ προσαύξων οὐ μικραῖς ταῖς προσθήκαις. Πολλῆς τε γὰρ καὶ ἀγαθῆς ἐκράτησε χώρας καὶ πολλὴν περιεβάλετο δύναμιν, πολλὰ τῶν τότε μὲν ὑπὸ Μακεδόνας, ὕστερον δὲ γενομένων ὑπὸ Ῥωμαίους τότε μὲν αὐτός, ἔπειθ᾽ οἱ μετ᾽ ἐκεῖνον δουλώσαντες. Ἀσίαν τε γὰρ Ῥωμαίων καὶ Βιθυνίαν καὶ Καππαδοκίαν καὶ Παφλαγονίαν ἀφεῖλον, ἦρχόν τε Πόντου τε καὶ Βοσπόρου καὶ μέχρι τῶν ὑπὲρ τὴν Μαιῶτιν ἀοικήτων, οὐδενὸς παρενοχλοῦντος. Ἐπεὶ δ᾽ οὐδὲν αὐτοῖς ὥριζε τὴν πλεονεξίαν, ἀλλ᾽ ἀεί τι ἐπικτώμενοι κἀπὶ τῆς ἀντιπέρας ἠπείρου διέβησαν, Θρᾴκην τε καὶ Μακεδονίαν ἐπὶ στρατῷ πολλῷ προσαγόμενοι καὶ μεγάλῳ, συμπάσης

could not come up with a plausible pretext for doing so; he thus decided to do away with Mithridates treacherously when he was present and in his company as an ally. He let his son Demetrios in on the plot, though he made him swear first under oath to keep it a secret and not so much as breathe a word of it to anyone. But Demetrios, who was bound by his friendship with the man and tormented by the thought of the injustice that he would suffer, sought a way to save Mithridates from his peril and avoid charges of perjury, while still keeping his word as best he could. And so he took Mithridates aside and, when they were alone, as Mithridates looked on, he wrote on the ground with the butt of his spear, "Run away, Mithridates." Mithridates immediately realized what was afoot and fled in the night to Cappadocia, escaping the danger that had been prepared for him.

From this point on, Mithridates was no friend of Antigo- 73
nos; he remained at odds with him and was his enemy, not only preserving and maintaining his own dominion, but also expanding it with sizeable additions. He seized much good land and attained great power, as first he himself and later his successors enslaved many areas which were then under Macedonian control but later came under the Romans. They seized Asia, Bithynia, Cappadocia, and Paphlagonia from the Romans, and ruled over the Pontos and Bosporos up to the uninhabited lands beyond the Sea of Azov, without anyone standing in their way. Since there was no limit to their greed, and they were always after more, they crossed to the opposite continent and acquired Thrace and Macedonia for themselves with a massive army, mastering the entire

τε θαλάσσης ἐπικρατοῦντες καὶ τὰς Κυκλάδας καταδουλούμενοι νήσους καὶ τὴν Εὔβοιαν ἔχοντες ἤδη ἔκ τε Ἀθηνῶν ὁρμώμενοι, τὰ μέχρι τῆς Θετταλίας ἔθνη τῆς Ἑλλάδος ἀφίστων, ἤγειραν μὲν καθ᾽ ἑαυτῶν τοὺς Ῥωμαίους, κατὰ δὲ τῆς οἰκείας ἤδη κεφαλῆς ἔγνωσαν πᾶν μηχανώμενοι, ἥ τε πλεονεξία προσαπώλεσεν αὐτοῖς καὶ τἀρχαῖα, καὶ τὸ κεφάλαιον αὐτὸ ζημιώσασα, ὥσπερ τοὺς ἐπὶ τόκοις μεγάλοις δανείζοντας, καὶ εἰς τοὐναντίον αὐτοῖς ἢ ἐβούλοντο περιέστη τὰ πράγματα.

74 Μάριός τε γὰρ καὶ μετ᾽ ἐκεῖνον ὁ Σύλλας πολλάκις Μιθριδάτῃ τε τῷ ἀπὸ τοῦ πρώτου ὀγδόῳ καὶ τοῖς ἐκείνου συρράξαντες στρατηγοῖς πόλεμον, οὐ τῆς Εὐρωπαίας γῆς διεώσαντο μόνον, ἀλλὰ καὶ Λούκουλλος μετὰ τούτους τῶν Ἀσιανῶν ἐθνῶν αὐτὸν οὐκ ὀλίγα ἀφείλετο. Ἐπεὶ δὲ τὸ πεπρωμένον ἀπῄτει καὶ ἡ μοῖρα τὴν Ῥωμαίων ἡγεμονίαν ἠνάγκαζεν ἐς τὰ γῆς ἔσχατα ἐκτετάσθαι καὶ τούτοις ὡρίσθαι σχεδὸν πέρασι, Πομπήιον Μάγνον ἀνέστησε, προθυμότερον μὲν τοῦ κατ᾽ αὐτῶν ἡμμένον πολέμου, μετὰ λαμπροτέρας δὲ καὶ εὐδαιμονεστέρας τῆς τύχης ὁρμώμενον. Ὃς Μιθριδάτῃ συμβαλὼν καὶ ἡττήσας, εἶτα φυγόντα μεταδιώκει, καί, μέχρι Κασπίων Πυλῶν ἀνελθών, κρατεῖ μὲν τῶν ἄλλων ἁπάντων ἐθνῶν, Σύρων τε καὶ Κιλίκων καὶ Παφλαγόνων καὶ τῶν ἐν Μεσοποταμίᾳ τε καὶ Φοινίκῃ καὶ Παλαιστίνῃ κατῳκημένων καὶ Ἰουδαίᾳ καὶ Ἀραβίᾳ, δουλοῖ δὲ Ῥωμαίοις Καππαδοκίαν, Μυσίαν, Κολχίδα, Ἰβηρίαν, Ἀλβανίαν, Ἀρμενίαν καὶ τὰ μέχρι Μαιώτιδος. Μιθριδάτῃ δ᾽ οὐ τὴν ἀρχὴν μόνον, ἀλλὰ καὶ τὴν ζωὴν αὐτὴν ἀφελόμενος, λαμπρὸς λαμπρῶς ἐπανῆλθε τῷ δήμῳ Ῥωμαίων

Aegean Sea and enslaving the Cycladic Islands. But when they already held Euboea and were basing their operations out of Athens, causing the nations of Greece as far as Thessaly to rebel, they provoked the Romans to move against them and soon realized that all their scheming had put their own necks on the line. Their greed even lost them their original territory and, since it deprived them of their capital itself, just as greed does when people borrow money at a high interest rate, things turned out contrary to what they wanted.

Marius and after him Sulla waged war many times on 74
Mithridates, the eighth of that name after the first, and his generals. They not only drove him out of Europe, but Lucullus, after them, deprived him of control over many peoples in Asia. But since fate demanded it and destiny required the Roman empire to extend to the ends of the earth and, in fact, scarcely to be contained by those boundaries, the Romans appointed Pompey the Great, who undertook the war against Mithridates even more zealously and who advanced with even more brilliant and happy success. He fought Mithridates, defeated him, and then pursued him when he fled. Pompey advanced as far as the Caspian Gates and prevailed over all the other peoples, including the Syrians, Cilicians, Paphlagonians, and those dwelling in Mesopotamia, Phoenicia, Palestine, Judaea, and Arabia. He subjugated for the Romans Cappadocia, Mysia, Kolchis, Georgia, Albania, Armenia, and the lands up to the Sea of Azov. After depriving Mithridates not only of his dominion but also of life itself, the glorious Pompey returned in glory to the Roman

εὐφημίαις τε καὶ θριάμβοις καὶ πᾶσι τιμῶν καταστεφόμενος εἴδεσιν.

Ἐντεῦθεν ἡ ἡμετέρα ἀσμένως τε ἣν ἐκ πολλοῦ ἐπίδοξον εἶχεν ἐλευθερίας εἶδεν ἡμέραν, καὶ τοῖς οἰκουμένης δεσπόταις εὐθὺς προσχωρήσασα Ῥωμαίοις καὶ τῇ κείνων ἡγεμονίᾳ ἑαυτήν τε καὶ τοὺς ἰδίους τροφίμους ἐνέδωκε φέρουσα, πολλὰ μὲν συνησθέντας σφίσιν αὐτοῖς ἀνθ᾽ ὧν τῆς βαρβαρικῆς ἐπιστασίας εὐτυχῶς ἀπηλλάγησαν, πολλὴν δὲ τῷ ἐλευθερίῳ θεῷ χάριν ὁμολογήσαντες τῆς ἐς τὸ κρεῖττον αὐτῶν τε καὶ τοῦ ξύμπαντος ἐπιδόσεως. Τὸ δ᾽ ἦν Ῥωμαίοις ὑποταγῆναι, Ἑλληνικῆς τε γῆς οὐ μόνον ἡγουμένοις ἁπάσης, ἀλλὰ καὶ μόνοις ἀξίως καὶ ὄντως ἄρχουσι, κηδεμονικήν τε καὶ πατρικὴν τὴν ἐς τοὺς ὑπηκόους ἐπιδεικνυμένοις εὔνοιαν καὶ τὸ κείνοις συμφέρον ἐκ παντὸς τρόπου μηχανωμένοις, ὅπερ ἐστὶν ἀληθῶς τε ἄρχοντος καὶ ἡγεμόνος τῷ ὄντι. Οὐ γὰρ δυνάμει γε μόνον καὶ περιουσίᾳ καὶ πλούτου καὶ στρατιᾶς κατεῖχον ὑπήκοα πάντα ἔθνη καὶ πᾶν γένος ἀνθρώπων, ἀλλ᾽ οὐδὲν ἧττον τῷ τε νομίμως ἄρχειν καὶ δικαίως αὐτοὺς ἐπήγοντο καὶ οἷς ὡς πρὸς παῖδας πατὴρ ὣς ἤπιος προσεφέροντο. Ἐντεῦθεν γὰρ αὐτοῖς καὶ παραμόνιμον τὸ τῆς ἀρχῆς διατετέλεκε γενόμενον πρόσχημα, ἅτε συνεχόμενόν τε εὐνοίᾳ καὶ φιλίᾳ συνδούμενον, καὶ μόνοι τοῦ χρόνου κρείττους ἐγένοντο, τοσούτου μὲν ἤδη τοῦ ἀπ᾽ ἐκείνου παραρρυέντος, οὐδὲν δ᾽ αὐτοῖς τήν τε εὐδαιμονίαν καὶ τὴν ἡγεμονίαν λυμηναμένου, ἀλλ᾽ ἄτρεπτόν τε καὶ ἀκίνητον σχοῦσιν, ἐφ᾽ ὅσον εἰκός, τὸ κατὰ πάντων κράτος καὶ τὴν ἀρχὴν τὴν βασίλειον.

people, crowned with acclamations, triumphs, and every kind of honor.

From this point onward, our city gladly saw its long- 75
awaited, glorious day of freedom and went over immediately to the Roman masters of the world, surrendering itself and those whom it nurtured to their rule. They were very pleased to be delivered with such good fortune from barbarian overlordship and expressed much gratitude to the god of freedom for giving them something that would better them and the whole world. That was to be subject to the Romans, who did not just have dominion over all Greek land, but also were the only ones to truly and worthily rule it, showing a protective and fatherly affection to their subjects and contriving to act in their best interests in every way, which is what truly defines a real ruler and sovereign. For it was not just by their strength and their abundance of both wealth and military might that they subjected all the peoples and every race of men; rather, they won them over no less by ruling them lawfully and justly, and by behaving towards them as a gentle father does to his children. Consequently, their form of rule became permanent and has endured, seeing that it was constituted by affection and bound by friendship. They alone became mightier than time for, although so much time has passed since that moment, it has done nothing to undermine their prosperity and dominion. Rather, it seems fair to say, they continue to hold an immutable and steadfast dominion and imperial rule over everyone.

76 Οἷς πολλῆς γῆς καὶ πλειόνων ἐθνῶν δηλωθέντων τὸ μέγιστόν τε καὶ κάλλιστον ἦν τὸ καὶ τὴν Ἑλλάδα τοὺς δεσπότας γνωρίσαι καὶ ζῆν ὑπὸ τούτους ἑλέσθαι τοὺς ἁπανταχῇ γῆς τὴν Ἑλλήνων τιμῶντας φωνήν. Πατρικήν τε γὰρ βασιλείαν καὶ νόμιμον καὶ σοφῶν ἐπιστασίαν ἀνδρῶν πόσων οὐκ ἄν τις ἐλευθεριῶν ἄσμενος πρίαιτο; Ἐντεῦθεν Ῥωμαῖοι μὲν ἦρχον, ὑπήκουε δὲ καὶ ἡ ἡμετέρα καὶ ἤγετο μετά γε τῶν ἄλλων Ἑλλήνων καὶ τῆς Ἀθηνῶν πόλεως καὶ μητρὸς Ἀττικῆς· καὶ σχῆμα μὲν εἶχον ὑπακουόντων, τιμῶν δ' εἵνεκα καὶ εὐνοίας καὶ ἧς ἐφύλαττον εἰς αὐτοὺς αἰδοῦς οἱ σφῶν ἄρχοντες συνάρχοντες μᾶλλον ἐδείκνυντο, ὥσπερ τις νεώτερος ἀδελφῷ πρεσβυτέρῳ συμβασιλεύων ἤ, ἵνα φῶ τἀληθέστερον, ὡς εὖ μὲν καὶ γνώσεώς τις καὶ φωνῆς ἥκων καὶ πείρας τῆς ἐς τὸν βίον, γήρᾳ δ' ἄλλως ἐξημβλωμένος τὸ δύνασθαι πράττειν, ἀδελφῷ ῥωμαλέῳ μὲν καὶ θαρροῦντι καὶ πολεμικῆς ἐπιστήμης ἱκανῶς ἔχοντι, δεομένῳ δὲ λόγων καὶ συμβουλίας συμπαρομαρτῶν τε καὶ συνεπόμενος.

77 Τήν τε γὰρ φωνὴν Ἕλλησιν ἐς τὸ ἀκριβέστατόν τε καὶ καθαρώτατον ἐξησκημένην Ῥωμαῖοι ἠπίσταντο, τήν τε γνῶσιν καὶ φρόνησιν καὶ τὸ περιὸν τῆς σοφίας αὐτά τ' ἐδείκνυ τὰ πράγματα καὶ ὅσα φθάσαντες διεπράξαντο, ὥστ' οὔτε βουλεύεσθαι συνετωτέρους ἄλλους ᾔδεσαν ὄντας ἢ μείζους τε καὶ καλλίους ἐξ ὧν ἔπραξαν ἀφορμὰς ἔχοντας, οὔτε, λόγον ἀποτεῖναι δεῆσαν σοφόν τε καὶ πιθανόν, προῆγον ἑτέρους, τῶν δευτερείων Ἕλληνας ἀξιοῦντες, ἀλλ' ὡς ἂν μόνους ἀξίους λόγοις κεκοσμημένους καὶ μόνους τὴν ἀνθρώπῳ προσήκουσαν φωνὴν ἀφιέντας,

Among the many lands and peoples mentioned above, this was the greatest and best for Greece to recognize as its master and choose to live under, since all over the world the Romans respected the Greek language. How many liberties would one not gladly trade for a fatherly and lawful imperial regime and the oversight of wise men? Henceforth, the Romans ruled and our city obeyed and was led by them along with the rest of the Greeks and the city of Athens, its Attic mother. However, while the Greeks were nominally their subjects, their rulers elevated them more to the position of corulers in terms of the honors, affection, and respect they retained for them. It was like a younger brother ruling jointly with an older brother or, to speak more truthfully, like a brother who has attained considerable knowledge, facility in speech, and experience in life, but who has otherwise grown too weary with age to be able to conduct business, accompanying and attending on his brother who is strong, confident, and very knowledgeable about warfare, but lacks words and counsel. 76

The Romans were aware that the Greeks had developed their language to the highest levels of precision and purity, while their history and accomplishments demonstrated their knowledge, rationality, and superior wisdom. As a result the Romans neither knew of anyone who could give wiser counsels than the Greeks, nor of anyone who had better or more virtuous grounds for their actions, nor, when they needed to make a wise and persuasive statement, did they prefer anyone else and deem the Greeks inferior. Rather, as though the Greeks alone were worthy of such esteem, given how well-spoken they were and that they alone spoke a language fit for humans (since they attained so much 77

ἅτε καὶ φύσεως ἀνθρώπων ἥκοντας ἐπὶ πλεῖστον καὶ τῷ ὄντι λογικοὺς ὄντας αὐτούς, προῆγόν τε τῶν ἄλλων ἁπάντων καὶ τιμῶν τῶν μεγίστων ἠξίουν καὶ σφῶν αὐτῶν ὁμολογοῦντες αὐτοὺς τῷ παντὶ διαφέρειν γλῶττάν τε τὴν αὐτῶν καὶ σοφίαν, ἄγοντες περὶ πλείστου καὶ σπουδάζοντες ἕκαστος ὅστις αὐτὴν ἐξησκηκὼς ἀκριβέστερον φθάσει. Οὕτως ἦγον Ἕλληνες μᾶλλον τοὺς ἄγοντας ἢ ὑπ᾽ αὐτῶν ἤγοντο, καὶ τοιοῦτον αὐτοῖς ἦν τὸ σχῆμα τῆς συμμαχίας.

78 Τούτῳ δὴ καὶ ἡ πόλις ἡμῖν τῷ τρόπῳ Ῥωμαίοις εἴξασα καὶ τῇ κείνων ἡγεμονίᾳ, τῆς γινομένης μὲν αὐτῇ τιμῆς τε καὶ θεραπείας ἐκεῖθεν ἀπήλαυε, τὴν δὲ προσήκουσαν αὖθις αἰδῶ τε καὶ πίστιν καὶ εὔνοιαν αὐτὴ τοῖς ἄρχουσιν οὐ μόνον ἐφύλαττεν, ἀλλὰ καὶ ἐς τόδε τηροῦσα διατελεῖ ὑφ᾽ οὓς εὔχετο τελέσαι δεσπότας καὶ οὓς ἐξ ἀρχῆς ἔγνω, οὐδενός τε τῶν ἄλλων ἀλλάξασα καὶ διατελοῦσ᾽ αὐτοῖς εὔνους οὖσα τὸν πάντα αἰῶνα. Ἐνιαυτοὶ γὰρ ἤδη πρὸς τοῖς πεντακοσίοις παρῳχήκεσαν χίλιοι Ῥωμαίοις ὑποταγείσης, καὶ πολλὰ μὲν ἔφυσαν ἐν τῷ μέσῳ, πλείω δὲ κέκρυπται, ἃ τῷ μακρῷ χρόνῳ προσήκειν ἔφη τις ἔργα, καὶ ὅμως ἄτρεπτος ἡ πόλις ἡμῖν οὖσα διαμένει καὶ ἀμετάβλητος, οὓς ἡγεμόνας εἵλετο στέργουσα καὶ τὴν γιγνομένην αὐτοῖς ἀποδιδοῦσα πειθώ. Καίτοι τὸ μὲν τῆς ἀρχῆς εἶδος μετεβλήθη Ῥωμαίοις· δικτάτωρες γὰρ ἐν τοῖς ἄνω χρόνοις καὶ ὕπατοι καὶ γερουσία καὶ στρατηγοὶ τὰ Ῥωμαίων ἦγον καὶ ἔφερον, εἶτα μονάρχης αὐτῶν ἐπελάβετο καὶ τὸ βασιλείας εἶδος ἐς τὸν ὄπισθεν χρόνον παρέπεμψε, καὶ τοῦτο τὸ σχῆμα τοῦ δήμου Ῥωμαίων καὶ τῶν αὐτοῖς ὑπηκόων ἐς

of what defines humanity by nature and were truly rational in the way they lived), the Romans advanced them over everybody else and deemed them worthy of the highest honors, admitting that the Greeks were superior to them in every way in terms of their language and wisdom, and, striving as much as possible and being eager, each outdid the other to practice this. So really it was the Greeks who led their Roman leaders rather than being led by them, and such was the configuration of their alliance.

In this manner, then, our city yielded to the Romans and 78
their empire, and as a result benefitted from their honor and care. In return, Trebizond not only maintained the proper degree of respect, faith, and allegiance to its rulers, but has constantly preserved these traits to this day under the rule of those whom it wished to have as its masters and whom it chose from the very beginning, not replacing them with anyone else and remaining loyal to them for this entire time. For although nearly one thousand five hundred years have passed since our city submitted to the Romans, and many things have arisen during this time and even more passed away (which someone once said was work befitting the long course of time), nevertheless, our city remains unshakeable and unchangeable, loving the masters whom it chose for itself and rendering them their due obedience. And yet the nature of the Roman regime has changed. In previous times, dictators, consuls, the senate, and generals led and directed the Roman state; afterward, a monarch took control and passed down to posterity the imperial regime. This form of government has been that preferred by the Roman people

τόδε προΐσταται, μεταβάσης τῆς βασιλείας ἐς τὸ Βυζάντιον καὶ τὴν ἑῴαν ἀπόμοιραν.

79 Ἡ ἡμετέρα δ᾽ ἐν πᾶσί τε τοῖς καιροῖς καὶ παντοίαις μεταβολαῖς ἡ αὐτὴ πρὸς αὐτοὺς μένει, τὸ Ῥωμαίοις ὑπείκειν προὔργου παντὸς εἶναι κρίνουσα καὶ μόνοις χρῆσθαι δεσπόταις αὐτοὺς ἀξιοῦσα, δυοῖν τε τοῦτο τοῖν καλλίστοιν ἐξάγουσα δεῖγμα τοῦ τε τῇ Ῥωμαίων ἡγεμονίᾳ μηδεμίαν ἑτέραν ἀξίαν εἶναι παραβεβλῆσθαι φιλανθρωπίας τε εἵνεκα καὶ ἡμερότητος. Οὐ γὰρ ἂν αὐτοῖς οὕτως εὐνόει τοῦ τε σφόδρα τε μέλειν αὐτῇ οἷς κρίνασα ὁμολογήσει καὶ ὑπακούσει ἀνδρείας τε περιεῖναι καὶ ῥώμης, ὑφ᾽ ὧν τοῖς μὲν ὡς ἀξίοις ὑπεῖκε, πολλῶν δ᾽ ἄλλων ἐθνῶν ἐπιόντων περιεγίγνετο, καὶ μάλιστα τῶν νῦν ἐπικρατούντων βαρβάρων, οἵ, τὰ κύκλῳ πάντα καταστρεψάμενοι καὶ περὶ τὴν ἡμετέραν κατῳκημένοι, πολλάκις μὲν ἐπέβαλον, τοσαυτάκις δὲ ἀπεκρούσθησαν, ὡς πέτρᾳ τινὶ προσρήξαντες ἢ ὡς κάλω ῥαγέντος ὑπανεχώρησαν.

80 Καὶ κατὰ μὲν τῶν ἄλλων ἴσχυσαν πάντων, μόνη δὲ ἡ ἡμετέρα κρείττων τε ὤφθη καὶ πᾶσιν ἀνάλωτος, καὶ τὰ μὲν περί που τὰ τῶν Ῥωμαίων βασίλεια καὶ ὅσα περὶ αὐτὸ τὸ Βυζάντιον ὡμολόγησαν τοῖς βαρβάροις καὶ τὴν δουλείαν ἐδέξαντο καὶ Ῥωμαίων οὐ πολὺν πεποίητο λόγον, ἡμεῖς δ᾽ ἐν ἐσχατιαῖς καὶ πρὸς αὐτοῖς τοῖς ὅροις καὶ πέρασι τῆς Ῥωμαίων ἀρχῆς ᾠκημένοι οὔτε τοὺς σφετέρους ἠρνήμεθα βασιλεῖς οὔθ᾽ ὑφ᾽ ἑτέρων, πολλὰ δυνηθέντων, ἡττήθημεν,

and their subjects to this day, even though the imperial capital moved to Byzantion and the eastern half of the empire.

Throughout all these circumstances and manifold changes, our city has maintained the same stance toward the Romans, judging obedience to them to be very beneficial and consenting to have them alone as its masters. For two most excellent reasons this provides an illustration as to why it was a good thing for our city to have given itself over to Roman rule rather than to any other: namely, Rome's benevolence and mildness. For without these our city would not thus otherwise be so obviously well-disposed to these Romans, whom it has judged, by its public declaration and its obedience, are superior in their manliness and strength, and for these reasons it has submitted to those whom it has thought worthy, but has stayed free from the many other peoples who have come against it, most especially the barbarians who have currently gained power. These people have destroyed all the surrounding lands and settled around our city. They have frequently attacked it, but just as frequently have been repelled and have retreated as though breaking apart on a rock or snapping like a cable. 79

Although the barbarians succeeded against everyone else, our city alone has proven superior and completely unconquerable. Even though the lands of the Roman empire and all the territory around Byzantion itself surrendered to them, accepted servitude, and did not show much concern for the Romans, we, by contrast, who live at the extremities, on the very borders and the outskirts of the Roman empire, neither rejected our own emperors, nor were we defeated by other rulers, even though they were very powerful. That is something which might well have happened, seeing as we 80

ὡς ἂν πόρρω τε ζῶντες Ῥωμαίων καὶ ἢ καθ᾽ αὑτοὺς ἄνευ τῆς ἐκείνων συμμαχίας ἀπειλημμένοι καὶ διὰ τοῦτο ὄντες εὐκαταγώνιστοι, ἢ τὴν ἐκείνων ἐξελόντες αἰδῶ τῆς ψυχῆς, ἀλλ᾽ ὡς ἂν πρὸς τοῖς αὐτῶν ὀφθαλμοῖς ἀγωνιζόμενοι, συνεπιρρωνύντων καὶ συμμαχούντων, οὕτω τήν τε πίστιν αὐτοῖς ἐτηρήσαμεν ἀκραιφνῆ καὶ τὴν εὔνοιαν ἀνδρείας τε μέγα σημεῖον ἐξενηνόχαμεν.

81 Οὓς γὰρ οὐκ Ἀσία, οὐ Συρία, οὐκ Αἴγυπτος ἀντιβλέψαι δεδύνητο καὶ ὑφ᾽ ὧν Παμφυλία καὶ Κιλικία καὶ Γαλατία δεδούλωτο καὶ οἷς τισι Καππαδοκία καὶ Ἀρμενία καὶ πᾶσα πόλις καὶ χώρα καὶ πᾶν γένος ἀνθρώπων ὑπεῖξαν, κατὰ μόνης οὗτοι τῆς ἡμετέρας οὐκ ἐνεανιεύσαντο πόλεως, οὐδ᾽ ἴσχυσαν καὶ ταύτην καταδουλώσασθαι, ἀλλὰ ταῦτα μὲν ἀφεῖλον Ῥωμαίων καὶ τούτοις τὴν ἐκείνων ἐμείωσαν δύναμιν (ἐῶ γὰρ εἰπεῖν ὡς καὶ τῶν Εὐρωπαίων ὑφ᾽ ἑαυτοὺς τὰ πλεῖστα πεποίηντο καὶ ὅσα νῦν οὐκ ἐν καιρῷ λέγειν), μόνης δὲ ταύτης τῆς ἡμετέρας ἡττήθησαν καὶ μόνην ἀνάλωτον ἔγνωσαν οὖσαν.

82 Οὕτω δυνάμεώς τε περιουσίᾳ καὶ πίστεως τὴν ἡμετέραν κατακοσμεῖ καὶ τῷ κεφαλαίῳ καλλωπιζόμεθα τῶν καλῶν, ἀληθείᾳ καὶ γενναιότητι. Τῶν τε γὰρ νυνὶ κρατούντων οὕτω περιεγένετο κἀν τοῖς ἀνωτέρω τούτων καιροῖς Πέρσαι τὸ κράτος ἔχοντες ἔτι πολλάκις μὲν ἐπειράθησαν, οὐδ᾽ ἅπαξ δὲ κατ᾽ αὐτῆς ἴσχυσαν. Τὴν γὰρ Κολχίδα καὶ Λαζικὴν γῆν, ἧς πάλαι τε προεῖχεν ἡ ἡμετέρα καὶ νῦν καθαρῶς ἄρχει, ὡς πάλαι τε σφῶν κατήκοος ἦν πεπυσμένοι καὶ ὡς μέγα σφίσι δουλωθεῖσαν αὖθις συντελέσειν τε καὶ συνδραμεῖσθαι πρὸς τὸ ῥᾳδίως ἐντεῦθεν τὴν Ῥωμαίων

live so far away from the Romans, so that either turning against them we would have been left without their aid, and consequently would have been easily conquered, or we might have lost our deep respect for them. Instead, as if we were right in front of their eyes, we have fought hard, helping and aiding them, and in this way we have maintained our loyalty and affection toward them unadulterated and have exhibited great proof of our courage.

Neither Asia, nor Syria, nor Egypt has been able to with- 81
stand the barbarians. Pamphylia, Cilicia, and Galatia have been enslaved by them. Cappadocia, Armenia, and every city, region, and race of men has yielded to them. Against our city alone have they failed to act with such insolence, nor were they strong enough to enslave it too. Though they seized those other places from the Romans and thereby diminished their strength (I will not relate, nor is it now an appropriate time to say, how they also subdued the greater part of Europe), they were defeated by our city alone, and recognized that it alone was impregnable.

In this way, our city is adorned with an abundance of 82
strength and loyalty, and we are embellished with those crowning virtues: sincerity and nobility. Just as Trebizond has overcome the barbarians who are now powerful, so in earlier times when the Persians still held power, although they made many attempts on the city, not even once did they prevail against it. For the Persians had heard that the lands of Kolchis, or Lazike, in which our city was preeminent in those times and which it now rightly rules, were once subject to them, and that this land's reenslavement would greatly facilitate and ease their endeavor to overrun and plunder the entire territory of the Romans. Indeed,

γῆν ἅπασαν καταδραμεῖν καὶ ληΐσασθαι, αὐτοί τε εἰδότες καὶ ἄλλων ἀκούοντες, οὐδὲ γὰρ οὐδ᾽ αὐτὸ Βυζάντιον ἐάσειν ἀπόρθητον, ἀλλὰ καὶ τοῦτο *αἱρήσειν, οὐδενὸς σφίσιν ἀντιστατοῦντος,* οὐδὲν ὅ τι μὴ κατ᾽ αὐτῆς ἐκίνησαν, καὶ σώμασι καὶ χρήμασι καὶ πλήθει στρατοῦ παρακινδυνεύοντες καὶ παραβαλλόμενοι ταῖς τε τῶν ὀρῶν δυσχωρίαις τοῖς τε στρατιώταις Ῥωμαίων, ἀπαντῶσιν ἐξ ὑπογυίου καὶ πειρωμένοις κωλύειν.

83 Ἐπὶ γοῦν Ἰουστίνου τοῦ πρώτου Ῥωμαίων βασιλεύοντος Καβάδης ὁ Περσῶν βασιλεὺς Ἴβηρσί τε καὶ Γουργένῃ τῷ βασιλεῖ τῶν Ἰβήρων ἐπιστρατεύσας μέχρι τε Λαζικῆς αὐτοὺς καταδιώκει φυγόντας καὶ δύο Λαζικῆς ἔσχεν οὐ πολλῷ πόνῳ φρούρια, πρὸς αὐτοῖς εἰσιόντι τοῖς Λαζικῆς τε καὶ Ἰβηρίας ὅροις δεδομημένα. Χοσρόης τε ὁ Καβάδου, τὰ Ῥωμαίων Ἰουστινιανοῦ διϊθύνοντος, ἠπείγετό τε προσωτέρω χωρεῖν καὶ σπουδὴν οὐ μικρὰν ἐποιεῖτο τὸ σύμπαν τε Λαζικῆς καὶ τὴν ἡμετέραν αὐτήν, εἰ οἷόν τε, καταδουλώσασθαι, ὡς τοῦτο ὂν αὐτῷ τῶν ἄθλων τὸ τελευταῖον καὶ τῆς ἀρχῆς ὁ ἔσχατος ὅρος, καὶ μεγάλῳ μὲν ἐσέβαλε πολλάκις στρατῷ, πλείω δὲ παθὼν ἢ δράσας, κακὸς κακῶς ἐκεῖθεν ἀπήλλαξεν. Οὐδὲ γὰρ οὐδὲν πλέον δυνηθεὶς ὅτι μὴ Πέτραν ἑλεῖν, φρούριόν τι νεόδμητον, Ἰουστινιανῷ τῷ βασιλεῖ δομηθέν, εἶτα μετὰ πολλῆς ἐκεῖθεν ἀπηλάθη ζημίας, πολλούς τε καὶ ἀγαθοὺς ἀποβαλόμενος τῶν Περσῶν, Ῥωμαίων τε καὶ τῶν ἡμετέρων ἀντικρουσάντων πατέρων καὶ τὴν σφοδρὰν αὐτῶν ῥύμην ἐπισχόντων σφοδρότερον. Ὥστ᾽ οὐχ ὅσον κακῶν ἀπαθὴς ἡ ἡμετέρα τετήρηται, οὐδ᾽ ἄχρι Ῥιζαίου καὶ Ἀθηνῶν αὐτῶν προελθεῖν τῶν Περσῶν

they themselves perceived and ascertained from others that they would not just be able to plunder Byzantion itself, but even *seize* it *without encountering any resistance.* Consequently, they made every possible attempt to seize it, endangering their bodies, resources, and a great number of troops as they exposed themselves to the difficult terrain of the mountains and to the Roman soldiers, who would suddenly attack and try to stop them.

Under the Roman emperor Justin I, the Persian king Ka- 83
vadh campaigned against the Georgians and Gourgenes, the king of the Georgians. He pursued them as far as Lazike as they fled and without much effort took two fortresses in Lazike, which had been built along the very borders of Lazike and Iberia as you enter them. When Justinian was governing the Romans, Khosrow, Kavadh's son, strove to advance farther and made a great effort to enslave all of Lazike and our city itself, if possible, as this would be his ultimate trophy and the farthest boundary of his domain. He attacked us many times with a great army, but suffered more than he accomplished, and that bad man came to a bad end there. Indeed, he was unable to take anything more than Petra, a small fortress recently built by the emperor Justinian. Later, he was driven from there with heavy losses and threw away the lives of many good Persians, as the Romans and our forefathers repelled their vehement assault with an even more vehement response. Consequently, our city remained unharmed by them, as the Persians had not even been able to advance as far as Rizaion and Athenai; nor for that matter

δυνηθέντων, ἀλλ᾽ οὐδ᾽ ἐπ᾽ ἐξουσίας αὐτοῖς πρὸς τὰ οἰκεῖα καὶ γῆν τὴν σφετέραν ἐπανελθεῖν συνεχώρησεν, ἐν κομιδῇ μὲν στενοῖς καὶ δυσόδοις ἀπειλημμένοις χωρίοις, ἀξίαν δὲ δοῦσι δίκην Ῥωμαίοις ὧν πεπαρῳνήκεσαν εἰς αὐτούς, τῆς σφίσι μὴ προσηκούσης ἐπιβατεύοντες γῆς καὶ ἀλλοτρίαν ἐπικτώμενοι δύναμιν.

84 Οὕτως αὐτῇ τῶν τε ἐναντίων εἵμαρτο περιγίνεσθαι καὶ μετὰ πολλοῦ τοῦ κρείττονος ἀπαλλάττειν, κρείττονι γινομένῃ τῶν πάντοθεν κατ᾽ αὐτῆς ἐπιόντων. Αὐτή τε γὰρ καθ᾽ αὑτὴν ἄμαχος ἦν καὶ ἀήττητος οἷς ἠγωνίζετο, μηδενὸς συμμαχοῦντος, τῷ τ᾽ ἐκ Βυζαντίου καὶ Ῥωμαίων στρατῷ κατὰ Περσῶν ἐνοχλούντων αὐτοῖς συμμαχοῦσα τοὺς μείζους τῶν ἀγώνων καὶ κρείττους οἰκεῖον ἑαυτῇ ἆθλον πεποίητο, ἡγουμένη τε καὶ παραδεικνῦσα καὶ τρόπους πολέμων καὶ τόπων εἰσόδους καὶ διόδους δυσχωριῶν, ὧν ἀκριβέστερον αὐτὴ πάντων πεπείρατο, ὡς ἂν τοῖς τε βαρβάροις ὅμορος οὖσα καὶ τὸν πρὸς αὐτοὺς πόλεμον πάλαι γεγυμνασμένη.

85 Ὥσθ᾽ ὧν αὐτή τε κατώρθου καὶ Ῥωμαῖοι ἐνίκων τὴν αἰτίαν αὕτη μόνη δικαίως ἂν ἀποφέροιτο, καὶ τοῖς ἐντεῦθεν κοσμοῖτο στεφάνοις, οὐχ ὅτι μόνον ἦρχε παντὸς ἀγαθοῦ καὶ παρεδείκνυ Ῥωμαίοις ἅπερ οὐκ ἦσαν εἰδότες αὐτοί, ἀλλ᾽ ὅτι κἀνταῦθα τοὺς ἁπανταχόθεν ὑποδεχομένη στρατιώτας Ῥωμαίων καὶ πολλὰ ταῖς ὁδοιπορίαις ταλαιπωρήσαντας ἀναπαύουσα τῶν τε ἐπιτηδείων μεταδιδοῦσα καὶ τῶν ἀναγκαίων ἁπάντων, ἀκμῆτας αὐτοὺς ἐντεῦθεν, ὡς ἔκ τινος ὁρμητηρίου καὶ ἐπιτειχίσματος ἐπιθέσθαι τε τοῖς ἐχθροῖς ἐδίδου καὶ τὰ πλείω νικᾶν. Ἐδύνατο γὰρ δὴ τοῦτο

could they even manage to return home to their own lands, for when they were on their way through the narrow, impassable, and deserted terrain, the Romans made them pay a fitting price for their wanton actions, trespassing upon a land that did not belong to them and seeking to extend their rule over someone else's territory.

Trebizond was thus fated to overcome its opponents and emerge much the stronger, becoming stronger than those who attacked it on all sides. On its own, the city was impregnable and invincible against those whom it fought, even when it had no allies. But when it was in alliance with the Roman army from Byzantion against the Persians who were harassing them, it won proper renown for itself in the more major and critical engagements. For it led the way, and showed the Romans various techniques of warfare, ways of gaining access to places, and passages through difficult country, since it had more experience than anyone else in all these matters, because it shared its borders with the barbarians and had long practice in warfare with them. 84

Consequently, our city alone should rightly receive credit for its own successes as well as for the Romans' victories, and should be adorned with the crown of victory for them, not only because it made everything go well and showed the Romans what they did not know themselves, but also because it harbored the Roman soldiers who came here from all around and offered them a respite when they were exhausted from their marches. It shared its supplies and all the necessities with them, and, when they were thus reinvigorated, it allowed them to attack the enemy and win the majority of their engagements, as if the city were a forward command post or frontier fortress. Our city, alone among all 85

μόνη τῶν ἄλλων ἡ ἡμετέρα, καὶ δυναμένη παντὸς μᾶλλον ἐβούλετο, τῶν ἄλλων τῶν μὲν ᾠκημένων ὡς πορρωτάτω Περσῶν, ὥστ᾽ οὐδὲν ἧττω τὸν πόνον εἶναι τῷ Ῥωμαίων στρατῷ, μέχρις αὐτῶν ἰοῦσι τῶν πολεμίων προκατειργασμένοις τε τὰ σώματα καὶ τὴν δύναμιν εὐχειρώτοις διὰ ταῦτα καθισταμένοις, τῶν δ᾽ ἐγγὺς μὲν κειμένων, τὰ ἴσα δ᾽ οὐ δυναμένων οὔτε μεγέθει καὶ κατασκευῇ πόλεως οὔτ᾽ ἀφθονίᾳ τῶν ἐπιτηδείων καὶ ὅσων ἄνθρωποι χρῄζουσιν, ἐπ᾽ ἀλλοτρίας οὐ διϊόντες μόνον, ἀλλὰ καὶ διατρίβοντες.

86 Εἰ δὴ κατορθοῦν μὲν οὐ μικρὸν οὐ μεῖζον ἔνι τῶν πολεμικῶν, μὴ πρότερον εὖ παρεσκευασμένους τὰ πάντα, πρὸς δὲ τὸ παρεσκευάσθαι καλῶς ἡ πόλις ἡμῖν οὐκ ὀλίγον Ῥωμαίοις παρ᾽ ἑκάστους συνεβάλλετο τοὺς καιρούς, πῶς οὐχὶ καὶ τῶν ἐκείνοις κατορθωθέντων προσήκοι τῇ Τραπεζοῦντι καὶ διχῇ πλέκοιτο ταύτῃ τῶν ἐπαίνων ὁ στέφανος οἷς τε καθ᾽ αὑτὴν διεγίνετο πάντων κρατοῦσα καὶ οἷς ἄλλοις ἐδίδου τὰς ἀφορμὰς τοῦ νικᾶν; Καὶ μήν, εἰ μὲν ἐν μέσῃ τῇ Ῥωμαίων ἀρχῇ κείμενοι κύκλῳ τε πόλεσι σφῶν ὑπηκόοις περιειλημμένοι, περιῆμέν τε τῶν ἐχθρῶν καὶ τοῖς ἐξ ἀρχῆς δεσπόταις τὴν εὔνοιαν καθαρὰν ἐτηροῦμεν, οὔτ᾽ ἂν ἡμῖν ἐπαίνων μεγάλων προσήκειν ἔφη τις ἄν, οὔθ᾽ ὡς ἐπὶ μεγάλῳ τινὶ κατορθώματι δικαίως ἂν ἐφρονοῦμεν. Τῶν τε γὰρ κύκλῳ συνεχόντων ἡμᾶς ἦν ἂν τὸ ἆθλον, *ἐν προβόλου* τε *μοίρᾳ* καθεστώτων ἡμῖν καὶ τοὺς ἐπιόντας γενναίως ἀποκρουομένων, ἡμῖν τ᾽ ἂν οὐδὲ πολλὰ βουλομένοις εἶχε καλῶς ἀφίστασθαι, μὴ ἔχουσι δίοδον· νῦν δ᾽ ἐπ᾽ αὐτοῖς ἤδη σχεδὸν τοῖς ὅροις Περσῶν καὶ Ῥωμαίων λαχόντες τὴν οἴκησιν αὐτοί τε προβεβλημένοι τῆς

others, could do this and, beyond merely being able to, actually wanted to do this. As for the other cities, some were so far away from the Persians that they were not worth the effort for the Roman army, since by the time they reached enemy lines from them they would already have been physically exhausted and thus easily defeated. Those that lay closer did not have comparable resources, such as the size and construction of the city, the abundance of supplies, and whatever else people need when they are not just passing through foreign lands but are actually staying there.

If, then, it is impossible to achieve either a minor or ma- 86
jor military success without everything being well prepared beforehand, and if our city greatly helped the Romans to be adequately prepared on every occasion, how could some part of their successes not be attributed to Trebizond? And should not the garland of its praise be woven from two strands, namely the victories that it continued to win on its own over everyone else and those which it allowed others to win by providing the resources? For if we had overcome our enemies and kept our loyalty untarnished to those who had been our masters from the start, when we were situated in the midst of the Roman empire and were surrounded by cities subject to them, no one would say that we deserved great praise, nor would we justly deem it a great success. In that case the prize would belong to all the people surrounding us, for they would have served *as a shield* for us and nobly repelled our assailants and we could not have really distinguished ourselves, even if we wanted to, because we would not have had the means. As matters stand, however, although we already lived virtually on the very border between the Persians and Romans and extended beyond the whole

Ῥωμαίων γῆς ὅλης, οὔτε πολλῶν καὶ πολλάκις ἐπιόντων ἡττήθημεν, ἀλλ' ὑφιστάμεθά τε τὰς προσβολὰς γενναιότατα, οὐ μόνον οὐδὲν ἄχαρι πάσχοντες, ἀλλὰ καὶ προσεργαζόμενοι τοὺς ἐχθρούς, εἰς ἀφρόν τε καὶ τὸ μηδὲν διαλυομένους ὡς κύματα *πέτραις προβλῆσι* προσράξαντα, οὔτε ῥᾴδιον ὂν βουλομένοις καὶ τοὺς ἀσμένως ἂν ἡμᾶς δεξομένους ἐπὶ ἴσῃ τε καὶ ὁμοίᾳ ἔχουσιν ἐγγυτάτω πρὸς ἀποστασίαν ἀπείδομεν ἢ γοῦν ἐννοῆσαί ποτ' ἐπῆλθε τοῖς πατράσιν ἡμῶν.

87 Καίτοι, εἰ πίστις ἐστὶν ἄνθρωπος καὶ ἀλήθεια καὶ τὸ τοῖς ἐξ ἀρχῆς δεδογμένοις ἐμμένειν καὶ τὰ ὀμωμοσμένα τηρεῖν, οὕτως ἐπὶ πλεῖστον τῆς ἀνθρώπῳ προσηκούσης ἀρετῆς οἱ ἡμέτεροι προκεχωρήκεσαν πρόγονοι, εἴτε καὶ ἀνδρεία τὰ γένη κοσμεῖ καὶ γενναιότης προσήκει ψυχαῖς ἀνθρωπίναις, οὕτω καὶ ταύτῃ τὸ συγκεχωρηκὸς εἶχον καὶ τὴν ἐντεῦθεν νίκην ἀναμφίβολον ἑαυτοῖς κατεστήσαντο. Πρὸς γὰρ δὴ τῷ ταῦτα δυνηθῆναι κατορθῶσαι, ἃ τοὺς ἐν μέσοις Ῥωμαίοις ἐχρῆν, ἔτι καὶ μεῖζον ἐκείνων δεδύνηνται, μείναντες αὐτῶν ἀπαθέστεροι καὶ πιστότεροι. Τἆλλα μὲν γὰρ ἅπαντα περιεῖλον οἱ βάρβαροι καὶ τοὺς Ῥωμαίους ἀφείλοντο, τὰ μὲν ἐξαιροῦντες νόμῳ πολέμου, τοὺς δ' αὐτοὺς προσθεμένους καὶ σφᾶς ἐνδόντας δουλώσαντες, μόνη δὲ ἡ ἡμετέρα ἐπεδίδου τε μᾶλλον καὶ ηὔξανε καὶ τὸ καθ' αὑτὴν ἀμείωτον ἐτήρει τὴν Ῥωμαίων ἡγεμονίαν, οὔτε πολέμου νόμῳ τῶν ἐχθρῶν ἡττηθεῖσα, οὔτε τῶν ἐξ ἀρχῆς ἀγαθῶν λογισμῶν καταγνοῦσα καὶ πρὸς τοὺς ἐναντίους ὥσπερ αὐτομολήσασα, ἀλλὰ μένουσα μὲν ἐφ' οἷς ἅπαξ ἔγνω μενετέον αὐτήν, ταῖς δὲ κατὰ μικρὸν αὐξομένη

Roman land, we were not defeated by our many, frequent assailants, but most nobly withstood their assaults. We not only suffered nothing untoward at the hands of our enemies, but even caused them to dissolve into foam and oblivion, like waves breaking *on rocks jutting out into the sea.* Nor did we ever consider rebelling, even though it would have been easy for us to do so, had we wanted to, and we had neighbors who would have warmly welcomed us as equals. The thought did not even occur to our forefathers.

Furthermore, if loyalty, sincerity, holding fast to one's original convictions, and abiding by oaths are what defines a human being, then our forefathers attained the highest possible degree of the virtue that defines humans. Or, if it is manliness that adorns races and nobility that befits human souls, then this also should be conceded to them and an unequivocal victory granted to them in this respect. For besides being capable of accomplishments that were fitting for people who lived amidst Romans, they actually proved themselves more capable than them by remaining less troubled and more steadfast than them. While the barbarians seized everything else and despoiled the Romans, destroying everything that they seized by right of conquest and enslaving those who joined them and surrendered themselves to them, our city alone grew, thrived, and maintained Roman hegemony undiminished over itself, neither being overcome by its enemies by right of war, nor repudiating the good principles it had held from the beginning and going over to its opponents, as if it were a deserter. Instead, it abided by the principles by which it had decided once and for all that it must abide, and little by little the city enlarged 87

προσθήκαις ἀνθρώπων τε πλήθει τῶν τε ἐκεῖ γεννωμένων τῶν τε ἄλλοθεν ἐπιγινομένων, οὓς πολλοὺς εἶναι ἀνάγκη, πολιορκουμένους μὲν πάντοθεν, εἰς αὐτὴν δ᾽ ὡς εἰς ἀσφαλὲς κρησφύγετον καταφεύγοντας καὶ ἄλλως εὑρόντας τῶν αὐτῆς ἀγαθῶν καὶ οἷς τὸ ἐνοικοῦν τρέφει καὶ ἀναψύχει τεχνῶν τε καὶ ἐπιτηδευμάτων ἀσκήσει παντοίων, ὅσαι τε τῶν βαναύσων καὶ ὅσαι τῶν ἐλευθερίων ἀνδρῶν καὶ ψυχῶν, οὐ πρὸς χρείαν συντελοῦσαι μόνον ἀνθρώποις καὶ αὐτὸ τὸ συνίστασθαι, ἀλλὰ καὶ τὸν μετιόντα κοσμοῦσαι καὶ ἦθος καὶ ἀγωγὴν καὶ πολιτείας βελτίωσιν, ἔτι τε τειχῶν παραυξήσει καὶ περιβολῇ μειζόνων μὲν ἢ τῶν πρίν, ἐχυρότητος δ᾽ εἵνεκα καὶ πολὺ προεχόντων.

88 Ἀπῆν γὰρ ὅλως οὐδὲν ἢ μᾶλλον ἦν οὐδὲ ἕν, ὃ μὴ τὸ μὲν ἤδη παρὸν ἦν αὐτῇ τῶν καλῶν, τὸ δ᾽ ἔμελλε. Τὸ γὰρ πεπρωμένον αὐτῇ καὶ ἡ μοῖρα συνεφόρει πᾶν ἀγαθόν, τὰ μὲν ἤδη καὶ προδεικνῦσα, πρὸς ἃ δ᾽ αὐτὴν εὐτρεπίζουσα ὅσα μήπω παρεῖναι τὸ τοῦ χρόνου συνεχώρει φερόμενον καὶ ἡ τοῦ μέλλοντος μέλησις. Καὶ γοῦν πολλὰ τῶν ἐν τῷ μέλλοντι ταττομένων καὶ ἃ ἂν οὐδεὶς ἤλπισε παρήγαγέ τε καὶ ὡς ἂν οὐδεὶς οὐδ᾽ ἂν ηὔξατο οὐχ ὅτι μὴ προσῆκεν αὐτῇ μηδὲ τὰ προσόντα οἱ κἀκεῖνα ἠνάγκαζον, ἀκόλουθά τε ὄντα καὶ οἷς φθάσασα ἔσχεν ἑπόμενά τε καὶ σύμφωνα, ἀλλ᾽ ὅτι, πάντων ἤδη σχεδὸν ἀπολωλότων τῶν τῇδε Ῥωμαίων, ταύτην οὐχ ὅσον περιγενέσθαι (ἀγαπητὸν ὂν καὶ τοῦτο καὶ οὐκ ἂν ἐλαχίστης εὐδαιμονίας τεκμήριον), ἀλλὰ κἀπὶ

its population and filled up, both with the people who were born there and those who migrated there from elsewhere. Inevitably there were many of the latter, who, besieged on all sides, sought refuge in our city as a safe haven and who in other ways discovered the good things with which it nourishes its inhabitants and refreshes its children by the practice of all manner of crafts and occupations, both those which pertain to common artisans and to free men. These not only provide for men's needs and their very existence, but also adorn the pursuit of morality, education, and the improvement of their state. And, even though this growth in population meant expanding the city's walls and enclosing a larger space than before, these still possessed very great strength.

The city lacked no good thing at all; or rather, there was 88
not one that it did not already have or that it would not have in the future. Destiny and fate were conferring all their blessings on it. Some they had already manifested, but there were others that they still had in store, which, though they had not yet come to pass, would come with the course of time and through the future's concern for us. Indeed, the future held many things in store for our city, which no one could have expected, and yet destiny and fate did produce them in a way for which no one could even have prayed. This is not because what the future held did not befit the city or because its previous situation made these things necessary. Rather, they were the logical consequences of, and conformed entirely to, what the city had already accomplished. This is because, when nearly all the cities of the Romans in these parts had fallen, ours not only survived (which in itself would have been admirable enough and proof of its signifi-

τοσοῦτον ἀρθῆναι καὶ δόξης καὶ εὐτυχίας οὐδ᾽ ἐλπίσαι γοῦν εἶχεν ἀσφάλειαν· ἀλλ᾽ ἡ συνέχουσ᾽ αὐτὴν ἄνωθεν ἀγαθὴ τύχη τοῖς τε ἄλλοις κεκόσμηκέ τε καὶ τιμῶσα διατελεῖ τῶν τε ἐς δόξαν φερόντων τὸ μέγιστον ἐπέθηκε φέρουσα, καὶ βασιλείας αὐτῇ περιθεμένη διάδημα καὶ ἀξίωμα, βασίλειον αὐτὴν ἡμῖν ὡς πάλαι τοῖς πράγμασι καὶ οἷς διετέλει ποιοῦσα, οὕτω νῦν καὶ τῇ κλήσει παρασκευάσασα λέγεσθαι.

89 Ἔδει γὰρ δὴ τὴν τοσοῦτο πίστει καὶ δυνάμει διενεγκοῦσαν, ὡς μήτε βιασθεῖσαν μήτ᾽ ἐθελοκακήσασαν προσθέσθαι τοῖς ἐναντίοις, αὑτήν θ᾽ ἑαυτὴν καὶ τὰς ἄλλας τὸ καθ᾽ αὐτὴν Ῥωμαίοις φυλάξασαν μὴ τῆς ἀρχῆς μόνον τοῖς βασιλεῦσιν ἡμῖν ὑπερασπιστήν τε καὶ πρόβολον, ἀλλὰ καὶ αὐτοῦ σώματος αὐτοῖς γεγονέναι, ἐν σωματοφυλάκων καθεστῶσαν αὐτοῖς μοίρᾳ. Εἴτε γὰρ εὐνοοῦσιν ἀνδράσι σφᾶς αὐτοὺς θαρρεῖν δεῖ τοὺς ἄρχοντας, οὕτω θαυμαστὰ πίστεως ἐν παντὶ τῷ χρόνῳ ἐξήνεγκε δείγματα, εἴτ᾽ ἀνδρείᾳ καὶ ῥώμῃ σωμάτων οὕτω διήνεγκε γενναιότητι, εἴτ᾽ ἀμφοῖν, καὶ δυνάμει καὶ πίστει, οὐκ οἶδ᾽ εἴ τις ἐς ἴσον ἔλθοι τῇ ἡμετέρᾳ.

90 Βασίλειά τε γοῦν ἐν αὐτῇ λαμπρῶς ᾠκοδόμηται, καὶ κρατεῖν ἀντὶ τοῦ δουλεύειν ᾑρέθη, καὶ βασιλέων διαδοχαὶ τῶν πάντα γενναίων ἡμᾶς κεκοσμήκασιν, αὐτοῦ τε τὸν πάντα χρόνον διατριβόντων ἐντεῦθέν τε κατὰ τῶν ἐχθρῶν ἐξιόντων καὶ ὡς ἡμᾶς αὖθις ἐπανιόντων, κἀντεῦθεν ἀρχόντων τῶν ὑπὸ χεῖρα καὶ βασιλέων οὐχ οἷς ἄν τις καὶ προστρίψαιτο μῶμον, οὐδὲ τῶν πάντα φιλοσκωμμόνων. Κομνηνιάδαι γὰρ ἡμῖν οἱ δεσπόται καὶ βασιλεῖς καὶ τῆς

cant prosperity), but even attained more glory and prosperity than one could safely have hoped for. However, the continuing good fortune from on high, which had adorned the city in other respects and honored it continually with everything that brings glory, also bestowed on it the greatest honor of all by crowning it with an imperial crown and rank. Previously, it had constantly bestowed imperial qualities on our city in terms of its deeds and accomplishments, but now it prepared it to receive the actual title itself.

For a city which had been so distinguished by its loyalty 89
and strength, so that it had not succumbed to force nor chosen to join Rome's enemies, but had preserved both itself and other cities for the Romans, necessarily had to become a defender and bulwark not only of the realm of our emperors, but also of their very bodies, taking on the role of bodyguard. For if rulers should entrust themselves to loyal men, our city has thus provided amazing examples of its loyalty throughout time, or if, rather, they should entrust themselves to manliness and physical strength, our city has thus been outstanding in its bravery, or if, again, to some combination of both strength and loyalty, I do not know of any city that could rival our own.

In any case, an imperial palace was lavishly built in the 90
city, and it was chosen to rule rather than serve. A succession of most noble emperors has adorned us. It is here that they make their permanent residence, marching out from here against our enemies and then returning to us again, and it is from here that they rule their subjects. And no one could possibly cast any blame on these emperors, not even those who delight most in making fun of other people. Our masters and emperors are the sons of the Komnenoi, the

τῶν Κομνηνῶν ῥίζης κάλλιστον ἔρνος, καὶ πρέμνος μάλα προσήκων τῇ ῥίζῃ καὶ οἷος ἂν γένοιτο πάνυ τοι συμβαίνων τῷ φύσαντι, οὐκ ἀπὸ γένους μᾶλλον ἢ τοῦ τρόπου τῆς ἀρχῆς ἄξιοι καὶ τοῦ τῆς βασιλείας ὀνόματος. Τό τε γὰρ γένος αὐτοῖς καὶ σφόδρα τῷ τῆς ἀρχῆς ὄγκῳ συνᾷδον, ἥ τε ἀρετὴ καὶ τῶν πράξεων ἡ λαμπρότης οὐδέσι προσῆκεν ὅτι μὴ βασιλεῦσι καὶ δεσπόταις ἀνθρώπων, ὥστ᾽ εἶναι καὶ τὸν τρόπον αὐτοῖς οἷον θαυμάζεσθαι, τό τε γένος οὐκ ὀλίγα κοσμεῖν ἔχειν αὐτούς τε καὶ τοὺς σφίσι δουλεύοντας, ὑφ᾽ ὧν τῆς τε βασιλείας ἐκρίθησαν ἄξιοι καὶ τῷ δήμῳ Ῥωμαίων ἀσμένῳ τε ἀνερρήθησαν, καὶ κριθέντες οὐκ ἔψευσαν τῶν ἐλπίδων τοὺς ἑλομένους, οὔτε μετάμελον παρέσχον αὐτῆς τῆς αἱρέσεως.

91 Ἄνδρες γὰρ οὗτοι καὶ πρὸ τῆς βασιλείας τὰ βασιλείας πράττοντες ἄξια, καὶ μήπω τὸ διάδημα περικείμενοι τῶν ἐν τηβέννῃ τε καὶ πορφύρᾳ περιειλημμένων οὐδὲν διαφέροντες ὅσα γ᾽ ἐς τὴν τῶν κοινῶν φροντίδα καὶ ἐπιμέλειαν καὶ στρατιωτικὴν ἐμπειρίαν καὶ πολέμους καὶ ἆθλα καὶ ἀγωνίσματα, μᾶλλον δ᾽ αὐτοὶ ταῦτα διαχειριζόμενοι πάντα, καθευδόντων τῶν βασιλέων καὶ βαθὺν ὕπνον ὑπνούντων, καὶ τοὺς μὲν πόνους οἰκείους αὐτῶν, τὰ δ᾽ ἆθλα τῶν βασιλέων ποιούμενοι, τόν τε δῆμον τῆς ἑαυτῶν ἀνῆψαν ἀγάπης, συνιέντας ὅστις ὁ ἀληθής ἐστι βασιλεὺς καὶ ὅτῳ προσήκει τὰ ἆθλα σφῶν τε αὐτῶν, αὐτοὺς δικαιοῦντας βασιλεύειν τε καὶ προΐστασθαι ὡς μόνους ἀξίους, αὐτοί τε ὑπέρ τε τοῦ γένους καὶ ὅπως μὴ παντελῶς ἀπόλωνται Ῥωμαίοις τὰ πράγματα τὴν ἡγεμονίαν ἐδέξαντο.

finest offshoot of the Komnenos root. They are a stem that springs directly from its root and is of the sort that corresponds completely to its progenitor, being worthy of the title of emperor not so much because of their lineage, but the manner of their rule. For their family is exceedingly well suited to the burden of rule, while their virtue and the brilliance of their actions befit no one but emperors and masters of men. Consequently, their manner of rule is something to be admired and their family has many ways in which to adorn itself and those who serve it. They were thus deemed worthy of imperial rank by them and were gladly proclaimed emperor by the Roman people and, once deemed worthy to rule, they did not betray the hopes of the people who chose them, nor give them any cause to regret their choice.

Even before these men came to the imperial throne, they 91
had performed deeds worthy of the imperial office. Even before they wore a diadem, they were not all that different from those who wore the purple toga in terms of their concern and care for public affairs as well as their military experience in wars, trophies, and contests. Rather, it was they who handled all of this while the emperors slumbered and lay fast asleep. By taking up these labors as their own, but pretending the trophies belonged to the emperors, they inflamed the people with love for them. The people understood who the real emperor was and who had really earned those trophies, and so they thought that it was right for the Komnenoi to become emperors and claim first rank as the only ones who were worthy to lead. For the sake of our people, and so that the Roman empire might not be totally lost, they accepted power.

92 Ἤδη γὰρ ἐπὶ γόνυ τε ἔκλιναν καὶ παντελῶς ἐκεκμήκει τὰ τῆς εὐτυχίας τῷ γένει καὶ ὑπορρεῖν ἤρξατο καὶ ἐνδιδόναι τῷ χρόνῳ καὶ ταῖς ἐκεῖθεν μεταβολαῖς, τῶν μὲν βασιλέων κατερρᾳστωνευμένον βίον βιούντων, τῶν δ' ἐναντίων ἀγωνιζομένων καὶ ἀγρυπνούντων. Ἀσίαν τε γὰρ κατέτρεχον οἱ βάρβαροι πᾶσαν καὶ τὰ ταύτης ἀδεῶς περιέκειρον κάλλη, μηδενὸς ἐμποδὼν ἱσταμένου, καὶ τὴν Σκυθῶν ἐρημίαν τὰ τῇδε πάντα πεποίηντο, οὐδαμοῦ τὴν οἰκείαν πλεονεξίαν ὁρίζοντες, ἀλλ' ἑξῆς πάντα καταστρεφόμενοι μέχρις αὐτῆς Χαλκηδόνος καὶ τῆς ἀντιπέρας ἠπείρου τῇ Βυζαντίδι, πρὶν ἐπ' αὐτὴν καταβῆναι τὴν θάλασσαν τῆς ἐπὶ τὰ πρόσω φορᾶς οὐκ ἀνακοπτόμενοι. Ἐκ μὲν γὰρ Αἰγύπτου Σαρακηνοί, Τοῦρκοι δ' ἐξ αὐτῆς τῆς Περσίδος ὁρμώμενοι καὶ τῶν ἔτι κατωτέρω μερῶν, οἱ μὲν Συρίαν καὶ Παλαιστίνην καὶ Παμφυλίαν, οἱ δὲ τὰ μεταξὺ πάντα μέχρις αὐτῆς Βιθυνίας ἐρημίᾳ τῇ τοῦ κωλύσοντος ὑποχείρια σφίσι καὶ δοῦλα πεποίηντο, ὡς καὶ αὐτὸν τὸν βασιλέα Ῥωμαίων ἀπαγαγεῖν δοριάλωτον Ῥωμανὸν τὸν καὶ Διογένην ἐπικληθέντα, τήν τε Εὐρώπην καὶ τὰ πρὸς ἥλιον δύνοντα πάντα λόγῳ μὲν εἶχον Ῥωμαῖοι, ἔργῳ δ' ἐκαρποῦντο Σκύθαι καὶ Οὖννοι καὶ Πατζινάκων τινῶν ἔθνος καὶ οὐκ οἶδ' εἴ τινες ἄλλοι, πάντοθεν ἐπιόντες καὶ Μυσῶν λείαν πάντα τιθέμενοι.

93 Ῥωμαῖοι δὲ καὶ Ῥωμαίων οἱ βασιλεῖς μέχρι τοῦ περιβαλέσθαι πορφύραν καὶ τὸ διάδημα ἀναδήσασθαι τῶν τε οἰκείων ἀπολαύειν ὀρέξεων τὴν βασιλείαν ὁρίζοντες, τά τε χρήματα οὐκ εἰς δέον ἀνηλωκότες ἐν στενῷ κομιδῇ τὰ ταμιεῖα σφίσι συνήλασαν, ὧν πολλῶν δεῖ πολέμῳ καὶ τοῖς

By now, the empire was already on its knees and our people's good fortune had been entirely exhausted and was starting to slip away, yielding to time and the changes that it wrought, because the emperors lived a life of luxury, while their enemies fought hard and remained vigilant. The barbarians overran all of Asia and ravaged its beauties fearlessly with no one standing in their way. They turned everything there into a proverbial Scythian wilderness, and their innate avarice knew no bounds. They destroyed everything in succession as far as Chalcedon itself and the land opposite Byzantion, and they did not halt their forward advance until they had reached the sea. With no one to hinder them, the Saracens who came from Egypt subjected and enslaved Syria, Palestine, and Pamphylia, while the Turks who came from Persia itself and regions even further distant did the same to everything in between, as far as Bithynia itself. They even took captive the emperor of the Romans himself, Romanos Diogenes. While in name the Romans possessed Europe and everything in the west, in reality the Scythians, the Huns, a tribe of Pechenegs, and I don't know who else, had free rein over it, attacking it from all sides and making of it the proverbial Mysian loot. 92

The Romans and their emperors had reduced the position of emperor to simply wearing the purple, putting on the diadem, and indulging their personal appetites. They had spent their funds inappropriately and left the treasury in dire straits, when a sizeable proportion of those funds should have been allotted for war and the military. Their 93

πολεμικοῖς πράγμασι. Τά τε τοῦ στρατοῦ καὶ λίαν αὐτοῖς εἶχε κακῶς, οὐδεμιᾶς ἀξιομάχου στρατιᾶς εὐποροῦσιν, οὔτε πλήθει νικώντων, οὔτε προυχόντων ἀσκήσει. Εἴς τε γὰρ εὐαριθμήτους αὐτοῖς ὁ στρατὸς συνηλάθη, ἀσκήσεώς τε ἕνεκα καὶ τῆς κατὰ πόλεμον ἐμπειρίας οὐδὲν αὐτοὺς γηπόνων ἀνδρῶν διαφέρειν ἡ τῶν βασιλέων τρυφὴ καὶ ῥᾳστώνη καὶ ὁ ἀνειμένος εἰργάσατο βίος. Ἐλπίς τε οὖν ἀγαθῶν ἦν οὐδεμία τῷ γένει, ἀλλὰ τόν τε περὶ ψυχῆς ἔτρεχον ἤδη κἀπὶ ξυροῦ σφίσιν εἱστήκει τὰ πράγματα καὶ ἔδει *καθῆσθαι, τὸν τελευταῖον ἀναμένοντας ὄλεθρον.*

94 Ἀλλὰ Θεός, ἄνωθεν ὑπερσχὼν χεῖρα καὶ λαβόμενος οἶκτον ἡμῶν, τούς τε Κομνηνιάδας ἡμῖν ἐβασίλευσε καὶ δι᾽ αὐτῶν ἐπανήγαγεν αὖθις τῷ γένει τὴν εὐτυχίαν καὶ τὴν ἧτταν ἀνεμαχήσατο καὶ τὰ ἀπολωλότα πάλιν ἐπανεσώσατο, τότε μὲν εὐθὺς Ἀλέξιον προβαλόμενος τὸν πάντ᾽ ἄριστον καὶ γενναῖον, ἆθλον ἀρετῆς καὶ ὧν στρατηγῶν κατωρθώκει τὴν βασιλείαν εὑράμενον, ἔπειτα δὲ τὴν ἐξ ἐκείνου *χρυσῆν* ὄντως *σειρὰν* ἐπιστήσας Ῥωμαίοις. Οἵ, τοῦτο δὴ τὸ τοῦ Δημοσθένους καλῶς εἰρῆσθαι νομίσαντες, πάντα δεῖν ἄνδρα καὶ πᾶσαν πόλιν τὴν αἰτίαν εὑρόντας ὅθεν ἥττους ἑαυτῶν ἐγεγόνεισαν, εἶτα βαδίσαι τὴν ἐναντίαν ὡς οὕτως ἐπανακαλεσομένους τὴν ἧτταν, σκεψάμενοί τε τοὺς πρὸ αὐτῶν βασιλεύσαντας ἀντὶ τρυφῆς καὶ βλακείας ὀλίγης τὰ πάντα διειργασμένους, αὐτοὶ βίον ἐργατικὸν καὶ πιναρὸν ἀνελάβοντο, λάβοντο καὶ σκηνήτην, ὀλίγα μὲν ἐν ταῖς πόλεσι, τὰ πλεῖστα δ᾽ ἐπὶ στρατοπέδου καθεύδοντες, καὶ τὸν πάντα βίον ἐπὶ πολέμου καὶ παρατάξεων διατετριφότες, ἐναγώνιόν τε ζωὴν ἔζησαν καὶ τὴν πολιτείαν

army was in an even more wretched condition and they had no battle-worthy troops at their disposal, lacking a host of superior soldiers and trained commanders. They had reduced the army to a paltry size. The luxury, easy living, and lazy lifestyle of the emperors had created a situation in which there was no difference in training and military experience between soldiers and farmers. Our people had no hope that our situation would improve, but they were instead running for their lives and their affairs stood upon the razor's edge. There was nothing left but *to sit down and await their final doom.*

But God stretched out his hand from on high, took pity 94
on us, and made the Komnenos clan our emperors, through them restoring prosperity to our people, reversing our defeat, and restoring what we had lost. At once, then, he appointed as a general Alexios, the best and most noble of men, who was prized for his virtue and all that he had accomplished for the empire, and subsequently he established Alexios's truly *golden lineage* over the Romans. The Komnenoi thought Demosthenes was right when he said that every man and every city must find the reason for their decline and then take the opposite course to reverse their defeat. They were of the view that the previous emperors had ruined everything for the sake of a little luxury and idleness, so they adopted a hardworking, austere way of life. They would spend most of their time in their tents, little in the cities, and would usually sleep in the army camp. Indeed, they devoted their entire life to war and battle formations, living a life full of struggle, but they set right the Roman

ὤρθωσαν ἤδη Ῥωμαίοις, τὸ πολέμιον ἅπαν περικαθήραντες, ἔκ τε Ἀσίας ἔκ τε Εὐρώπης αὐτοὺς ἀπήλασαν ὡς πορρωτάτω καὶ πολλὴν ἀνακωχὴν καὶ βαθεῖαν γαλήνην ἡμῖν ἐπορίσαντο, ἐναυσάμενοί τε τὰ πράγματα καὶ πνεῦμα ζωῆς ὥσπερ ἐμπεπνευκότες τοῖς πράγμασιν ἤδη νενεκρωμένοις καὶ τελέως ἀπεσβηκόσι.

Ταύτης δὴ τῆς πάντ᾽ ἀρίστης καὶ γενναίας μὲν ῥίζης, γενναιοτέρων δὲ πρέμνων καὶ οἱ τὴν ἡμετέραν κοσμοῦντες ἤρτηνται βασιλεῖς καὶ πρὸς τοιούτους ἔχουσιν ἀναφέρειν προγόνους, οὕτω μὲν τὴν πολιτικὴν ἐπιστήμην ἀρίστους, οὕτω δὲ τὰ πολεμικὰ πάντων κρατίστους, οὕτω δὲ διὰ πάντων διήκοντας καὶ καλῶν ἄγαλμα πάντων τὴν σφετέραν καταστησαμένους ψυχήν. Ἀλέξιος μέν γε καὶ ἡμῖν, ὁ πρῶτος τῆς γῆς ταυτησὶ βασιλεύσας (καὶ τοῦτο δὴ τὸ γλυκὺ πάντων ὄνομα καὶ ἡμῖν, ὡς τοῦ τῆς βασιλείας ὀνόματος), οὕτω δὴ καὶ πάντων κατῆρξε καλῶν. Οὗτος υἱωνὸς μὲν ὑπῆρχεν Ἀνδρονίκου τοῦ Κομνηνοῦ, βασιλεύσαντος μὲν καὶ αὐτοῦ τῶν Ῥωμαίων, τὸ δ᾽ οἰκεῖον ἀναφέροντος γένος οὗ καὶ ὁ πρῶτος Ἀλέξιος· μέγας δὲ Κομνηνὸς κεκλημένος, οὐδὲν ἧττον καὶ τοῖς ἔργοις ἦν μέγας, οὐ μᾶλλον ὀνόματος ἢ τῆς τῶν Κομνηνῶν ἀρετῆς αὐτός τε κληρονόμος γενόμενος καὶ τοὺς ἐξ ἑαυτοῦ τοιούτους ἑτέρους ἡμῖν ἀναφήνας, ἀγαθοὺς ἐξ ἀγαθῶν καὶ ἐξ ἀρίστων ἀρίστους, πάντας βασιλικούς, πάντας τῷ γένει συμβαίνοντας, πάντας ἐκείνου τοῦ χαρακτῆρος καὶ τῆς ὁμοίας εἰκόνος, πάντας ἀλλήλοις ἐρίζοντας, ἀλλήλοις ἁμιλλωμένους ὅστις αὐτὸς φθάσει πλείω κατωρθωκὼς ἀγαθὰ καὶ μεταδώσει τοῖς ὑπὸ χεῖρα. Τήν τε γὰρ πόλιν ἡμῖν οὐ

state and purged it of all its enemies, driving them as far away as possible from both Asia and Europe. They thus provided us with a long cessation of hostilities and a profound calm by rekindling the affairs of the state and, as it were, breathing a new spark of life into something that was already dead and completely extinguished.

Therefore, it is from this best and most noble root, and 95
from its even nobler stems, that the emperors who adorn our city have sprung. They can trace their ancestry back to men of this sort, who had such an excellent command of political science, who were so much better at war than everyone else, so outstanding, and who made their souls a model of every virtue. An Alexios (we find this the most pleasing name of all for an emperor) was thus the first emperor of this land, Trebizond, and the source of all our blessings. He was the grandson of Andronikos Komnenos, who had himself ruled the Romans and traced his ancestry back to Alexios I. He was called Grand Komnenos, and he was no less grand in his actual deeds, as he inherited not so much the name as the virtue of the Komnenoi. And he produced for us others like himself, good men born of good men, excellent men born of excellent men, all of them of imperial quality, all of them befitting this family, all of them with its character and of a similar stamp, and all emulating each other, competing over who could outstrip the others in accomplishing greater good and bestowing it upon his subjects. For they significantly increased the territory con-

μικροῖς ὅροις ἐπηύξησαν, ἀντ᾽ ἀρχομένης ἄρχουσαν καταστήσαντες καὶ ἀντὶ τοῦ δουλεύειν ἑτέροις πολλοὺς ἄλλους δουλώσασαν, σχῆμά τε μητροπόλεως πρὸς τὰ κύκλῳ πάντα καὶ τὴν σύμπασαν Λαζικὴν σχοῦσαν, τό τε ὑπήκοον ἐννόμου βασιλείας ἐπιστασίᾳ καὶ πλήθει καὶ πλούτῳ καὶ τῇ κατὰ πολέμους ἀνδρείᾳ καὶ γενναιότητι βέλτιον αὐτὸ ἑαυτοῦ ἀπειργάσαντο καὶ προήγαγον εἰς ἐπίδοσιν.

96 Φιλοῦσι μὲν γὰρ αὐτοὺς οἷα παῖδας πατήρ, οὐ μᾶλλον ἀρχόντων ἢ γονέων ἐπιδεικνύμενοι σπλάγχνα, φροντίζουσι δὲ τῆς αὐτῶν βελτιώσεως καὶ μᾶλλον ἢ παίδων γονεῖς, τὸ μὲν αὐτῶν τι κηδόμενοι, τὸ δὲ καὶ σφῶν αὐτῶν προνοούμενοι. Μᾶλλον γὰρ ἂν οἴονται καὶ καθαρώτερον βασιλεύσειν, ἂν ὡς ὅ τι βελτίστων κρατῶσι τῶν ἀρχομένων. Τοσοῦτο γοῦν εὐνοίας ὅ τε δῆμος εἰσφέρει τοῖς βασιλεῦσιν οἵ τε τῶν ἐν τέλει, μὴ καταψευδόμενοι τοῦ ὀνόματος, ὅσον οὐκ οἶδ᾽ εἰ παῖδες πατράσιν, ἀνθ᾽ ὧν οὔθ᾽ ἡμῖν οἱ κρατοῦντες ἠλλάξαντο τὸ ὑπήκοον, ὡς ἂν ἡμῶν καταγνόντες, ὅτι μὴ μᾶλλον σφίσι προσαύξουσι τὴν ἀρχήν, ἐντεῦθεν τὰ βάρβαρα γένη φοβοῦντες, οὔθ᾽ ἡμεῖς ἠλλαξάμεθα τοὺς δεσπότας, ἑτέρους ἐπιζητήσαντες ὡς ἂν ἀχθεσθέντες αὐτοῖς.

97 Ἀλλὰ τὸ Κομνηνῶν γένος καὶ οἱ ἐξ αὐτῶν ἡμῶν ἄρχουσι χρόνον ἤδη τοσοῦτον καὶ τοσαύτης διαδοχῆς παρελθούσης, ὃ μόνον αὐτῶν ἴδιον καὶ οὐκ ἄλλῳ τῳ προσῆκον εὕροι τις ἂν ἐξετάζων. Τοὺς γὰρ ἐν ἁπάσῃ τῇ γῇ καὶ πάσαις πόλεσιν ἄρχοντας μέχρι τετάρτης ἢ πέμπτης γενεᾶς προϊόντας ἕτερον διαδέχεται γένος, καὶ τοῦτο πάλιν πάσχει ταὐτὰ καὶ πρὸς ἄλλους τὴν ἀρχὴν παραπέμπει καὶ οὕτως

trolled by our city. Instead of it being ruled, they have made it rule, and instead of it being enslaved to others, they have enabled it to enslave many others. They have made it into the capital city of everything around it and even the whole of Lazike. They have made the subjects of this lawfully ordained empire greater than they were before in authority, number, wealth, manliness in war, and bravery, and they have brought about their overall advancement.

For they love their subjects as a father does his children, 96 displaying the affections not so much of a ruler but of a parent. In fact, they are more concerned for their betterment than a parent is for his child, by watching over them and looking to their future interests. This is because they believe more effective government results from ruling the best possible subjects. The people, along with public servants, who do not belie the term, bear such goodwill toward the emperors that I do not know whether children actually possess this much goodwill for their parents. Our masters would consequently never exchange their subjects for anyone else, since, were they to disdain us, they would not be able to expand their domain for fear of the barbarian races, nor would we ever change our masters and seek out others, as we would be aggravated by them.

The fact that the Komnenos family and their descen- 97 dants have already ruled us for so long and so many of them have succeeded each other is a unique characteristic and without parallel, as one can confirm through investigation. In every other land and city, once a family of rulers has continued for four or five generations they are succeeded by another family. The same happens to the latter in turn and they pass their power on to yet others, and so it always is. It

ἀεί, καὶ οὐκ ἔστιν εὑρεῖν γένος οὐδὲν οὐκ ἀρχόντων, οὐ τυράννων, οὐ βασιλέων μέχρι παντὸς ἐπὶ ταὐτοῦ παραμεῖναν. Οἱ δ᾽ ἡμέτεροι δεσπόται καὶ βασιλεῖς κἀν τούτῳ καλῶς ποιοῦντες τῶν ἄλλων ἐκράτησαν, καὶ ἧς ἅπαξ ἐλάβοντο γῆς καὶ βασιλείας ἐπέβησαν, ταύτης οὐ χρόνος, οὐ τύχη, οὐ πραγμάτων μεταβολαὶ τούτους ἀπήγαγον, ἀλλ᾽ ὥσπερ ἀθάνατοι ἄρχοντες διαιωνίζουσιν ἡμῖν οἱ αὐτοὶ καὶ ταὐτοῦ γένους ὄντες καὶ αἵματος, παῖς πατέρα διαδεχόμενοι καὶ τὴν οἰκείαν ἕκαστος ἡγεμονίαν κρατύνοντες. Εἴη δὲ δὴ καὶ τοῦ λοιποῦ τοῖς αὐτοῖς χρῆσθαι δεσπόταις καὶ ὑπὲρ τῶν αὐτῶν βασιλεύεσθαι, καὶ συνέχοις αὐτὸς ἄνωθεν, Θεὲ ἡγεμόνιε, τὸ γένος τῶν βασιλέων καὶ ἰθύνοις μὲν τὴν βασιλείαν αὐτοῖς, εὖ δὲ τὰ ἡμέτερα διαθείης καὶ δι᾽ ἀλλήλων ἀλλήλους κρατύνοις, τῇ τε πόλει τοὺς βασιλεῖς καὶ τοῖς βασιλεῦσι τὴν πόλιν τε καὶ τὸ γένος ἡμῖν.

98 Ὑπὸ δὴ τοιαύτῃ βασιλείᾳ καὶ τοιούτοις ἄρχουσιν ἡ πόλις ἡμῖν ὀρθουμένη ἑαυτῆς τε βελτίων γεγένηται καὶ συμφώνως τοῖς πρὶν εὐτυχήμασιν τούς τε τῆς ἀρχῆς ὅρους ηὔξηται τῇ τε περιβολῇ τῶν τειχῶν καὶ τῆς ἄλλης κατασκευῆς νεῶν τε καὶ οἰκημάτων καὶ ἀγορῶν καὶ πάσης τῆς τῇδε φιλοτιμίας, τῷ τε τῶν πολιτῶν πλήθει καὶ πλούτῳ καὶ εὐδαιμονίᾳ ὑπερεβάλετο ἑαυτήν, τοὐναντίον παθοῦσα ἢ τῶν πόλεων αἱ πολλαί. Αἱ μέν γ᾽ εὐτυχήσασαι πρῶτα, εἶτα τῆς ἐναντίας τύχης πειρῶνται, καὶ παρακμάζει σφίσι τὰ τῆς αὐξήσεως, ἡ δ᾽ ἀπὸ ταπεινοῦ καὶ σμικροῦ τὸ πρῶτον ἠργμένη οὐ κάμνει προκόπτουσα οὐδ᾽ ἐπιδιδοῦσα.

99 Ὄντος γοῦν αὐτῇ τὰ πρῶτα τοῦ περιβόλου στενοῦ, καὶ

is impossible to find a family of rulers, tyrants, or emperors that has remained in power forever. But our masters and emperors have done well even in this respect and have surpassed the others. Once they took possession of this land and ascended this throne, neither time, nor fortune, nor a change of circumstances has swept them away. Instead, as if they were immortal rulers, the members of this same family and its bloodline have continued to reign perpetually over us. Son succeeds father, and each further consolidates his own rule. May we have the same masters for the rest of time and may we be ruled by them. And may you, Almighty God, protect this family of emperors from on high and guide their rule. May you manage our affairs well and strengthen each of us through one another: the emperors through the city, the city through the emperors, and their family through us.

Under such an empire and such rulers our city has been 98
exalted and has become better than it was. In accordance with its previous successes, it has increased the boundaries of its dominion and has surpassed itself in increasing the area bounded by its walls as in the construction of churches, houses, markets, and every other mark of distinction, as well as in the number of its citizens, their wealth, and their prosperity. It has thus experienced the opposite of many other cities. For while they prospered at first and then fell on hard times and saw their growth decline, our city has not wearied of developing and growing ever since it first got its start from humble and modest origins.

For example, the circuit wall used to encompass only a 99

δεύτερος περιήχθη, καὶ προσεσκεύασται τρίτος, καὶ πρὸς μέγα μέτρον ἡμῖν τὰ τῶν τειχῶν παρατέταται. Τὴν γὰρ νῦν μὲν ἀκρόπολιν, πάλαι δὲ πόλιν, εἰσόδους παρεχομένην διττάς, τὴν μὲν ἀπάγουσαν ἔξω τε καὶ ὡς πρὸς τὴν ἤπειρον, θατέραν δ᾽ ἐκ τοῦ πρὸς θάλατταν αὐτῆς μέρους, προσαυξῆσαι θελήσαντες οἱ πατέρες ἡμῖν, οὐ κύκλῳ περιέλαβον ἅπασαν, ὡς εἴσω τοῦ δευτέρου τείχους ὅλην ποιήσασθαι· ἀλλ᾽ ἐπεὶ κατιέναι μέχρις ἐς θάλασσαν ἦν αὐτοῖς προὔργου μετά γε τοῦ τὸν περίβολον παραυξῆσαι, τὴν μὲν ἐς μεσημβρίαν καὶ ἔξω βλέπουσαν πύλην ἀφεῖσαν ἔξω πάλιν αὐτῆς εἶναι, τὸ δέ γε πρὸς θάλασσαν αὐτῆς μέρος ἀπολαβόντες ἀπό τε τῶν γωνιῶν ἑκατέρας ἠργμένοι, τείχη τε παρέτειναν ἑκατέρωθεν ἕτερον πολλάκις τὸ μῆκος τοσοῦτον ὅσον τὸ τῆς ἀκροπόλεως ὅλης, εἶθ᾽ ἑτέρᾳ πλευρᾷ ἐγκαρσίῳ ταῦτά τε συνῆψαν ἀλλήλοις καὶ τὸν ἐντὸς ἅπαντα τόπον τοῦ λοιποῦ καὶ πρὸς τῷ αἰγιαλῷ διωρίσαντο, καὶ πύλαις μὲν παρ᾽ ἑκατέρᾳ μιᾷ ἀνεπέτασαν, ἐκ δὲ τοῦ πρὸς θάλατταν αὖθις ἑτέρᾳ, περὶ ἥν, ἐπείπερ ὁ τῇδε φέρων χῶρος ὁμαλὸς καὶ ἐπίπεδος, οὔτε περιειργάσαντο, οὔτ᾽ ἐπολυπραγμόνησαν.

100 Περὶ δὲ τὰς παρ᾽ ἑκατέρας πύλας καὶ πολὺν κατεβάλοντο πόνον καὶ οἷον ἂν ἄξιον διηγήσασθαι. Οἱ γὰρ ἄνωθεν κατιόντες παρ᾽ ἑκάτερα φάραγγες, ἐνταῦθα βαθυνόμενοί τε καὶ τραχυνόμενοι μᾶλλον, οὔτ᾽ ἀνθρώποις εὐζώνοις, οὔτε πολλῷ μᾶλλον βουσὶν ἢ ζεύγεσιν ἢ φορτηγοῖς ζῴοις ῥᾳδίαν παρεῖχον τὴν εἴσοδον. Ἔδει δὴ καθομαλισθῆναι τὴν φάραγγα καὶ τὸν κρημνώδη χῶρον ἴσον τε καὶ ἐπίπεδον γεγενῆσθαι καὶ τὴν ὁδὸν εὐθεῖαν ἀπ᾽ αὐτῶν τῶν

limited area at first, so a second wall was put up around it and then a third was constructed, so that our walls extend over a great distance. Since the city in ancient times, which is the current acropolis, used to have two entrances, with one leading out toward the land and the other leading out of the section of the city by the sea, our ancestors, who wanted to expand the city, did not entirely encircle it in such a way as to encompass the whole of it within the second set of walls. Instead, since they thought that it would be beneficial to have it extend down to the sea by expanding the circuit wall, they let the gate to the south, which looked out from the city, still remain as an outer gate for it and focused on the part facing towards the sea. Starting from each of the corners, they built another wall on either side which was many times longer than that of the whole acropolis. Then, with another oblique side, they joined them with each other and separated off all the area within, by the beach. They also pierced it with gates, one in each side wall, and installed another gate in the sea walls. Since the area next to that gate is smooth and flat, they did not concern themselves with it or spend much time on it.

They expended a great deal of effort on the gates on the 100
sidewalls, however, and this is worth describing. For on each side the ravines descend from above and become so deep and rugged here that it was not easy for an unencumbered man, let alone oxen, yoked animals, or beasts of burden, to enter there. For this reason, they had to level the ravine and make the steep area level and flat, straightening out the road

πυλῶν μέχρις ἐς γῆν τὴν ἀντιπέρας αὐτήν. Ἀπ᾽ αὐτῶν γοῦν τῶν μυχαιτάτων ἠργμένοι τοῦ φάραγγος ἀνέστησαν πάχει διαφέροντα τείχη καὶ εἰς ὕψος ἀνήγαγον, μέχρις αὐτῶν τε τῶν πυλῶν φθάνοντα καὶ τῆς ἀντιπέρας τῶν ὀχθῶν ἑκατέρας.

101 Καὶ τὰ τείχη διττὰ παρ᾽ ἑκάτερα, τὸ μὲν ἀπ᾽ αὐτῶν πυλῶν ἐς αὐτὸ τὸ ποτάμιον ῥεῦμα, ὃ τοὺς φάραγγας δίεισι, τὸ δ᾽ ἀφ᾽ ἑκατέρας ὄχθης ἐς αὐτὸ δὴ τὸ ῥεῦμα, τὸ δὲ τούτοιν ἀμφοῖν μεταξὺ χάος τε καὶ κρημνὸς ὑπολέλειπται καὶ οὐκ ἔστι διελθεῖν οὔτ᾽ ἐξιόντα τῆς πόλεως οὔτ᾽ ἐσιόντα, ἀφαιρεθέντος τοῦ ζεύγματος καὶ τοῦ ἐπικειμένου ξυλίνου γεφυρώματος. Τοῦ γὰρ ἀσφαλοῦς προνοούμενοι παρ᾽ αὐταῖς τε ταῖς ὄχθαις πύργους ἀνήγειραν, ὅθεν ἂν τοῖς πολεμίοις τὰς εἰσόδους ἀποτειχίζοιεν, καὶ τὰ γεφυρώματ᾽ αὐτὰ ὑπέθεσαν ξύλινα, ὡς ἄν, ἐν τῷ παρισταμένῳ τῆς χρείας ῥᾳδίως αἰρόμενα, ἄβατον τοῖς ἐναντίοις τὴν εἴσοδον καταλίποιεν.

102 Ἐπεὶ δ᾽ αὐξομένης ἀεὶ καὶ ἧς εἴληχε μοίρας ἐπὶ τὸ βέλτιόν τε καὶ μεῖζον ἀγούσης αὐτήν, ἔδει τόν τε περίβολον ἐκτετάσθαι καὶ ἀκριβῶς γενέσθαι θαλάττιον, τῶν κυμάτων αὐτῆς περικλυζόντων τὰ τείχη, ἐν ὑστέρῳ καιρῷ καὶ τοῦτο δὴ προσεγένετο. Ἐκ γοῦν τοῦ πρὸς δυσμὰς φέροντος ἠργμένοι, οὗ τὸν πύργον ἐπ᾽ αὐτῇ δεδομῆσθαι τῇ εἰσόδῳ προέφημεν καὶ τὴν ἐνταῦθα φάραγγα εἴσω ποιησάμενοι πᾶσαν καὶ πολὺ παρεξιόντες μέχρι τὰ θαλάσσης κατῆλθον αὐτῆς, τῶν κυμάτων αὐτῶν ἐπιβάντες, καί, περιαγαγόντες τὸ τεῖχος, εἰς αὐτό γε τὸ πρὸς ἔω τῆς πόλεως μέρος προσενήρμοσαν φέροντες, τῆς τε

from the gates as far as the land on the other side of the ravine. Starting from the innermost parts of the ravine, they erected walls of remarkable thickness and raised them up until they reached the level of the gates themselves and the banks on the other side.

There are two sets of walls on each side. One runs from 101
the gates to the stream which flows through each ravine, while the second starts from each bank and runs to the same stream. Between each set of walls, however, there remains a deep chasm and cliff, so that it is impossible for a person entering or leaving the city to cross it when the platform and the wooden bridge which lies over it is removed. Our forefathers thus provided for the security of the place by erecting towers along the banks in order to fortify these points of entry against any enemies and also by laying down these wooden bridges, so that they could be easily raised up when necessary and make the entrance impassable for the enemy.

Since the city was continually growing and its destiny was 102
leading it to bigger and better things, the circuit wall again had to be extended and had truly to become a sea wall, that is with the waves washing up against the city's walls. This was added at a later time. Starting from the wall toward the west, where, as we have already said, they had built a tower near the entrance gate, they incorporated the entire ravine there and built a wall alongside it over a great distance right down to the sea, advancing into the waves themselves. Then they looped the wall around and joined it to the one at the eastern part of the city. Thus they encompassed the part of

προειρημένης ὀλίγῳ κάτωθεν πόλεως εἴσω τε τῆς ἐνταῦθα φάραγγος πάσης τοσούτῳ μεῖζον τοῦ δευτέρου περιβαλλόμενοι τεῖχος, ὅσῳ τοῦτο διαφέρον τοῦ πρώτου, πύλαις τε καὶ πυλίσιν ἀναπεπταμένον παντοδαπαῖς, καὶ πανταχοῦ φέρον πολλαῖς ταῖς αὐταῖς τοῦ τε μεγέθους πρὸς λόγον ὃ περιβέβληται καὶ τοῦ πλήθους τῶν ἐνοικούντων. Ἐς αὐτήν τε γὰρ θάλατταν δυσὶ καὶ τρισὶν ἀνέῳγε πύλαις καὶ αὖ παρ᾽ ἑκάτερα ταῖς ἴσαις καὶ πλείοσιν εἰσιέναι παρέχεται, ὥστε διπλοῦν ἀνθ᾽ ἁπλοῦ τὸν περίβολον ἡμῖν εἶναι καὶ τὰ ἴσα πολλαῖς ἄλλαις μεγέθους εἵνεκα δύνασθαι.

103 Τοσούτου δὲ παντὸς ὄντος τοῦ περιβόλου καὶ τοσοῦτον περιέχοντος χῶρον ἐντός, ὅμως οὐδὲν ἧττον τὸ τῆς πόλεως πλῆθος στενοχωρεῖται καὶ κρεῖττον ἢ κατὰ τὴν πόλιν ὑπάρχον εὑρίσκεται. Τό τε γοῦν πλεῖστον ἐκτὸς παρ᾽ ἑκάτερα κέχυται καὶ οὐδ᾽ ὀφθαλμοῖς ὁρίζει τὸ τῶν οἰκιῶν πλῆθος, ὅσαι πρός τε τὴν ἕω καὶ τὴν ἐς δυσμὰς φέρον δεδομημέναι προαστείων τε τῇ πόλει φέρουσι λόγον, καὶ οὓς ὁ περίβολος οὐ χωρεῖ δεχόμεναι ἀναπαύουσι λειμῶνές τε καὶ παράδεισοι καὶ δένδρα παντοδαπὰ καρποῖς βρίθοντα, τά τε ἄλλα καὶ ἐλαιῶν πλῆθος ὥσπερ τι συνηρεφὲς ἄλσος τὸν τῇδε πάντα χῶρον σκιάζοντα, προκεχυμένα τῆς πόλεως, τούς τ᾽ ἐσιόντας μετὰ πολλῆς παραπέμπει τῆς ἡδονῆς καὶ πυκνὰ τοὺς τῶν ἐξιόντων ὀφθαλμοὺς ἐπιστρέφει τε πρὸς αὐτὰ καὶ οἷον ἐπιλαθέσθαι τῆς προκειμένης ὁδοῦ πείθοντα, ὅλους πρός τε θαῦμα τοῦ ἑαυτῶν κάλλους ἀπάγει, καὶ πεδητῶν τρόπον αὐτοῦ πάντας κατέχει, ἐμπόριόν τε καὶ ἀγορὰ πᾶσα καὶ κάπηλοι πάντες ἔξω τῆς πόλεως,

the city, mentioned above, that is a little further down and is bounded by the whole ravine there, with a wall which was as much larger than the second circuit wall as the second had been when compared to the first. This third circuit wall was pierced by all sorts of gates and posterns; there are many of both kinds along its entire length on account of its size and the multitude of the city's inhabitants. Two or three gates open onto the sea itself, and the wall features the same number of gates, or more, by which to enter the city on each side, so that our circuit wall is actually a double rather than a single one and is comparable in size to those of many other cities.

Although the whole circuit wall is so large and encloses 103
such a large space within it, nevertheless the population of the city is closely packed and larger than the area inside the walls can accommodate. The greater part of the population has thus overflowed outside the walls on either side, where the number of houses stretches farther than the eye can see. The houses that have been constructed there extend from the suburbs to the east and west and bring repute to the city. Those whom the wall cannot accommodate are welcomed and offered repose by meadows, gardens, and all sorts of trees brimming with fruit. In addition to so much else, there are also many olive trees, which like a canopied grove cast shade on the whole area there. Flowing out from the city, these trees send people who are heading into it on their way with much delight and, closely packed, they attract the gaze of people who are leaving it, almost making them forget the road ahead, drawing every eye to the wonder of their beauty and keeping everyone captivated by it. In addition, a trading hub, an entire marketplace, and dealers are all outside the

καὶ ταῦτα πάντα τὸ πρὸς ἕω μέρος αὐτῆς φέρει, ἀπ' αὐτῶν μὲν ἀρχόμενα τῶν τειχῶν, ἀπιόντα δ' ἐς μῆκος ὅσον ἐνῆν πλεῖστον οὐκ ἐπ' εὐθείας μόνον, ἀλλά πῃ καὶ κάμπτοντα πολλαχοῦ καὶ παρεκδρομὰς οὐκ ὀλίγας ποιούμενα.

104 Παρ' ἑκάτερα δὲ ἐργαστήριά τε δεδόμηται πάμπολλα καὶ *γέρρα τῶν ἐργαστηρίων* ἐξέχει καὶ ἄνδρες ἐργάται καθήμενοι ἐμπορεύονται, τὰ τιμιώτατά τε καὶ κάλλιστα πιπράσκοντες καὶ ὠνούμενοι καὶ ὅσα ἡ πᾶσα γῆ φέρει. Ἔτι δ' ἐπιτηδεύματα πάντα καὶ τέχνας παντοίας, ὅσαι τε βάναυσοι ὅσαι τε ἄπυροι, καὶ ὅλως ὅσων ἀνθρώποις οὐ πρὸς ζωὴν μόνον, ἀλλὰ καὶ πρὸς διαγωγὴν δεῖ, πάσας ἂν εὕροις ἐνταῦθα καὶ οἵας οὐκ ἄλλοθι γῆς, ὥστε τὸ τῶν τεχνιτῶν ἡμῖν πλῆθος ἀντ' ἄλλης εἶναι πληρώματος πόλεως.

105 Πλήθει γοῦν ἡμῖν ἡ ἀγορὰ καὶ αὐτὸ τὸ ἐμπόριον οὐ τῇδε ἢ τῇδε τῶν πασῶν ἡμερῶν, οὐδὲ τῷδε ἢ τῷδε μέρει ἡμέρας καὶ ὥρας ὁποιασοῦν, ἀλλὰ πάσαις μὲν ἡμέραις ἐνιαυτοῦ, πάσαις δὲ ὥραις ἡμέρας, σύμμικτον ἀεὶ φέρουσα πλῆθος καὶ μόλις χωροῦσα τοὺς διϊόντας. Τό τε γὰρ ξενικὸν οὐκ ὀλίγον ἐνταῦθα καὶ ὅσον κατ' ἐμπορίαν τῇ ἡμετέρᾳ συμμίγνυσιν οἵ τε πολῖται τῷ τῆς πόλεως μεγέθει συμβαίνοντες καὶ οἱ αὐτὸ τοῦτο ἔμποροι, οὓς οὐκ ἔνι μὴ ἀγοράζειν ἀεί, ἀρκοῦντες τὴν ἀγορὰν πλήθειν ἀνθρώπων ποιεῖν, ὥστε τριχῇ τὸ πλῆθος ἐνταῦθα συρρεῖν, αὐτῶν τε τῶν ἐπηλύδων καὶ ὅσοι κατ' ἐμπορίαν ἴασιν ἐνταῦθα διατριβόντων ἀεί, τῶν τ' ἐγχωρίων, τῶν μὲν διὰ παντὸς ἐπιχωριαζόντων αὐτοῦ, ὡς ἂν τούτου τοῦ ἐπιτηδεύματος ὄντων, τῶν δ' οὐδ' αὐτῶν διὰ τὴν χρείαν ἀπόντων ἐκεῖθεν.

city. All this is on the eastern side of the city, starting from the walls themselves and stretching away as far as possible, not only in a straight line, but also often winding around all over the place and making many detours.

On either side of the road, numerous workshops have been constructed and *booths* spread out *from these workshops* where artisans sit and trade, buying the most precious and finest wares and selling the products of the whole land. Here you can find practiced all the professions and all sorts of trades, all those which both do and do not use fire, in a word all those that are not only necessary for life, but also for its enjoyment. Indeed, you would not find such variety anywhere else on earth, so that the multitude of our artisans is enough to fill up another city. 104

The marketplace and commercial center is full of people not only on this or that day, or at this or that particular time of day or hour, but on every day of the year and during every hour of the day. It is always crowded and there is hardly space for people to pass. There are also many foreigners there for trade, and their citizens mingle with our own people, increasing the size of the city, and their traders do the same. These people, who always have to be in the marketplace, suffice to make the market teem with people. The crowd that converges on the market can thus be divided into three parts. There are the newcomers to the city and those who came to it to trade but have then stayed on; and then there are the locals, some of whom practically live in the market all the time as if this was their job; while others never leave because they have to be there. So, given the 105

Ὥστε τῷ τε πλήθει τῶν ἀγοραζόντων τῷ τε μέτρῳ τοῦ τόπου, ὃν ἡμῖν ἡ ἀγορὰ περιλαμβάνει καὶ ἐς ὅσον ἐκτέταται, κατ' οὐδὲν εὐθενουμένης ὅλης λείπεται πόλεως.

106 Ἀλλὰ μὴν οἰκιῶν πλήθη καὶ κάλλη αἷς ἄμφω ταῦτα χορηγεῖ δαψιλῶς ἥ τε τῶν παρ' ἡμῖν τεκτόνων σοφία, οἷς μόνοις ἄν τις ἔφη προσήκειν τὸ "*σοφὸς ἤραρε τέκτων,*" οὕτως ἐς τἀκριβὲς τουτουὶ τοῦ ἐπιτηδεύματος ἧκον, ἥ τε παρὰ τῶν ὀρῶν φορά, παρεχομένων ὑλοτομεῖν δαψιλῶς ὕλην παντοίαν τε καὶ ποικίλην καὶ οἵαν οὐκ ἄλλοθι, ταῦτα μὲν οὖν ἐάσω· καὶ γὰρ ἔχοι τις ἂν τοῖς ὁμοίοις καυχήσασθαι· αὐτῶν γε μὴν τῶν βασιλείων πέρι, τρυφὴν ἀνακτορικὴν καὶ πολλὴν ἐνδεικνυμένων ἁβρότητα, κἂν μὴ δύναιτο λόγος ἱκανῶς παραστῆσαι, μικρὰ ἄττα διαληψόμεθα ὅμως καὶ ὅσον ἐνδείξασθαί φασιν *ἐκ τοῦ κρασπέδου θοιμάτιον.*

107 Τὰ γὰρ δὴ τῶν βασιλέων οἰκήματα ἐν αὐτῇ μὲν ἵδρυται τῇ νῦν ἀκροπόλει, αὐτὰ δ' ἐστὶν οὐδὲν ἧττον ἀκρόπολις τοίχων τε ὀχυρότητι καὶ ποικιλίᾳ κατασκευῆς καὶ μεγέθει καὶ κάλλει τῶν ἁπανταχοῦ διαφέροντα. Τὸ μὲν γὰρ πρὸς δύνοντα ἥλιον τεῖχος αὐτῶν, αὐτῇ τε τῇ ἀκροπόλει καὶ τοῖς ἀρχείοις κοινὸν ὄν, ἐς τὴν αὐτὴν ἀμφοῖν ἓν καὶ ταὐτὸ χρείαν παρείληπται, ἀνιὸν μὲν ἐς πρῶτον καὶ δεύτερον ὄροφον τῆς τ' ἀκροπόλεως τῶν τε βασιλείων αὐτῶν εἵνεκα, τὸ δ' ὑπὲρ τοῦτο πᾶν ἤδη καθαρῶς ὑπὲρ αὐτῶν μόνον ἀνυψούμενον τῶν ἀρχείων, τοσούτῳ τοῦ τῆς ἀκροπόλεως ὑπερανιστάμενον τείχους, ὅσον ἐκεῖνο σχεδὸν ὑπερανέχει τῆς γῆς. Τὸ δέ γ' ἐπὶ θάτερα τεῖχος, ὕψους τε καὶ παχύτητος καὶ τῆς ἄλλης οἰκοδομίας εὖ ἔχον, ἄνωθεν

number of people in our marketplace, the size of the area encompassed by it, and the distance it extends, it is practically an entire thriving city in and of itself.

As for the number and beauty of the city's houses, the wisdom of its builders provides amply for both. For them alone could you use the phrase "*a wise builder raised it up,*" since they have cultivated this profession so highly. The other contributing factor is the resources that come down from the mountains, for the latter provide an abundance of manifold and diverse trees, unlike those that grow anywhere else, for us to cut down. But I will pass over this point, as someone else might also be able to boast about similar things. Concerning the palace, which displays lordly luxury and great splendor, even if no words could possibly do it justice, we will, nevertheless, mention a few things, which make *the cloak* recognizable *by the hem,* as they say. 106

Although the palace structures are situated on what is now the acropolis, they are still no less an acropolis in their own right, as they stand out from everything else in the strength of their walls, the diversity of their construction, their size, and beauty. The western wall is shared between the acropolis and the imperial residence and serves the same purpose for both. It thus rises up to a first and then a second story on account of the acropolis and the palace itself. But everything further above that was raised up purely for the imperial residence alone and it rises as far above the acropolis wall as the latter rises above the ground. The wall on the other side is excellent in terms of height, thickness, and the other aspects of construction, running downhill. Although 107

κάτω διηγμένον, ὑπὲρ τὸ ἥμισύ τε τῆς ἀκροπόλεως ἀφαιρεῖται, καὶ τῷ τῶν βασιλείων μέρει προστίθησιν, ὡς καὶ μόνον ἀρκεῖν ἐπιόντα τε πολέμιον ὑποστῆναι ἐν ἀσφαλεῖ τε φυλάττειν οὓς ἂν εἴσω ποιήσαιτο, διτταῖς δὲ τὴν εἴσοδον συγχωροῦν πύλαις καὶ πυλίδι μιᾷ, παντὶ τῷ λοιπῷ ἑαυτοῦ ἀσφαλῶς τε δεδόμηται καὶ τοὺς προσιόντας ἀποτειχίζει τε καὶ ἀπείργει.

108 Τούτου παρ' ἑκάτερα μὲν ψιλός τις ὑπολέλειπται τόπος αἰθουσῶν τε εἵνεκα καὶ τοῦ δέχεσθαι τοὺς ὑπηρετουμένους τοῖς βασιλεῦσιν· ἐπ' αὐτοῦ δὲ τοῦ μέσου τὰ βασίλεια ἵδρυται, εἴσοδον μὲν παρεχόμενα μίαν, ἀναβαθμοῖς προσανεσπασμένην καὶ κλίμακι, καὶ ποιούμενα τὴν εἴσοδον ἄνοδον. Εἰσιόντα δ' εὐθὺς ἔνθεν μὲν πρόδομοι καὶ δόμοι λαμπρῶς ὑποδέχονται, κάλλους τε καὶ μεγέθους ἱκανῶς ἔχοντες καὶ χωρεῖν οὐκ ὀλίγους δυνάμενοι, ἐξῶσταί τε κύκλῳ τοὺς δόμους περιειλήφασι, πανταχοῦ τετραμμένοι καὶ πᾶσιν ἐκκείμενοι πνεύμασιν· ἐκ δέ γ' ἐπὶ θάτερα μήκει τε μήκιστος οἶκος καὶ κάλλει κάλλιστος παρατέταται, τοὔδαφος μὲν λευκῷ λίθῳ σύμπας ὑπεστρωμένος, χρυσῷ δὲ τὴν ὀροφὴν καὶ ποικιλίᾳ χρωμάτων καὶ τοῖς τῆς γραφῆς καταστραπτόμενος ἄνθεσιν, ἄστρα τε προδεικνῦσαν ἐν τῷ ξύμπαντι ἑαυτῆς κύτει καὶ αὐγὰς ἀποπέμπουσαν ὡς ἂν οὐρανοῦ μίμημα καὶ πολλὴν ἐπιδεικνυμένην τῆς γραφῆς περιττότητα καὶ τρυφήν· τά τε κύκλῳ καὶ πρὸς τοῖς τοίχοις αὐτοῖς γέγραπται μὲν ὁ τῶν βασιλέων χορὸς ὅσοι τε τῆς ἡμετέρας ἦρξαν ὅσοις τε προγόνοις ἐχρήσαντο, γέγραπται δὲ καὶ εἴ τινα κίνδυνον ἡ πόλις ἡμῖν περιστάντα

it cuts off more than half the acropolis, it adds to the palace area, so that it is sufficient to withstand an attacking enemy and keep safe any people who may be inside. The walls permit entry through two gates and one postern, and they are constructed securely in every other regard so as to exclude and ward off attackers.

On either side of this enclosed area, there is a space left 108
open for halls and quartering the emperors' servants. But in the very middle of this area stands the palace, provided with a single entrance, with a stairway that can be pulled up, making the entrance impassable. As you enter, you are at once exquisitely welcomed on the one side by vestibules and halls, which are quite beautiful and large and able to accommodate a great many people. Balconies surround the halls, facing in all directions, and exposed to all the breezes. On the other side as you enter there extends a building of very great length and very great beauty. Its floor is paved entirely with white marble, while its ceiling gleams with gold, a variety of colors, and masterpieces of painting. The entire vault shimmers with stars casting their light in imitation of the sky and displaying the extraordinary refinement and luxury of the painting. In a circle around the walls of the building they have had painted a procession of both the emperors who have ruled our city and of their ancestors, and there are also scenes depicting the dangers which the city has had to

διήνεγκε καὶ ὅσοι κατ᾽ αὐτῆς ἐπιόντες καθ᾽ αὐτῶν ἔγνωσαν ἐγχειρίσαντες.

109 Ἄνω δὲ αὐτοῦ καὶ πρός γε τῷ ἄκρῳ βῆμα κατηρεφὲς προφαίνει βασίλειον, ὀροφὴν μὲν ἀποτεῖνον εἰς πυραμίδα, τέτρασι δ᾽ αὐτὴν κίοσιν ὑπανέχον, λευκῷ δὲ καὶ αὐτὸ λίθῳ κύκλῳ τε καὶ πρὸς τῷ ὀρόφῳ περισκεπόμενον, τούς θ᾽ ὑπηκόους ἀποτειχίζον τῶν βασιλέων ὥσπερ τισὶν ἄλλαις κιγκλίσιν, οὗ βασιλεὺς αὐτὸς μάλιστα προφαινόμενος χρηματίζει τε τοῖς ἐν τέλει καὶ πρέσβεσι διαλέγεται καὶ λόγον δίδωσι καὶ λαμβάνει. Προϊόντι δὲ βῆμά τε βασίλειον ἕτερον, εὖρει καὶ ὕψει πολλῷ προέχον, κατηρεφὲς καὶ περίστυλον· ἀναβαθμοί τ᾽ ἐν τῷ βήματι ἀνιόντας τοὺς βασιλέας ἐς ὕψος ἀνάγοντες καὶ πεποικιλμένον γραφαῖς οἴκημα, ἔνθα τοὺς ἐν τέλει τε καὶ τὸ λοιπὸν ὑποχείριον λαμπρῶς ἑστιᾶν βασιλεὺς εἴθισται. Ἐντεῦθεν ἐπὶ μὲν ἀριστερὰ ἄλλοις τε δωματίοις παμπόλλοις ἐστὶν ἐντυχεῖν καὶ τῶν ἄλλων ἑνὶ διαφέροντι, τέτρασι μὲν ἴσαις διῃρημένῳ πλευραῖς καὶ σχῆμα πλαίσιον σῴζοντι ὑπομνήματά τε τῆς τῶν ὅλων γενέσεως φέροντι καὶ ὡς τὴν ἀρχὴν ἄνθρωπος γέγονε γενόμενός τε ὡς τὰ καθ᾽ αὐτὸν ἐπολίτευσεν. Ἐπὶ δεξιὰ δὲ δόμοι καὶ πρόδομοι καὶ ἐξῶσται καὶ κοιτῶνες καὶ θάλαμοι, διαιρούμενοι μὲν στοαῖς, ἑκάστης πρὸς ἐγκαρσίαν τελευτώσης ἑτέραν, μέτρον δὲ φέροντες μεθ᾽ ὃ πλέον οὐχ ὑπάρχει λαβεῖν, μεγέθει μὲν μείους τε καὶ μείζους ἀλλήλων, πάντες δὲ μετὰ κάλλους ἀρρήτου καὶ τῆς πρεπούσης ἁρμονίας ἐσκευασμένοι. Καὶ νεὼς ἐκεῖ ἱερὸς ἵδρυται, γραφῆς τ᾽ ἀγλαϊζόμενος κάλλεσι καὶ ἱεροῖς ἀναθήμασιν οὐ

undergo as well as those who have attacked it, only to recognize that they were fighting a losing battle.

Beyond this building, close to the top of the acropolis, 109
there appears a canopied royal structure with a pyramidal roof supported by four columns. It is covered all around by white marble up to the roof, which separates the emperors from their subjects as though by some kind of latticed gates. It is from here especially that the emperor makes his appearance to conduct business with his ministers, hold audiences with ambassadors, and give and receive statements. Continuing further, there is another imperial inner sanctum of great width and height, which has a vaulted roof and is surrounded by columns. Ascending a staircase in the sanctum, the imperial family mounts on high to a chamber bedecked with paintings, and here the emperor customarily holds lavish feasts for his ministers and the rest of his subjects. Thereafter one encounters on the left a great many other rooms, one of which stands out from the rest. Divided up by four ribs of equal size, it has a rectangular shape and contains depictions commemorating the creation of the universe, how man first came into existence, and his subsequent history. On the right, there are vestibules, halls, terraces, chambers, and rooms separated by colonnaded porticoes, each set across from the other. They are all of a size greater than one can imagine, some larger, some smaller than each other, but all constructed with ineffable beauty and appropriate harmony. A holy church has also been set up there, shimmering with beautiful paintings and decorated with sacred offerings; although the latter are not very

μᾶλλον πλήθει πολλοῖς ἢ κάλλει καλλίστοις κοσμούμενος, ὅσῳ τοῦ μεγέθους λειπόμενος τοσοῦτον τοῦ κάλλους πλεονεκτῶν.

110 Οὕτω κάλλιόν τε ἢ εἰπεῖν ἐσκεύασται τὰ βασίλεια καὶ μόνη ταῦτ᾽ ἂν ἀκριβῶς ὄψις κατανοήσαι, τά τε ἄλλα καὶ ὅσα ὑπό τε τὸν πρῶτον καὶ δεύτερον ὄροφον μηκικῶς τε διῃρημένα καὶ πλατικῶς καὶ πολλὴν ἐνδεικνύμενα ποικιλίαν τε καὶ τεκτόνων σοφίαν οὐδεὶς ἂν ἀξίως παραστήσειε λόγος πλὴν ὅσα γε πειραθῆναι. Οὐ μὴν ἀλλὰ τούτοις αὖ καὶ τὰ πανταχοῦ τῆς ἡμετέρας ἱερὰ συμβαίνει καὶ οἱ νεῴ, ὥς γ᾽ ἐν ὀλίγῳ τὸ πᾶν εἰπεῖν, οἵ τ᾽ ἐν αὐτῇ τῇ πόλει οἵ τ᾽ ἐκτὸς τῆς πόλεως, οἱ μὲν ἐγγύς τε ὄντες καὶ ἐπ᾽ αὐτῶν ᾠκοδομημένοι τῶν περιβόλων, οἱ δὲ δὴ καὶ πορρωτέρω πᾶσαν κύκλῳ διαλαβόντες τὴν χώραν, ὡς μηδὲν αὐτῆς εἴη τοῦ τοιοῦδ᾽ ἀγαθοῦ τε καὶ κόσμου καὶ τῆς ἐντεῦθεν χάριτος ἄμοιρον, μᾶλλον μὲν ὄντες καλοὶ ἢ πολλοί, μᾶλλον δὲ τῷ πλήθει προέχοντες ἢ διαφέροντες κάλλει, τοσοῦτοι μὲν ὄντες ὡς, εἰ καὶ μὴ κάλλους μετεῖχον, οὐδὲν ἧττον φέρειν εἰς δόξαν ἡμῖν, οὕτω δ᾽ ἐσκευασμένοι καὶ περιττῶς ἔχοντες κάλλους ὡς, εἰ καὶ μὴ πλήθει προεῖχον, μέγα ἂν δύνασθαι μόνῃ τῇ διὰ πάντων εὐαρμοστίᾳ καὶ συμφωνίᾳ καὶ οἷς οὐδὲν ἄπεστι τῶν εἰς θαῦμα φερόντων, περὶ ὧν ἰδίας ἐδέησεν ἂν ὑποθέσεως βουληθέντι διαλαβεῖν καὶ πραγματείας ἑτέρας.

111 Οὕτω πάντοθεν ἥ τε φύσις, ἥ τε τῶν πατέρων φιλοκαλία, ἥ τε τῶν βασιλέων ἡμῖν ἐπιστασία πᾶν ἀγαθὸν ἠρανίσατο καὶ τῇ σφετέρᾳ προσεπορίσατο. Ἀλλὰ τὰ μὲν περὶ τὴν ὅλην τῆς πόλεως κατασκευήν τε καὶ θέσιν καὶ τὴν

numerous, they are extraordinarily beautiful. What the church lacks in size, it makes up for in beauty.

The palace is thus constructed in a way that is too beautiful to describe. Only seeing it could do it justice. As for everything else that is below the first and second level of the palace, it is divided up by length and width in a way that reveals the diverse skill and great wisdom of the architects; no description could adequately present it all, however much it tried. Moreover, the rest is no different from these areas, for every part of our city has churches and shrines. To make a long story short, the churches inside the city and outside it, both those constructed close to and even abutting the very walls, or those farther away that are built in a ring around the whole region, none of them lack the same sort of quality, decoration, or the grace that stems from those things. In some areas they are beautiful rather than numerous, while in others they stand out for their number rather than their particular beauty, but there are so many that, even when they are not beautiful, they may nevertheless bring us glory. They are thus built in such a way and have such an abundance of beauty that, even if they did not stand out for their sheer numbers, they would still be able to do so, due solely to their agreeable and harmonious appearance in every way; indeed, they lack no admirable qualities. But someone wishing to describe them would require a separate treatment and a separate work. 110

In these ways, then, nature, our forefathers' love of beauty, and the protection afforded by our emperors have provided us with every blessing in every regard and have further enriched their city. I have already discussed the overall construction and location of the city as well as the 111

τῆς πολιτείας οἰκονομίαν καὶ διαχείρισιν εἴρηται. Τό γε μὴν αὐτῆς μάχιμον καὶ τὰ κατὰ στρατείας καὶ πόλεμον θαυμαστὴν ὅσην σοφίαν τε καὶ ἀνδρείαν αὐτῇ μαρτυρεῖ. Ἀποκέκρινται μὲν γὰρ τοῦ λοιποῦ πλήθους οἱ προβεβλημένοι τῆς πόλεως καὶ τεταγμένοι στρατεύεσθαι, μόνον ἔχοντες ἔργον καὶ ἓν ἐπιτήδευμα, τὴν τῶν τακτικῶν γυμνασίαν καὶ τὸ κατὰ πολέμους εὐδοκιμεῖν, οὐδὲν δ' ἧττον καὶ σύμπας ὁ δῆμος καὶ τὸ πᾶν τῆς πόλεως πλήρωμα οὐ μᾶλλον ὑφ' ἑτέρων φυλάττεσθαι ἢ φυλάκων ἀξιοῦντες, αὐτοὶ σχῆμα σῴζειν τοῖς ἄλλοις διαχειρίζονται μὲν καὶ ἣν ἕκαστος ἔτυχεν ἠσκηκὼς τέχνην καὶ ἐπιτήδευμα, γυμνάζονται δὲ καὶ τὰ ἐς πολέμους καὶ μάχας καὶ στρατιωτικὴν ἐμπειρίαν, ὡς ἂν ῥώμης τε ἱκανῶς ἔχοντες καὶ ἀνδρείας ἥκοντες ἐπὶ πλεῖστον, τῆς γῆς ὥσπερ ἐπίτηδες θάρσος ἀνείσης καὶ τόλμαν τοῖς ἐξ αὐτῆς ἔμφρονα καὶ ῥώμην σωμάτων, ὥστ' οὐ μᾶλλον ἄν τις αὐτῶν τὴν καρτερίαν θαυμάσαι ἢ τὸ τοῦ σώματος ἐν τοῖς πόνοις ἀνάλωτον. Γενναιότητι μὲν γὰρ τοὺς ἀνδρείους, ῥώμῃ δὲ νικῶντες τοὺς ἰσχΰϊ προέχοντας ἢ μᾶλλον τοὺς μὲν ῥωμαλέους ἀνδρείᾳ, ῥώμῃ δὲ τοὺς τὴν ψυχὴν ἀηττήτους, ἐν πᾶσι δ' ἀμφοῖν εὐδοκιμεῖν ἔχουσι καὶ τὸ κατὰ πάντων ἀποφέρεσθαι κράτος.

112 Πρόσεστι δὲ καὶ ἡ ἄσκησις, πρᾶγμα τοσοῦτον οὐκ ἐν τοῖς κυνηγεσίοις γυμναζομένων μόνοις καὶ τῇ πρὸς τὰ τῶν θηρίων ἀνυπόστατα μάχῃ, ἃ τῶν πολεμικῶν ἀγώνων εἰσὶ πάντως προτέλειαι, ἀλλὰ μάλιστα μὲν αὐτοὶ κατὰ τῶν πολεμίων συνεχῶς καὶ τῆς ἐκείνων χώρας εἰσβάλλοντες καὶ τοὺς ἀληθινοὺς ἐν τούτοις μελετῶντες ἀγῶνας, σχολῆς δ'

management and administration of the state. The city's warlike qualities, on campaigns and on the battlefield, attest how admirable are its wisdom and courage. For those who have been assigned to protect the city and to serve in the army have been selected from the rest of the people, having only a single job to do and one profession: practicing battle tactics and earning a good reputation in war. Nevertheless, the entire populace and the masses of the city would rather guard themselves than be guarded by others and so, although they nominally entrust their protection to others, whatever craft or profession each of them practices, they also train in the skills necessary for wars, battles, and military service. As a result they are very strong and have attained a considerable degree of bravery. It is as if this land has deliberately produced courage, wise audacity, and physical strength in her children, so that one would not admire their endurance any more than their indefatigability in their exertions. For they defeat the courageous with their nobility, and the powerful with their strength, or rather they defeat the mighty with their courage, and men of unconquerable spirit with their might, having an ample store of both these qualities and the ability to prevail over everyone.

Then there is also their training, which does not just con- 112
sist of hunting and fighting invincible beasts for exercise, which are assuredly the preliminaries to military contests. Rather, most of the time they are constantly attacking their enemies and invading their lands and practicing actual combat through these activities. When they are free from these

οὔσης ἐκεῖθεν καὶ εἰρήνης πολέμων αὐτοί τε ἐφ' ἑαυτῶν ἔν τισι συγκειμέναις ἡμέραις παμπληθεὶ *τὰ τῶν πολεμούντων ἐπιδεικνύμενοι* καὶ τὰ τακτικὰ γυμναζόμενοι καὶ ὅλως τοῦθ' ἕν τε καὶ προὔργου διὰ βίου μετιόντες ἐπιτήδευμα, εὖ τε καὶ καλῶς παρεσκευάσθαι πρὸς πόλεμον, ὡς ἐπιόντα τε πολέμιον ὑποστῆναι καί, δεῆσαν κατ' ἄλλων αὐτοὺς ἐπιέναι, δυνηθῆναι λυπῆσαι. Ὅπλοις τε γοῦν ἀγχεμάχοις κεχρῆσθαι καὶ συστάδην ἀγωνίζεσθαι τίνος οὐκ ἀκριβέστερον ἤσκηνται πάλλειν τε δόρυ καὶ τόξοις λυπεῖν τίς ἂν ἐς ἴσον αὐτοῖς ἔλθοι ποτέ; Τόξοις μὲν γὰρ Τεῦκρον νικῶσι καὶ Πάνδαρον, *ἵππους δέ τε κοσμῆσαι καὶ ἀνέρας ἀσπιδιώτας* Μενεσθέα ἀπέκρυψαν, παῖδα δὲ τὸν Ὀϊλέως ἀπέδειξαν ποδωκείᾳ τε καὶ τῷ εὐζώνῳ τοῦ σώματος, καὶ ἄλλῳ ἄλλον τῶν ἀγωνισμάτων καὶ πᾶσι παρευδοκίμησαν ἅπαντας.

113 Αὐτοί τε γὰρ καθ' αὐτοὺς πρὸς πᾶν εὐφυῶς ἔσχον, ἡγεμόνων τε καὶ κορυφαίων τοιούτων ἐτύχομεν, τῶν ἀρίστων ἡμῖν βασιλέων, ὡς, εἰ καὶ πρὸς μηδὲν ἐπεφύκειμεν, ἱκανοὺς ἂν αὐτοὺς εἶναι τῷ καθ' αὐτοὺς ὑποδείγματι παιδαγωγῆσαί τε καὶ ῥυθμίσαι καὶ πρὸς ἅπαν εἶδος ἀρετῆς ἐμβιβάσαι καὶ τῶν καλῶν ὀρεχθῆναι ποιῆσαι, ὥστε τὴν νῦν τῆς πολιτείας κατάστασιν καὶ ἣν ἔχουσι πεῖραν οἱ πολῖται καὶ γυμνασίαν ἐν τοῖς πολεμικοῖς οὐκ ἔξω τοῦ εἰκότος εἶναι λόγου, οὔτε τῆς τ' αὐτῶν εὐφυΐας τῆς τε τῶν βασιλέων παιδαγωγίας.

114 Οὔκουν θαυμαστόν, εἴ τινες καθ' ἡμῶν ἐπιόντες καθ' αὐτῶν ἔγνωσαν ὁρμηθέντες καὶ κακοὶ κακῶς ἀπήλλαξαν ἢ εἰ πρὸς τὴν τῶν ἐναντίων αὐτοὶ τὸν πόλεμον μετατιθέντες βλάψαι ἰσχύσαμεν, ἀλλὰ τοὐναντίον ἔδει θαυμάζειν, εἰ, οὕτως ἐφ' ἑαυτῶν ἄριστα προμεμελετηκότες τὰ τῶν ἐν

tasks and there is peace from wars, they gather together on certain prearranged days *to display how to wage war* and practice their tactics. In short, they share this one important mission in life: to be thoroughly prepared for war, so that they may withstand an enemy's attack and, when occasion demands that they attack others, to be able to cause them harm. Who else has been trained to use weapons and fight in hand-to-hand combat more precisely than they have? Who would ever be their equal in throwing a spear or harassing their enemies with arrows? They would prevail over Teukros and Pandaros as archers, outstrip Menestheus when it comes to *marshalling horses and shield-bearing warriors,* show up the son of Oileus in speed and in physical fitness, and overcome anyone else in any other feats, surpassing everyone in every way.

On their own terms, they are naturally well suited for any 113
task, and we have such rulers and leaders in our most excellent emperors that, even if we were by nature good for nothing at all, they would still be capable of tutoring and training us by their own example, as well as guiding us in acquiring all manner of virtue and making us hunger for what is good. Consequently, my description of the present condition of the state and of the experience and military practice of the citizens is not improbable, nor that of their natural abilities and the training afforded by our emperors.

No wonder, then, that some of those who attacked us re- 114
alized that they were fighting a losing battle and being bad men, came to a bad end, or that, by shifting the theater of war to our opponents' land, we succeeded in harming them instead. On the contrary, it would have been a cause for wonder if, with all our best preemptive training for military

πολέμοις ἀγώνων, ἔπειθ᾽ ἥττους τῶν ἐπιόντων ἐφαινόμεθα γινόμενοι καὶ κατ᾽ ἄλλων αὐτοὶ στρατευόμενοι μετὰ τῆς ἐλάττονος ἐπανήειμεν μοίρας.

115 Δύο γοῦν ὑπερφυῆ καθ᾽ ἡμῶν εἰσελάσαι βαρβάρων καὶ μέγιστα τῶν πώποτε στρατεύματα μνημονεύεται, μυριάσι μὲν ἀνδρῶν δεδιττόμενα, τῇ πάσῃ δὲ παρασκευῇ φοβοῦντα καὶ ἐξιστῶντα τοὺς ἐναντίους, οὐδέτερον δὲ καθ᾽ ἡμῶν ἴσχυσεν οὐ πλήθει στρατοῦ, οὐκ ἀνταγωνιστῶν ἐμπειρίᾳ, οὐκ ἄλλῳ τῳ τῶν ἐφ᾽ οἷς μέγα φρονοῦσι πολέμιοι. Ἀλλὰ τὸ μέν, ὡς ἀνηνύτοις ἐπιχειρεῖν ἔγνω καὶ πλείω κακῶς ἔπασχεν ἢ ἡμᾶς ἔδρα, τοῖς πᾶσιν ἀηττήτους ὀφθέντας, ὡς εἰς τελευταίαν κατέφυγον ἄγκυραν καὶ ὧν εἶχον τὸ βιαιότατον, ἐμπρῆσαι τὴν πόλιν, πρᾶγμα τῶν τε πειρωμένων πολλὴν ἀνανδρίαν μαρτυροῦν καὶ νίκης ἀπόγνωσιν, καθ᾽ ὧν τε ἐμηχανᾶτο ἡττηθεῖσι μὲν οὐδεμίαν ἐπιφέρον δικαίως κατηγορίαν, εἴπερ τῶν ὑπὲρ ἄνθρωπον πάντας ἑξῆς ἡττᾶσθαι πᾶσα ἀνάγκη, περιγενομένοις δὲ πάντα τὰ κάλλιστα καὶ περιουσίαν ἀνδρείας καὶ εὐτυχίας ἐπάγον. Πῦρ γοῦν ἐνῆκαν μὲν ταῖς οἰκίαις, οἱ δὲ πολῖται, καὶ πρὸς τὸ πῦρ καὶ τοὺς ἔξω πολεμίους ἀγωνιζόμενοι, οὐδὲν ἧττον καὶ τούτους ἐτρέψαντο καὶ τοῦ πυρὸς ἐγένοντο κρείττους οὐχ ὅσον ἐντεῦθεν βλαφθέντες οὐδέν, ἀλλὰ καὶ μᾶλλον ἀποφανθέντες λαμπρότεροι ὅσῳ πάσας τὰς τῶν ἐναντίων ἐλπίδας καὶ τὴν δυνατὴν αὐτοῖς πεῖραν ἀπήλεγξαν τὸ μηδὲν οὔσας καὶ παιδίων πρὸς ἄνδρας ἀθύρματα.

116 Τὸ δέ γε λοιπόν τε καὶ δεύτερον στράτευμα ὅσῳ δεινότερόν τε καὶ φοβερώτερον ἦν, τοσούτῳ καθ᾽ ἑαυτοῦ δεινότερον ὤφθη γενόμενον καὶ τοὔνομα ἀπηνέγκατο καὶ

combat, we had then appeared to be in worse shape than our attackers and, when campaigning against our enemies, we had returned worse off.

Let us recall two of the most enormous and strongest barbarian armies to have ever attacked us. Although they frightened their opponents with their myriads of men, terrified them with all their preparations, and confounded them, none of this made any impression on us, not the size of their army, their experience in fighting their opponents, or anything else in which enemies take so much pride. As for the first army, when they realized that they were attempting the impossible and that they had suffered more harm than they had inflicted upon us, although they appeared invincible to everyone else, they fell back on their final option and the most vicious tactic they had at their disposal: to set fire to the city. This act testifies to the great cowardice of their enterprise and their despair of winning; it could bring no just criticism for the people whom they contrived to defeat in this way (since everyone must necessarily in turn be defeated by superhuman factors), but could bring out all that is best in the survivors, including an abundance of manliness and prosperity. So they set fire to the houses, but the citizens, who were combatting both the fire and their enemies outside the city, nevertheless routed them and prevailed over the fire, suffering no harm as a result, but even gaining greater repute by dashing all of their opponents' hopes and thwarting their powerful attempt, making them as nothing and as child's play for men. 115

The second army turned out to be as terrible for itself as it had been more terrible and formidable than the first one; its name was obliterated, it gained notoriety everywhere for 116

περιβεβόηται πανταχοῦ οἷς πανωλεθρίᾳ παντελεῖ παραδέδοται κἀκ τῆς ἰδίας συμφορᾶς γέγονε γνώριμον. Ἅμα τε γὰρ εἰσήλασαν καὶ πέρα δεινῶν αὐτοῖς ἀπηντήκει τὰ πράγματα, οὐδὲ γνοῦσιν ὅθεν ὁ ὄλεθρος, ὥστε μηδ' ἀγγελιαφόρον ἤ, τοῦτο δὴ τὸ λεγόμενον, *ὑπολελεῖφθαι πυρφόρον*, ἀλλ' αὐτοῦ πεσεῖν μὲν ἅπαν τὸ στράτευμα καὶ τὸν ἐς Ἅιδην ὑπνῶσαι, τὸν δ' ἄρχοντ' αὐτοῖς καὶ ἡγεμόνα τῆς στρατιᾶς δέσμιον ἀπαχθῆναι, τὴν προτέραν ἀλλαξάμενον τύχην καὶ ὧν ὠνειροπόλει κατὰ τῆς πόλεως ὕπαρ ἀποτίνοντα δίκας. Ὅπερ εἴθ' ἡ τῶν ἐνοικούντων ἀνδρεία κατώρθωσεν εἴτε τις δύναμις θειοτέρα (λέγεται γὰρ οὖν καὶ πιστεύεται), εἴτε καὶ ἄμφω ταυτὶ συνδραμόντα, Θεοῦ συνεπιρρωννύντος τοὺς ἡμετέρους πολίτας, ποίαν οὐκ ἂν ὑπερβολὴν ἀγαθῶν παρενέγκοιεν;

117 Ὥσπερ δὲ πεπρωμένον ἡμῖν ὂν εὐδοκιμεῖν πανταχοῦ καὶ τοῖς πᾶσι νικᾶν, οὕτω μετὰ πολλοῦ τοῦ κρείττονος ἐπιόντων τε καθ' ἡμῶν ἀπαλλάττομεν τῶν ἐχθρῶν καὶ αὐτοὶ κατ' αὐτῶν ἐκστρατεύοντες διὰ πάντων κρατοῦμεν, καὶ ψυχὰς αὐτῶν δουλούμενοι καὶ τὰ σώματα, ἅτε μὴ μόνον εὖ παρεσκευασμένοι τοῖς πᾶσι καὶ ὅσων δεῖ πολέμῳ καὶ μάχῃ, ἀλλὰ καὶ μετὰ παντὸς τοῦ δικαίου πρὸς τοὺς πολεμικοὺς ἀγῶνας ἥκοντες καὶ παλαίσματα. Ἄρχομεν γὰρ μάχης οὐδ' ἅπαξ, ἀμυνόμενοι δὲ τὰ ὀμωμοσμένα παραβαίνοντας τοὺς ὁμόρους ἑκάστοτε, τόν τε τοῦ δικαίου λόγον ἡμῶν αὐτῶν προβαλλόμεθα, καὶ μετὰ τοιαύτης ὡρμημένοι τῆς συμμαχίας οὐκ ἀπεικότως περιγινόμεθα τῶν ἐχθρῶν καὶ τοῖς τῆς μάχης ἄθλοις κοσμούμεθα, ὥστ' ἀμφοτέρων ἡμῖν ἄριστα τῶν καιρῶν

its utter destruction, and became widely known for its own misfortune. For at the moment these people attacked, things went horribly wrong for them. They did not even recognize the source of their destruction, so that there was no one left to bear news of what happened or, as the saying goes, *not one sacrificial fire-bearing priest was left.* Instead, the entire army fell in battle and sank into a deathly slumber, while their commander, the leader of the army, was carried off in chains, exchanging this fate for his previous good fortune and, now that he was wide awake, paying the price for what he dreamed of doing to the city. Either the bravery of the city's inhabitants or (at least, so it is said and believed) some other more divine force brought about this victory; or perhaps both these factors converged, for with God empowering our citizens, what abundance of virtues might they not exhibit?

It is as if we are fated to succeed in every regard and de- 117
feat everyone. Thus we dismiss enemies who attack us, even when they have a great advantage over us, and we ourselves always prevail when we campaign against them, enslaving their minds and bodies, because we are not only prepared for everything and whatever is necessary in war and battle, but also because we come to the contests and struggles of war with righteousness on our side. We never initiate the fight, but always defend ourselves against our neighbors whenever they break the oaths they have sworn. We make a point of having our own just cause, and setting forth with it as our ally, we naturally overcome our enemies and are rewarded with the spoils of battle, so that we can live well

ἐξεῖναι πολιτεύεσθαι εἰρήνης τε ἀπολαύειν βαθείας, τὰ πλείω τῶν πολεμίων τρεμόντων καὶ ἠρεμούντων· εἰρηνεύει γὰρ μάλιστα ὃς μάλιστα πρὸς πόλεμον παρεσκεύασται καί, πολέμου δεῆσαν, κουφότατα περιγίνεσθαι καὶ τὴν νικῶσαν ἀποφέρεσθαι πανταχοῦ.

118 Ὥστ᾽ οὐχ ὧν ἡ ἡμετέρα κατὰ τῶν βαρβάρων, πεζῇ τε κατ᾽ αὐτῶν ἐκστρατεύουσα καὶ τριήρεσι καὶ θαλάττῃ χρωμένη, κατώρθωκε μόνον, εἰς τὴν αὐτῶν ἀποβαίνουσα καὶ τὸν περὶ τῆς σφετέρας ἀναγκάζουσ᾽ αὐτοὺς ἀγωνίζεσθαι, ἀλλὰ καὶ ὧν οὐ κατορθοῖ δικαίως ἂν θαυμασθείη, τὸ μὲν πολλῶν ὧν ἠρίστευσεν ὄντων καὶ πάντων ἀξίων αὐτῇ, τὸ δ᾽ ὅτι καὶ μὴ κατορθοῦσα τὴν σφετέραν οὐδὲν ἧττον ἐπιδείκνυται γενναιότητα, ἅτε περιουσίᾳ δυνάμεως συνέχουσά τε τοὺς ἐχθροὺς καὶ ἄκοντας ἠρεμεῖν δέει τῷ ἐς αὐτὴν καὶ τῆς ἀνάγκης αὐτὴ τοῦ πολεμεῖν ἀφειμένη. Τοῦ γὰρ ἐν μάχαις εὐδοκιμεῖν, ἀνάγκης ἡκούσης, οὐδὲν ἧττον εἰς εὐφημίαν εἰρήνην ἑαυτῷ πορίσασθαι πάντοθεν, δεδιότων τῶν ἐχθρῶν συμβαλεῖν. Ὥσθ᾽ οὕτως ἄν τις μὴ κατορθῶν πολλῷ μέσῳ τοὺς κατορθοῦντας νικῴη καὶ τὰ τῶν ἀγωνιζομένων ἀποφέροιτ᾽ ἂν ἔπαθλα, μὴ παλαίων, μηδὲ μαχόμενος. Οἷς γὰρ πρὸς πόλεμον παρεσκεύασται καὶ κρατεῖν μεμελέτηκεν ἀφεῖται μὴ πολεμεῖν.

119 Τὴν οὖν οὕτω μὲν δυνάμεως, οὕτω δ᾽ ἀγαθῶν πάντων ἀσκήσεως, οὕτω δὲ τῆς ἐν πολέμῳ δεινότητος καὶ τοῦ κατὰ πάντων ἔχουσαν κράτους καὶ κοσμουμένην μὲν ἀρχαιότητι, θέσει δ᾽ ἀγαλλομένην καὶ ὡρῶν ἁρμονίᾳ καὶ κάλλει κατασκευῆς καὶ οἰκοδομίας παντοδαπῆς καὶ τῇ διὰ

during both war and peace. We enjoy prolonged peace, as most of our enemies are terrified and keep quiet. He who is most prepared for war is most at peace, since when war becomes necessary, he easily overcomes his opponents and gains the benefit of victory in every case.

Consequently, our city not only wins victories over the 118
barbarians, both marching against them on foot and using triremes at sea to go to their land and force them to fight for what is theirs, but it should also be rightly admired when it is *not* successful; for in the former case it performs many noble deeds, all of them worthy of itself, while in the latter case, even though our city does not succeed in its intentions, it nevertheless displays nobility, since it keeps its enemies in check with its ample strength and compels them, even against their will, to be at peace out of fear of our city and also the anguish that would result from attacking it. Our city fares well in battle when need presses, and yet it is no less to its credit that it secures peace for itself on all its fronts, as its enemies are afraid to meet it in battle. In this way, even if one did not succeed, he would still outdo those who were successful and take home the competition's prizes, without even actually wrestling or fighting. For those who are prepared for war and have practiced getting the upper hand can avoid making war in the first place.

Thus, when our city is so powerful, so practiced in all 119
good things, so formidable in war, so superior to everyone else, a city adorned by its antiquity, beautified by its location, the harmony of its seasons, the beauty of its construction, and the variety of buildings, as well as by its harmony

πάντων εὐαρμοστίᾳ καὶ συμφωνίᾳ, τίς ἂν λόγος πρὸς ἀξίαν κοσμήσειεν ἢ ποία τῶν αὐτῇ προσηκόντων ἐφίκοιτ᾽ ἂν γλῶττα;

120 Ὃ γοῦν ἐν τοῖς ἄνω μέν ἐστι λόγοις, οὐδὲν δ᾽ ἧττον καὶ νῦν ἁρμόζει ῥηθῆναι, ὅτι, τῶν ἄλλων ἁπάντων τῶν ὡς ἐγγυτάτω τε καὶ πόρρω τῆς Ῥωμαίων ἀρχῆς ὄντων δεδουλωμένων καὶ νῶτα τοῖς ἐχθροῖς δόντων, ἡ ἡμετέρα τούτου τε κρείττων ἐγεγόνει, καὶ πρός, ἄλλων ἄρχειν ἠξίωται, τοῦτ᾽ αὖ ὑπειπὼν καὶ δὴ πεπαύσομαι. Εἰς κόσμον μὲν γὰρ ἡμῖν φέρει καὶ θαύματος λόγον καὶ τοῦτο δὴ τὸ κοινὸν καὶ κατὰ πάντων κρατῆσαν, μόνης αὐτῆς ἡττηθέν, ὅταν δὲ καὶ τὰς εὐδαιμονηκυίας τῶν πόλεων ἴδοις τις ἂν ἑαλωκυίας δεινῶς καὶ ταὐτὸ τοῦτο παθούσας ὃ κατὰ πάντων ἐνίκησεν αἷς καὶ μόνον ἀντιπαρεξετάζεσθαί τινα φέρει πρὸς ἔπαινον, τότ᾽ αὔξεται καὶ μᾶλλον τῇ περιγενομένῃ τὸ θαῦμα, καὶ μείζων ὁ ἔπαινος αὐτῇ γίνεται.

121 Εἰς ἃς οὖν ἀναφέρειν ἔχομεν πόλεις καὶ αἷς ὥσπερ πατρίσι κοσμούμεθα, ταύτας εἰς ἔσχατον ἐν τοῖς ἄνω χρόνοις ἡκούσας εὐκλείας ἀρχῆς τε εἵνεκα καὶ δυνάμεων καὶ πάντων τῶν ἄλλων, οὐδ᾽ ὅσον εἰπεῖν ἡ ἡμετέρα πόλις ὑπερεβάλετο. Μιλήτου μὲν γὰρ καὶ Σινώπης αὐτῆς, τῆς μὲν οὐδὲ τοὔνομα λέλειπται, τὴν δὲ δακρύσαις ἂν ἰδὼν ὑφ᾽ ὅτων οἰκεῖται καὶ οὓς ἄρχοντας στέργει, ὑπὲρ δὲ Ἀθηνῶν καὶ τῆς Ἀττικῆς χώρας ἁπάσης κἂν αἰσχυνθείη τις· οὕτω πονήρως πεπράγεσαν. Ἡμῖν δὲ χωρεῖ τὰ πράγματα κρεῖττον ἢ κατ᾽ εὐχήν, καὶ ὁ *πάντα* μὲν *γηράσκων χρόνος*, αὐτὸς δ᾽ ἀκμάζων ἀεὶ καὶ νεάζων, ἡμῖν μόνοις τῆς ἑαυτοῦ μετέδωκε φύσεως, ἐν ἀκμῇ τὰ τῆς εὐτυχίας τῇ πόλει

and agreement in every matter, what oration could properly praise it, or what tongue truly represent its features?

What I have said above, then, deserves no less to be re- 120
peated now: when all others, both those closest to and farthest away from Roman rule, were being enslaved and were turning tail before their enemies, our city overcame the threat and, furthermore, was deemed worthy to rule other cities. On this note, I will end my speech. For it is to our credit and a matter for admiration that, when this threat prevailed in general and overcame everyone else, it was vanquished by our city alone. When one sees how cities that were once prosperous have fallen into such straits and have suffered from exactly the same threat that has defeated everyone else, and if one simply tries to compare Trebizond to them in terms of deserving praise, then one's amazement at its survival is definitely increased and one's praise for it becomes even greater.

And thus, regarding those cities which we have had cause 121
to mention and by which we are adorned as our progenitors, in the end, although they were renowned in the old days for their rule and on account of their power and everything else, our city has, to say the least, surpassed them. Considering Miletos and Sinope, not even the name of the former remains, while you would weep if you saw what kind of people inhabit the latter and what rulers it loves. Even Athens and the whole land of Attica are a cause for shame, they have fared so miserably. Yet our affairs have gone better than we could possibly have hoped, and *time, which makes everything old,* but itself is always in its prime and youth, has shared this aspect of its nature with us alone and kept our city always

συνέχων, καὶ ταῦτα πλείων παραρρυεὶς ἤδη σχεδὸν ἀφ᾽ οὗ Μίλητον ὑφ᾽ ἑαυτὸν ἐποιήσατο καὶ Ἀθήνας ἢ ὅσον ἔφθασαν ἐκεῖναι οἰκισθεῖσαι τὴν ἡμετέραν. Γένοιτο δὲ καὶ τὸν ἔπειτα χρόνον μετὰ τῆς ὁμοίας ἡμᾶς ὑποδέξασθαι τύχης καὶ τοῖς δυνατοῖς ἅπασι κοσμῆσαι τὴν ἡμετέραν, ἀθάνατον αὐτῇ τὴν ἀγαθὴν συνέχοντα μοῖραν.

122 Ὁ μὲν οὖν πρὸς τὴν ἐνεγκοῦσαν ἐξείργασται λόγος, ἄνδρες πολῖται, καὶ τὸ χρέος ἐκτέτισταί μοι τὸ πρὸς αὐτήν, τῆς μὲν δυνάμεως ἴσως οὐδὲν ἧττον, τῆς δ᾽ ἀξίας τε καὶ βουλήσεως οὐδ᾽ ὅσον εἰπεῖν. Εἰ δὲ τῷ λέγοντι τὸν λόγον, οὐ τῇ πόλει παραμετρήσαντες, οὕτω τὴν ψῆφον ἐξοίσετε, κατ᾽ ἀγαθούς τε κρινεῖτε κριτὰς καὶ δικαίους καὶ τοὺς ἐνταῦθα λόγους ὑπὲρ ὑμῶν ἔργοις αὐτοῖς βεβαιώσετε.

prosperous and in its prime. And that, when almost more time has already passed since it subdued Miletos and Athens than when they first settled our city. May the future too grant that we may continue to enjoy a similar fate and honor our city with the very best attributes it can, maintaining its immortal good fortune.

And so, I have now completed this speech for the city 122
which bore us, my fellow citizens, and discharged my debt to her. I have tried to do my very best, but I have not been able to do it justice or say as much as I would have liked. But if you evaluate the person who has given the speech rather than the city and you cast your vote on that basis, you will issue a verdict befitting good and just judges and confirm with these acts the words spoken here on your behalf.

Abbreviations

CPG = Ernst Leutsch and Friedrich G. Schneidewin, eds., *Corpus paroemiographorum Graecorum,* 2 vols. (Göttingen, 1839–1851; repr., Hildesheim, 1958)

EI^2 = Peri J. Bearman et al., eds., *Encyclopaedia of Islam,* 2nd ed., 12 vols. (Leiden, 1960–2005)

LbG = Erich Trapp et al., eds., *Lexikon der byzantinischen Gräzität* (Vienna, 1994–2017)

ODB = Alexander P. Kazhdan et al., eds., *Oxford Dictionary of Byzantium,* 3 vols. (New York, 1991)

PG = Jacques-Paul Migne, ed., *Patrologiae cursus completus: Series Graeca* (Paris, 1857–1866)

PLP = Erich Trapp, ed., *Prosopographisches Lexikon der Palaiologenzeit,* 12 vols. (Vienna, 1976–1996)

Thiriet, *Régestes* = Freddy Thiriet, *Régestes des délibérations du Sénat de Venise concernant la Romanie,* 3 vols. (Paris, 1958–1961)

Note on the Texts

Michael Panaretos's *On the Emperors of Trebizond* survives in a single manuscript, Marcianus graecus 608/coll. 306, which was copied around 1440 by two scribes on the basis of a now lost exemplar (Peter Schreiner, "Bemerkungen zur Handschrift," in *Mare et Litora* [Moscow, 2009]). It was acquired by John Zacharias, who lived in either Crete or Venice, during the latter half of the sixteenth century and eventually passed into Venice's Biblioteca Marciana in 1734 through a bequest of Giambattista Recanati. The chronicle was discovered by Jakob Fallmerayer during the 1820s. Citing from the manuscript, he deployed Panaretos to powerful effect in his seminal *Geschichte des Kaiserthums von Trapezunt* (Munich, 1827). After Fallmerayer's *Geschichte* was published, he initially gave the text to his colleague Gottlieb Tafel, who published a faulty edition as an appendix to his edition of the works of the twelfth-century scholar Eustathios of Thessalonike. Based on this edition, Marie-Félicité Brosset translated the text into French in an appendix to Charles Le Beau's *L'histoire du Bas Empire* in 1836. In 1844 Fallmerayer published an improved edition of the text, complete with a German translation, along with many other texts relating to the empire of Trebizond that he had discovered during his travels in the Orient. In 1905, the Russian scholar Alek-

sandr Khakhanov republished the text with a Russian translation; the numbering and abbreviations used in the manuscript proved problematic, however. A 1907 edition by Spyridon Lampros greatly improved the text, but it was not without its faults. Iordanis T. Pampoukis subsequently published a corrected edition of Lampros's text in 1947. However, the text had to wait for Odysseas Lampsides's 1958 edition to finally be transcribed correctly.

Panaretos's chronicle was recently translated into English for the first time by Annika Asp Talwar in 2016 based on Lampsides's edition. My translation includes the Greek text, detailed notes, a map of the empire of Trebizond, and a genealogy of the Grand Komnenoi, to aid and spur further research on the empire of Trebizond.

In contrast to Panaretos, Bessarion's *Encomium on Trebizond* was not published until Spyridon Lampros produced an edition in 1916 based on Bessarion's autograph copy of his youthful works, Marcianus gr. 533. About seventy years later, in 1984, Odysseas Lampsides published a corrected and more accurate transcription of the text. Thanasis Georgiades published a modern Greek translation in 2000 based on Lampsides's edition. As both Lampros and Lampsides were working from Bessarion's autograph copy, neither examined an additional copy of the text, Madrid gr. 4619, which once belonged to the Renaissance humanist Constantine Laskaris. In fall 2014, I examined the fifteenth-century manuscript and determined that it was an apograph of Marcianus gr. 533.

The Greek text of both *On the Emperors of Trebizond* and the *Encomium on Trebizond* presented here is based on Lampsides's texts without the critical apparatus of these two fine editions. In some places, I have amended the text and punc-

tuation of both in order to clarify the text for the reader. These changes are signaled in the Notes to the Texts. Numbers presented an issue with Panaretos, as the manuscript of the text is inconsistent in its use of cardinal and ordinal numbers. As a matter of principle, I have remained as close to Lampsides's transcription of the manuscript as possible in order to convey to the reader the customs of the time and idiosyncrasies of Panaretos's text. I have only corrected egregious errors. I have also introduced new chapter divisions to both texts for ease of reference.

Notes to the Texts

Michael Panaretos, *On the Emperors of Trebizond*

7 ͵ςψϟʹ: *I have corrected the MS* ͵ς″ψ″ϟ″.

55 βάρκας: *I have corrected the MS* βάλκας.

83 ἐν ἡμέρᾳ: *I have corrected the MS* ἐνήμερα.

85 διακαινησίμου: *I have corrected the MS* διακαινισήμου.

Bessarion, *Encomium on Trebizond*

title Εἰς Τραπεζοῦντα: *Bessarion also titled the text* ἐγκωμίον εἰς Τραπεζοῦντα *in his autograph table of contents for Marcianus gr. 533. See Saffrey, "Recherches," 287.*

7 ἡττηθέντα: *I have added a paragraph break here.*

26 ᾗ: *I have added a paragraph break here.*

34 συρρηγνύντος: *I have corrected the MS* συρρηγνύντας.

74 ὀγδόῳ: *I have corrected the MS* ὀγδόου.

Μυσίαν: *I have corrected the MS* Μοισίαν.

75 ἀσμένως: *I have corrected the MS* ἄσμενός.

86 ἀσμένως: *I have corrected the MS* ἄσμενος.

Notes to the Translations

Michael Panaretos, *On the Emperors of Trebizond*

1 *Alexios I*: Alexios (*ODB*, 1:63–64) was the grandson of the Byzantine emperor Andronikos I Komnenos (r. 1183–1185). For the sake of clarity, I give regnal numbers for each ruler when first mentioned, even though they do not appear in the Greek text.

Tamar: Tamar, queen of Georgia (r. 1184–1213).

indiction 7, 1204: The dates in the Greek text follow the Byzantine calendar, which dated events from the supposed creation of the world in 5509 BCE. Their calendar year began on September 1. The modern Common Era year is calculated by subtracting 5,508 for dates falling between January and August, and 5,509 for dates falling between September and December. If the chronicler does not specify the month in which an event happened, it may have occurred in either of (our) two years. Thus, a date of 6712 could fall between September 1203 and August 1204 CE. For the convenience of the reader, in the English translation I have rendered the Byzantine dates in the year of the Common Era. An indiction is any year in the Byzantines' fifteen-year tax cycle. Thus, indiction 7 refers to the seventh year in the fifteen-year cycle.

Sunday of Orthodoxy: The Sunday of Orthodoxy is the first Sunday of Lent.

2 *Andronikos I Gidos Komnenos*: The Greek form of Andronikos's name is variously rendered as Gidos and Gidon. I retain Panaretos's variations in spelling, which result from confusion in the Pontic Greek dialect between the noun termination -ων, -ωνος and -ος, -ωνος. The latter tends to replace the former.

Melik Sultan came to attack Trebizond: This incident is also described more fully in Lazaropoulos, *Synopsis,* miracle 23, and perhaps even in Bessarion, *Encomium on Trebizond,* chapter 116. The person referred to as Melik Sultan may have been the son of the Seljuk sultan Kayqubad I (r. 1220–1237), but his identity is uncertain. For a recent study of the event, see Andrew C. S. Peacock, "The Saliūq Campaign against the Crimea and the Expansionist Policy of the Early Reign of 'Alā' al-Dīn Kayqubād," *Journal of the Royal Asiatic Society* 16 (2006): 133–49.

After reigning for six years he died . . . in 1238: In fact, John I reigned as sole emperor for only three years. The chronicler may be including an extra three years when John I was Andronikos's coemperor. *ODB* (under "Grand Komnenos") and Grumel, *La chronologie byzantine,* 372, both give John I's death as 1238, though without providing a month or explanation. *ODB* specifies that its date is "based on Grumel, but with modifications."

polo grounds: A field *(tzykanisterion)* where people played *tzykanion,* a game similar to modern polo.

3 *Ioannikios*: Some have seen him as the son of John I who was tonsured so that his uncle Manuel could take the throne. However, it is also possible that he was John I and Ioannikios was his monastic name, as several Byzantine emperors were tonsured before they died, such as the emperors John VI Kantakouzenos (r. 1347–1354) and Manuel II Palaiologos (r. 1391–1425), who took the monastic names Ioasaph and Matthew, respectively.

Manuel I: Almost nothing is known of the reign of Manuel (*PLP* 12113), but the emperor probably gained the title "the greatest general" after he reconquered Sinope from the Turks in 1254. Byzantine rule was brief, as the city fell to the Turkmens in 1265. See Maria Nystazopoulou, "La dernière reconquête de Sinope par les Grecs de Trébizonde (1254–1265)," *Revue des études byzantines* 22 (1964): 241–49.

5 *George Komnenos*: George Komnenos (*PLP* 12094) reigned from 1266 until his *archontes* and family betrayed him to his Ilkhanid overlord Abaqa Khan (r. 1265–1282) in 1280. The meaning of the phrase ἐν τῷ ὄρει τοῦ Ταυρεζίου, which we have translated

as "at the mountain of Tabriz," is a mystery because there is no mountain of Tabriz. Some have suggested emending ὄρει to ὄρῳ: "the boundary of Tabriz." If the manuscript reading is correct, the mountain of Tabriz may be Mount Ararat, to the north of Tabriz, where the khan is known to have had a summer palace. See Anthony Bryer, "The Fate of George Komnenos, Ruler of Trebizond (1266–1280)," *Byzantinische Zeitschrift* 66 (1973): 332–50.

6 *John II*: John (*PLP* 12106) reigned from 1280 until 1297.

Papadopoulos's rebellion: Nothing else is known about Papadopoulos (*PLP* 21747) or his rebellion.

Michael Palaiologos: Michael VIII Palaiologos reigned at Constantinople from 1261 until 1282. He had usurped the throne from the Laskarid dynasty. For his marriage alliance with the Grand Komnenoi, see Pachymeres, *History* 6.34.

Eudokia Komnene Palaiologina . . . born in the purple: *PLP* 12064. The imperial title *porphyrogennetos* means "born in the purple." It designated a son or a daughter born after their father had become emperor.

when Palaiologos died: Michael actually died on December 11.

condemning his father: Michael attempted to reunify the Churches (Catholic and Orthodox) at Lyons in 1274 in order to nullify the ambitions of Western rulers against him. His son Andronikos II (r. 1282–1328) rejected the Union upon his accession to the throne.

7 *After 1282, in April*: The chronicler presumably means that after the Byzantine year 6790 ended on August 31, 1282, David attacked in April 6791 (that is, 1283 CE). For more on the calculation of the Byzantine year, see the Introduction, and the note to Panaretos chapter 1 above.

the king of Georgia, David: David VI Narin (*PLP* 5017) was king of Georgia from 1245 until 1293. He ruled Imireti, the western half of Georgia, from 1259 onward.

8 *Alexios II*: Alexios (*PLP* 12084) became emperor in 1297 after his father's death and died in 1330. His reign was one of the most successful in Trapezuntine history.

the raid and capture of lord George Komnenos: After being held in

captivity by the Mongol khan, George Komnenos either escaped or was set free. The latter is likely because his captor Abaqa Khan died in 1282. Presumably, this event refers to an unsuccessful attempt to retake the throne.

Theodora Komnene: Theodora (*PLP* 12067) was the daughter of the emperor Manuel I and Rusudani of Georgia. It has been suggested that her mother was only a mistress of Manuel. Little is known about Theodora's brief reign (1284–1285), the only record of which appears to have been the production of coinage with her name and image. On her reign, see Michel Kuršanskis, "L'usurpation de Théodora Grande Comnène," *Revue des études byzantines* 33 (1975): 187–210.

Kaloïoannes Komnenos: That is, John II the Grand Komnenos. Kaloïoannes was his nickname, meaning something like "Handsome John."

Limnia: The stronghold and trading port of Limnia was located somewhere on the coast of the Yeşil Irmak delta, roughly two hundred miles west of Trebizond. Its precise location is unknown and has elicited much scholarly discussion. See Bryer and Winfield, *Pontos*, 1:96–97.

Chalybia: The region of Chalybia lies in the mountainous hinterland of modern Ünye, roughly 150 miles west of Trebizond. Famous in antiquity for its mines, the region fell under Turkmen domination and was subsequently ruled by the emirate of Chalybia, on which see the note to chapter 13.

he was still warm: The Greek here is problematic. It would imply that John's body was still warm when it reached Trebizond, two hundred miles distant from Limnia. Most bodies reach the temperature of their surrounding environment two to eight hours after death when exposed, so this seems unlikely. Earlier editors such as Fallmerayer and Lambros emended the text reading to σῶν instead of ζῶν, which would yield "His remains were still uncorrupted when they were brought . . ." This is plausible and perhaps preferable. However, it is not impossible that John's body remained warm for some time after his death. For an overview of body temperature after death, see Burhard

Madea, ed., *The Estimation of the Time Since Death in the Early Postmortem Period,* 3rd ed. (London, 2015), chaps. 2, 6.

Theotokos Chrysokephalos: The church is now a mosque named Ortahisar Fatih Büyük Camii. It lies inside Trebizond's walls and was used as a burial site for the imperial family. Andronikos I Gidos and Theodora Kantakouzene (d. 1426) were also laid to rest in the church. See chapter 110 below.

9 *the daughter of Pekaï*: Pekaï has been identified as Bekha Jaqeli (*PLP* 22252), the semiautonomous ruler of the mountainous region of Samtskhe (mod. Meskheti) in Georgia. Andronikos II Palaiologos of Constantinople, Alexios II's guardian, intended to marry his ward to the daughter of his minister Nikephoros Choumnos, but Alexios had married the daughter of Bekha Jaqeli before Andronikos could finalize the marriage alliance. See Pachymeres, *History* 10.7. On Bekha Jaqeli, see Kalistrat Salia, *Histoire de la nation géorgienne* (Paris, 1980), 242–43.

10 *still a widow*: When Eudokia visited Constantinople, her brother, the emperor Andronikos II, attempted to wed her to the Serbian king Stefan Uroš II Milutin (r. 1282–1321), but she refused. On her stay in Constantinople, see Pachymeres, *History* 9.29–30, 10.7.

11 *Kerasous*: Modern Giresun, located 109 miles west of Trebizond.

Koustouganes: The identity of this individual is a mystery.

12 *the shipyard was burned by the Latins*: The Latins on this occasion were the Genoese, who refused to pay high tariffs on their goods to the emperor of Trebizond. After failing to convince him to lower the tariff, they tried to leave the city without paying. Alexios sent his troops to stop them, and a battle ensued, resulting in a fire that burned the harbor area. The Genoese ships were destroyed, and Alexios's forces ultimately prevailed. For a more detailed account of this event, see Pachymeres, *History* 11.29. Bessarion may also allude to this event in his encomium: chapter 115.

13 *Bayram*: Bayram (Pariamis and Pairamis in Greek) was the emir of Chalybia. He and his son Hacı Emir frequently attacked Trebizond and later become its ally under Alexios III (r. 1349–

1390); see chapter 69 below. His dynasty is called the Hacimiroğulları in later Turkish sources, that is, the sons of Hacı Emir. On the emirate, see Shukurov, "Between Peace and Hostility," 43–47.

14 *Sinope*: Modern Sinop. See Bessarion's description of the city in chapters 23 to 25. Located three hundred miles west of Trebizond, the city had been lost under Alexios I in 1214 and then was briefly reconquered by Manuel I. At this time, it was ruled by the Turkmen Isfendiyarid dynasty, which allowed piracy to flourish. See *EI*², 4:108.

15 *Alexios II the Grand Komnenos passed away*: Panaretos's date is confirmed by a contemporary obit of the emperor. See Gregorio de Andrés Martínez, *Catálogo de los códices griegos de la Real Biblioteca de El Escorial* (Madrid, 1965), 3:71. Alexios's death was also the subject of a funeral epitaph by Constantine Loukites. See his *Funeral Oration for Alexios Komnenos.*

16 *Andronikos III*: *PLP* 12088. A contemporary obit on the death of Alexios II (see previous note) records that Andronikos was eighteen at the time of his succession. However, this is implausible if Andronikos's son Manuel II was eight in 1332 (see the following chapter).

17 *Asomatos*: The location of this place is uncertain. A church of the Asomatos (the Incorporeal One, that is, an archangel) in Matzouka is suggested by Bryer and Winfield in preference to Asomatos in Platana: Bryer and Winfield, *Pontos,* 1:263.

18 *Basil the Grand Komnenos . . . seized the imperial office*: Basil (*PLP* 12092) ruled from 1332 until 1340. Presumably, he fled to Constantinople after his brother Andronikos III of Trebizond murdered their brothers. After Andronikos III died, the way was open for Basil to return and take his revenge on the previous regime.

chief admiral: The office of *megas doux,* commander in chief of the navy.

commander in chief of the army: The office of *megas domestikos,* supreme commander of the army after the emperor.

They stoned to death Syrikaina, the wife of the chief admiral: Stoning was a punishment often reserved for adulterers. However, we know nothing of the backstory surrounding Syrikaina and her husband, Lekes Tzatzintzaios. Her official title of *megale doukaina* designated her as the consort of the chief admiral *(megas doux)*. Presumably, she was related to Manuel I's wife, Eirene Syrikaina (see chap. 5).

the chief admiral, the eunuch John: John (*PLP* 8597) served the emperors of Trebizond throughout the 1330s and 1340s. He was later a key supporter of the empress Eirene Palaiologina and held the emperor Michael Komnenos hostage until his death in 1344, either by the assassin's sword or natural causes. See chapters 26, 37.

19 *Eirene Palaiologina*: Eirene (*PLP* 12061) was the illegitimate daughter of the emperor Andronikos III Palaiologos (r. 1328–1341) and Basil's second cousin once removed. Her marriage to Basil is celebrated in a contemporary poem written in a manuscript of the Gospels now preserved in the Bodleian Library; see Alexander Turyn, *Dated Greek Manuscripts of the Thirteenth and Fourteenth Centuries in the Libraries of Great Britain* (Washington, D.C., 1980), 45–46.

20 *the sheikh Hasan*: Panaretos's sheikh Hasan (Sichasanes in Greek) is the Çobanid Hasan-i Küçük, ruler of Şebinkarahisar from 1338 to 1343. On the emirate of Şebinkarahisar, see Shukurov, "Between Peace and Hostility," 28–32.

ravine of Saint Kerykos: What the chronicler means by εἰς τὸν ἀχάντακαν τοῦ ἁγίου Κηρύκου is unclear. Bryer ("Greeks and Türkmens," 144) identifies the toponym as the palisade of Saint Kerykos, albeit without explanation. Presumably, he assumed that ἀχάντακας was the same as the modern Greek χαντάκι (gutter, ditch), ultimately derived from the Arabic *khandaq* (moat, ditch). Bryer and Winfield (*Pontos,* 1:206) tentatively suggest that this location is associated with a chapel near modern Soğuksu, about three miles southwest of Trebizond, where the city's western ravine begins. I suggest that the ἀχάντακας

was not a palisade, but the city's western ravine, whose name is otherwise unattested. Trebizond's eastern ravine was named after Saint George.

Minthrion: Modern Boz Tepe, a hill about one mile southeast of Trebizond.

'Abd-al Rahīm: Nothing is known about 'Abd-al Rahīm (Aftouraïmes in Greek) or why his death was important to the chronicler. Shukurov ("Between Peace and Hostility," 29) suggests that he may have been a Kurdish supporter of Hasan-i Küçük.

23 *lady Eirene from Trebizond*: Eirene from Trebizond (*PLP* 12060) should not be confused with Basil's first wife, Eirene Palaiologina. Basil's bigamous second marriage to Eirene of Trebizond outraged the Trapezuntine community, provoking civil war when he died (see chap. 25 below); it is described by Gregoras, *Roman History*, 2:548–51. The metropolitan of Trebizond turned a blind eye to the issue, earning a sharp rebuke from the patriarch of Constantinople. See Caroline Cupane, Herbert Hunger, Ewald Kislinger, and Otto Kresten, *Das Register des Patriarchats von Konstantinopel, Edition und Übersetzung der Urkunden aus den Jahren 1337–1350* (Vienna, 1995), vol. 2, no. 129.

25 *chief quartermaster*: Known as the *megas stratopedarches*, this official oversaw the provisioning of the army and commanded some army contingents.

the monastery of Saint Eugenios: The monastery and church of Saint Eugenios is now a mosque named Yeni Cuma Camii. It lies due east of Trebizond's citadel and the imperial palace, just outside the city walls on a hill overlooking the eastern ravine.

while the Amytzantarantai . . . seized the citadel with the empress: The Amytzantarantai were apparently the officials who supported the captain of the bodyguards *(amyrtzantarios)*. Naturally, the bodyguards stood by their empress against the faction led by John Tzanichites (*PLP* 27771), a powerful rich man. From their respective positions at Saint Eugenios and the citadel, the factions effectively engaged in a staring match across the eastern ravine for several months until the chief admiral *(megas doux)*

John arrived. The event is also described, at greater length, by Gregoras, *Roman History,* 1:549, and Libadenos, *Travels,* 63–64.

26 *lost their lives there*: As described in chapter 29 below, the *archontes* imprisoned at Limnia were executed one year later, in June 1341.

27 *Ak Koyunlu Turks*: The Ak Koyunlu (Amitiotai in Greek) or White Sheep Turkomans were an Oghuz Turkmen clan that later ruled present-day Azerbaijan, Armenia, eastern Turkey, part of Iran, and northern Iraq, in the fifteenth century. In the fourteenth century, they seem to have been a minor state, ranging over an area extending from the Pontic Alps in the north to the Syrian bend of the Euphrates River. See John E. Woods, *The Aqquyunlu: Clan, Confederation, Empire* (Salt Lake City, 1999).

sons of Dolinos: The identity and importance of these individuals are uncertain. Rustam Shukurov has suggested that the Duhar tribe may be represented by the Greek Dolinos. A later Turkmen source alleges that Kutlu Bey marched against Trebizond because the Trapezuntines killed a certain Yusuf of the Duhar tribe; see his *Velikye Komnini i Vostok (1204–1461)* (Saint Petersburg, 2001), 243.

30 *Anachoutlou*: *PLP* 12059. This nickname is perhaps a Turkish/Greek hybrid. Kutlu in Turkish means "blessed." Thus, Anachoutlou may stand for Anna Kutlu, "Blessed Anna."

Lazia: Lying east of Trebizond between the modern city of Rize and the Georgian border, Lazia was a mountainous region, home to the Laz. The Laz region had first become a Roman client kingdom under Hadrian and later became a Byzantine theme. See further Bessarion, *Encomium on Trebizond,* chapter 82 and note.

31 *Michael Komnenos*: Michael (*PLP* 12117) reigned briefly in 1341 and then from 1344 until he was deposed in 1349.

Niketas Scholaris and lord Gregory Meizomates: This is the first appearance of Niketas (*PLP* 27305) and Gregory (*PLP* 17618), who would control the empire off and on throughout the civil war.

The Laz seized the galleys: A longer report is given by Gregoras, *Roman History,* 2:680. Eirene Palaiologina had requested that her father, Andronikos III, send a husband to help her rule Trebizond. Andronikos died before he could grant her request. The commander in chief of the army *(megas domestikos),* the future emperor John VI Kantakouzenos (r. 1347–1354), selected Michael Komnenos for the task. When he arrived, Trebizond's ruling elite welcomed him under false pretenses and then imprisoned him when he let his guard down, since they were eager to maintain their dominance over the machinery of government.

33 *Oinaion*: Modern Ünye, 150 miles west of Trebizond, on the Black Sea coast.

35 *Meitzomates's brother*: In the Greek text, Meizomates sometimes is rendered as Meitzomates, as here.

John III Komnenos: John (*PLP* 12107) had been left behind in Constantinople by his father.

when the whole region from all around had gathered: The meaning of the Greek is unclear. Presumably, the chronicler is describing the massacre of dissidents at John III's coronation, which was followed by persecutions, public confiscations, and executions. After the betrayal of Michael Komnenos by the ruling elite, John III's ministers purged and replaced them; see Gregoras, *Roman History,* 2:681.

lord George's mother, Sargale: Presumably, Sargale was the mother of George Achpougas, who was slain by his brother Andronikos III (see chap. 16). Sargale is probably the Greek version of the name Sargul, which is attested in modern Turkey and Armenia.

37 *the cave of Saint Sabas*: Saint Sabas was a church built in the caves on Boz Tepe; see Bryer and Winfield, *Pontos,* 1:231.

38 *treasurer of the wardrobe*: The office of *protovestiarios.* Originally the highest financial position in the Byzantine empire, by the time of the Grand Komnenoi it had become an important honorary position.

chief comptroller: The office of *megas logariastes,* general comptroller of expenses for the empire.

chamberlain: Known as the *parakoimomenos,* this official originally served as imperial chamberlain and later as the commander of the imperial guard. Under the Palaiologoi at Constantinople, there were two *parakoimomenoi:* the *parakoimomenos* of the *koiton* continued his function as commander of the imperial bodyguard, while the *parakoimomenos* of the *sphendone* controlled the state seal. The role played by the official under the Grand Komnenoi is unclear.

head of the imperial bodyguard: The Greek term for this office, *amyrtzantarios,* derived from the Turkish *emir çandar* (captain of the bodyguards).

39 *arrested by the emperor lord Michael*: Gregoras, *Roman History,* 2:682, reports that Michael effectively gave up his authority as emperor to the Scholarioi. They ruled for him until a popular revolution restored the emperor to power.

Saint Andreas and Oinaion were taken: Saint Andreas was perhaps a monastery on Cape Jason (mod. Yason Burnu), roughly 130 miles west of Trebizond. There were several monastic communities in the region, which was a popular retreat for the imperial family (see chap. 62). On the region, see Bryer and Winfield, *Pontos,* 1:119–20.

40 *In September, indiction 1*: This is the year 1346.

the plague: The Black Death.

42 *Akhi Ayna Bey from Erzincan*: Akhi Ayna Bey (Aches Aïnapak in Greek) ruled the semi-independent emirate of Erzincan, having purchased it from his predecessor. On his relations with Trebizond, see Shukurov, "Between Peace and Hostility," 32–34.

Machmat Eikeptaris from Bayburt: The identity of this ruler of Bayburt is uncertain. Shukurov ("Between Peace and Hostility," 32) suggests that his name was Muhammad *rikābdār.* A *rikābdār* originally was a groom, but under the Turks he came to hold important powers in the army and royal court; see *EI*[2], 8:529–31.

Tur Ali Bey and Boz Doğan from the Ak Koyunlu: Tur Ali Bey (Tou-

ralipek in Greek) was the chief of the Ak Koyunlu Turkmens. Boz Doğan (Posdoganes in Greek) is the name of a tribe rather than a personal name. Boz Doğan must have been an important member of the tribe or the chieftain, working in tandem with the Ak Koyunlu; see Shukurov, "Between Peace and Hostility," 53.

the Çepni: The Çepni (Tziapnides in Greek) were a clan of Turkmens who had entered Anatolia with the Seljuks in the eleventh century, eventually settling in the Pontos region; see Rustam Shukurov, *The Byzantine Turks, 1204–1461* (Leiden, 2016), 284–90.

43 *two Frankish galleys*: Presumably Genoese.

Caffa: Modern Feodosia in the Crimea. It was a Genoese colony at the time.

Daphnous: Daphnous, a suburb to the east of Trebizond, served as one of the city's three harbors.

44 *Aminsous*: More commonly known as Amisos, Aminsous lay on the Black Sea coast to the west of modern Samsun, roughly two hundred miles west of Trebizond.

Leontokastron: Literally, "the castle of the lions," it lay at the corner of Daphnous, just east of Trebizond.

Kenchrina: Alternatively spelled Kechrina, the fortified town's exact location is uncertain. Kalecik-Hisarüstü, some seventy miles west of Trebizond, has been proposed as a potential candidate; see Bryer and Winfield, *Pontos,* 1:135–36. It lay along the coast on a high rock visible from all around. It is described in detail by Libadenos, *Travels,* 81–82.

Sampson's daughter: This Sampson is the *tatas* Michael Sampson mentioned in the following chapter. He is otherwise unknown. At this point, Niketas Scholaris had fallen from favor and been replaced as chief admiral *(megas doux)* by John Tzanichites. The reign of Alexios III marked Scholaris's resurgence.

47 *Michael Sampson left on a galley*: This is the same journey to Constantinople to arrange a marriage alliance as that described above, in chapter 45.

48 *Tripolis*: Modern Tirebolu, some fifty-five miles west of Trebizond.

49 *the empress Komnene Kantakouzene*: Her full name was Theodora Komnene Kantakouzene (*PLP* 12068). Panaretos does not mention her name initially.

John VI Kantakouzenos: This Byzantine emperor, who reigned from 1347 to 1354, was instrumental in Alexios III's elevation to the throne, according to Lazaropoulos, *Synopsis,* miracle 25. This marriage sealed the alliance of the Kantakouzenoi and the Komnenoi.

50 *the emperor's mother*: That is, Eirene the Grand Komnene, the wife of Basil Komnenos.

51 *In January of that same year*: That is, the Byzantine year 6860, which corresponds with the Common Era year of September 1351 to August 1352. The events described by Panaretos in this chapter thus take place in 1352 CE. For more on the conversion of Byzantine dates, see the Introduction, and the note to Panaretos chapter 1 above.

Tzanicha: Modern Canca, northwest of Gümüşhane, roughly sixty miles south of Trebizond.

52 *emir*: From the Arabic word for "commander." A number of Turkish and Turkmen rulers of minor principalities used the title following the dissolution of the Seljuk Sultanate of Rum in the thirteenth century.

54 *who could possibly describe*: Thus, Panaretos the secretary complains about all the messages he had to draft and send to Scholaris. Similarly, see chapter 100.

56 *a settlement was reached*: Libadenos, *Travels,* 74–75, also describes Scholaris's time in Kerasous. After Scholaris's failed coup, Alexios III urged the Scholaris faction to return to Trebizond, but they dithered, fearing for their lives. As diplomacy was proving ineffective, Alexios sailed against the city with his fleet and attacked it. Libadenos accompanied Scholaris's fleeing partisans, escaping the city by impersonating a soldier.

a battle: Libadenos, *Travels,* 82–83, was again present. The siege

lasted until September, when Scholaris and his partisans decided to make peace with Alexios III.

57 *governor of Chaldia*: Originally the commander *(doux)* of the military district of Chaldia. Under the Grand Komnenoi, the title became semihereditary and was often held by the Kabazitai family, who guarded the Pontic Alps against invaders.

Cheriana: Modern Şiran, roughly ninety miles southwest of Trebizond. The town lies in the southern foothills of the Pontic Alps, guarding one possible approach to Trebizond from Şebinkarahisar and Erzincan. Because it was easy to approach and strategically valuable, it changed hands a number of times under Alexios III. He himself attacked it unsuccessfully several times; see chapters 60, 96.

Sorogaina: Modern Yalınkavak, some seventy miles southwest of Trebizond and about forty miles north of Şiran. The fortress lay along the road to Trebizond from Şebinkarahisar and Erzincan. John Kabazites's conquests aimed to retake control of the route through the mountains.

58 *Michael the Grand Komnenos left Constantinople*: Presumably, the Byzantine emperor John V (r. 1341–1391) released Michael from captivity, lending his support to Michael's bid for the Trapezuntine throne.

Soulchation: Soulchation (Solkhat) was in the Crimea. Now known as Staryi Krym, the city was the capital of the Crimean Khanate at this time; see Alexander A. Vasiliev, *The Goths in the Crimea* (Cambridge, Mass., 1936), 164.

59 *They took Scholaris . . . into their custody*: Libadenos, *Travels,* 83–84, testifies that "a truly God-loving aim" overtook the Scholaris faction to make peace with Alexios III. In September 1355, they sent an embassy to Trebizond to treat for peace. Meizomates and Sampson then arrived and offered favorable terms, to which the supporters of Scholaris assented. Together, they all returned to Trebizond, where Alexios III received them on October 28, thus ending his war with Niketas Scholaris.

61 *lord Andronikos*: Andronikos (*PLP* 12086) died prematurely in March 1376. Panaretos is mistaken about the date of Androni-

kos's birth, which was actually 1353/54. See note on chapter 99 below.

62 *Cape Jason*: The modern Yason Burnu lay roughly 130 miles west of Trebizond. See note on chapter 39 above.

63 *that same year 1357*: That is, the Byzantine year 6865 (September 1356–August 1357).

66 *Hacı Emir, Bayram's son*: Hacı Emir (Chatzymyris in Greek, *PLP* 30732) was the emir of Chalybia. See note above on chapter 13.

Matzouka: The region of Matzouka lay directly south of Trebizond in the valleys between the coast and the Pontic Alps.

Palaiomatzouka: The castle lies below modern Hamsiköy, roughly thirty-five miles southwest of Trebizond.

Dikaisimon: Now called Maçka after Matzouka, the town lies roughly twenty miles southwest of Trebizond. The emir effectively raided a fifteen-mile stretch of land in the Prytanis river valley.

67 *that same year 1358*: That is, the Byzantine year 6866 (September 1357–August 1358).

John Leontostethos: Leontostethos (*PLP* 14724) was the ambassador of John V Palaiologos to Alexios's court. He may have been sent to open negotiations for a marriage alliance between the Grand Komnenoi and Palaiologoi, as outlined in chapter 74.

70 *He was named Basil*: For Basil, son of Alexios III, see *PLP* 12089.

71 *Koukos*: According to Bryer and Winfield, *Pontos,* 1:310–11, this is the fortress of Koukos (mod. Koğ Kale), which lies about nine miles southeast of the modern city of Gümüşhane near Esenyurt and roughly eighty miles from Trebizond. It is on the road to inner Chaldia and Trebizond from Bayburt. Hence, *hoca* Latif, the ruler of that city, was eager to prevent its construction.

hoca Latif: The Turkish *hoca,* from the Persian *khōja* or *khwaja,* means master. The so-called *hoca* Latif ruled Bayburt from at least 1355. He was killed by the people of Matzouka in 1361 (see chap. 76 below). Further on *hoca* Latif, see Shukurov, "Between Peace and Hostility," 32–34.

Alexios III removed John Kabazites: In chapter 60, Kabazites was captured by the Turks. He appears to have been ransomed

or escaped, subsequently resuming his tenure as governor of Chaldia.

72 *the Soumela monastery*: Built on a steep cliff, the world-famous monastery (mod. Sümela Manastırı) lies about thirty miles south of Trebizond. The emperors of Trebizond and in particular Alexios III were patrons of the monastery. Alexios III bestowed a chrysobull on the monastery in 1364; see Franz Miklosich and Joseph Müller, eds., *Acta et diplomata graeca medii aevi sacra et profana,* 6 vols. (Vienna, 1860–1890), 3:276–81. For an image of the chrysobull, see Anthony Bryer, *Peoples and Settlement in Anatolia and the Caucasus, 800–1900* (London, 1988), ii.

73 *In the same year . . . 1360*: That is, the Byzantine year 6869 (September 1360–August 1361).

74 *John V Palaiologos*: John V Palaiologos reigned from 1341 to 1391, albeit with several interruptions. After the removal of John VI Kantakouzenos from power, the Palaiologoi seemingly sought to reaffirm their friendly relationship with the Grand Komnenoi through a new marriage alliance.

76 *Lacharane*: Modern Akarsu, a town about twenty-five miles south of Trebizond. The town is not to be confused with the Larachane River mentioned in chapter 87.

Chasdenicha: Bryer and Winfield (*Pontos,* 1:285) tentatively identify this place with Hortokop Kale, a few miles south of Maçka and roughly thirty miles south of Trebizond.

hoca Latif . . . beheaded: The defeat of *hoca* Latif was celebrated by Libadenos in two poems, *Verses on the Death of the Virgin Mary,* 70–89, and *Iambs for the Birthday of the Mother of God,* 72–96.

78 *the citadel of Golacha*: This stronghold is in the modern town of Bahçelik, formerly known as Çolaşana, about six miles west of modern Gümüşhane and roughly sixty miles southwest of Trebizond. See note below on chapter 91.

Kordyle: Modern Akçakale. It lies several miles west of Trebizond and only a few miles east of modern Akçaabat.

80 *Mesochaldia*: The location of this place is uncertain. Some have placed it at the modern Torul, but Bryer prefers the formidable Keçikaya Kalesi, some fifteen miles east of Gümüşhane

and roughly eighty miles distant from Trebizond; see Bryer and Winfield, *Pontos,* 1:312.

departed . . . because of the plague: Mesochaldia in the mountains south of Trebizond was presumably free of plague. It also would have been safe from Alexios's conspiring *archontes,* who attempted a revolution against Alexios, as indicated later in this chapter.

Saint John the Sanctifier: The church lies on the summit of Boz Tepe.

çelebi Taccedin: The title *çelebi* means gentleman, designating nobility. Taccedin (Tatzatines in Greek) ruled Niksar (Neokaisareia in Greek), the Phanaroia valley, Sonusa, and Iskefser. His rule extended as far as Oinaion and Limnia on the coast. In 1379 he married a daughter of Alexios III; see chapter 100. For his emirate, see Shukurov, "Between Peace and Hostility," 41–43.

81 *chief secretary*: The office of *protonotarios,* chief of the imperial secretaries and possibly even the emperor's own private secretary.

Ioasaph Kantakouzenos: The emperor John VI Kantakouzenos assumed the name Ioasaph when he took the monastic habit after his abdication in 1354.

the patriarch lord Kallistos: Kallistos (*PLP* 10478) was patriarch of Constantinople from 1350 to 1353 and from 1354 to 1363.

the empresses: That is, Helena Kantakouzene (*PLP* 21365), the wife of John V, and probably Eirene Asanina (*PLP* 10935), the wife of John VI Kantakouzenos.

the emperor's sons: That is, Andronikos IV (*PLP* 21438), Manuel II (*PLP* 21513), Theodore (*PLP* 21460), and Michael (*PLP* 21522).

capetan: A Venetian official in Constantinople. Panaretos and Scholaris met with him in order to reestablish Venetian commercial ties with Trebizond after they had terminated in the 1340s during the civil war; see Thiriet, *Régestes,* 1:413.

chief magistrate of the Genoese . . . Leonardo di Montaldo: Also called Leonardo Montaldo, he briefly served as the chief magistrate *(podestà)* of the Genoese in Pera, leaving Constantinople at the

end of 1363. He later served briefly as doge of Genoa from 1383 until his death from plague in 1384. The *podestà* (Italian for "authority") oversaw the Genoese colony of Galata (Pera) across from Constantinople.

a marriage agreement: This marriage alliance never came to fruition.

82 *the Saint Gregory River*: Bryer and Winfield, *Pontos,* 1:161, identify the Saint Gregory River with Kalenima Dere, which runs about eight miles west of Trebizond. The location of Katabatos is unknown.

Kabazitai archontes: The Kabazitai were a powerful family throughout the empire's history. They held several high offices and are presumed to have originated in Chaldia.

Nephon Pterygionites: Nephon (*PLP* 23889) was metropolitan of Trebizond from 1351 until his death in 1364; see chapter 83. Soumela in Trebizond is an otherwise unattested *metochion,* that is, an urban base of operations for the Soumela Monastery in Matzouka. On the *metochion,* see Alice-Mary Talbot, "Metochion," *ODB,* 2:1356–57.

Dzianotes Spinoula and Stephanos Daknopines: The identification of these individuals is uncertain. The former could be a member of the powerful Genoese Spinola family. Dzianotes may be a form of the Italian name Giannoti.

83 *In that same year, 1364*: That is, the Byzantine year 6872 (September 1363–August 1364).

the metropolitan, lord Barnabas: Barnabas (*PLP* 2301) was metropolitan of Trebizond from 1311 to 1329.

skeuophylax Joseph Lazaropoulos: *PLP* 14320. The future metropolitan (r. 1363–1367), whose baptismal name was John, was a native of Trebizond. He fled to Constantinople during the Trapezuntine civil war and played a role in the elevation of Alexios III to the throne in 1349. After becoming metropolitan, he wrote an *Oration on the Birthday of Saint Eugenios* and a *Synopsis of the Miracles of Saint Eugenios,* which are invaluable sources for this period. A *skeuophylax* is a high patriarchal official.

85 *the same year, 1365*: That is, the Byzantine year 6873 (September 1364–August 1365).

marketplace: Panaretos uses the Turkish word *meydan* instead of the classical Greek *agora*. For a detailed description of the *meydan* of Trebizond, see Bessarion, *Encomium on Trebizond*, chapters 104–5.

Venetian ambassador: Known as the *bailo*, this official was the resident ambassador of the Venetian republic. The *bailo* administered courts for Venetian citizens, collected taxes and dues, and supervised Venetian trade.

87 *Spelia*: Modern Ispela, about twenty-seven miles southeast of Trebizond. See Bryer and Winfield, *Pontos*, 1:285.

Phianoe: Modern Fikanöy Yayla, near Sındıran, roughly twenty-five to thirty miles southwest of Trebizond.

Gantopedin: This has been identified with Zanha Kale, between modern Çeşmeler and Köprüyanı, roughly thirty miles south of Trebizond; see Bryer and Winfield, *Pontos*, 1:285.

Marmara: Location unknown. Bryer and Winfield (*Pontos*, 1:259) suggest that it was pasture land north of Spelia.

We then went up to Achantakas, crossing over Saint Merkourios: The location of both sites is unknown. Bryer and Winfield (*Pontos*, 1:258) suggest that they lay on the coast near Trebizond. But this identification is problematic because ἀνήλθομεν implies that Alexios and his army ascended the Pontic Alps rather than descending to the coast. I propose that the site of Saint Merkourios lay instead along the summer road (Stenon), which began at Dikaisimon (Maçka) and passed via Hortokop Kale (Chortokopion) up into the mountains before rejoining the main road near Tzanicha (Canca). Describing Andronikos Gidos's stationing of troops along the Stenon route, John Lazaropoulos (*Synopsis*, miracle 23, ll. 1210–11) mentions Saint Merkourios as one of the sites chosen for a guard unit to watch the movements of Melik Sultan. Labeled "difficult to take" (δύσληπτον χῶρον), Saint Merkourios was probably a fortified location or pass overlooking the road. On the summer road, see Bryer and Winfield, *Pontos*, 1:256–57.

the emir: Presumably, this is the emir of the Ak Koyunlu, Kutlu Bey, who stayed with Alexios at Trebizond, according to chapter 86.

Bagrat Bagration: Bagrat V (*PLP* 21273) was king of Georgia from 1360 until 1393. His surname, Bagration, designates that he was a member of the Bagratid dynasty, which had ruled Georgia since the early Middle Ages. The Abasgians are the modern Abkhazians who inhabit the northern coastal region of Georgia.

Makrou Aigialou: That is, the "long beach." Makrou Aigialou has been located near the modern city of Kemalpaşa, about 115 miles east of Trebizond. The town is only a few miles from the modern border with Georgia and lies along a wide stretch of beach.

along the Larachane River, namely to Limnion: Alexios III followed the Akarsu Dere south of Dikaisimon (mod. Maçka) to the summer pastures about thirty miles south of Trebizond. I tentatively suggest the high-altitude lake Çakır Gölü as a potential candidate for Limnion. It lies about forty miles south of Trebizond along the road south from Maçka and the Soumela Monastery. From there, Alexios would have descended back into mountainous Chaldia.

88 *the Eleousa monastery*: The monastery of the Panagia Eleousa, just east of Trebizond near the Daphnous harbor; see Bryer and Winfield, *Pontos,* 1:243.

89 *the same year, 1368*: That is, the Byzantine year 6876 (September 1367–August 1368).

the pirate ships: The term *azapika paraskalmia,* which I have tentatively translated as "pirate ships," is obscure. A *paraskalmion* was a type of war vessel, but in later Byzantine writers *azapika* appears to refer to Ottoman pirates. As Bryer pointed out in "Greeks and Türkmens," 146n137, *azapika* might also represent corsairs who came from Sinope, or local Turkmens. Sinope seems the most likely point of origin here. In 1360, the Venetian Senate had ordered its deputies in the region to minimize the threat posed by Sinope to their Black Sea traders; see Thiriet, *Régestes,* 1:360.

the Araniotai: They were the inhabitants of Ares island (mod. Giresun Adası) a few miles east of modern Giresun. There was a monastery on the island; see Bryer and Winfield, *Pontos,* 1:126, 133–34.

my beloved son Constantine . . . my other dearest son Romanos: Constantine Panaretos must have been born between August 6, 1353 and August 6, 1354, dying August 6, 1368. Romanos was born between summer 1351 and summer 1352 and died during the fall of 1368. It is odd that in these entries Panaretos briefly switches into perfect tense rather than the usual aorist. He may do so to emphasize the vividness of the event.

feast of the Transfiguration . . . Saint Sophia: The feast falls on August 6. The monastery of Saint Sophia is three miles west of Trebizond.

90 *Kılıç Arslan*: The emir of Şebinkarahisar (d. 1380/81). Formerly the Greek Koloneia, the city lies approximately sixty-five miles south of Kerasous (mod. Giresun) and 150 miles southwest of Trebizond.

91 *Golacha*: Modern Bahçelik, it guarded the route over the Pontic Alps and was the key to controlling Chaldia, as other Turkish attempts on the fortress (chaps. 78, 98) indicate. There is a large cave just south of Golacha where its people must have sought refuge after the fortress fell. It is unclear why Panaretos labels it "treacherous." For Golacha, see Bryer and Winfield, *Pontos,* 1:302. For an image of the cave, see Bryer and Winfield, *Pontos,* vol. 2, plate 240.

93 *Hagarenes*: A term used by the Byzantines to refer to Muslims, whom they believed to be descendants of Hagar, the maidservant of Abraham. Here the reference is probably to Turkmens.

94 *the metropolitan lord Theodosios*: Theodosios (*PLP* 7166) was metropolitan of Trebizond from 1370 until 1380. He actually came from Koressos, near Kastoria, and not Thessalonike. His ordination as metropolitan probably took place between late 1369 and early 1370.

Holy Mountain: Mount Athos.

95 *Bathys*: Modern Batumi, roughly 130 miles east of Trebizond.

the Gurieli: Title of the ruler of Guria, a Georgian state near the

border of Trebizond and Georgia. Panaretos evidently did not know his actual name. On Guria, see Bryer and Winfield, *Pontos,* 1:344.

97 *lord Michael*: Michael Palaiologos (*PLP* 21522) was the governor of Mesembria at this time and attempted to seize the throne of Trebizond at the instigation of his father-in-law, Dobrotica, a Bulgarian noble who operated a powerful fleet on the Black Sea; see Thiriet, *Régestes,* 1:576.

John Andronikopoulos: Nothing else is known about Andronikopoulos (*PLP* 951).

98 *Golacha was taken by the Chaldians*: See above, chapter 91, on its devastation five years before. The theme of Chaldia was nominally ruled by the emperor of Trebizond, but his local officials (often drawn from the Kabazitai family, for example, John Kabazites in chaps. 57, 60, 71) ruled semiautonomously. Thus, the governor *(doux)* of Chaldia, whoever this was at the time, reclaimed Golacha only to lose it again a short while later.

99 *despot lord Andronikos the Grand Komnenos*: Andronikos (*PLP* 12086) was Alexios III's illegitimate son (see chap. 61). His death was commemorated in a now lost funerary epitaph recorded by Jakob Fallmerayer when he visited Trebizond in the nineteenth century. See the corrected edition of the text by Spyridon Lampros, "Ἐπιτύμβιον Ἀνδρονίκου νόθου υἱοῦ Ἀλεξίου Γ′ Κομνηνοῦ Αὐτοκράτορος Τραπεζοῦντος," *Νέος Ἑλληνομνήμων* 13 (1916): 50–55, here 54. The inscription says that Andronikos was twenty-two when he died (τὸν εἰκοστὸν δεύτερον ἀνύων χρόνον). Panaretos (chap. 61) notes that Andronikos was born around 1355/56, which would put his age at death between twenty and twenty-one. Since Panaretos is not specific about his year of birth, the funerary inscription is to be preferred. This would place Andronikos's birthdate between March 1353 and March 1354.

Theoskepastos monastery: Modern Kızlar Manastırı, less than a mile southeast of the city, and outside its walls.

David of Tbilisi: David IX of Georgia (r. 1346–1360), on whom see *PLP* 5016. He was the father of Bagrat V, mentioned in chapters 87, 95, and 105.

Achpougas: Presumably, George Achpougas, the son of Alexios II Komnenos, mentioned in chapter 16.

Manuel III: Manuel (r. 1390–1416) was the younger son of Alexios III; see *PLP* 12115. It is uncertain what happened to Manuel's older brother Basil, whose birth is noted in chapter 70.

Makraigialous: The same location as in chapter 87 above. Alexios III stayed there until the feast of the Dormition, on August 15.

Gonia: The modern Gonio fortress in Georgia, about 120 miles east of Trebizond. This probably marked the border between Trebizond and Georgia.

Eudokia: Eudokia (*PLP* 6231) was empress until her death in 1395 (see chap. 108). Koulkanchat stands for *Gulkhan hatun,* that is, lady Gulkhan.

marriage crowns: Normally, in an Orthodox wedding, the bride and groom are given marriage crowns by the priest, symbolizing their participation in Christ's kingdom. In the context of an imperial wedding, it was probably appropriate for the emperor to perform this action.

100 *talks and delegations*: This is the consummation of marriage talks first alluded to in chapter 80. The emperor traded his daughter for control of Limnia, which had apparently been taken by Taccedin sometime after the emperor's visit in 1369 (see chap. 92).

the lady Eudokia: Eudokia (*PLP* 12062) had an eventful life as a princess of Trebizond. First, she was married to Taccedin, but sometime after his death in 1386 (on which, see chap. 104) she married Konstantin Dragaš, the grandfather of John VIII Palaiologos (r. 1425–1448) and Constantine XI Palaiologos (r. 1448–1453). After he died in 1395, she returned to Trebizond once more (see chap. 109).

Kılıç Arslan was about to descend on Trebizond: After Golacha was retaken by the Turks in 1374, the road from Şebinkarahisar to Trebizond lay open to the emir.

101 *Petroman*: About three miles south of the modern town of Halkavala at the mouth of the Harşit River is the fortress of Petra Kale, or Bedrama Kalesi, built on rock, hence Petroman; see Bryer and Winfield, *Pontos,* 1:139–40, 143. It lies about fifty miles west of Trebizond.

conveyed them: Περνίζω, meaning "convey someone across a river," is a peculiarity of the Pontic dialect. See Anthimos A. Papadoulos, *Ἱστορικὴ γραμματικὴ τῆς Ποντικῆς διαλέκτου* (Athens, 1955), 182.

Philabonites River: The modern Harşit River, the Philabonites, begins in the Pontic Alps, flowing through Torul and Özkürtün to the Black Sea. Its mouth lies near modern Tirebolu (Greek Tripolis), roughly fifty-five miles west of Trebizond.

winter quarters: Where one would expect εἰς τὰ χειμαδία in Greek, Panaretos has εἰς τὰ χειμαδίας. The use of the neuter plural article with the feminine plural is a feature of the modern Pontic dialect. See Papadoulos, *Ἱστορικὴ γραμματικὴ τῆς Ποντικῆς διαλέκτου*, 45–46.

Simylika: The Greek *Simylika* defies translation. Fallmerayer and Bryer thought it was a village called Simylika (mod. Sümüklü) or a neologism; see Bryer, "Greeks and Türkmens," 147n138. He revisits this question subsequently in Bryer and Winfield, *Pontos,* 1:140–41. I follow him here with some reservation. Sümüklü lies high in the Pontic Alps near the modern Özkürtün close to the Harsit River, roughly sixty-five miles southwest of Trebizond.

Sthlabopiastes: Tentatively identified as Vakfıkebir by Bryer and Winfield, *Pontos,* 1:47. The town lies about twenty-five miles west of Trebizond on the coast.

Kotzauta: Bryer and Winfield (*Pontos,* 1:141) were unable to locate this fortress, proposing that it lay among the cultivable lands flanking the Philabonites River.

close to the beach of Sthlabopiastes: Alexios III employed a two-pronged assault on the Çepni. First, he ascended the Harşit river valley, probably as far as Chaldia, returning to Sthlabopiastes. The other army traversed the land along the coast, expecting to rendezvous with the emperor there. It is unclear why the emperor was not at Sthlabopiastes. Perhaps the army traveling along the coast was late for the rendezvous.

102 *They called him Basil*: For this Basil, see *PLP* 12090.

103 *Trikomia*: A *bandon,* that is, administrative region, of the empire

of Trebizond. The region began at Platana (mod. Akçaabat) and stretched several miles east to Trebizond.

Sourmaina: Modern Sürmene, about twenty-five miles east of Trebizond.

Dryona: Modern Yomra, about ten miles east of Trebizond.

104 *Süleyman Bey*: The Turkish emir was Alexios's nephew. In the scholarship, there has been some confusion as to his relationship with the emperor due to a misplaced comma. In my text I have adopted the correction of Elizabeth Zachariadou, "Trebizond and the Turks (1352–1402)," *Ἀρχεῖον Πόντου* 35 (1978): 333–58, here 351n3.

105 *who had a khan in his power*: Because he was not descended from Genghis Khan, Timur could not lay claim to the title of khan, so he set up a descendant of Genghis Khan as a puppet. Timur ruled but officially held the title emir and acted in the name of his khan.

Timur: Alternatively known as Tamerlane (as here to Panaretos), he was the Turco-Mongol conqueror of much of Asia and founder of the Timurid Empire. He reigned from 1370 to 1405. The emperors of Trebizond would later submit to Timur. His defeat of the Ottoman sultan Bayezid I (r. 1389–1402) at the battle of Ankara in 1402 temporarily checked the growth of the Ottoman empire.

her son David: Anna Komnene's son David (*PLP* 5028) should not be confused with David IX, king of Georgia (*PLP* 5016), mentioned in chapter 99.

106 *died on Sunday, March 20*: This is confirmed by an obit scribbled in the margins of a contemporary manuscript. See Anthony Bryer, "Some Trapezuntine Monastic Obits," *Revue des études byzantines* 34 (1976): 125–38, here 131.

He . . . was fifty-one: From here on, different individuals seem to have added to the chronicle, since the chronology of entries breaks down between chapters 107 and 108.

107 *Manuel III the Grand Komnenos died*: Manuel III actually died in 1417. The chronicler's year is incorrect, but not his reckoning of how long Manuel reigned. An Armenian inscription records

that Manuel was still alive in 1415; see William Miller, *Trebizond: The Last Greek Empire* (London and New York, 1926), 79.

108 *Alexios IV*: Alexios (*PLP* 12082) was the son of Manuel III. He reigned from 1417 to 1429.

109 *Saint Phokas*: This is the monastery west of Trebizond mentioned in chapter 78.

another boat: The Greek term *gripiares* apparently refers to a kind of fishing boat.

Philanthropenos's daughter: This Philanthropenos is Alexios Angelos Philanthropenos (*PLP* 29750), who ruled Thessaly from around 1390 until its conquest by the Turks in 1394.

the lady Theodora: Theodora (*PLP* 12069) was empress of Trebizond until her death in 1426 (on which, see chap. 110). Bessarion commemorated her death with three monodies addressed to her grief-stricken husband, Alexios IV.

110 *in the vault . . .* : Between chapter 110 and 111, there are ten lines left blank in the manuscript. The text of the chronicle of Trebizond was copied by two hands in the 1440s based on an earlier exemplar. It thus seems likely that a gap was left here because there was also a gap in the exemplar. See Peter Schreiner, "Bemerkungen zur Handschrift der trapezuntinischen Chronik des Michael Panaretos in der Bibliotheca Marciana (Marc. gr. 608/coll. 306)," in *Mare et Litora: Essays Presented to Sergei Karpov for his 60th Birthday*, ed. Rustam Shukurov (Moscow, 2009), 613–25, here 616–18.

111 *In November of that same year*: The date of Maria's marriage to David is uncertain, having taken place sometime between 1426 and roughly 1440. The terminus ante quem for the marriage is set by the date at which the manuscript of Panaretos was copied, on which see the previous note.

Theodoro: Modern Mangup in the Crimea, it was an independent Greek principality (alternatively known as Gothia) from the fourteenth century until its conquest by the Turks in 1475. For an account of this state, see Vasiliev, *The Goths in the Crimea*, 182–266.

David the Grand Komnenos: David (*PLP* 12097) was the last em-

peror of Trebizond (r. 1459–1461). He surrendered the empire of Trebizond to Mehmed II (r. 1451–1481) in 1461 and was subsequently executed along with his family in 1463.

Bessarion, *Encomium on Trebizond*

1 *For as a human being, the only free animal that loves both receiving honor and giving gifts*: See Xenophon, *Hiero* 7.1–4, for a definition of how man's desire for honor sets him apart from animals.

he should not only . . . do something good in return for them: See Libanios, *Letters* 1193.2.

father of his fathers: See Aristides, *Panathenaic Oration* 1.

2 *but the earth alone . . . anything by anyone*: See Libanios, *Antiochian Oration* 12.

3 *let everyone contribute . . . to his fatherland*: See Libanios, *Antiochian Oration* 9.

Let some act as patrons: Literally, "Let some act as a *choregos*." The *choregos* paid the costs of the chorus and dramatic productions in ancient Athens.

let some serve as trierarchs: The trierarch paid to outfit triremes for the Athenian navy.

4 *I shall adorn my fatherland with words*: Bessarion alludes to his education, on which, see Introduction, pp. xi–xii.

God the Word: In Greek, the adjective *logios* means "educated," hence "scholar." Bessarion employs wordplay here on the idea of God the Logos, or Divine Word. Throughout chapter 4, Bessarion plays on multiple meanings of *logos* as both "word" and "reason."

6 *It is customary . . . I really do need to use these kinds of tactics*: Bessarion, like many other rhetors, begins his speech with a discussion of the customary tactics used by rhetoricians to seek the goodwill of their audience, the so-called *captatio benevolentiae,* on which, see Menander Rhetor, *On Epideictic Rhetoric* 368 (ed. Russell and Wilson). Bessarion's *captatio benevolentiae* shows some affinities with Libanios, *Antiochian Oration* 6.

my speech's style is difficult, heavily ornamented, and irksome to read: See the strikingly similar qualification in Aristides, *Panathenaic Oration* 3. Bessarion labels his speech λαμπρός (brilliant), which I have translated somewhat loosely as "heavily ornamented." In Byzantine stylistics, the brilliant style was distinguished by lengthy clauses and a figurative manner of speech. The speaker is confident in his assertions because what he is saying is generally accepted (for example, everyone thinks it is right to offer something to the fatherland), employing direct denials (for instance, "For I do not need to be told . . ."). On the brilliant style, see Hermogenes, *On the Types of Style*, 264–69.

8 *Moreover, most information about it happens to be obscure, so where to start*: See Aristides, *Panathenaic Oration* 7. Aristides employs a similar phrase but affirms that most information about Athens is well known and that there are many possible points of departure for his speech.

its mother city . . . through some other intermediaries: Athens is the mother city. The intermediaries are Miletos and Sinope, as Bessarion establishes in chapter 13 below.

11 *as long as water flows and tall trees are in bloom*: A poetic phrase quoted by Plato, *Phaedros* 264d, attributed to Homer or Kleoboulos in the *Greek Anthology* 7.153, and subsequently used for rhetorical ornamentation throughout Greek literature.

13 *Sinope*: Modern Sinop, which lies on the northern coast of Turkey along the Black Sea. The city is described in greater detail in chapters 23 to 25.

Miletos: The ruins of Miletos lie near the modern village of Balat, in the Aydın province of Turkey.

The Milesians were a powerhouse in Asia and the gem of the Ionians: See Herodotus, *Histories* 5.28.

coastal Greece: Bessarion means the coast of Asia Minor.

were they mighty once upon a time: Bessarion puns on the proverb "Once the Milesians were strong": *CPG* 1.152.

17 *the many peoples on this side of the Halys River*: Compare the similar phrasing of Herodotus 1.6.2.

Gyges . . . who killed his master Kandaules: According to Herodotus

1.8–10, Kandaules was proud of his wife's beauty and decided to show her off to his minister Gyges. He contrived to bring Gyges to the palace and hide him behind a tapestry. Unfortunately, Kandaules's wife noticed Gyges's presence and delivered an ultimatum to Gyges: kill Kandaules and rule, or die. Gyges chose the former.

The Phrygians and the Mysians . . . Carians: Phrygia lay in west central Anatolia. Mysia was situated above it to the northwest, near the Sea of Marmara. Bithynia and Paphlagonia lay to the north and northeast, near the Black Sea coast. Chalybia, famous for its iron, lay even further east, in the Pontos region and Cappadocia. Pamphylia occupied south central Anatolia, along the Mediterranean coast. Caria lay west of Phrygia and east of mid-Ionia, near the coast. The region's most famous city is Halikarnassos.

18 *as the historian says*: Herodotus, *Histories* 6.6.

19 *skin the air and make rope out of sand*: Proverbial expressions for impossible tasks: see *Suda,* α 554, ε 1536.

They seized Kolophon . . . took control of Klazomenai: Cities along the west coast of Asia Minor in Ionia.

they too spent eleven years pressing a siege: The Lydian war with Ionia lasted from 624 BCE to roughly 613 BCE. See Herodotus, *Histories* 1.18.

who endured . . . without any external support: As above, Bessarion is drawing on Herodotus, *Histories* 1.18–19. However, he embellishes the resistance of Miletos, as Herodotus notes that the people of Chios sent men to the aid of the Milesians.

21 *buffeted by the wheel of life*: Miletos was conquered by the Lydians under Kroisos and subsequently passed to the Persian king Cyrus when he conquered Kroisos; see Herodotus, *Histories* 1.141.

The Milesians continued to be . . . the saviors of the king's affairs: Bessarion appears to be extrapolating the history of Miletos from Herodotus, who notes that Cyrus showed the Milesians special privileges when he allowed them to keep the same terms they had had with Kroisos; see *Histories* 1.141. This may

be the source of the notion that the Persian king highly honored them. The assertion that the Milesians were saviors of the king during his time of need refers to Darius I (r. 522–486 BCE) and his campaign against the Scythians. After the Scythians outmaneuvered Darius's forces, they tried to persuade the Greeks guarding the Hellespont bridge to break it up and strand Darius in Europe, but Histiaios, the tyrant of Miletos, convinced the Greeks to remain loyal to the king and guarded the bridge until Darius and his men had crossed back to safety (4.133–42). For his loyalty, Histiaios was rewarded and became Darius's companion and counselor (5.24).

22 *They were thus the first to revolt*: Bessarion alludes to the Ionian revolt (499–493 BCE) instigated by Aristagoras and Histiaios of Miletos for reasons that would appear to have more to do with those two men's egos and finances than a desire for liberty, at least according to Herodotus: see *Histories* 5.35. Strangely, Bessarion does not allude to the Athenians' involvement in the affair, as one of the arguments Aristagoras used to convince the Athenians to join the revolt was their role as mother city of their colony Miletos; see *Histories* 5.97.

23 *At that time, it was not possible to cross from the Aegean Sea to the Black Sea*: Bessarion's prehistory of the Black Sea derives from Strabo, *Geography* 7.3.6, who holds that the sea was difficult to navigate because of the barbarian tribes living along the coast, until the Ionians (that is, Miletos) established colonies there.

24 *The city of Sinope*: The city of Sinope (mod. Sinop) lies roughly four hundred miles east of Constantinople and three hundred miles west of Trebizond. It is situated on a peninsula that is very narrow at its thinnest point (roughly one thousand feet) and then expands to a triangular shape about one to two miles across. It was founded by Miletos in the seventh century BCE.

The site projects out into the sea . . . granting rest and safety to them: The statement is modeled on Aristides's description of Attica: *Panathenaic Oration* 10.

25 *Peirene*: Scholars have been unable to conclusively identify the location of this city in modern Germany. Bessarion would not have known where the city was either.

The Danube has its source . . . mountainous Cilicia: Bessarion's description of the Danube is modeled after Herodotus, *Histories* 2.33–34.

26 *These people, who had been compelled . . . to leave*: See Herodotus, *Histories* 1.15; Strabo, *Geography* 11.2.5.

although they had not been living there for more than two generations: See Herodotus, *Histories* 4.12.

27 *Diogenes of Sinope*: Founder of the Cynic sect in the fourth century BCE.

showed himself off publicly to everyone like the public blessing that he was: It is hard to convey the comic punch of Bessarion's final turn of phrase in chapter 27. There is nothing overtly humorous about the line taken within the context of Bessarion's speech. But for anyone familiar with Diogenes Laertios's account of Diogenes the Cynic, the phrase "showed himself publicly" (πᾶσι κοινὸν ἑαυτὸν εἰς μέσον) recalls that Diogenes the Cynic did everything in public, including masturbate. Bessarion comically delays the ἀγαθὸν (blessing) until the end of the clause, turning his audience's mind away from the gutter at the last moment.

28 *being surpassed . . . fathers can only hope*: See Libanios, *Letters* 369.2.

30 *For this is certainly true of only one city and one place*: See Libanios, *Antiochian Oration* 14–15. Bessarion imitates Libanios, amplifying his arguments on the pointlessness of emphasizing a city's centrality in an encomium.

31 *Persians, Medes, Sabiri, and people of Kolchis*: The term "Medes" originally referred to a people who inhabited northwestern Iran. The Sabiri were originally a Turkic people inhabiting the steppes by the Caspian Sea. By the "people of Kolchis," Bessarion most likely means his contemporary Georgians.

collect it in both hands: *CPG* 1.31. The expression signifies that someone does something eagerly. Here it means that these people are eagerly importing Trapezuntine goods.

a sea of bounties: *CPG* 1.3.

33 *the name of the Black Sea*: In Greek, the Black Sea is known euphemistically as the Euxine or "Friendly" Sea. Bessarion's description of the Black Sea is somewhat inaccurate. The sea is

given to weather extremes and waves more reminiscent of the Atlantic Ocean than the Mediterranean. July and August are generally safe for sailing, but winter storms can be particularly harsh.

34 *a Scylla or a Charybdis*: Two monsters believed to dwell in the treacherous Strait of Messina, in Sicily, where they sink unsuspecting boats.

hidden reefs and shoals: See Pollux, *Onomasticon* 1.15.2.

35 *and thence accepts being conquered only where to conquer would not be to its advantage*: Aristides (*Panathenaic Oration* 18) similarly argues Athens has the favorable attributes it should, but has escaped unfavorable ones.

While it may not be the first or last among the ten known seas of notable size: For the list of ten seas, see Markianos, *Circumnavigation of the Outer Sea* 1.7.

36 *The Black Sea is and is called both a "sea" and an "open sea"*: Throughout this passage, Bessarion draws a distinction between the terms θάλαττα (sea) and πέλαγος (open sea). A πέλαγος was generally considered a part of a θάλαττα. As Bessarion defines it below, the Black Sea is a πέλαγος because it lacks islands and other bodies of land breaking it up, so there are no places for ships to dock.

as a "sea" does: Thus, a sea like the Mediterranean is filled with inhabited islands and peninsulas, but not the Black Sea.

this sea: In this context, Bessarion most likely means the Mediterranean. He appears to have written the encomium while at Mistra or Constantinople.

41 *no cities or minds of men about which we do not know*: See Homer, *Odyssey* 1.3.

And yet I have heard someone say: See Plato, *Laws* 704d–5b, where the Athenian Stranger condemns coastal cities for having moneymen and businessmen who destroy their virtue. Compare how Bessarion uses Plato's *Laws* to support his argument for Trebizond as a coastal city in chapter 44. Bessarion may also draw on Libanios, *Antiochian Oration* 38.

42 *learning a great deal results from experiencing a great deal*: *CPG*

2.600, 772. The expression survives in modern Greek as το πάθημα γίνεται μάθημα.

virtue in the proper sense: Virtue in the proper sense is a philosophical concept borrowed from Aristotle's *Nicomachean Ethics* 1144b. Here Aristotle discusses the interaction of natural (inborn) virtue with virtue acquired through habit and practice. He makes the point that natural virtue exists in everyone, but that it takes prudence *(phronesis)* to attain virtue in the true sense of the word. Thus, people who live in coastal cities obtain virtue in the proper sense through constant interaction with and experience of foreigners.

where is the need for all these absences and excuses: Bessarion seems to be either imagining an opponent or facing a real opponent who avoided conversations on the value of coastal cities.

44 *Furthermore, if Plato praises*: Plato, *Laws* 7.794d–95d.

45 *Sarmatians, Kolchians, Albanians, and Iberians*: As always, identifying ethnonyms in Byzantium is problematic. By Sarmatians, Bessarion perhaps refers to the Russians or Mongols of the Golden Horde. The Kolchians and Iberians may both refer to Georgians of his day. By Albanians, he presumably means the Caucasian people inhabiting roughly what is now Azerbaijan.

as if our city were a common emporium or marketplace for the whole world: See Aristides, *To Rome* 11–13.

46 *Serian silk threads . . . Sinese baskets*: For the Greeks and the Romans, the Chinese were two separate peoples. They situated the Seres in northern China and associated them with the production of silk. The Sinai (or Sinoi) were associated with the peoples of southern China and Vietnam.

the products of the lands around the Phasis and Tanaïs rivers: The Phasis River is the modern Rioni River in Georgia, while the Tanaïs is the modern Don in Russia.

49 *being truly seasonable*: Bessarion puns on the root (ὥρα, "season") of the adjective ὡραῖος (timely, seasonable).

Astronomers and teachers of astronomical and heavenly phenomena will attest: Ptolemy, *A Sketch of Geography* 5.6.5.

50 *In northern cities . . . living their lives like prisoners*: Bessarion al-

ludes to Libanios's description of northern cities, where people live like prisoners shut up in their houses: *Antiochian Oration* 215.

51 *transcends what is normal according to the name of the season*: See Aristides, *Panathenaic Oration* 18.

53 *smooth and cleared roads on our appointed course*: See Herodotus, *Histories* 8.98.

in the mountain highlands: What Bessarion means by the phrase τοῖς τ' ἀνέχουσι τῶν ὀρῶν is uncertain. I interpret this phrase to refer to the mountain highlands of the Pontic Alps, where the emperors of Trebizond frequently vacationed during the summer.

55 *Antitauros Mountains*: The Antitauros Mountains (mod. Aladağlar) are a mountain range in southeastern Turkey that curve north from the Tauros Mountains in Cilicia near the modern city of Adana, reaching their pinnacle at Mount Erciyes, near Kayseri, before splitting off to the east and the west. The mountains that surround Trebizond are the Pontic Alps, which run east-west from Georgia to the Sea of Marmara along the North Anatolian Fault. Bessarion incorrectly makes the Pontic Alps a subrange of the Antitauros Mountains.

56 *the mountains are terribly inaccessible . . . than there should be*: The Pontic Alps were notoriously inaccessible, especially during the winter, before the advent of modern transportation and roads.

Gates into Greece: That is, Thermopylai, the "Hot Gates."

who could then do nothing but show how to die nobly: See Aristides, *Panathenaic Oration* 131. The battle of Thermopylai in 480 BCE is recounted in Herodotus, *Histories* 7.201–34. In order to halt the advance of Xerxes, the Spartan king Leonidas (r. 490/89–480 BCE), an army of three hundred Spartans, and his Greek allies held the pass of Thermopylai for seven days. Upon learning from a deserter that there was a northern route over the pass, Xerxes sent several men via that route and surrounded Leonidas and his men on both sides, slaughtering the Spartans and their king.

57 *Thyrea*: Lying between Lakonia and the Argolid, the Thyrea

mountain range divides the two regions. Bessarion might have known this route personally, as he lived in Lakonian Mistra for several years. On his time in the Peloponnese, see p. xiii in the Introduction.

Cilician Gates: Now known as Gülek Pass, the Cilician Gates are a mountain pass leading from mountainous Cappadocia to coastal Cilicia. They were long a major trade thoroughfare between the coast and inland Anatolia.

This mountain range . . . like a great boundary marker: Throughout this passage, Bessarion puns on ὅρος (boundary) and ὄρος (mountain). In Byzantine Greek, they would have sounded identical.

59 *The hill is rounded at the top*: Trebizond was founded on top of a mesa, hence came the city's Greek name Trapezous (from *trapeza,* table).

as the Spartans once did a long time ago: The mythical Spartan lawgiver Lykourgos, when asked about city walls, famously advised the Spartans that "a city is well fortified when it is surrounded by a wall of men and not bricks." See Plutarch, *Lykourgos* 19. Bessarion's reference to the Trapezuntines using weapons as walls refers to phalanx formations, in which an army would form a wall of shields.

60 *We know what kind of response*: A reference to Herodotus's story of the Athenians putting Persian envoys to death: *Histories* 7.133.

62 *the Ten Thousand and Klearchos*: The march of the Ten Thousand with Cyrus is recounted in Xenophon's *Anabasis.* Upon the death of king Darius II (r. 424–405/4 BCE), Cyrus's older brother Artaxerxes II (r. 405/4–359/58 BCE) assumed the throne. Cyrus, then governor of Lydia, made a bid for the Persian throne, accompanied by an army of Greek mercenaries commanded by the Spartan general Klearchos (d. 401 BCE). The armies of Artaxerxes and Cyrus clashed at Kounaxa in 401 BCE, with Artaxerxes eventually emerging victorious. After Cyrus's defeat, the Greek mercenaries began their long return march to the Black Sea.

64 *arranging for them to pass . . . through friendly and Greek cities*: The

Trapezuntines provided the Ten Thousand with guides, who took them as far as Sinope: Xenophon, *Anabasis* 5.5.15–16.

65 *Xenophon the Athenian*: Xenophon was an Athenian historian and philosopher. He served in the Ten Thousand and wrote an account of the expedition known as the *Anabasis of Cyrus.* He later wrote a history of the Greek world continuing the *Histories* of Thucydides. A follower of Socrates, he also wrote several philosophical works.

commander of commanders: For the phrase "commander of commanders" (ἄρχων ἀρχόντων), see Aristides, *Panathenaic Oration* 148, where Athens is described in this way before the battle of Salamis. It originally derived from Thucydides, *Histories* 5.66.3–4, where it was used to describe Spartan kings.

Furthermore it was he who . . . bears witness: See Xenophon, *Anabasis* 4.8.22–23.

66 *if we admire the Athenians*: The sons of Herakles (the Herakleidai) fled the Peloponnese when Eurystheus, king of Tiryns, attempted to murder them following Herakles's death. They found refuge at Athens, which protected them even when Eurystheus besieged the city. After Eurystheus died during the siege, Athens restored them to their birthright, the rule of Argos, Sparta, and Pylos. The Herakleidai were a popular *topos* in Greek literature and especially in encomia, where they were frequently used to show the selflessness and kindness of Athens. See Herodotus, *Histories* 9.27.2; Isocrates, *Panathenaicus* 194; Aristides, *Panathenaic Oration* 49–50 and 59; Libanios, *Antiochian Oration* 56.

the Persian peoples are more terrible . . . than a single man, such as Eurystheus: Besides the comparison of scale, a nation to a single king, Bessarion may be comparing the Persians and Eurystheus, because both were believed to be descendants of the Greek hero Perseus in Greek mythology. On the connection between Perseus and the Persians, see Herodotus, *Histories* 7.61.

69 *Our ancestors demonstrated this principle*: See Aristides, *Panathenaic Oration* 249, where Aristides deploys the same basic argument that a people can be physically subdued without being men-

tally (γνῶμαι) conquered to explain why Athens could be destroyed by Xerxes and captured by Sparta without really being "defeated." However, Bessarion goes a step further, seeking to prove the point philosophically with generalizations about the relationship of the mind and the body. His discussion of the difference in freedom between the two is probably inspired by Aristotle's *Politics* 1254a–55b. Here Aristotle lays out the principle that the mind rules the body and applies the idea to the master-slave relationship.

70 *Mithridates*: Mithridates I (r. 281–266 BCE) was the founder of the kingdom of Pontos, along the Black Sea.

So the people of Trebizond made peace with them: Bessarion's history of the Trapezuntines and their distress at being ruled by the various kings named Mithridates is mostly hypothesis. Ancient sources do not discuss what happened to Trebizond between the time of Xenophon and Roman rule. Strabo (*Geography* 12.3.1) notes that Mithridates VI seized the Anatolian coast from the Halys River (mod. Kızılırmak) to Kolchis. From this vague indication, Bessarion appears to have extrapolated the city's subjection to Mithridates.

71 *Mithridates, son of Ariobarzanes*: The uncle of Mithridates I of Pontos, executed by the Macedonian king Antigonos (see below). Bessarion seems to confuse Mithridates I and his uncle.

Antigonos, the king of Syria and most of Asia: Antigonos I Monophthalmos was one of Alexander the Great's generals who went on to rule the Syrian and Anatolian portion of Alexander's conquests following Alexander's death, declaring himself king in 306 BCE. He was the founder of the Antigonid dynasty of Macedon.

For he had conjectured from the actual circumstances . . . and, from a dream: According to Plutarch, *Demetrios* 4, Antigonos had dreamed that he was crossing a field and sowing gold dust, from which gold crops sprouted up. When he went away and came back, the crops were cut down. He heard that Mithridates had reaped the crop and gone off to the Black Sea. See also Libanios, *Antiochian Oration* 81, where a similar anecdote

is recounted with Seleukos, another of Antigonos's rivals, in place of Mithridates.

72 *his son Demetrios*: Demetrios I Poliorketes, ruler of Macedon from 294 to 288 BCE and son and right-hand man of Antigonos I.

73 *ruled over the Pontos and Bosporos*: Bessarion here refers to the so-called Cimmerian Bosporos, a region centered on the straits of Kerch between modern Ukraine and Russia.

deprived them of their capital itself, just as greed does when people borrow money at a high interest rate: See Demosthenes, *First Olynthiac* 15.

74 *Marius and after him Sulla*: Marius (d. 86 BCE) was a distinguished Roman general and statesman, whose conflict with his fellow citizen Sulla (d. 78 BCE) upset the Roman state. Command in the Mithridatic War was a flashpoint in their rivalry. The Roman senate awarded Sulla, as consul, command of the war in 88 BCE, but Marius, envious of his rival's position, convinced the popular assembly, which had the ultimate say over commands, to award it to him instead. Before Marius could move against Mithridates, however, Sulla marched on Rome and forced Marius into exile. Thus, assuming his command, Sulla waged war with Mithridates from 87 BCE until 85 BCE. Bessarion distorts events somewhat by asserting that Marius actually fought Mithridates.

Mithridates, the eighth of that name after the first: Mithridates VI, king of Pontos from about 120 to 63 BCE. Bessarion follows Appian (*Mithridatic War* 112) in naming him as the eighth and not the sixth Mithridates.

Lucullus . . . deprived him of control over many peoples in Asia: Lucullus (117–57/56 BCE) was a Roman general and statesman who fought Mithridates VI from 73 to 66 BCE.

the Romans appointed Pompey the Great: Pompey the Great (106–48 BCE) was a famed Roman general who had originally been elected to fight pirates in the Mediterranean but expanded his mandate to prosecute the war against Mithridates to its end. He fought Mithridates from 66 BCE until Mithridates's death in 63 BCE.

the Caspian Gates: The location of the Caspian Gates is unknown.

Presumably, they were either in modern Derbent or the Darial gorge.

He subjugated for the Romans Cappadocia, Mysia: Mysia lay near the Sea of Marmara on the northwest coast of Asia Minor. On Albania in the Caucasus, see above, note to chapter 45.

75 *They were very pleased to be delivered . . . from barbarian overlordship*: Trebizond did not technically become a part of the Roman empire until over one hundred years after Mithridates's defeat. It formed part of the Polemonian kingdom, a client of Rome. Bessarion would have known this from the geographer Strabo (*Geography* 11.2.18), who informs us that Polemon I Pontos (d. 8 BCE) ruled over the Pontos and Trebizond in his day.

78 *although nearly one thousand five hundred years have passed*: Bessarion's calculation of the years since Trebizond became Roman seems to go back to the death of Mithridates in 63 BCE. However, he is speaking generally, so we cannot definitely establish the year. See Introduction, pp. xvi–xvii.

work befitting the long course of time: The source of this remark appears to be Libanios, but which of his texts is unclear. Compare Libanios, *Letter* 1114.1 and *Oration* 24.12.

the imperial capital moved: Bessarion refers to the foundation of Constantinople (formerly Byzantion) by Constantine the Great (r. 306–337 CE) in 324.

79 *These people . . . settled around our city*: Bessarion no doubt refers to the various Turkoman states that surrounded Trebizond and frequently attacked the city.

81 *Neither Asia, nor Syria, nor Egypt has been able to withstand the barbarians*: Bessarion refers to the Arab conquest of part of the Byzantine empire in the seventh century.

Pamphylia . . . has yielded to them: This refers to the Turkish conquest of Anatolia in the eleventh century.

82 *Kolchis, or Lazike*: Kolchis, the legendary location of the golden fleece, was identified by Byzantines with the Pontos region from Sinope to modern-day Georgia. Lazike lay along the coast of the Black Sea about fifty miles east of Trebizond. The region extends to the Pontic Alps, and in Late Antiquity the

kingdom of Lazia included parts of the coast of modern-day Georgia. The Laz, who gave their name to Lazike and Lazia, are a Kartvelian-speaking language group who still speak a distinctive language.

they would not just be able to plunder Byzantion itself . . . without encountering any resistance: The sentiment is echoed in Prokopios, *History of the Wars* 2.28.23, and Agathias, *Histories* 2.18.7.

Consequently, they made every possible attempt to seize it: Compare Bessarion's description of the Persians with the Lydians in chapter 20 above.

83 *Under the Roman emperor Justin I, the Persian king Kavadh*: Justin I (r. 518–527 CE) was the uncle of the emperor Justinian. The Sassanid shah Kavadh I reigned from 488 to 496, and from 498 to 531.

Gourgenes, the king of the Georgians: The identity of Gourgenes is uncertain. He has tentatively been identified with the shadowy Georgian king Vakhtang I (d. 502 or 522/23 CE).

He pursued them: For this campaign, see Prokopios, *History of the Wars* 1.11.28–12.19.

Khosrow, Kavadh's son: Khosrow I (r. 531–578/79 CE) ruled over the Persians and waged several wars against the emperor Justinian I (r. 527–565 CE) for control of Lazike and the Caucasian region.

Petra: This fortress, the modern Tsikhisdziri, is situated on the coast of present-day Georgia, about 140 miles east of Trebizond. In Justinian's time, it was in the hands of the Laz. For the fall of Petra, see Prokopios, *History of the Wars* 2.17.18–28, and on the city's recent construction by Justinian, 2.29.20.

Later, he was driven from there with heavy losses: For the recapture of Petra, see Prokopios, *History of the Wars* 8.12.14–20.

Rizaion and Athenai: Rizaion (mod. Rize) lies about fifty miles east of Trebizond, while Athenai, not to be confused with Athens, is about twenty miles further east; both are on the Black Sea coast and lay near Byzantine Lazike. If the Persians successfully passed Lazike, they would have been able to gain access to these settlements.

84 *For it led the way*: Bessarion's claims about Trebizond's involve-

ment in the Persian Wars under Justinian are problematic. Prokopios mentions the city only once in a nongeographical sense (*History of the Wars* 8.4.6), where Roman soldiers stationed in Abkhazia dismantled and fled their outposts for Trebizond, an episode that perhaps gave rise to Bessarion's claims in the following chapter about the city as a resting place for Roman soldiers. More intriguingly, the ambush he mentions at the end of chapter 83 was actually facilitated through Laz knowledge of the rough terrain (see Prokopios, *History of the Wars* 2.30.34–48). It appears that Bessarion is laying claim to the actions of the Laz, who were a semi-independent kingdom at the time, for his own Trapezuntines.

86 *served as a shield for us*: See Aristides, *Panathenaic Oration* 8.

rocks jutting out into the sea: See Homer, *Iliad* 16.407. For the metaphor, compare chapter 79 above.

Nor did we ever consider rebelling: In fact, Trebizond had been a thorn in the side of the Komnenos dynasty at the end of the eleventh century and the beginning of the twelfth. The Gabrades family had revolted against them and had ruled semi-independently.

87 *While the barbarians seized everything else*: Bessarion is probably referring in a general sense to the Arab conquests of the mid-seventh century and the Turkish conquest of much of Asia Minor in the late eleventh century.

90 *an imperial palace was lavishly built in the city*: Bessarion refers to the foundation of the empire of Trebizond in 1204.

progenitor: The Byzantine emperor Alexios I Komnenos (r. 1081–1118) founded the Komnenian dynasty. Bessarion discusses him further below.

91 *so that the Roman empire might not be totally lost, they accepted power*: Bessarion refers to the accession of the Komnenian dynasty in 1081. They found the empire wrecked by internal chaos and Turkish invasion and put it back on firm footing.

92 *a proverbial Scythian wilderness*: *CPG* 1.453, 2.208, 2.643.

Chalcedon: The town lay opposite Constantinople in Asia Minor. It roughly corresponds to the modern Kadıköy district of Istanbul.

the Saracens who came from Egypt: The Fatimids. At the beginning of the eleventh century, multiple Byzantine emperors competed with the Fatimid caliphate for control of northern Syria. Bessarion appears to be collapsing several different historical events in this passage.

the Turks who came from Persia itself and regions even further distant: Bessarion is referring to Seljuk Turks, who migrated to Persia from Central Asia, seizing control over much of Persia and then Iraq. Under Alp Arslan, they expanded into Georgia and Armenia, wresting most of Asia Minor from the Byzantines, as Bessarion describes below. On their conquest and its nature, see, most recently, Alexander Beihammer, *Byzantium and the Emergence of Muslim-Turkish Anatolia, ca. 1040–1130* (London, 2017).

They even took captive . . . Romanos Diogenes: Romanos IV Diogenes (r. 1068–1071) was captured by the Turkish sultan Alp Arslan at the battle of Mantzikert in 1071.

the Scythians, the Huns, a tribe of Pechenegs: It is unclear what tribes Bessarion is referring to with the ethnonyms Scythians and Huns. The Pechenegs were a nomadic tribe that periodically crossed the Danube and raided Byzantine Thrace and Macedonia. During the 1070s shortly before Alexios I's succession, they had seized Byzantine fortresses on the Danube and were menacing lands to the south.

the proverbial Mysian loot: *CPG* 1.122, 2.38, 538, and esp. 762–63.

93 *Their army was in an even more wretched condition*: See Michael Attaleiates, *The History* 17.1–2, for a description of the decline of the Byzantine empire and the sorry state of its army in the later eleventh century. Bessarion's description of the army has some similarities to Attaleiates's.

they were instead running for their lives: *CPG* 2.193. I have translated ψυχῆς as "lives," though Bessarion may intend this word to resonate with his idea of the divide between mind and body, in chapter 69.

to sit down and await their final doom: Bessarion employs the same expression in his *Second Monody for Theodora Komnene*, 357.

94 *But God . . . made the Komnenos clan our emperors*: See Nikephoros

Bryennios, *Material for History* proem.10. Bessarion probably used Bryennios interspersedly for ideas such as the contrast between the lazy emperors who stayed in the capital and the active Komnenoi out on the battlefield. Bessarion may even have had a full copy of Bryennios in front of him at some point. An excerpt from Book 1.7–11 on the rise of the Turks is preserved among the manuscripts in his library: see Albert Failler, "Le texte de l'Histoire de Nicéphore Bryennios à la lumière d'un nouveau fragment," *Revue des études byzantines* 47 (1989): 239–50.

Alexios: As noted previously, Alexios I Komnenos (r. 1081–1118) was the first emperor of the Komnenian dynasty.

golden lineage: See Homer, *Iliad* 8.19.

every man and every city . . . to reverse their defeat: See Demosthenes, *First Olynthiac* 11 and *On the Crown* 95. Bessarion appears to have confused the two speeches.

95 *An Alexios . . . was thus the first emperor of this land*: Alexios I of Trebizond (r. 1204–1222) fled Constantinople and seized Trebizond in April 1204, shortly before the fall of Constantinople to the Fourth Crusade in May.

Andronikos Komnenos: The last emperor of the Komnenos dynasty, his brief reign (r. 1183–1185) was marked by its cruelty and violence, but prior to that he had a most remarkable life.

Alexios I: Alexios I Komnenos (r. 1081–1118) was the founder of the Komnenian dynasty (1081–1185) and the great-great-grandfather of Alexios I of Trebizond.

He was called Grand Komnenos: Grand Komnenos (Μέγας Κομνηνός) was a title adopted by the Komnenoi of Trebizond.

he was no less grand in his actual deeds, as he inherited not so much the name as the virtue: See Libanios, *Antiochian Oration* 121, where Antiochos III the Great (ὁ Μέγας), who ruled the Seleucid empire from 222 to 187 BCE, is described in similar terms with the same pun on the word μέγας. See ibid., 124, where Libanios says that the Seleucids inherited not just the name but also the virtues of their family.

good men born of good men . . . all emulating each other: See Libanios, *Antiochian Oration* 105.

96 *they believe more effective government results from ruling the best possible subjects*: A principle outlined in Aristotle, *Politics* 1254a.

who do not belie the term: The meaning of the Greek here is uncertain. Bessarion may be playing off the phrase τῶν ἐν τέλει (those in power) and the adjective ἐντελής (mature, full grown), that is, between the people and public servants as children and the emperors as parents.

98 *our city has not wearied . . . from humble and modest origins*: See Herodotus, *Histories* 1.58, where a variation of the phrase is used to describe the rise of the Greek race at its very beginnings. Bessarion may intend to emphasize the similarity of the Trapezuntines with early Greeks through the intertext.

99 *circuit wall*: On the walls of Trebizond, see Bryer and Winfield, *Pontos,* 1:86–95.

102 *This was added at a later time*: Alexios II of Trebizond (r. 1297–1330) was responsible for building the city's seawall when he expanded the citadel, on which see Bryer and Winfield, *Pontos,* 1:187–90.

104 *booths . . . from these workshops*: See Libanios, *Letters* 255.6.

105 *full of people . . . every hour of the day*: See Libanios, *Antiochian Oration* 171.

their citizens . . . who always have to be in the marketplace: Presumably, Bessarion alludes here to the Genoese and Venetians at Trebizond, whose citizens resided and traded in the city, possessing their own quarters. On Trebizond's relations with its Italian neighbors, see Sergei Karpov, *L'impero di Trebisonda, Venezia, Genova, e Roma, 1204–1461: Rapporti politici, diplomatici, e commerciali* (Rome, 1986).

106 *a wise builder raised it up*: See Pindar, *Pythian Odes* 3.113–14; Homer, *Iliad* 23.712. Bessarion has probably conflated the two.

Concerning the palace: On the imperial palace, see Bryer and Winfield, *Pontos,* 1:184–86, 191–96. For an alternative translation, see Mango, *The Art of the Byzantine Empire,* 252–53. I differ from Mango on a number of points but am indebted to his translation.

which make the cloak recognizable by the hem, as they say: An old

Byzantine proverb, similar to *CPG* 1.252 and Aristides, *To Capito* 316.9–10. Here it means "and show a few things (the hem) that make Trebizond (the cloak) distinctive."

109 *a canopied royal structure . . . supported by four columns*: Bessarion appears to be describing a ciborium.

depictions commemorating . . . his subsequent history: No doubt, Bessarion describes a mural of the creation of man and his downfall as described in Genesis 1–4. The Grand Komnenoi seem to have had a particular fascination with the Genesis cycle; we find friezes of it on the Church of Hagia Sophia in Trebizond and a bastion attached to the palace complex. Anthony Eastmond suggests that the exile of man from Paradise and the promise of redemption particularly resonated with the Grand Komnenoi, who thus alluded to their exile from Constantinople and ambitions to retake the capital: *Art and Identity in Thirteenth Century Byzantium: Hagia Sophia and the Empire of Trebizond* (Burlington, Vt., 2004), 73. On the bastion frieze, see Bryer and Winfield, *Pontos,* 1:193.

A holy church: Bessarion may be referring to the imperial chapel located at the south of the palace complex. For more on the chapel, see Bryer and Winfield, *Pontos,* 1:184–86, 215.

112 *to display how to wage war*: See Achilles Tatios, *Leukippe and Kleitophon* 3.14.2.

Teukros and Pandaros as archers, outstrip Menestheus: Heroes during the Trojan War. Teukros was the son of king Telamon of Salamis and the legendary founder of Salamis in Cyprus. Pandaros was a renowned Trojan archer. Menestheus was a legendary king of Athens and suitor of Helen of Troy.

marshaling horses and shield-bearing warriors: Homer, *Iliad* 2.554. The line is also discussed by Aristides, *Panathenaic Oration* 377, who sees the mention of Athens in the catalog of ships as a sign of its greatness compared to the rest of the Greeks.

son of Oileus: Ajax the Lesser. He was the leader of the Locrian contingent at Troy and an important figure in the Trojan war.

114 *being bad men, came to a bad end*: See Bessarion's use of the same phrase in chapter 83 above.

115 *So they set fire to the houses*: There has been some debate as to which historical episode this passage alludes. The encomium's first editor, Spyridon Lampros, identified it with the Turkoman attack on the city in 1341, described in Panaretos, *On the Emperors of Trebizond* 30, and Andreas Libadenos, *Travels* 64–66; see Lampros, *Ἐγκώμιον εἰς Τραπεζοῦντα* (Athens, 1916), 60–61. Given the amount of horror and carnage described by both these authors, Odysseas Lampsides was, however, probably right to identify the event with the Genoese attempt to burn down the Trapezuntines' arsenal in 1302, as described in Panaretos, *On the Emperors of Trebizond* 12, and George Pachymeres, *Andronikos Palaiologos* 5.29; see Lampsides, "Zu Bessarions Lobrede auf Trapezunt," *Byzantinische Zeitschrift* 35 (1935): 15–16.

116 *not one sacrificial fire-bearing priest was left*: A proverbial expression; see *CPG* 1.134–35. In English we would say "and not a soul was left alive," or "there were no survivors." Sacrificial fire-bearing priests would accompany Spartan armies when they marched to war and would not let the fire go out.

this victory: Lampros, *Ἐγκώμιον εἰς Τραπεζοῦντα,* 61, suggests that Bessarion is referring to the Turkish attack on Trebizond in 1224 led by the son of the sultan of Rum, which is discussed in Panaretos, *On the Emperors of Trebizond* 2. More details are found in Lazaropoulos, *Synopsis,* miracle 23, ll. 1411–13, where the Turkish commander allegedly dreamed of conquering Trebizond only to awaken and find his army defeated. Lampsides, "Zu Bessarions Lobrede," 16–17, has again disputed the dating of this event and suggests reassigning it to Alexios II's recapture of Kerasunt from the Turks in 1301; see Panaretos, *On the Emperors of Trebizond* 11. However, Lampsides's suggestion is weakened by the fact that an attack on the actual city of Trebizond is implied.

117 *He who is most prepared for war is most at peace*: A paraphrase of Dio Chrysostom, *Oration* 1.27. The phrase also recalls Vegetius's famous maxim (*De Re Militari* 3.proem), "He who desires peace will prepare for war."

120 *then one's amazement at its survival*: Alternatively, "Then one's amazement at its superiority."

121 *not even the name of the former remains*: Bessarion exaggerates. Up to 1425, Miletos (Turkish Balat) was home to a number of Turkish emirates, under which it prospered. It was a site of east-west trade with rich pottery traditions and had several mosques and even a *madrasa*—an Islamic school for the study of scriptures and theology. By the Ottoman period its harbors had silted up, but it remained home to a small hamlet. See Alan Greaves, *Miletos: A History* (London, 2002), 143–50. Perhaps Bessarion meant that the place had become thoroughly Turkish, so that no one remembered it was once Miletos. In any case, his language deceptively implies more than that.

you would weep if you saw . . . what rulers it loves: Sinope was ruled at this time by the Turkish beylik of the Isfendiyarids. In the fourteenth century, it had been home to pirates who harassed Black Sea trade routes. They even attacked Trebizond itself in 1318/19. See Panaretos, *On the Emperors of Trebizond* 14.

Even Athens and the whole land of Attica are a cause for shame: Athens and Attica had already become something of a backwater during Byzantine times, though the city was visited often by tourists and pilgrims wanting to see its sights. In the wake of what came to be called the Fourth Crusade, at the start of the thirteenth century, it fell to the Franks and was subsequently ruled by Burgundians, Catalans, and then the Florentine Acciajuoli family into the fifteenth century. During Bessarion's day, the city did see an increase in Greek and western visitors, such as Cyriaco d'Ancona, curious to see the sights of the city. On Athens during this period, see Kenneth Setton, *Athens in the Middle Ages* (London, 1975).

time, which makes everything old: Aeschylus, *Prometheus Bound* 981.

122 *But if you evaluate the person . . . you will issue a verdict befitting good and just judges*: A statement modeled on Theodoretos of Kyrrhos, *Questions on Kings and Chronicles* 832.43–45.

CRIMEA
Black Sea
Sinope
Cherson
Theodoro
Alouston/Lusta
GOTHIA
Symbolon/Cembalo
Zalichos
Paurai
Amisos
LIMNIA
Vezirköprü
Oinaion
Phadisane
Cape Jason
Kotyora
Kerasous
CHALYBIA
Amasya
Erbaa
Niksar
Zile
Tokat
Gümenek
Şebinkarahisar
ANATOLIA
Sivas
0
30 mi
0
50 km

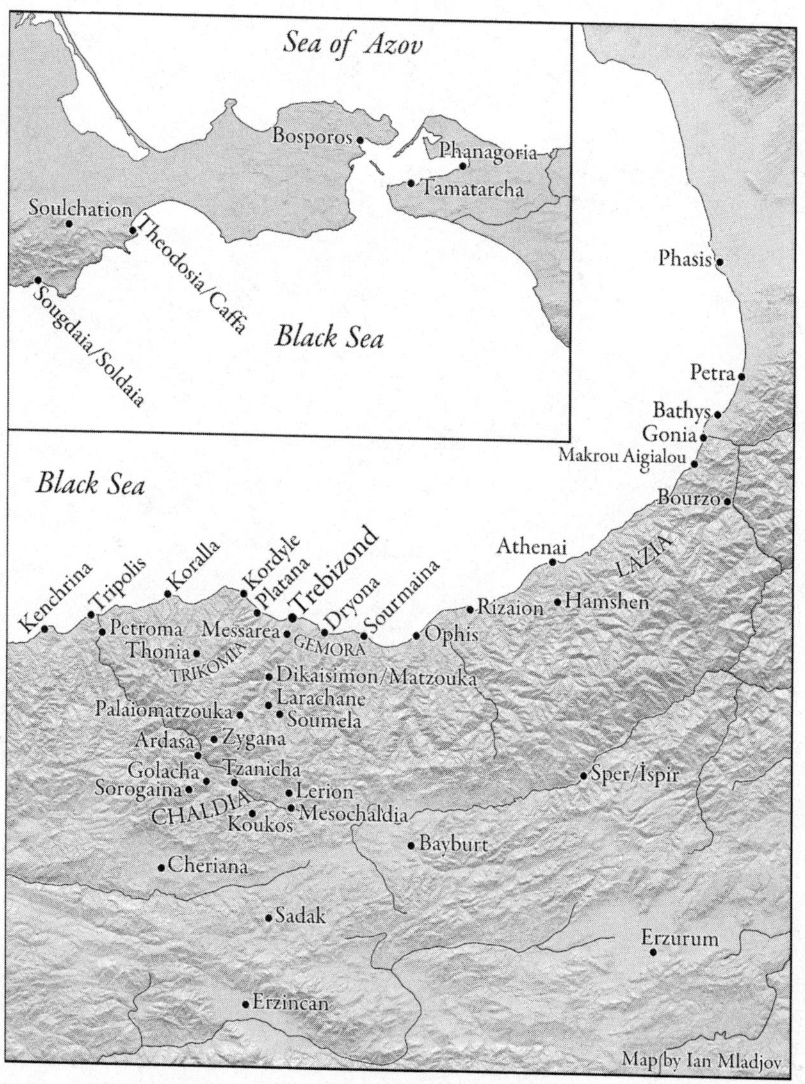
Sea of Azov
Bosporos
Phanagoria
Tamatarcha
Soulchation
Theodosia/Caffa
Sougdaia/Soldaia
Black Sea
Phasis
Petra
Bathys
Gonia
Makrou Aigialou
Black Sea
Bourzo
Athenai
LAZIA
Kenchrina
Tripolis
Koralla
Kordyle
Platana
Trebizond
Dryona
Sourmaina
Rizaion
Hamshen
Petroma
Messarea
GEMORA
Ophis
Thonia
TRIKOMIA
Dikaisimon/Matzouka
Larachane
Palaiomatzouka
Soumela
Ardasa
Zygana
Golacha
Tzanicha
Sorogaina
Lerion
Sper/İspir
CHALDIA
Mesochaldia
Koukos
Bayburt
Cheriana
Sadak
Erzurum
Erzincan
Map by Ian Mladjov

Glossary of Offices, Titles, and Technical Terms

Most of the following information is based on the relevant entries in the *Oxford Dictionary of Byzantium*, ed. Alexander Kazhdan (New York, 1991). This glossary, however, focuses on the nature of these offices and titles as they had evolved at the court of the Grand Komnenoi at Trebizond in the late Byzantine period. The glossary also includes some foreign titles that Panaretos employs while describing the empire's foreign relations.

archontes: the term was used for the powerful elite in the medieval Roman world. The *archontes* consisted of the emperor's officials and members of influential families.

çelebi: Turkish for "gentleman" or "lord."

despoinachat: a fusion of Greek *(despoina)* and Turkish *(hatun)* words for "lady," often used to refer to Trapezuntine princesses married to Turkish lords.

epikernes (*pikernes*): more commonly rendered *pinkernes* by most Byzantine authors, but we maintain Panaretos's spellings. Originally, this individual was the emperor's cupbearer. By the time of the Grand Komnenoi, *epikernes* had become a high honorific title.

grand konostaulos: originally, the commander of the Latin mercenaries in the Byzantine army. In the fourteenth century, the title had presumably become a military honorific.

grand logothetes: originally, an official created to coordinate the various offices of imperial administration. He was in charge of drawing up laws and preparing imperial documents sent to foreign governments.

protosebastos: a dignity resulting from the inflation of the honorific epithet *sebastos.* He ranked between the *grand logothetes* and the *epikernes.*

sebastokrator: a combination of the titles *sebastos* (the old Greek translation of "Augustus") and *autokrator* (a Greek version of *imperator*). The dignity was primarily reserved for the emperor's close relatives.

skeuophylax: a high patriarchal official.

tatas: the title does not appear to have had a clearly defined function. Some define the *tatas* as the pedagogue of the emperor's children, while others see it as high court title holder.

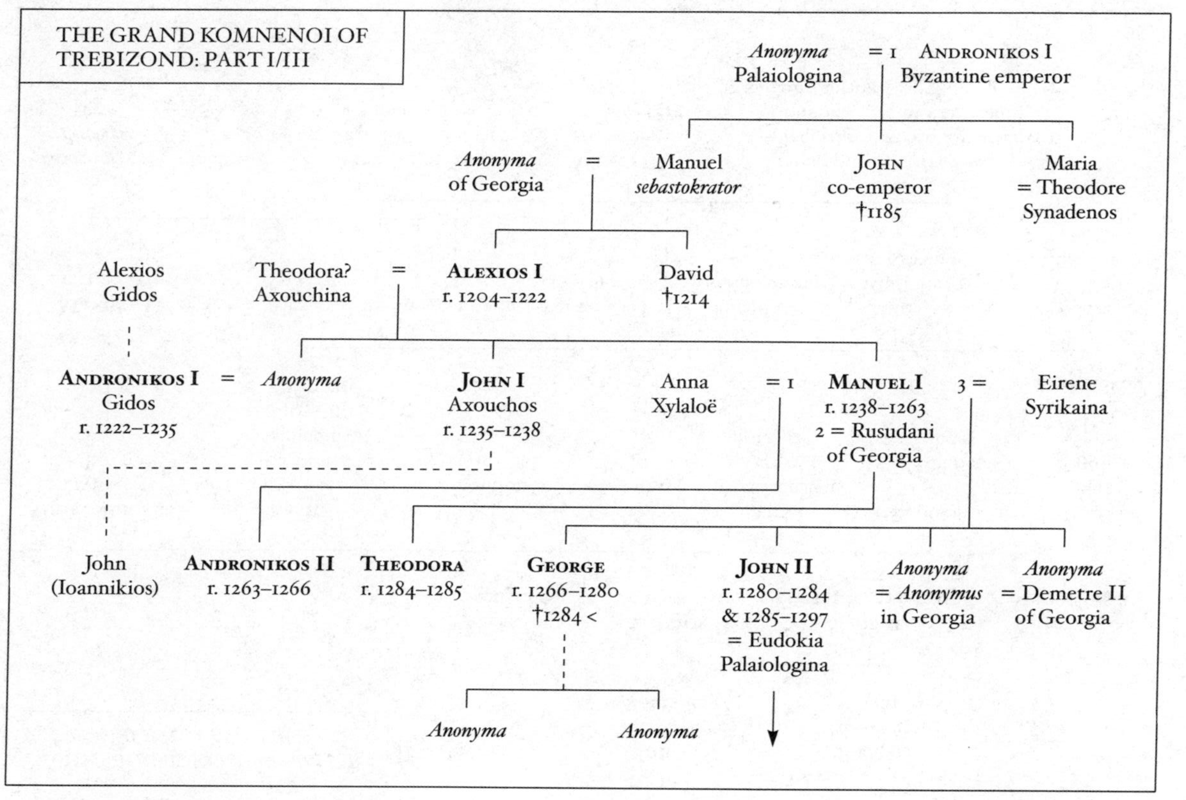

THE GRAND KOMNENOI OF TREBIZOND: PART I/III
Anonyma Palaiologina = 1 Andronikos I Byzantine emperor
Anonyma of Georgia = Manuel sebastokrator
John co-emperor †1185
Maria = Theodore Synadenos
Alexios Gidos
Theodora? Axouchina = Alexios I r. 1204–1222
David †1214
Andronikos I Gidos r. 1222–1235 = Anonyma
John I Axouchos r. 1235–1238
Anna Xylaloë = 1 Manuel I r. 1238–1263 2 = Rusudani of Georgia 3 = Eirene Syrikaina
John (Ioannikios)
Andronikos II r. 1263–1266
Theodora r. 1284–1285
George r. 1266–1280 †1284 <
John II r. 1280–1284 & 1285–1297 = Eudokia Palaiologina
Anonyma = Anonymus in Georgia
Anonyma = Demetre II of Georgia
Anonyma
Anonyma

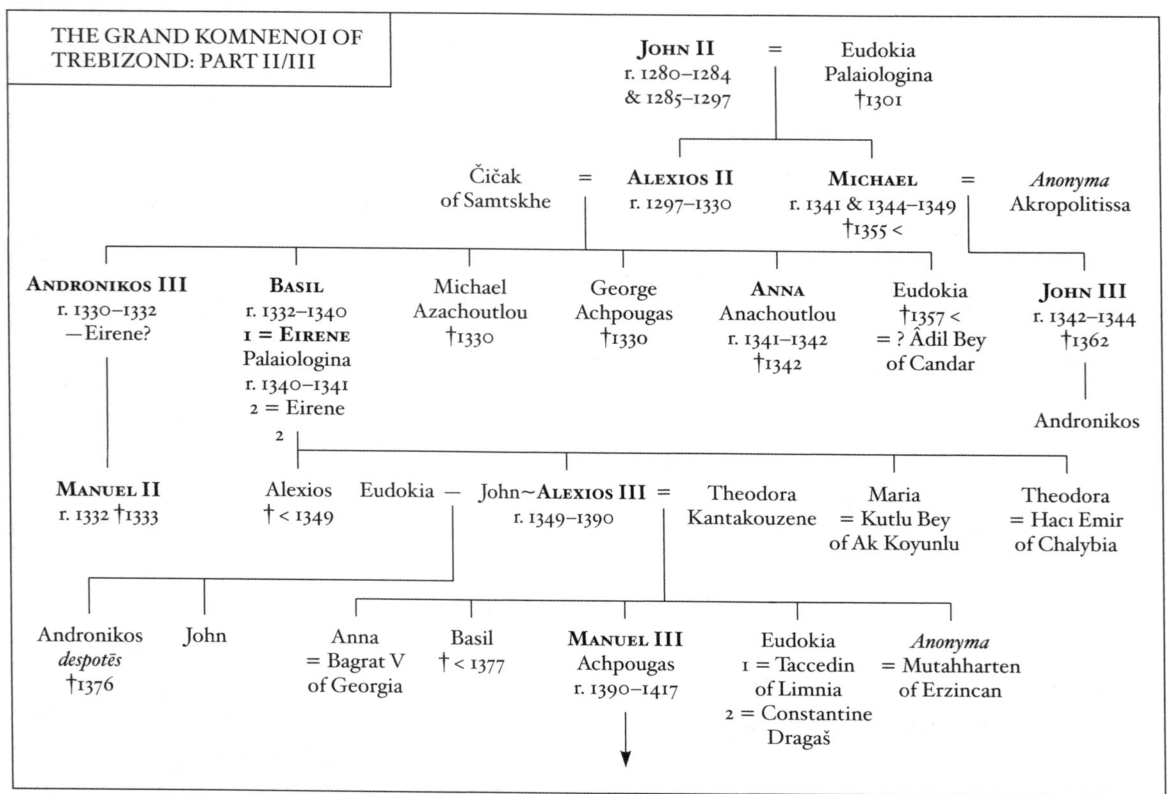
THE GRAND KOMNENOI OF TREBIZOND: PART II/III
John II
r. 1280–1284
& 1285–1297
=
Eudokia
Palaiologina
†1301
Čičak
of Samtskhe
=
Alexios II
r. 1297–1330
Michael
r. 1341 & 1344–1349
†1355 <
=
Anonyma
Akropolitissa
Andronikos III
r. 1330–1332
—Eirene?
Basil
r. 1332–1340
1 = Eirene
Palaiologina
r. 1340–1341
2 = Eirene
2
Michael
Azachoutlou
†1330
George
Achpougas
†1330
Anna
Anachoutlou
r. 1341–1342
†1342
Eudokia
†1357 <
= ? Âdil Bey
of Candar
John III
r. 1342–1344
†1362
Andronikos
Manuel II
r. 1332 †1333
Alexios
† < 1349
Eudokia —
John~Alexios III =
r. 1349–1390
Theodora
Kantakouzene
Maria
= Kutlu Bey
of Ak Koyunlu
Theodora
= Hacı Emir
of Chalybia
Andronikos
despotēs
†1376
John
Anna
= Bagrat V
of Georgia
Basil
† < 1377
Manuel III
Achpougas
r. 1390–1417
Eudokia
1 = Taccedin
of Limnia
2 = Constantine
Dragaš
Anonyma
= Mutahharten
of Erzincan

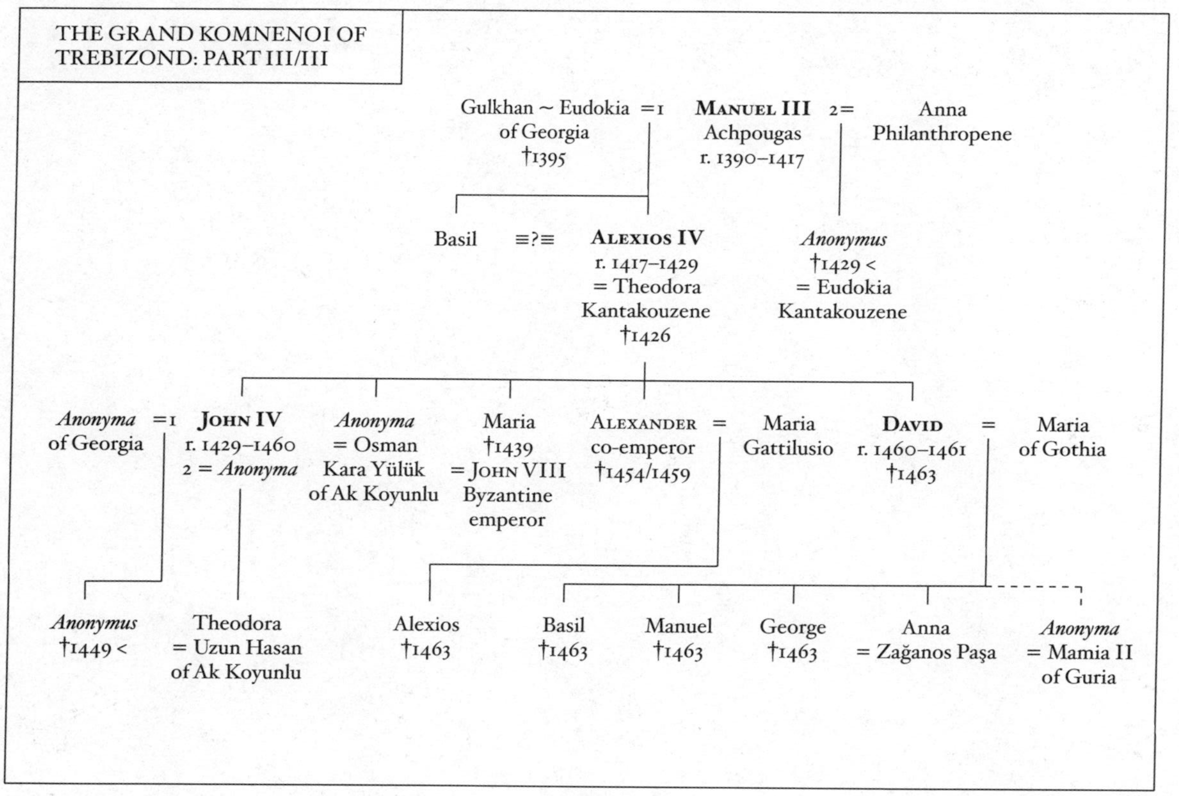

THE GRAND KOMNENOI OF TREBIZOND: PART III/III
Gulkhan ~ Eudokia of Georgia †1395
=1
Manuel III Achpougas r. 1390–1417
2=
Anna Philanthropene
Basil
≡?≡
Alexios IV r. 1417–1429 = Theodora Kantakouzene †1426
Anonymus †1429 < = Eudokia Kantakouzene
Anonyma of Georgia
=1
John IV r. 1429–1460 2 = Anonyma
Anonyma = Osman Kara Yülük of Ak Koyunlu
Maria †1439 = John VIII Byzantine emperor
Alexander co-emperor †1454/1459
=
Maria Gattilusio
David r. 1460–1461 †1463
=
Maria of Gothia
Anonymus †1449 <
Theodora = Uzun Hasan of Ak Koyunlu
Alexios †1463
Basil †1463
Manuel †1463
George †1463
Anna = Zağanos Paşa
Anonyma = Mamia II of Guria

Bibliography

Panaretos Editions and Translations

Asp-Talwar, Annika. "The Chronicle of Michael Panaretos." In *Byzantium's Other Empire: Trebizond,* edited by Antony Eastmond, 173–212. Istanbul, 2016.

Brosset, Marie-Félicité. "Chronique de Trébizonde, composée en grec par Michel Panarète." In Charles Le Beau, *L'histoire du Bas-Empire.* Revised by Antoine-Jean de Saint-Martin and Marie-Félicité Brosset, 482–509. Vol. 20. Paris, 1836.

Fallmerayer, Jakob P. "Original-Fragmente, Chroniken und anderes Materiale zur Geschichte des Kaiserthums Trapezunt." *Abhandlungen der historischen Klasse der königlich bayerischen Akademie der Wissenschaften* 4.2 (1844): 11–40.

Gamqrelidze, Alekhandre. "Mikhel Panaretosis Trapizonis Khronika." *Masalebi Sakharthvelosa da Kavkasiis istoriisathvis* 33 (1960): 1–98.

Khakhanov, Aleksandr. *Michail Panaret: Trapezountskaya khronika.* Moscow, 1905.

Lampros, Spyridon. "Τὸ Τραπεζουντιακὸν Χρονικὸν τοῦ πρωτοσεβάστου καὶ πρωτονοταρίου Μιχαὴλ Παναρέτου." *Νέος Ἑλληνομνήμων* 4 (1907): 266–94.

Lampsides, Odysseas. "Μιχαὴλ τοῦ Παναρέτου Περὶ τῶν Μεγάλων Κομνηνῶν." *Ἀρχεῖον Πόντου* 22 (1958): 5–89.

Pampoukis, Iordanis T. *Ποντιακά.* Vol. 2. Athens, 1947.

Tafel, Gottlieb Lukas Friedrich. "Panareti chronicon Trapezuntinum (e cod. Ven.)." In *Eustathii metropolitae Thessalonicensis opuscula,* 362–70. Frankfurt, 1832.

Bessarion Editions and Translations

Georgiadis, Thanasis. *Εγκώμιον εις Τραπεζούντα κατά τον Μαρκιανόν κώδικα.* Athens, 2000.

Lampros, Spyridon. "Βησσαρίωνος Εἰς Τραπεζοῦντα." *Νέος Ἑλληνομνήμων* 13 (1916): 145–204.

Lampsides, Odysseas. "Ο 'Εις Τραπεζούντα' Λόγος του Βησσαρίωνος." *Αρχείον Πόντου* 39 (1984): 3–75.

Mango, Cyril. *The Art of the Byzantine Empire, 312–1453: Sources and Documents,* 252–53. Englewood Cliffs, N.J., 1972.

Primary Sources

Agathias. *Histories.* Edited by Rudolf Keydell, *Agathiae Myrinaei historiarum libri quinque.* Berlin, 1967.

Apostolis, Michael. *Funeral Oration.* PG 161:128–40.

Aristides. *To Capito.* Edited by Wilhelm Dindorf, *Aristides,* 2:415–36. Leipzig, 1829; repr., Hildesheim, 1964.

Attaleiates, Michael. *History.* Edited by Inmaculada Pérez Martín, *Miguel Ataliates: Historia.* Madrid, 2002. English translation by Anthony Kaldellis and Dimitris Krallis, *The History: Michael Attaleiates.* Cambridge, Mass., 2012.

Bessarion. *Address to the Emperor Alexios Komnenos.* Edited by Chrysanthos, "Βησσαρίωνος προσφώνημα πρὸς τὸν εὐσεβέστατον βασιλέα τῆς Τραπεζοῦντος Ἀλέξιον τὸν Μέγαν Κομνηνόν." *Ἀρχεῖον Πόντου* 12 (1946): 117–30.

———. *Encomium of Saint Bessarion.* Edited by Pierre Joannou [= Periklis Petros Ioannou], "Un Opuscule inédit du cardinale Bessarion: Le panégyrique de Saint Bessarion anachorète égyptien." *Analecta Bollandiana* 45 (1947): 107–38.

———. *Epitaph for Cleofa Malatesta.* Edited by Spyridon Lampros, *Παλαιολόγεια καὶ Πελοποννησιακά,* 3:176. Athens, 1926.

———. *Epitaph for Manuel Palaiologos.* Edited by Spyridon Lampros, *Παλαιολόγεια καὶ Πελοποννησιακά,* 3:284–90. Athens, 1926.

———. *Monody for Cleofa Malatesta.* Edited by Spyridon Lampros, *Παλαιολόγεια καὶ Πελοποννησιακά,* 3:154–60. Athens, 1926.

———. *First Monody for Theodora Komnene.* Edited by Alexander Sideras, *Die byzantinischen Grabreden,* 529–36. Vienna, 1994.

——. *Second Monody for Theodora Komnene.* Edited by Alexander Sideras, *25 unedierte byzantinische Grabreden,* 349–59. Thessalonike, 1990.

——. *Third Monody for Theodora Komnene.* Edited by Alexander Sideras, *25 unedierte byzantinische Grabreden,* 361–68. Thessalonike, 1990.

Bryennios, Nikephoros. *Material for History.* Edited and translated by Paul Gautier, *Nicéphore Bryennios: Histoire.* Brussels, 1975.

Capranica, Nicolò, *Funeral Oration.* Edited by Ludwig Mohler, *Kardinal Bessarion,* 3:404–14. Paderborn, 1942.

Choniates, Niketas. *History.* Edited by Jan Louis van Dieten, *Nicetae Choniatae historia.* Berlin, 1975.

Doukas. *History.* Edited and translated by Vasile Grecu, *Istoria turcobizantină (1341–1462).* Bucharest, 1958.

Gregoras, Nikephoros. *Roman History.* Edited by Immanuel Bekker and Ludwig Schopen, *Nicephori Gregorae historiae Byzantinae.* 3 vols. Bonn, 1829–1855.

Hermogenes. *On the Types of Style.* Edited by Hugo Rabe, *Hermogenis opera,* 213–413. Leipzig, 1913.

Komnene, Anna. *Alexiad.* Edited by Athanasios Kambylis and Dieter R. Reinsch, *Annae Comnenae Alexias.* Berlin, 2001.

Lazaropoulos, John. *Oration on the Birthday of Saint Eugenios.* Edited and translated by Jan Olof Rosenqvist, *The Hagiographical Dossier of St. Eugenios of Trebizond: A Critical Edition with Introduction, Translation, Commentary and Indexes,* 246–359. Uppsala, 1996.

——. *Synopsis.* Edited and translated by Jan Olof Rosenqvist, *The Hagiographical Dossier of St. Eugenios of Trebizond: A Critical Edition with Introduction, Translation, Commentary and Indexes,* 204–45. Uppsala, 1996.

Libadenos, Andreas. *Iambs for the Birthday of the Mother of God.* Edited by Odysseas Lampsides, *Ἀνδρέου Λιβαδηνοῦ βίος καὶ ἔργα,* 109–12. Athens, 1975.

——. *Travels.* Edited by Odysseas Lampsides, *Ἀνδρέου Λιβαδηνοῦ βίος καὶ ἔργα,* 39–87. Athens, 1975.

——. *Verses on the Death of the Virgin Mary.* Edited by Odysseas Lampsides, *Ἀνδρέου Λιβαδηνοῦ βίος καὶ ἔργα,* 105–8. Athens, 1975.

Libanios. *Antiochian Oration.* Edited by Richard Foerster, *Libanii opera,* 1.2:437–535. Leipzig, 1903.

——. *Letters.* Edited by Richard Foerster, *Libanii opera.* Vols. 10–11. Leipzig, 1921–1922.

Loukites, Constantine. *Funeral Oration for Alexios Komnenos.* Edited by Athanasios Papadopoulos-Kerameus, *Ἀνάλεκτα Ἱεροσολυμητικῆς Σταχυολογίας,* 1:421–30. Saint Petersburg, 1891.

Markianos. *Circumnavigation of the Outer Sea.* Edited by Karl Müller, *Geographi Graeci minores,* 1:515–62. Paris, 1855.

Pachymeres, George. *History.* Edited and translated by Albert Failler and Vitalien Laurent, *Georges Pachymérès. Relations historiques.* 5 vols. Paris, 1984–2000.

Platina. *Panegyric.* In PG 161:113–16.

Pollux. *Onomasticon.* Edited by Erich Bethe, *Pollucis onomasticon.* 3 vols. Leipzig, 1900–1937.

Prokopios. *History of the Wars.* Edited by Jakob Haury, *Procopii Caesariensis opera omnia;* revised by Gerhard Wirth. 2 vols. Leipzig, 1962–1963.

Sphrantzes, George. *Chronicle.* Edited by Riccardo Maisano, *Giorgio Sfranze: Cronaca.* Rome, 1990.

Suda. Edited by Ada Adler, *Suidae Lexicon.* 5 vols. Leipzig, 1928–1938.

Zosimos. *New History.* Edited by François Paschoud, *Zosime: Histoire nouvelle.* 3 vols. Paris, 1971–1989.

Secondary Sources

Akışık, Aslıhan. "Praising A City: Nicaea, Trebizond, and Thessalonike." *Journal of Turkish Studies* 36 (2012): 1–36.

Bryer, Anthony. "Greeks and Türkmens: The Pontic Exception." *Dumbarton Oaks Papers* 29 (1975): 113–48.

Bryer, Anthony, and David Winfield. *The Byzantine Monuments and Topography of the Pontos.* 2 vols. Washington, D.C., 1985.

Fatouros, Georgios. "Bessarion und Libanios: Ein typischer Fall byzantinischer Mimesis." *Jahrbuch der österreichischen Byzantinistik* 49 (1999): 191–204.

Giarenis, Ilias. "Ο λόγιος και ο γενέθλιος τόπος: Η Τραπεζούντα με τον τρόπο του Βησσαρίωνος." *Επετηρίς Εταιρείας Βυζαντινών Σπουδών* 53 (2007–2009): 265–80.

Grumel, Venance. *La chronologie.* Vol. 1 of *Traité d'études byzantines.* Paris, 1955–1958.

Janin, Raymond. *Les églises et les monastères des grands centres byzantins.* Paris, 1975.

Lampsides, Odysseas. "Datierung des Ἐγκώμιον Τραπεζοῦντος von Kardinal Bessarion." *Byzantinische Zeitschrift* 48 (1955): 291–92.

——. "L' éloge de Trébizonde de Bessarion." *Jahrbuch der österreichischen Byzantinistik* 32 (1982): 121–27.

——. "Περὶ τὸ 'ἐγκώμιον εἰς Τραπεζοῦντα' τοῦ Βησσαρίωνος." *Ἀρχεῖον Πόντου* 37 (1982): 153–81.

Lauritzen, Frederick. "Bessarion's Political Thought: The Encomium to Trebizond." *Bulgaria Mediaevalis* 2 (2011): 153–59.

Rosenqvist, Jan Olof. "Byzantine Trebizond: A Provincial Literary Landscape." In *Byzantino-Nordica 2004: Papers Presented at the International Symposium of Byzantine Studies Held on 7–11 May 2004 in Tartu, Estonia,* edited by Ivo Volt and Janika Päll, 29–51. Tartu, 2005.

Saradi, Helen. "The Monuments in the Late Byzantine Ekphraseis of Cities." *Byzantinoslavica* 69.3 (2011): 179–92.

Shukurov, Rustam. "Between Peace and Hostility: Trebizond and the Pontic Turkish Periphery in the Fourteenth Century." *Mediterranean Historical Review* 9 (1994): 20–72.

Index

P = Panaretos, *On the Emperors of Trebizond;* B = Bessarion, *Encomium on Trebizond*